Best wishes, Malcolm Miles,
September 2004.

Newport People

A History of a Shropshire Market Town

Malcolm Miles

2004

Published by Malcolm Miles

The Birches, Avenue Road South, Newport, Shropshire TF10 7DY

e-mail   susanmiles.newport@virgin.net

First published 2004

© Malcolm Miles 2004
All rights reserved.   No part of this publication may be reproduced in any form or by any means, graphic, electronic, or mechanical, including photocopying, recording, taping or information storage and retrieval systems – without the prior written permission of the publisher.

ISBN 0-9548531-0-5

Printed and bound in Great Britain by Advertiser Printing Works, Newport, Shropshire

Front Cover Photograph Newport May Fair

NEWPORT PEOPLE.

Contents.

	Index of Photographs and Inserts	2
	Foreword	4
	Introduction	5
1	The Lilleshall Estate	7
2	The Bougheys of Aqualate.	26
3	The Poor of Newport	63
4	The Newport Patrole	91
5	The Chetwynd Estate and the Burton Boroughs	99
6	Longford and the Leekes.	116
7	The Harrop Diaries.	124
8	William John Fieldhouse.	130
9	The Surgeons of Newport.	133
10	Mary Roddam and District Nursing.	149
11	Tom Collins.	158
12	Sarah Jane Mills and Merevale.	175
13	The Silvesters of Newport.	186
14	The Underhills.	207
15	Audco and Jobs.	218

Photographs and Inserts

1. The Lilleshall Estate   Page

Song to commemorate the Birth of Lord Gower	11
1890 New Drive Constructed on Old Canal	12
Marquis and Duchess of Sutherland	14
Coming of Age of Marquis of Stafford 1909 Ox Roast	14
Lilleshall Estate Sale Catalogue	15
Lovely Lilleshall Band and Special Attractions 1929	16
Bomb dropped on Lilleshall Golf Course 1941	17
Programme of Opening Ceremony by HRH The Princess Elizabeth	18
Lovely Lilleshall Guide Book Cover	19
Lilleshall Hall	21
West Terrace	22
Woodland Railway	23
Gardens and Fountain	24
Map Newport 1775	25

2. The Bougheys of Aqualate

The Original Tudor House C1630	26
The Nash Sketches for Aqualate 1803	29:30:32
Aqualate Hall	33
A New Song for the Coming of Age of Sir Thomas F. Boughey Esq.	37
Programme of Procession for the coming of Age	38
Programme of Public Diner for the coming of age	39
Programme of A Banquet for Gentlemen for the coming of age	39
Hall and Stairway of Aqualate Hall	41
Aqualate Gardens	41
Skating on The Mere	42
Otter Hunting	43
Funeral of the late Sir T. F. Boughey Bart. Forton	44
Sir T.F. Boughey Bart J.P.	45
The Boughey Memorial	45
Annabelle Lady Boughey	46
Laying of Commemorative Stone, Newport Church Porch	47
Funeral of Annabelle Lady Boughey, Newport	48
Family Gathering with Ethel Morris	48
Wartime Nissan Huts at Aqualate	51
The Paddock Family at Fernhill 1905	52
Aqualate Hall and Stables c 1925	53
Estate Workers c 1925	54
Boughey Family Tree	57
Fire at Aqualate 1910	59
Mr. Morrey, estate employee, inspects rebuilding of the hall c1928	60

3. The Poor of Newport

Plan of Poor Law Institute	70
Mr. & Mrs. Buck, Master and Matron 1912	73
Workhouse Group c.1912	74
Arial View of Audley House and surround area	75
Matron and Nursing Staff taking Tea Outside The Infirmary c 1920	78
Cast Iron Sliding Laundry Rails	82
Tommy The Donkey	85
The Workhouse Bell	88
The Old Infimary – Now Combat Stress	89
Audley House – Now Converted into Apartments	89
Audley House Mews	89

4. The Newport Patrole

The Guardroom in Middle Row	92

5. The Chetwynd Estate

Chetwynd Park	100

Chetwynd Lodge	102
Chetwynd Church	104
J.S.B. Borough. B.A., D.L., J.P.	109
Col. Borough with Walter Wheat in 1935	110
Map Chetwynd Park	111
Dovecote	112
Estate Plan	113

6. Longford and The Leeks

Longford Hall and Park	117
Longford Hall 1935	118
The Kitchen Garden	118
Col. Ralph Leeke	120
Longford Hall - Military Hospital 1917	121
Sale Catalogue of 1935	122
Public Ball to Celebrate Coming of Age of Ralph Merrick Leeke Esq.	123

7. The Harrop Diaries

John Harrop	125
Edgmond Hall – Once the home of John Harrop	126
John Harrop Memorial Card.	129

8. William John Fieldhouse

9. The Surgeons of Newport

Baddeley Wells near Millwood Mere	137
E.A. Ernest Elkington M.B., M.R.C.S.	138
Window of 47 Upper Bar	145
Gable End, Granville Street	145
Baddeley Family Tree	147

10. Mary Roddam and District Nursing

Girls' Home, Edgmond	149
Summerhill, Edgmond	150
Mary Roddam	152
Roddam House	153

11. Tom Collins

T. Collins M.A.	158
"The Grammar School, Newport"	161

12. Sarah Jane Mills and Merevale

Mark and Sarah Mills	177
Merevale College	178
School Games 1908	179
Staff of Merevale c 1922	181
Sarah Mills and Dainty'	182
Merevale College	183

13. The Silvesters of Newport

The Silvester Monument in Newport Cemetery	191
The Horne Family	195
C.W. Smallman M.J.I.	200
The Advertiser Offices, 23 High Street, Newport	201

14. The Underhills

Highfield, Church Aston	208
Map - St. Mary's Iron Works 1902	210
Advert - Underhill, Agricultural Engineers	213

15. Audco and Jobs

The Audley Engineering Company	220
Aerial Photo c 1930	223
Hurst Engineering Co. - Light Drilling Section	228
Core Shop 1951	229
Aerial Photo c 1950	230
Serck Audco Valves	231
Underhill Close	233
Commemorative Lamp c 1992	236

FOREWORD.

This is a book many years in the writing from the time in the mid-eighties when I began reading and researching the Newport and Market Drayton Advertiser from 1855 to 1954.

The newspaper opened up a vast store of historical information, accurate, revealing and eminently readable, such a wealth of local history that would overwhelm any attempt at a single *"history"*.

This book therefore is highly selective, deliberately biographical under a general heading of *"People"*, which avoids the usual categories such as "trade", "transport", "education" while allowing the major economic and social elements of 19th Century history to be discussed not only in a local but also a national context.

So Newport did understand the threat from Napoleon; it did see the rise and decline of the landed estate; its doctors did understand the work of Pasteur and the necessity of clean water; they knew the value of child welfare in alleviating poverty; by the end the products of the industrial skills of Newport had made a unique contribution to the international economy.

By 1900 the rural market town had declined as had its agricultural environment, to be revived by the arrival of the commuter age. In this it is typical of many rural communities. Limited horizons and ambitions may seem a flaw but they were also an attraction, as they are today, and do not mean that people lived in a vacuum. Astride the A41, to take one example, Newport saw the troops marching to Ireland and saw the result of that policy in the flood of refugees after the Irish famine. We can see how they tried to adapt the vast, national bureaucratic structure of the Poor Law to the needs of their own people.

However the main purpose is to provide an enjoyable account of local history which will enable the many new Novaportans to identify with their past and surroundings.

As many contemporary accounts are included as possible to give the flavour and style of the times and because the modern reader is quite capable of assessing original evidence.

Thanks are due to the owners and staff of the Newport and Market Drayton Advertiser for allowing access to their archives over many years and for permission to use extracts. An even deeper debt is to the original journalists such as the Silvester brothers, Charles Horne, editor and owner, and T.P.Marshall and many others unknown, who had such dedication and literary skill.

Acknowledgement must be made to Shropshire Records and Research Centre, to Staffordshire Record Office and the Salt Library and the staff at Newport Library. Also to Vicky Langford for insight into the history of the Serck Audco Company; to Clare and William Boughey for details of the family and particularly the diaries of Ethel Morris and finally to Sue Miles who has prepared the manuscript for publication and suffered my ignorance of computers.

Malcolm Miles. Newport. August 2004.

Introduction.

The English market town was bound up with agriculture, with markets and fairs and with labourers and farmers often resident in the town. Their prosperity fluctuated with that of farming, an upswing to 1815 then a downturn through 1820-40 with a golden age from 1850 followed by a long depression from 1870.

If there was a market or a fair the place would be described as a market town despite population though there was no guarantee, markets failing to grow into towns and towns failing despite markets and charters. Shropshire had at least eight planned medieval, market towns, not all survive.

Though rural, market towns were influenced by changes in industry from both directions; they served the needs of developing industrial areas as Newport did the mining area of east Shropshire; they also were affected by the mass-produced industrial goods that replaced traditional crafts. Transport technology left some towns stranded and overtaken by neighbours who did let in canals and railways. Newport had both but on the edges of town leaving the medieval centre untouched.

Agriculture was the key, usually a radius of five miles, with corn and cattle; specialised fairs; retail markets and business serving rural needs.

Corn markets were held in the open market place or inns usually by sample. There were some "pitched" markets where all the produce was brought in but this was costly in space, labour, transport and time. Sample markets were customary. During the mid 19th Century special corn exchanges were built as more corn was produced while good accommodation free from the weather attracted trade from neighbours. Railways could mean business going to the main towns where prices might be higher. There was a rash of building from 1850 often combined with community facilities and frequently around the £12,000-13,000 mark. This was exactly the case in Newport. After 1870 exchanges became less profitable as farmers carried on trade away from the monopoly of the market companies and their restricted selling hours.

There were different markets for different animals, and fairs that lasted for several days on specific dates. These were accommodated in the streets and were gradually replaced by specialist centres as numbers increased and townsfolk objected to the nuisance. This happened in Shrewsbury in 1850 and Newport in 1860. In 1845 the tax on auction markets was lifted and auctioneers began to sell in the established markets until by the end of the century, like the corn markets, farmers began to sell on the farm or privately to butchers at times, of course, chosen by themselves. Today Newport cattle market has ceased to operate the final blow being foot and mouth disease.

With large-scale production of goods indoor markets replaced fairs. In Newport the Corn Exchange, the indoor retail market and the livestock market were combined on one new site in 1860, commonly referred to as the Town Hall though it never served that purpose being, and still is, a private company. Fairs from the 1870's became restricted to amusements dominated by regional giants such as Pat Collins. Retail markets were for food often on a casual basis with farmers' wives and smallholders and customers were mainly the poor. Other goods such as haberdashery were in shops. Many towns with covered markets retained open street markets but not in Newport where the Market Act prohibits such trading still, despite legal challenges.

There were traditional hiring fairs variously described as "mops", "statute fairs" or "gawby" markets but these broke down as hiring by the year became unpopular and uneconomic for both sides. In Newport this was kept going by Pat Collins for legal reasons by having just one stall at Christmas.

As the century wore on, shops got a wider range of consumer goods but continued to include workshops for production and packaging as well as domestic accommodation. By 1900 many shops were retailing from large-scale manufacturers or wholesalers from "ready-made" goods and branded packages. Even saddlers and clockmakers were selling goods wholly or partly made elsewhere though labelled "Newport". By 1895 larger premises in Newport were installing plate glass often adorned with national advertising and the larger town houses that had been intermixed with shops were now being converted. Brittains the grocers were building up a local empire buying in bulk sometimes from abroad, and re-packaging to their smaller outlets. But W.H.Smith, Woolworths and Boots gradually found their way on to the High Street.

There were innumerable inns and beershops providing refreshment and parking for vehicles and horses though they declined with the decline of drinking after 1870. The dominant class were the lawyers, agents and doctors serving the adjacent estates and they were behind the huge civic improvements of the 1850's. With the abolition of stamp duty in 1855 most towns had their own newspaper, the Newport Advertiser eventually covering a wide area of Shropshire and Staffordshire.

Industry was based on local raw materials, leather, timber, malting, dairying and the area was usually self-sufficient. Some small towns developed products of national importance such as brewing, biscuits or shoemaking, in Newport it was valves.

Towns were a focal point of communications; in Newport this was not just local but national being on the main route to Ireland, the present A41. Turnpikes, coaches and carriers were important and new hotels, like the Royal Victoria Hotel (1830) were built for the trade. In fact a count of the number of carriers to the feeder villages indicates the importance of a town. Railways were a mixed blessing upsetting traditions and bringing competition but most were welcomed and brought opportunities for trade and travel and wider horizons. If towns did decline it was not because of them.

For most market towns population growth stopped between 1831-61 and even after that was either constant or declined. Few towns grew at the rate of the natural average. In Newport there was stagnation until the 1960's. The greatest surge of growth was in the 1850's with new public buildings, for example the town hall and police station, new roads like Stafford Street, Granville Avenue and New Street, with new industries such as Underhills.

Any increase in population was catered for, not by expansion beyond the medieval boundary into the open fields, but by infilling mainly of poor housing with no clean water or sanitation mixed in with noxious trades. The hazards of disease were understood but cost and no distinct system of local government were the main obstacles rather than ignorance. Even gas, there from 1835, was restricted to street lighting. By 1914 market towns such as Newport were paved, drained, lit and watered, with cemeteries and markets improved and removed.

By the 1890's the former boisterous sports had gone replaced by touring mechanical fairs, circuses, agricultural shows, carnivals and excursions. Employers and gentry encouraged the mass-appeal sports such as football and cricket and even golf and cycling while the race meeting was a local affair on the long enclosure road of the marsh, with a motley collection of horses hardly able to sustain two days of racing. The gentry elevated the mind with libraries, theatre, mechanics and literary institutes and left money for welfare and hospitals.

Business up to 1914 was often conducted in the manner of a village but the telephone and the car brought the world rushing down the A41 to stay.

1. THE LILLESHALL ESTATE.

By the 19th Century Newport was surrounded by large estates that came right to the back door of the town, determining its size and development. The vivary and the open fields at Norbroom had gone making the town dependent on its rural hinterland. The few fields that remained were for pasture, for hay or fattening cattle, forming a small green belt. These estates exerted a powerful influence on the town and this is obvious in the deference shown and the respect paid to these landed families until at least the First World War. Every notable event in their lives was celebrated whether it was the coming of age of Thomas Boughey in 1857 as depicted in the towns most familiar painting or the coming of age of the Marquis of Stafford the eldest son of the Duke of Sutherland in 1909, this time captured by the camera.

Beginning in the south-west is the largest estate, the Lilleshall estate of the Dukes of Sutherland. This dates from the dissolution of the monasteries the lands of Lilleshall Abbey being purchased in 1539 by James Leveson ["Luson"], a Wolverhampton wool merchant. Nearby is Woodcote, a smaller estate, of the Cotes family. On the west between the Lilleshall estate and the town was the Longford estate of the Talbots, Earls of Shrewsbury, sold in 1789 to Ralph Leeke of Wellington who had made his fortune with the East India Company. To the north was the Chetwynd estate of the Pigotts bought in 1803 by Thomas Borrow of Derbyshire who changed his name to Borough. The Aqualate estate to the east lies mostly in Staffordshire. At the end of the 18th Century its owners Charles Baldwyn and his son Mr W.Childe were in debt, and the estate was bought by John Fenton Fletcher from industrial Staffordshire. He changed his name to "Boughey" on succeeding to his cousins' estates. In 1812 he succeeded to the baronetcy created for his father in 1798.

In this small area around Newport we have the intermingling of trade, industry and land which created so much of the English "gentry".

The Lilleshall estate was based on the privatisation of monastic lands, but its success comes from the exploitation of its mineral wealth and the investment of this wealth in agricultural improvement and management. Careful marriages also helped, the family having "a talent for absorbing heiresses". One generation married into the Granvilles of Cornwall, the next the Egertons of the Duke of Bridgwater and finally, which brought the Dukedom, the Countess of Sutherland. This enabled the Leveson family, by now the Leveson-Gowers ["Luson-Gores"], to acquire numerous titles peaking with the Dukedom of Sutherland in 1833, and becoming by far the greatest owner of land if not the wealthiest landowner in the kingdom over 1,380,000 acres with a rent roll of £141,000 a year.

The wealth of their mines, forges and furnaces in the northern part of the Coalbrookdale coalfield created by the Lilleshall Company, was literally ploughed into the drainage of the wetlands or Weald Moors to the west of Newport, creating fine agricultural land out of summer grazing. In 1673 the newly inducted Vicar of Kynnersley, Ralph Thoresby, described the isolation of the population on their little islands which were impassable in winter, covered in woods which had rotted to form a thick black soil, and with the remains of the stumps and large trees resting on sunken ground with the roots as stilts. Names in the area ending with EI, EA or EY indicate places surrounded by water.

In June 1801 the Duke (though technically not the "Duke" until 1833), obtained an Act of Parliament to divide, allot, enclose, drain and improve the common moors called Sydney Moor, Small Moor, Waters Upton Moor and other common and waste lands. John Bishton, a business partner of the Duke was one of the Commissioners appointed to carry out the Act.

" [The Weald Moors] consisted of an extensive tract, amounting with the land similarly circumstanced, to near twelve hundred acres. The soil is composed of a fine, black peat, incumbent on a bed of red sand full of water. They are bounded chiefly by the upland part of these estates, and surround the parish of Kynnersley, which also belongs to it, and which is composed of some of the finest turnip and barley soil in the kingdom. They had evidently formed the bottom of an extensive lake. The different brooks from the surrounding country held their course through them. These brooks are known in the country by the name of Strines, being distinguished from each other by the name of the places from which, or past which, they flow. Their course to the Tearn was devious and crooked in the extreme, injuring to a great extent, the land through which they ran. A great proportion of these moors was occupied by the tenants of the adjoining farms, who turned their stock in upon them for a portion of the summer season only. During the rest of the year it was impossible to use them. They afforded but a small quantity of food, and were in most places so wet, that it was at all times difficult to walk over them, it being necessary to select the hardest places to step on. They were covered in water after almost every severe rain owing to which the inhabitants of the neighbourhood were subject to frequent attacks of ague. The adjoining lands, besides, to an extent exceeding six hundred acres were kept in nearly a state of nature, owing to there being no level by which they could be drained, while this extensive district was subject to such inundations.

This district has been subsequently divided into regular enclosures, by great ditches, which fall into the main drains; and wherever it has been possible, these ditches have been made to serve this purpose, as well as that of a fence to the new roads which have been constructed across these moors. In one instance, one of these roads had been carried in a straight line for about two miles. On each side of this road trees have been planted at regular intervals, which will soon form one of the finest avenues in England".

This was how James Loch, the Duke's agent, described the area in 1820, land which had originally been purchased from the Earl of Shrewsbury. It has to be remembered that this was the landscape over which Newport was designed as a crossing. The Sutherlands were an exceptional family in their financial resources and in their recruitment of able men such as James Loch, the Gilbert Brothers and their partners in industrial enterprises. Loch for instance managed three other noble estates, was an MP, and involved in railways and canals. The Gilbert brothers were agents to the Duke of Bridgewater as well and brought his knowledge of canals to Shropshire. The Lilleshall estate was only a small part of his responsibilities and with the other English estates formed only 4% of the total family acreage though it provided most of the rental and capital. From about 1790 the second Marquess, the first Duke, through agents such as Loch and Bishton, pursued a radical and revolutionary policy of estate management on the most "improved" lines. This involved every aspect of the rural economy, drainage, roads, enclosure, rotation, leases, buildings, equipment and implements.

> *"In consequence of the complete state of ruin in which the farm buildings on these estates were found, it was necessary to incur a serious expense in constructing new ones. In this way it has been necessary to erect thirty seven new, and to repair throughout eight other extensive sets of farm offices, besides the smaller repairs which such estates necessarily require. They have been executed in the most substantial manner. They are built of the best possible brick work, covered with slates or tiles; and their cost, including the expence of those thoroughly repaired, may, on the average, be stated at from fifteen to sixteen hundred pounds each……….To almost every one of these homesteads is attached a threshing machine, constructed on the best principles; wherever water could be obtained, that has been made use of as the impelling power. Of late some of the more extensive farms have been provided with steam engines for that purpose".*

James Loch 1820.

The logistics of the improvements are impressive. It was estimated that between 1815 and 1820 17,000 yards of embankments were constructed; 27,000 yards of watercourses deepened and scoured; 46,000 yards of main ditches made or deepened; 30,000 yards of new hedges planted and 462,000 yards of underground draining laid with tiles and filled with stones. Several miles of estate roads or "drives" were made at the same time. Meanwhile in Sutherland new coastal villages were being built along with roads and bridges though these "clearances" were more contentious.

The impetus came from within the family, from its desire to maximise the benefits for future years and the belief in trusteeship of the land and the obligations to the rural economy ownership of land involved. Another incentive to both the Lilleshall and the Trentham estates was the growth of the nearby urban markets and their demand for a mixed range of agricultural products. Before 1815 investment was encouraged by fifty years of rising prices and profits, after this date investment continued though diminished, to offset low prices by improved practice particularly in the balance of crops. The family also had a personal need to invest for in 1803 the then Lord Stafford inherited the wealth of his uncle the Duke of Bridgewater of canal fame. This wealth would on the death of Stafford go to the second son and would therefore be lost to the estate. It therefore had to be invested and invested well for future consumption. On his death in 1833, Stafford had received an income of £2,084,373 from this source alone. Despite economic conditions investment in the west midlands estates was essential to offset the loss of the Bridgewater income, to provide capital for the unprofitable Scottish estates, for railways and canals and for the conspicuous consumption of Stafford House in London, Cliveden, Dunrobin (cost £54,000) Castle, Trentham Hall (£172,000) and Lilleshall Hall. Lilleshall Hall was designed by Sir Geoffrey Wyatville and completed in 1837. It reflected the new wealth and status of the Sutherlands. Previously they had lived in a half-timbered building known as the Old Lodge and from the 1750's the Old Hall which is still in the centre of Lilleshall village.

In 1833, when the second Duke succeeded, James Loch drew up a statement of the English estates; they show the financial magnitude of such undertakings and how they could absorb a whole local economy.

	Gross Rental	Permanent Expenditure	Net Income	Allowance For Improvement	Income
	£	£	£	£	£
Trentham	18,032	15,304	2,727	700	2,027
Newcastle	2,956	477	2,478	-	2,478
Wolverhampton	5,899	158	5,807	-	5,807
Lilleshall	25,899	8,440	17,459	2,000	15,459
Stittenham	52,854	24,381	28,473	2,700	25,773
	1,886	114	1,772	-	1,772
	54,740	24,495	30,245	2,700	27,545

Income Sutherland English Estates 1833. James Loch.

Such wealth and nobility made the Sutherlands national figures and the companions of royalty, particularly the Prince of Wales, a friendship frowned upon by Queen Victoria.

Though they did not have the involvement of the local gentry, it would be wrong to think of them as absentee landlords as they were frequently in residence at Lilleshall and concerned themselves with the welfare of their tenants and workers, as the epitaph on the memorial to the first Duke shows and as do the solid cottages and lodges in which they housed their employees. Each cottage, in a distinctive "Sutherland" style, had to have a large garden, pigsty and a walnut tree.

The Sutherlands had shared the Lordship of the Manor since 1579 and became the sole Lords when they purchased the moiety of the sixteenth Earl of Shrewsbury for £600 in 1829. Though much of this became meaningless, for instance the meeting of the Newport Court Leet was really the excuse for a substantial meal, the Lord of the Manor had to be compensated for the loss of rights whether in money or land when the marsh was enclosed in 1764 and again in 1860 when the cattle were taken off the streets into the new cattle market and the Lord lost his tolls. As late as 1924 C.W.S.Dixon, who had bought the Lordship from the Sutherlands was insisting on the payment of "Chief Rent" by the Urban District Council.

The estate had enormous influence on the local economy. The letter book of 1879, the year Lord Roberts invaded Afghanistan and the Zulus defeated the British at Isandhlwana in Natal, shows the scale of the commercial enterprise with property extending from Lilleshall to Sherrifhales, Kynnersley, Tibberton as well as the industrial parts of what is now north Telford. It is estimated that over 150 people were employed in supporting Lilleshall Hall; there were 30 men employed in the woodlands; 14 gamekeepers; 10 lodge keepers; 10 men on the Home Farm; gardeners and nurserymen (there were fifty-five gardeners at Trentham as well); bricklayers, sawyers, carpenters and labourers. The book lists 62 men receiving wages of up to £1 per week with Joseph Francis, head gardener, getting £60 pa. Outsiders were brought in to do specialist work, Messrs Sambrook, Butters, Middleton, Morris and Massey carrying out land drainage an endless task in the wetter parts of the Weald Moors. Joseph Bromfield of Upper Bar, Newport, had men whitewashing and cleaning for five days for £1.12. The carriage builder, W.B.Dawson, repaired four wheels on a dog cart for 20p. The Royal Victoria Hotel hired out a wagonette, two horses and a driver for £2.35 with 25p for the driver, as they had done since the hotel opened under William Liddle in 1830.

There was also seasonal employment on the land and the roads and during shoots and also on social occasions such as rent dinners which with the meals, drinks and cigars, brought business to local hostelries.

Contractors and shopkeepers in Newport were retained for plumbing and painting, for animal feeds and medicines, for leather goods (William Fishwick, saddler), dairy utensils (Eliza James, St Marys Street), ironmongery (Underhills and Jones and Aston), tarpaulins used for covering haystacks (R.J.Cooper, St Marys Street), groceries and household furnishings. Horne and Bennion in the High Street provided the office stationery.

The estate provided community services; churches; schools, Miss Marshall at Lilleshall school being paid £30 pa and her colleague, John Tomlinson, £60 pa; it provided the building for the workhouse at Lilleshall and later Donnington – and the income through the poor rates; it also supplied the drinking water and the fire engines.

The Dukes were great patrons, the 1879 book listing the Salop Infirmary, Shropshire Rifle Association, Shropshire Archaeological Society and Shropshire Agricultural Society. They were Presidents of Newport Agricultural Society in 1893, 1909 and 1912.

> **SONG**
> IN COMMEMORATION OF THE BIRTH OF
> **LORD GOWER,**
> Aged 21 Years, August 8th, 1807.
>
> TUNE,—*Liberty Hall.*
>
> As Time flies away o'er life's roundabout course,
> Velocid as *Childers*,* though mightier in force,
> Abundance of pleasure th' old fellow extends
> To each one who duly his progress attends.
>
> Hours, minutes, and seconds are plumes in his wings,
> Of bliss they're the source,—and, to energy, springs:
> And these, if applied and attended-to right,
> Will be found fully charg'd with extatic delight.
>
> The dawn of that day which to GOWER gave birth,
> Was a moment abounding with new-budding mirth,
> Which now, fully ripen'd, gives general joy,
> Enliv'ning the heart and delighting the eye.
>
> May each future year, that flies over his head,
> With the roses of pleasure his paths overspread;
> While sorrow's base thorns never poison the gale,
> But ever be strangers to *Trentham's* fair vale.
>
> In the praises of GOWER be tun'd ev'ry lay,
> To gladden the moments and honor the day;
> To the tip charge your goblets—your toasts be display'd—
> Your King and your Country, Lord GOWER and Trade.
>
> * Flying Childers, the fleetest horse that ever ran at Newmarket.
>
> G. DAVIS.
>
> SILVESTER, TYP. NEWPORT.

Many in Newport became prominent businessmen and community leaders through their contacts with the Lilleshall estate. Dawson and Bromfield have been mentioned. When the Sutherlands moved to London for the "season" their coach would pick up meat and tripe from Blakemans the butchers in the High Street in white cane baskets under white boiled cloths, to take to the capital. Joseph Whittingham came down from Lancashire to manage the building of Lilleshall Hall in 1829 and remained to manage the stone masonry on the estate and build the monument on Lilleshall Hill. He resided in Newport for fifty-five years and established a successful business erecting private and public buildings throughout the county, especially churches. Such was the patronage of the Dukes.

The Dukes also received appeals for justice, one in 1835 from Mr Wilson, a schoolmaster in Newport, who was owed £54 in school fees by one of the Dukes tenants, Mr Adams of Cherrington.

The accounts of the tenant farmers show the same involvement with the town. They sold produce - hams, bacon, and cheeses - to the grocers; bought and sold cattle in the livestock market; used the canal for lime and guano; they employed labour especially unskilled, Irish, labour; they purchased their luxuries - cigars and household china - as well as education for their children, and music lessons to enhance the social graces of their daughters.

Lilleshall Hall was meant to be the residence of the eldest son, and three dukes lived there prior to their inheritance and continued to visit afterwards for the shooting. The third Duke was the friend of the Prince of Wales and shared his love of shooting, fires, fire engines, trains and mistresses. Queen Victoria implored her son not to stay with the Duke at Dunrobin (30 December 1865) explaining that *"he does not live as a Duke ought"*. She thought him uncouth. The Prince replied *"he is a clever and most straightforward man in spite of certain eccentricities and formerly, faults."* The Duke arranged all the royal trips and hosted Garibaldi, the Shah of Persia and Disraeli. He had a mistress Mrs Blair whom he married when the Duchess died in 1886. In 1892 Mrs Blair was imprisoned in Holloway for a short time after destroying a letter, the Duke having died, in the presence of the Duke's solicitor and her own. The family later compromised and settled her in her own castle in Scotland.

1890 New Drive Constructed on Old Canal

The Prince and Princess of Wales visited Lilleshall on 23 January 1866 and the Prince was there again in 1890 when he ceremoniously opened the grand addition to the Hall of a two mile drive from the Newport Road, with three lodges and a set of "Golden Gates", replicas of those at Buckingham Palace. The lodges were equipped with apparatus which allowed the lodge gates to be opened by levers from under the lodge veranda. The drive was built over several hundred yards of the Duke of Sutherland canal which had linked Pave Lane with Donnington bringing cheap coal to Newport. The old bridge which spanned the canal can still be seen over the drive along with the marks of the tow ropes. The Duke had to compensate his neighbour, John Cotes of Woodcote, to the tune of £250 when closing the canal, since the Cotes family had the right to run a boat on the canal for 500 years!

The Prince was in a royal shooting party at Lilleshall on 6 January 1897. By now shooting was a large-scale distraction for the bored rich, with the military organisation of beaters, bearers and keepers who at Lilleshall had to be at least 6'2" tall and of proportionate physique and character.

John Grass was one of fourteen keepers in 1897 at £1 a week, a rent free house - Doublegates Lodge - coal, milk and butter and a horse and trap for his rounds as well as a gun, dog allowance and an annual payment of £3 in lieu of tips. He was clothed and had a livery for special occasions.

The fourth duke, Cromartie, and his wife Millicent, though over-indulgent and self-important, had a social conscience and provided a sick pay scheme, social club and health provision, looked after the elderly and were generous at Christmas. They built tin churches at Muxton and Granville and a substantial one at Donnington Wood.

Royal Shooting Party held at Lilleshall on January, 6th. 1897.

Guns: H.R.H. The Prince of Wales.
Duke of Sutherland.
Marquess of Ormond.
Earl of Dartmouth.
Lord Wolverton.
Lord Herbert Vane-Tempest.
Captain. A. Holford.
W.H.Mildmay, Esq.
Bag: 919 pheasants, 4 partridge, 67 hares, 70 rabbits.
Game distribution: Trentham, Wolverhampton Orphan Asylum,
Staffordshire General Infirmary, Shropshire General Infirmary,
Tenants, Servants, Gamedealer.

The landed estate was pre-eminent in the two decades before 1914 and the Sutherlands were part of that small circle of landed aristocracy surrounding Edward V11, as he now was, who made the social rules. On Saturday 26 November 1907 Edward motored through Newport to have lunch with the fourth duke. He came from Ingestre in Staffordshire where he had been visiting the Earl of Shrewsbury, whose Talbot Company had built the cars they were travelling in, through Stafford, where he paused to receive an address from the Mayor and Corporation. Newport had been quickly decorated when it was heard that the king had unexpectedly decided to visit, and people from a wide area stood in pouring rain as the procession of nine limousines, elegantly upholstered in crimson and grey, reached Newport at 1pm. After lunch, the royal party, including Mrs George Keppel, left Newport station in a special train of five saloons and two vans. A select few, including Lady Boughey from Aqualate Hall, were admitted to the platform by ticket.

The final flourish was the celebration of the Coming of Age of the Marquis of Stafford, later the fifth duke, in 1909. His father had had a similar celebration for his majority and in December 1828 the burgesses' minute book shows the bailiffs paying the Newport bell-ringers £1 for their ringing for the birth of a son and heir to the Earl Granville. The 1909 celebrations were elaborate and widespread, with more than a hint of a last, indulgent fling. The date for Newport was Monday 25 October. A small committee had raised £100 by subscription a small amount compared to previous events and reflecting the agricultural depression. The money was used to buy an ox from the Earl of Bradford. Roasting equipment was borrowed from Stratford on Avon. The ox was slaughtered and weighed in at the railway station at 27 score and 7 pounds. It was drawn in a procession around the town to the Square where it was put on a pole which took eight men to lift onto the cradle. It was adorned with horns and rosettes. The pole was turned by a large wheel, the hearth beneath consisting of iron hurdles with huge drip pans. The crowd was kept back by blocks and stalls from the market hall. The town was decorated from end to end. At 2.30 a procession of 600 children from the National School, led by a silver band, proceeded to the Square to await the Marquis and his parents. He was welcomed by the Chairman of the Urban District Council and presented by the Rector with an illuminated address in book form, gold and embossed and bound in Russian leather. He also received eight silver candlesticks. The Marquis carved the first piece of the ox and the meat was distributed in sandwiches. The children had tea in the Market Hall and there was a moonlit carnival at 6pm from the school with bands, yeomanry, scouts, cycles, floats and tableaux. It was accompanied by a lavish torchlight display watched by huge crowds. Throughout the day the church bells rang and the day ended with a dance in the Town Hall

The Square, Newport.
Marquis and Duchess of Sutherland in Centre
Coming of Age of Marquis Of Stafford 1909 Ox Roast

Behind the scenes the economies were beginning. The family became over indulgent and ran short of money - by their standards! In 1900 they still had 55 gardeners at Trentham all with comfortable lodgings. In 1909-10 they sold pictures from their collection of over 1,000. In 1911 Trentham was pulled down and in 1912, Stafford House in London was sold to become national property as "Lancaster House". Then began the sale of the estates in Shropshire and

Yorkshire. In July 1912 the northern parts of the Lilleshall Estate including the villages of Cherrington, Crudgington, Shray Hill and Tern went for £180,685.

In July 1914, 2,400 acres were sold between Wellington and Newport; 9 dairy farms, smaller farms, smallholdings, 70 cottages and gardens, residential properties and building land. Also sold were three public houses and a brick and tile works. In January 1917 the Duke, now the fifth duke, wrote to his tenants telling them of his decision to sell the remainder of the estate and giving them notice to quit on Lady Day 1918. He blamed the burden of taxation and death duties and hoped all the tenants would become owners, as many of them did. The sale in July 1917 included Lilleshall Hall, elaborately built in 1829 by Sir Geoffrey Wyatville, and Lilleshall Abbey, where the story began. In total there were 7,800 acres with 30 farms, 45 holdings, 150 cottages and 1,000 acres of woodland bringing in a rental of £20,000 pa. It covered the villages of Lilleshall, Sheriffhales and Heathhill. The three days realised £217,611, the Hall, Abbey and grounds being bought by a syndicate for £45,000.

It is difficult in this modern age to find anything comparable to the role and function of these estates. Certainly there was nothing immediately to replace them. One incident from the 1917 sale shows how inter-dependent the estate and the community were. Near Newport is Lilleshall Hill, a prominent feature on which stands the obelisk to the first Duke from his grateful tenants. The hill was sold. The local people were now denied a traditional open space but more important the hill contained the reservoir. Since 1902 the Dukes had supplied water to the area but now the estate was in private hands there was no such obligation. Uproar and a public meeting ensued and the problem was only solved when the Duke re-purchased the hill and sold it, except for the site of the monument, to the Newport Rural District Council.

In 1919 the Hall and the Abbey were purchased by Sir John Leigh who was reputed to have been left £2 million made in the cotton industry of Altrincham by his father, one of those men who had "done well in the war". He added the 4,000 acres of Woodcote in 1920. In the 1914-18 war Sir John was a generous benefactor with donations to funds and hospitals. In 1921 he purchased the "Pall Mall Gazette and Globe". In 1923 he placed the Lilleshall property in the "Pall Mall Trust". In 1925 at the Royal Victoria Hotel the estate and the farms were again sold but there was no offer for the Hall. In 1927 another attempt only reached £25,000 so much had property and agricultural values declined.

LOVELY LILLESHALL

Band Engagements for Season 1929 and Special Attractions.

SATURDAY, MAY 18th.—LILLESHALL PARK RACES.
UNDER PONY TURF CLUB RULES.
Admission to Course, 1/2.   First Race, 3.30 p.m.
SUNDAY, MAY 19th.—JACKFIELD PRIZE SILVER BAND.
MONDAY, MAY 20th.—BAND OF THE 5th BATT. ROYAL WARWICK'S REGT. (T.A.).
SUNDAY, MAY 26th.—LILLESHALL COLLIERIES PRIZE BAND.
SUNDAY, JUNE 2nd.—BOLAS VICTORY SILVER BAND.
SUNDAY, JUNE 9th.—THE BAND OF THE 243rd LEEK (H) BATTERY, R.A. (T.A.).
SUNDAY, JUNE 16th.—DONNINGTON WOOD COLLIERY SILVER PRIZE BAND.
SUNDAY, JUNE 23rd.—REVO ELECTRIC WORKS PRIZE BAND.
MONDAY, JUNE 24th.—LILLESHALL PARK RACES.
UNDER PONY TURF CLUB RULES.
Admission to Course, 1/2.   First Race, 3.30 p.m.
SUNDAY, JUNE 30th.—THE NORTH STAFFS. "IMPERIAL" MILITARY BAND.
SUNDAY, JULY 7th.—LILLESHALL COLLIERIES PRIZE BAND.
SUNDAY, JULY 14th.—JACKFIELD PRIZE SILVER BAND.
SUNDAY, JULY 21st.—DONNINGTON WOOD COLLIERY SILVER PRIZE BAND.
SUNDAY, JULY 28th.—THE BAND OF THE 54th (WEST RIDING AND STAFFS.) MEDIUM BRIGADE ROYAL ARTILLERY (T.A.).
SUNDAY, AUGUST 4th.—THE NORTH STAFFS. "IMPERIAL" MILITARY BAND.
MONDAY, AUGUST 5th.—BOLAS VICTORY SILVER BAND.
LILLESHALL PARK RACES.
UNDER PONY TURF CLUB RULES.
Admission to Course, 1/2   First Race, 3.30 p.m.
TUESDAY, AUGUST 6th.—LILLESHALL FLOWER SHOW.
Admission to all Parts, 1/3.
JACKFIELD PRIZE SILVER BAND.
SUNDAY, AUGUST 11th.—LONGTON TOWN PRIZE BAND.
SUNDAY, AUGUST 18th.—ALDRIDGE COLLIERY SILVER PRIZE BAND.
SUNDAY, AUGUST 25th.—DONNINGTON WOOD SILVER PRIZE BAND.
SUNDAY, SEPT. 1st.—THE BAND OF THE 243rd LEEK (H) BATTERY, R.A. (T.A.).
SUNDAY, SEPT. 8th.—LILLESHALL COLLIERIES PRIZE BAND.
SUNDAY, SEPT. 15th.—LONGTON TOWN PRIZE BAND.
SUNDAY, SEPT. 22nd.—BOLAS VICTORY SILVER BAND.
SUNDAY, SEPT. 29th.—JACKFIELD PRIZE SILVER BAND.

"ADVERTISER" PRINTING WORKS, NEWPORT, SALOP.

A handbill from 1929. It indicates the wide range of entertainment at Lilleshall Hall in the 1920's before becoming the National Sports Centre in 1950.

An advertisement of 6 August 1927 announced that the Hall was to be open to the public daily from 15 August. Attractions included the gardens, walks and the abbey. There would be lunches and parking and bus services from Newport and Shifnal at 5p both ways. Lilleshall Estates Ltd, whose Managing Director was Herbert Ford, aimed at providing a public amusement centre for the new car-owning classes. At a hearing in February 1928 for a restaurant license it was stated that between the previous August and October there had been 30,000 visitors eating 20,000 meals. In 1928 200,000 visitors were expected. It was argued that the estate and the house would otherwise have been broken up and that the new enterprise would bring money into the district. It was envisaged as the *"Mecca of the Midlands"*. As well as the abbey and the Hall there was the famous, and still existing, tree collection; there were sports facilities, catering, a ballroom, horseracing, a miniature railway and golf. There were floodlights of 1,000 watt capacity covering the whole forty acres of gardens. Thousands of coloured bulbs lent by the West Bromwich Electricity Department draped the trees from September to the end of October. There were many "Special Events". In September 1927 tennis was staged with British players Joan Fry and H.K.Lester; in July 1932 Amy Johnson flew in with her husband. But there were problems. On January 18 1932 Lilleshall Racing Club Ltd went into voluntary liquidation and the facilities were sold including the grandstand and the winning post. In September of that year publicity was whipped up by the mystery of a secret passage from the Abbey to Longford Church, nearly three miles away. There were excavations and diviners and various psychics descended on the Abbey. The Estate offered £50 to the person who discovered the passage and a book was published *"The Mystery of Lilleshall Abbey"*.

In June 1939 the last nine holes of the golf-course were completed after two years work. The first nine holes had been built over parkland, the last nine through a *"primeval forest"*. Thousands of trees were uprooted, pulled out or blown up using 17cwt of gelignite. The scene was reminiscent of Ypres; thousands of tons of soil were removed by heavy machinery. The cost was estimated at £1,000 per hole. It is now a private members club.

Bomb Dropped on Lilleshall Golf Course 1941

The Second World War put an end to the entertainment venture, the Hall being occupied by Cheltenham Ladies College and, until September 1947, 400 children of Dr Barnardos.

Already in October 1945 Herbert Ford, who had remained in the Hall during the war and had transferred his West Bromwich factory to the Audco premises, had sold livestock and machinery; in August 1947 negotiations took place for the Hall to become a Country Club for Coddon Sports and Social Club this was the huge ordnance depot hurriedly transferred from Woolwich to Donnington just before the outbreak of war. In March 1948 Ansells Brewery gave up the license at the Hall and transferred it to a new hotel *The White House* at Muxton. In December 1949 Shifnal Rural District Council received an application to develop *"Lilleshall Hall as a PT Centre"*. Herbert Ford sold the catering equipment and outside effects and on 13 January 1950 the Central Council for Physical Recreation purchased the Hall with money from the South African *"Aid to Britain Fund"*, after a three year search for premises. Ford stayed on in part of the house. As a national sports centre it is back in the national and international limelight as it was in the heady Victorian days of the third Duke and the Prince of Wales.

THE DAY'S ARRANGEMENTS

H.R.H. THE PRINCESS ELIZABETH'S PROGRAMME

Her Royal Highness will arrive at the Golden Gates (11.20 a.m.), be welcomed by a Reception Party at the front door of the Hall and unveil a plaque commemorating the opening of the Centre (11.25 a.m.), receive certain guests in the common room (11.30 a.m.), see round the grounds (11.40 a.m.), perform the Opening Ceremony (12.20 p.m.), return to the Hall for lunch (12.40 p.m.) and leave by the Shifnal drive (1.45 p.m.).

INFORMATION BUREAU

Guests are invited to visit the Information Bureau in the Orangery (near the ornamental garden), where information about the day's arrangements, the work of the C.C.P.R. and the activities of the Centre will be available, and publications and photographs will be on display.

ACTIVITIES

The following activities will be in progress from 10.15 to 11.15 a.m., 11.35 a.m. to 12.5 p.m. and 2 to 3 p.m., the associations named being responsible for their organisation :—

- Archery (Grand National Archery Society)
- Association Football (The Football Association)
- Athletics (Amateur Athletic Association)
- Basket Ball (Amateur Basket Ball Association of England and Wales)
- Fencing (Amateur Fencing Association)
- Indoor Cricket School
- Judo (British Judo Association)
- Lawn Tennis (Lawn Tennis Association)
- Netball (All England Netball Association)
- Weight-Lifting (British Amateur Weight-Lifters' Association)

Guests are cordially invited to join in American Square Dancing from 2 to 3 p.m. on the South Lawn, led by a representative of the English Folk Dance and Song Society.

REFRESHMENTS

Refreshments will be on sale in Marquee A from 10.30 a.m. onwards.

INSPECTION OF THE CENTRE

Guests wishing to see over the Hall between 2 and 3 p.m. will find guides stationed near the front door.

14

THE OPENING CEREMONY

Guests are asked to take their places (according to the directions on their admittance cards) by 12 noon.

H.R.H. THE PRINCESS ELIZABETH DUCHESS OF EDINBURGH

will come out on to the Terrace at 12.20 p.m.

A bouquet will be presented to Her Royal Highness

The National Anthem

THE RT. REV. THE LORD BISHOP OF LICHFIELD

will dedicate the centre

VISCOUNT HAMPDEN

President of the C.C.P.R., will welcome The Princess

H.R.H. THE PRINCESS ELIZABETH

MR. C. H. TORRANCE

Deputy High Commissioner for the Union of South Africa, will respond

The South African National Anthem

15

Centre pages of Official Opening Souvenir Programme June 1951

NOTES

One: The Lilleshall Estate.

1. Loch, James, *An account of the improvements on the estates of the Marquess of Stafford*, (1820).
2. Stamper, Paul, *The Farmer Feeds Us All*, Shropshire Books, (1989).
3. Richards, Eric, *Leviathan of Wealth, Sutherland fortune in the Industrial Revolution*, Routledge, (1973).
4. Magnus, Phillip, *King Edward the Seventh*, Penguin Books, (1964)
5. Jones, David. S., *The Dukes Gamekeeper*, Shropshire Magazine, February, 1994.
6. Williams, W. Howard, *The Lilleshall Estates and the Leveson Gowers*, Shropshire Magazine, August 1958.
7. Williams, W. Howard, *The First Duke Of Sutherland Was The Man Who Tamed The Wild Moors*, Shropshire Magazine, September 1958.
8. Trinder, Barrie, *The Industrial Revolution in Shropshire,* Phillimore, (1973) for the definitive description of the industrial aspects of the estate. This chapter deals only with the Newport connections.
9. *Lilleshall Estate Letter Book 1879-80,* Newport and District History Society, archives.
10. Newport and Market Drayton Advertiser, [NMDA]. Coming of Age of Marquess of Stafford, 1909; estate sales from 1912; sale 1927; Lovely Lilleshall from 1927; Lilleshall Marvels 1928; National Recreation Centre from 1948; Lilleshall Hill, 1964.
11. Pevsner, N., *The Buildings of England – Shropshire*, (1958), p. 166.
12. *Lovely Lilleshall,* various guides and souvenir booklets.
13. Lead Peter, *Agents of Revolution – John and Thomas Gilbert.* University of Keele 1989.

Lilleshall Marvels

Many new attractions.

Aeroplanes, Stage Coach, Light Railway and Racing.

The thousands who visited Lilleshall Hall and grounds last year were greatly impressed not only by the natural beauties of the place but by the remarkable way in which, through the enterprise and ingenuity of Mr. R. Ford, Managing Director of the Lilleshall Estates Ltd, the condition of the grounds were being improved and fresh attractions being added. These visitors however will be astonished when they return as they are certain to do during the coming season and discover the wonderful progress that has been made in rendering the whole place more attractive and in catering for practically every variety of taste.

In the first place it will be possible from Easter onwards to arrive at Lilleshall by aeroplane, the Air Ministry having granted a full license for part of the extensive grounds to be used as a civil aerodrome so that from Easter throughout the summer a regular air service will operate between Lilleshall and Castle Bromwich. It is likewise hoped to work a regular service between Castle Bromwich, Wolverhampton and Lilleshall provided a suitable landing ground can be obtained on the outskirts of Wolverhampton. In addition passenger flights from the ground will also be given so that all desirous of seeing what the district looks like from the air, or who have longed to experience the delights of a flight, will be able to do so. For a short flight the fee will be 5/- [25p], for a local flight 10/- [50p] and for a long distance flight, £1. The service will be provided by the Henderson Flying School Ltd and will be under the charge of Col. Henderson who recently arranged the air service between Johannesburg and Capetown for the South African government. It is also hoped to form a light aeroplane club with headquarters at the Lilleshall aerodrome. Private owners of aeroplanes all over the country are being invited to visit Lilleshall and several of these in the south have already intimated that they will run up for a Saturday or Sunday trip.

At the same time for the benefit of those who prefer less modern forms of travelling and who love the romantic past, the syndicate have arranged to subsidise a daily stage coach service from Birmingham to the Hall and back, a distance of about 32 miles each way. The coach which is a genuine and typical relic of olden days, black and yellow in colour, was constructed by Windover the famous coach builders and had been acquired from Lord Knaresborough. It will be driven by a former coachman of Lord Lonsdale who will be attired in the correct uniform as also will be the guard, the latter being equipped with the traditional horn. The start will be made from the centre of Birmingham the journey being made along the old coaching road through Soho and Handsworth, rich with associations of James Watt, Matthew Boulton, William Murdoch, Josiah Wedgewood and many other historical characters who must have traversed it, and thence to the Black Country to Wolverhampton. From there the route lies along the Tettenhall Road past the Old Green where the horses will be changed at an old country inn. The coach will next process along the Shifnal Road to Albrighton and Tong through old fashioned villages practically unaltered since the days when the stagecoach to Chester and the north daily passed through them, where stops will be made at old world inns for the purpose of watering the horses.

Tong it will be recalled possesses a fine old church the scene of the last days of Little Nell and her grandfather immortalised by Dickens. The church was actually attacked by the Roundheads during the Civil War but was saved from destruction by a pre-emptory message from Cromwell who was a friend of the Local Squire. From Tong the journey continues along the Newport to Chester Road, over the Watling Street and so on to the Golden Gates presented by the people of Trentham to the late Duke of Sutherland. The final stages being through the magnificent private drive to the Hall two miles in length and bordered for a considerable distance by magnificent trees. It is rumoured that the re-incarnated spirit of Dick Turpin, mounted on Black Bess will hold up the coach in the course of its journey and will levy a voluntary contribution from the travellers in the cause of local charity. People coming to the Hall from Newport or Shifnal railway stations, will be met there by motor buses.

No one need be deterred by bad weather from visiting the Hall for innumerable attractions are provided indoors for both old and young. In the main entrance hall stands an oriental bazaar where all sorts of useful and handsome souvenirs may be purchased and where also the official, detailed history of Lilleshall can be obtained. This contains a full description of Lilleshall Abbey and its siege by the Parliamentary forces during the Civil War, in which it was reduced to ruins.

A splendid luncheon and tea room overlooking the terrace accommodates at one sitting over 750 persons, while overhead, approached by a magnificent staircase, is a tea room, providing seating for at least 200 and this will also make a fine ballroom for parties. From its window a superb view of the surrounding countryside for many miles is available.

By arrangement with the Morris Motor Company an excellently furnished Club Room, together with a writing room, is placed at the disposal of owners with Morris cars, who may become members of the new Morris Club and be entitled to the full use of these rooms simply by supplying their names and addresses, together with the numbers of their engine and registration numbers, to the Company. All the rooms are lit by electric light shining through alabaster shells.

On descending to the amusement basement which has been formed out of the extensive subterranean regions, one finds games and slot machines providing enjoyment for both old and young. A new rifle range has just been installed, the rifle used being 2.2 repeaters. There are also two Ski Board tables, a Stradla game for parties, a Whirler Ball, a bowling game with prizes offered for the highest score, a punch ball, a cycle race for which two people mount stationery cycles and pedal as hard as possible to see who can register the fastest speed, and other games. The principal attraction here however will certainly be the electric racing train the only game of its kind in the world being most fascinating and scientific and yet easily learnt. It can be played by as many as six individuals at a time each player having under his control a model electric train on a model railway track. The prizes are for the competitor who succeeds in getting his train to the goal first. More games will be added in due course for the management are sparing no pains in supplying high class amusements for both parents and children. Boxes have been placed in various rooms for visitors to place in them any suggestions they may care to make concerning the undertaking, all of which will receive careful consideration.

It is the aim of the management to maintain the extensive grounds in all the beauty and order in which they were kept in the days of their former owner the Duke of Sutherland and so that this high standard may be realised they have wisely secured the services and vast experience of Mr George Adams of Lilleshall the Dukes` former head gardener, who is now actively engaged in supervising the numerous improvements being carried out, having already laid out new shrubbery's. A handsome statue of Cupid has been erected in the Dial Garden and another of Psyche in the Rose Garden while once more the fountains play.

The extensive greenhouses are not open to the public but are being used for the production of tomatoes, a special feature, peaches, cucumbers, melons, grapes, flowers etc, all of which will be on sale to the public in the orangery being also available at meals. Vegetables for the luncheons are being grown in the Hall kitchen garden so these will always be fresh.

The first class catering for lunches and teas is in the hands of the well-known firm of Pattison, Hughes and Company of Birmingham.

Tennis, bowls, clock golf, putting greens and American skittle alleys, a most interesting game, are provided out of doors, while swings, seesaws, giant slides etc are to be found in the children's playground.

The management being out to support local talent and industry as much as possible, have engaged some first class bands in the district to play on Saturdays and Sundays during the coming season, among these being the Lilleshall Colliery Prize Band and the Bolas Victory Silver Band, the latter will be in attendance on Easter Monday.

A further feature bound to provide considerable enjoyment is the Lilleshall Abbey Woodland Railway now in course of construction by Messrs Bagley of Burton on Trent. This will be a miniature railway starting at the station at the Lilypond garden and running nearly to the Abbey through some of the most charming woods and gardens and back again. The route, which is a mile in extent is being planted with Rhododendrons and other flowers in order to make it of even greater beauty. The line is a two foot gauge and the locomotive weighing two tons capable of drawing a train with 36 passengers. Although the work of laying the rails has only started a fortnight ago it is already almost completed and will be running shortly.

Woodlands Railway – Lovely Lilleshall

Those who prefer to wander through the grounds on foot will be charmed with the Lovers Walk, a delightful path near to the Abbey running along the edge of a small stream containing a fine waterfall.

Lovers of animals will be interested in the dog cemetery where lies the remains of several of the former owners dogs, each grave having a miniature headstone. Memories of the old regime in Russia are recalled by the largest and most imposing of these bearing the following inscription: "Csar a Russian wolfhound lies here. He was given at Moscow in 1856 to the Marchioness of Stafford by Alexander II Emperor of all the Russias. This stone is erected here by his mistress in memory of his devotion to her and as an act of sorrow at his death".

The Abbey ruins have now been completely cleared of the undergrowth which hid their majestic proportions, these being now completely visible. Evidence of the seriousness with which the management regard their responsibilities as custodians of the Abbey on behalf of the nation is shown by the fact that recent labour there has cost them a considerable sum.

With the co-operation and support of the Lilleshall Estate Ltd as owners it is proposed to lay out and equip a racecourse on the side of the former Ducal polo ground, with such additional land as may be necessary in Lilleshall Park, for the purpose of racing under the rules of the Pony Turf Club. The patron of the Turf Club is the Earl of Derby KG, while amongst the Stewards are Viscount Lascelles, the Earl of Caernavon, Sir William Bass, General Gurson and Major Alexander. It is intended to hold six meetings each year those of 1928 having been fixed for June 2, July 7, August 8, September 8, October 11 and October 13. The racing will be rigidly governed by local Stewards and these will include Viscount Edenham, Sir Edward Hanmer, Brig. General Hickman, Brig. General R Hoare, Col. H.B.Sykes, Mr.J.Reid-Walker and Major E.M.Vaughan.

A private Ltd Company is in course of formation of which the following have agreed to act as its first Directors Messrs J.M.Belcher, Tibberton, H.Ford, Lilleshall, W.S.Lane, Birmingham, Chartered Accountant, R.P.Liddle, Church Aston and J.Royle, Sutton. The above named Stewards and Directors are taking a pecuniary interest in the Company. An agreement between the proposed Company and the Lilleshall Estate Ltd will in due course be completed, with the main object of placing the undertaking on a secure footing. In lieu of rent the Lilleshall Estate Ltd will participate in the takings on race days. Any pony up to and under 15 hands is eligible for the above races provided it is registered with the Pony Turf Club. This can be done on application to the Secretary, Mr.A.M.Knight, Lilleshall Park.

The course, which will be a mile in length all but 130 yards, the last quarter of a mile being straight, is already in course of preparation. The stands and paddocks will be situated at Pear Tree Lodge upon an eminence where an uninterrupted view of the whole course is obtainable. There will also be a grandstand. Pear Tree Lodge will be used as a meeting room for the Stewards and a ladies cloakroom, while any amount of stabling will be available at Lilleshall Hall and Mr.J.M.Belchers, Lillyhurst. Excellent quarters for the stable boys will be provided at the Hall these being the original quarters used by the Dukes stable boys.

At the first meeting £250 will be given in stakes and six races will be held, the distances of which will vary from six furlongs to 1.5 miles. The price of admission to the course will be 2/-, to Tattersalls ring 10/-, the Silver Ring 5/- and the additional ring 2/6.

A grass track meeting for motor cycles and motorcycles with sidecars will be held in the Hall grounds from May 19 under the auspices of the Wolverhampton Motorcycle and Car Club, this being followed by speed events on May 26. On April 21 a motorcycle football match will be played between teams from Coventry and Wolverhampton.

The management have kindly consented to open the grounds on a Friday in June in aid of the Queen Alexandra Hospital Garden Fund. The price of admission will be 1/- per head and Mr Ford has also prevailed upon the caterers to give 20% of their takings on that day to the Fund.

Gardens and Fountain – Lovely Lilleshall

There is no doubt that the management headed by Mr Ford are doing all in their power to provide a thoroughly enjoyable time at small expense, to all *who care to visit the Lilleshall Estate. Mr Ford`s carefully thought out plan being admirably translated into action by an expert staff under the skilled direction of the able manager Mr Rabjohn. One cannot but feel that the public owes to the Lilleshall Estate Ltd, a deep debt of gratitude on having made available to them on easy terms the opportunity of enjoying the splendid house and grounds. If the Company had not purchased the property it is more than probable that the Hall would by now be in the hands of the housebreakers, so they have succeeded in preventing a great act of vandalism.*

Newport and Market Drayton Advertiser 6 April 1928.

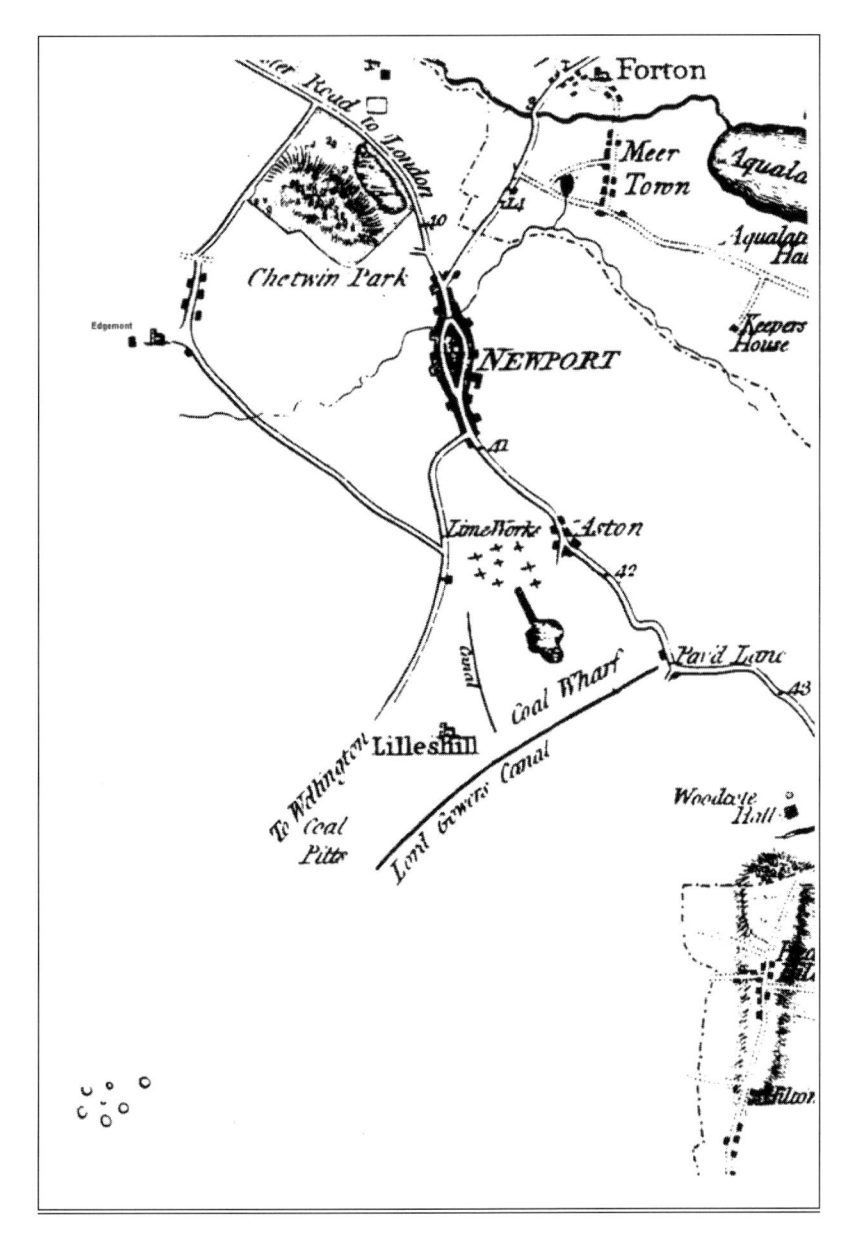

Newport 1775

2. THE BOUGHEYS OF AQUALATE

Aqualate is in Staffordshire just a short walk over the county boundary from Newport, Shropshire. Its history is closely associated with the market town though few locals have ever seen the Hall, its deer-park or the Mere except distant views from Forton, Meretown or the road to Stafford. More visible is the decayed monument at Forton, the "castle" on the Meretown road and the ruined lodges facing Newport and Coley Mill.

The mere, the central feature of the estate, is glacial in origin and the largest sheet of water in Staffordshire, a mile long and 600 yards wide, covering 220 acres. Over the years changes in farming and silting from the three feeder streams have made it smaller and shallower so that it is now about 4-5 feet deep in most places. In the past the nature of the mere and the necessity for water in a rural economy led to disputes between neighbours and users, the watering of hemp and flax for instance, polluting the water for fish, while keeping the level artificially high to drive the mill, led to complaints about the water-logging of the surrounding land. In 1877 there was a legal dispute with the Shropshire Railway and Canal Company over the discharge of water from the canal into the Mere causing flooding. In 1851 it was described as:

> "....abounding in pike, and other fish of very large dimensions, pike having been caught in it, weighing 36 lbs., and carp as heavy as 15lbs."

Today its value is more scenic but the setting led to the siting of the Hall nearby and must have been one of the attractions to the Bougheys apart from being a good investment.

The Original Tudor House c1630

Sir Thomas Skrymsher purchased the estate in 1547 and erected the first Hall on a low hill above the mere. He died in 1633 his tomb being in the north aisle of Forton Church. They were related to the Barnfield family great benefactors of Newport who built the Butter Market and supported almshouses and the Royal Free English School. Dr Johnson was also a Skrymsher. The male line ran out in 1689 with the death of Edwin Skrymsher and the property went to two sisters the eldest, Mary, getting Aqualate. Mary married Nicholas Acton in 1654 and they had a daughter Elizabeth. Mary married for her second husband Sir Timothy Baldwyn. He died in 1696 and there were no children. Elizabeth Acton, Mary's daughter, married Charles Baldwyn nephew of Sir Timothy, an MP, barrister and Recorder of Ludlow. Their eldest son, Acton Baldwyn married Eleanor Skrymsher of Norbury. Their third son, Charles, succeeded to Aqualate and his father's Shropshire estates. Neither Mary nor Elizabeth resided at Aqualate. Charles married Catherine Lacon Childe and had three children

William, Charles and Catherine all baptised at Forton. He married a second time to a Mrs Palmer. Charles lived at Aqualate as the other estates were entailed to the children. He was often in dispute with his son and heir. Charles had financial difficulties despite marrying the heiress of the Lacon Childe family. He was extravagant and built on a large scale from 1772 some, described by Twemlow, as *"good and solid"* and some *"rather tawdry and purposeless"* such as the *Monument* and *Castle*. Charles added the stable courtyard to the east with room for fifty horses and twelve grooms also the fish stews and farm buildings, a walled garden and paddocks. In 1788 there was a meeting of creditors at the *Red Lion*, Newport, to decide whether to sell Aqualate to pay the debts of Charles Baldwin [Baldwyn] and his son Mr W Childe. In 1795 he got the consent of Parliament to sell Aqualate. This was necessary as he was depriving his heir. In 1796 the estate was valued at £69,584 and contained 2,326 acres, including £4,281 for 6,284 trees of which 60% were oak, Aqualate means *"Oak-track"*. His son William had gone his own way taking the name Lacon and marrying into the Leighton family. Charles` creditors were after him and he became bankrupt. He died in 1801.

> *"The Mansion House consists on the ground floor of a Hall 28 by 23 feet; anti room 24 by 15; Dining room 36 by 23; Drawing room 24 by 18; Library 24 by18; Breakfast parlour 18 by 15 with exceeding good Stewards and housekeepers room and Butlers pantry and large servants hall and kitchen with Brewhouse, washroom, laundry and other offices complete. On the first floor four bed chambers and four dressing rooms and on the second floor seven bed chambers and three dressing rooms.*
>
> *There are capital stables for upwards of fifty horses over which are twelve good lodging rooms with coach house, granaries, barns and all other outbuildings necessary for the management of a large house. In view of the Mansion House are upwards of sixty acres of rich ornamental plantation beautifully disposed besides a quantity of timber growing on the premises and at a proper distance is a most noble natural lake or piece of water remarkable for pike and fish of various kinds called Aqualate Mere containing upwards of 200 statute acres which for extent and beauty has not its equal in the that part of the Kingdom, so that there is no place in England more desirable for the residence of a Nobleman or Gentleman of large fortune.*
>
> *The whole of the estate lies together and is situated within two miles of the market and post town of Newport in the County of Salop and the same distance from the great turnpike road between London and Chester ten miles from Stafford and twenty miles from Shrewsbury. It is near inexhaustible mines of excellent coals and limestone to both which there is a very good road.*
>
> *The present yearly costs of all the above estate are only £1500.5.10 but upon a survey and valuation lately taken by Mr Bishton of Walsall on a very moderate valuation the estates are worth to be let at the yearly sum of £2197.19.0.*
>
> *The chief rent payable by the copyhold tenants amount annually to £13.19.10. The annual value of such copyhold estates exceed £1,400 a year.*
>
> *The Glebe Land belonging to the Rectory consists of 45a.3r.24p and the annual value of the Rectory including Glebe Land is upwards of £340 a year.*

The land tax payable out of the whole estate is only £54.4.8

The present incumbent of the Rectory of Forton is the Reverend Mr Oakley aged about 80. The next presentation is disposed of and subject thereto the Advowsen is to be sold."

1797 Valuation. Staff. S.S.T.A.S.. D645/5

The valuation lists the tenants. Francis Wedge, who was to act as agent, had Fernhill, Coley and Aqualate Hall farms. There was also Forton Farm, Sutton and Lower Sutton Farms and Lodge Farm. In all 2,299 acres an attractive proposition for a father with the duty of setting up a son as a landed gentleman.

Thomas Fletcher married Anne Fenton of Newcastle under Lyme whose mother, Anastasia, was a Boughey. Thomas, like his father, was a banker and business partner of the Fentons an influential Newcastle family. He was an autocrat who was also musical and played the violin. He became a leading citizen, active magistrate and was knighted in 1798 for his public work buying his title as he had no landed estate to qualify in the traditional way. He inherited Betley Court and the few acres that went with it from his father-in law and only moved there from his town house in 1792. Sir Thomas Fletcher died in 1812 and his monument is in St Margaret's, Betley, where the Bougheys remained considerable landowners into the twentieth century.

John Fenton Fletcher was born on 1 May 1784. His cousin George Boughey of Audley, a wealthy lawyer and the last of the Boughey line, died in 1788 when John was four years old. George was one of four sons from Audley, his brother John being a lawyer in Newcastle, William was a clergyman and Thomas an apothecary in London. All died without issue before 1750. George inherited all the property formerly in the hands of the Cradocks, Fentons and Fletchers. George a barrister of the Inner Temple, was a man of some standing involved in several famous cases. At his death he had property in Stafford, Wiltshire, Sussex and London. There was no direct heir so the Staffordshire estates went to cousins Catherine Tollet and Anastasia Fenton and the remainder to John Fenton Fletcher. When Anastasia and Catherine died their property mainly in Audley but also in Stoke and Cheshire also passed to John.

Being a lawyer the details of the legacy were precise, £20,000 to accumulate until he came of age and then to be invested in land. John was to adopt the Boughey coat of arms and the name. The property in Wiltshire went to the boy immediately and the London property was sold and the proceeds invested in land in the counties. The trustees purchased land in Audley and the Aqualate family continued as Lords of the Manor and owners of most of the land at Audley where there are still the "Boughey Arms" and the Sir Thomas Boughey High School. In 1797 the trustees, of whom his father was one, bought Aqualate for £64,728 with the funds accumulated during the minority. The trustees also paid £10,500 for the Lordship of Audley and 426 acres. The legacy was tied up in a Chancery Account specifically for the purchase of land

On the 9 February 1808 he married Henrietta Dorothy eldest daughter of Sir John Chetwode of Oakley, Stafford, on the Cheshire border. The Chetwodes were well connected and this was a good marriage and a further step into the landed gentry. She brought with her a marriage settlement of £60,000 in consols controlled by the trustees and entailed with the estate. John Boughey had to match this funding with £20,000 which he appears to have borrowed. These restricted funds handicapped development of the estate.

The Fletchers had political ambitions as Whigs and stood in the Newcastle constituency against the powerful Leveson-Gower interest. In 1812 John Boughey took the seat. In 1815 his father-in-law, Sir John Chetwode won the other Newcastle seat in a by-election. They were both defeated in 1818. Letters from John in 1820 show him pledging support to the new King and seeking advice and signatures for the forthcoming election and agonising with his cousin Twemlow as to whether he should stand. Stand he did in such a manner that the Earl Gower withdrew rather than face defeat and humiliation. Despite the wealth of the Gower interest John Boughey won his victories relatively cheaply and approached the role seriously not just as a further step up the social ladder. He was on a first visit to the house he had leased in London as a base for his parliamentary work when he heard of the death of his son in 1823 a death that ended any political ambitions.

The estate had become neglected by the Baldwyns and in the next two years Thomas Fletcher spent £500 on immediate repairs with the help of Francis Wedge a tenant who also acted as agent and lived in the Hall up to 1805. Thomas Fletcher brought in John Webb who produced the first plans for the house and gardens and constructed new roads, fencing and bridges using local sub-contractors and labour like Thomas Crump a bricklayer, John Cobb a builder from Chetwynd End and Fieldhouse a family from Forton.

To enlarge the park and make the house and mere more secluded the existing road in front of the Hall which went through Forton to Newport, was moved to a new turnpike along the line of the present, more direct, Newport-Stafford road. This new turnpike was approved by Quarter Sessions in 1807. This was a familiar feature of emparkment and occurred at Attingham Park about the same period where John Nash and Humphrey Repton were also involved.

Between 1805, when he came of age, and 1812, John became more involved in the remodelling, rebuilding and enlarging of the Hall and church and redesigning of the park. Don Yale in his study *"The landscaping of Aqualate Park 1805-13"* shows the problems and intrigues involved. Haycock of Shrewsbury was engaged in the early building work but acrimonious correspondence led to a final payment of £70 and rejection. John Nash was being consulted by October 1805 but a letter on War Office notepaper and dated 29 December 1803 includes sketches by Nash. Does this suggest earlier secret approaches or was it just an old envelope?

The Nash Sketches for Aqualate 1803

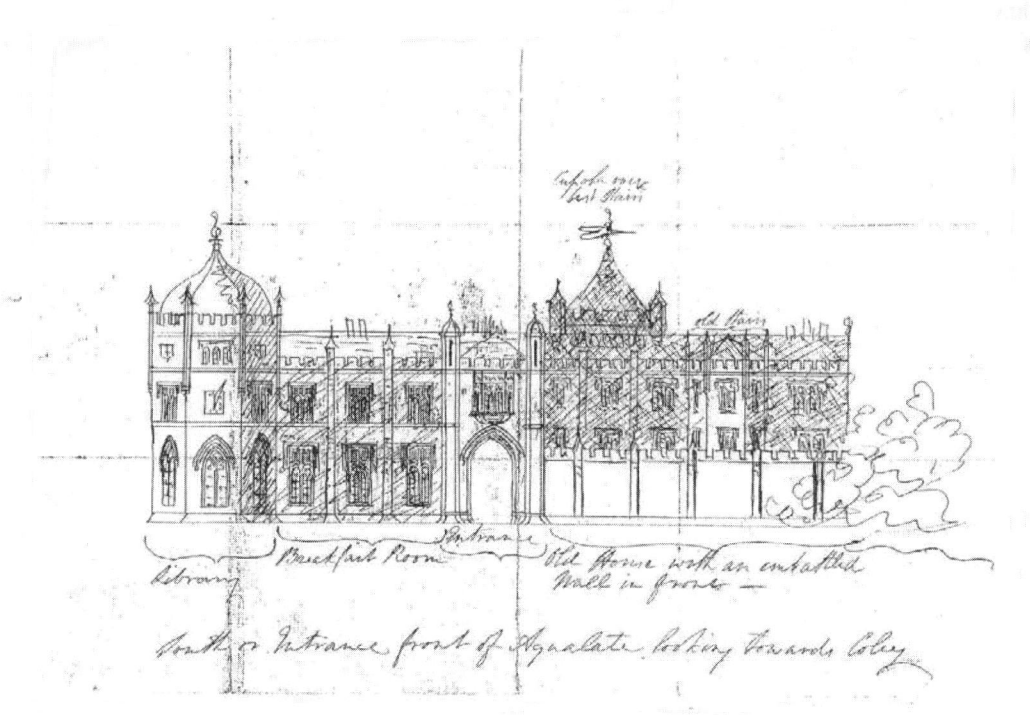

The rough sketches show towers, cupolas and embattled walls reminiscent of the Pavilion at Brighton and also the layout of the old building and the proposed internal changes and frontages, the south or entrance front, the north towards the mere and the end or west front. They are endorsed, *"..this Mr Nash thinks will be the handsomest and most picturesque."*

The letter on the rear of the drawings is unsigned.

> *" Dear mother, In addition to what I told you in my letter the room sat in an evening is made into a bedroom. The little dark room a partition put up at the bottom into a butlers pantry – the Partition in the hall taken away and divided more equally. To the Water a Dressing Room, to the front a Butlers sleeping room. The old*

> *Drawing room a bath and Powdering room and the ante Room into both them – This is what Mr Nash proposes doing with the old house – being as little as possible – from the second landing of the next stairs you go into the first floor rooms of the old house and into the attics above by the present old staircase. The new rooms on the ground floor are 18 feet high – part of the Library and Drawing room is 3 times high all the rest of the new 2 only. The new building ? ? Nash contains 933 square feet less than Haycocks House."*

The letter continues apologetically with some local gossip:

> *"My dear Mother*
> *I think I have returned you a belly Full of Building in return for the good feed you have just sent me by Captain Harding – but yours like stewed carp – boiled Tench or a haunch of Venison improves on the palate and the longer the dinner continues the better – I hope you have ? this received the letter I sent you on Tuesday from Woore so now for some news for you. Perks ? the butcher of this place has gone off – taking my Auntie for upwards of 70£, Salmon ? for 22 – John Armitshead ? 10 – Greaves the Tanner 30 and old Madam Kelsall and Hopkins of Lea for something considerable. Mrs Sneyd has got another girl, Mrs Southern? A girl too – Yesterday I dined at Barretts meeting – W Sneyd – Davis – Yates _ (the father I suppose) B`s mother and Mrs Edwards – a pleasant day enough but…"*

The writer could be John Fletcher who did not assume the name Boughey until 1805 and continued to live with his parents at Betley Court until 1810 even after his marriage in 1808. Thomas Fletcher Fenton Boughey, the eldest son of John and Henrietta, was baptised at Betley on 2 January 1809, one of only three entries in the register.

Whatever the timing Nash accepted the work which was completed by 1808 at a cost of £22,300 of which Nash took 5.5% commission while Boughey provided materials costing £1,281. In the 326 acres of parkland 53,000 trees were planted at a cost of £2,296 including thousands of quicksets especially hawthorn cuttings for hedges. These to join the many famous oaks already there. It took ten horses and two wagons four days to fetch the trees from Birmingham. Meanwhile Webb was completing roads, bridges and planting, the final cost being £1,397. There were 2.5 acres of garden with heated walls and glasshouses and 127 acres of deer park which he stocked locally.

Nash made the house three times its original size. It was covered in stucco ornamented with pinnacles, buttresses and gothic window tracery. There were polygonal turrets, castellated parapets and ogee domes with an entrance porch on the south side. Inside there was plaster work by Bernasconi, a great gallery, a hall with scagliola [imitation] marble columns and water closets.

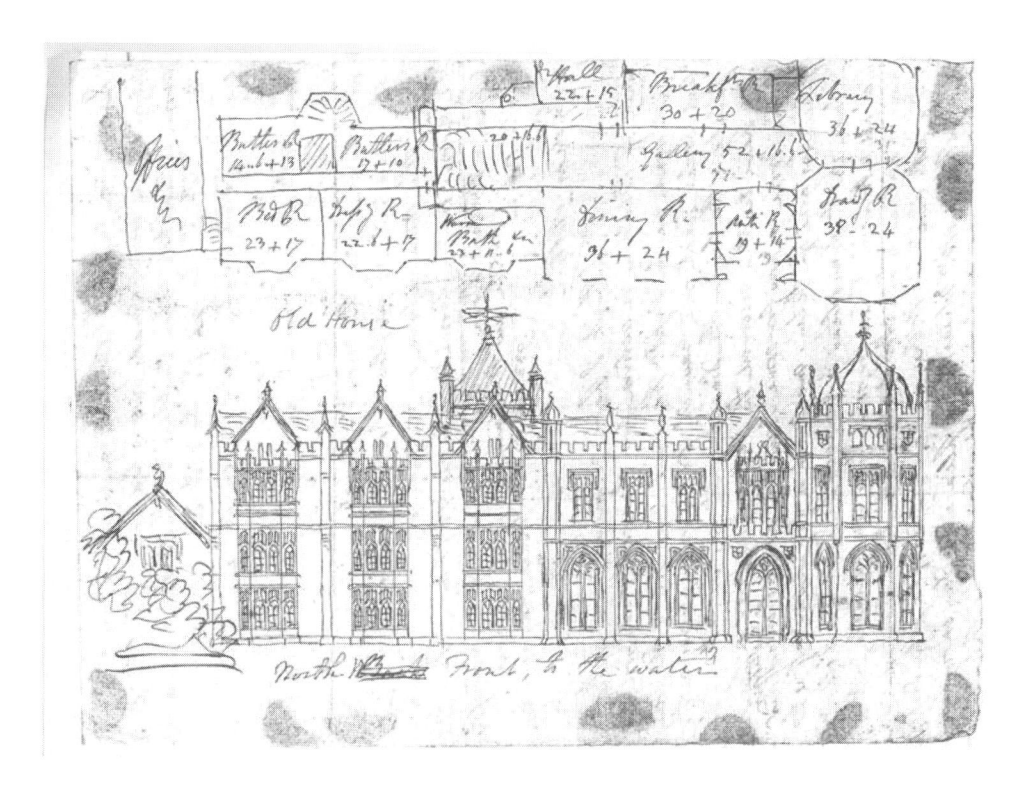

The sweep of the carriage drive was designed to enhance the surprise view of the mere. The Victoria County History describes Aqualate as a *"good example of Nash's extravagant gothic style."*

John Nash also recommended Humphrey Repton but by 1802 this partnership had finished and it was Reptons fourth son, George Stanley Repton, who was assistant to Nash until 1820 and it is in this Repton's *Pavilion Notebook* that the plan of Aqualate Hall appears. Whichever Repton it was relations were not easy with acrimonious correspondence over fees and ideas. Repton was abandoned. Boughey did the work himself partly using Reptons plans for which a payment was made in 1812. The contribution of Repton is now thought to have been small. Webb did the spade work while Boughey, a vigorous young man, used Haycock, Repton and Nash, but was in charge and responsible for the house, the deer fencing and park, the glasshouses and kitchen garden and for incorporating farmland. The customer, John Boughey, executed the ideas of the professional advisers, a not uncommon practice.

Over the next sixteen years John produced nine sons and four daughters. His son had twelve children so that throughout the nineteenth century the Bougheys went forth to serve the Empire and populate the shires. Each son was allocated a role in a strict pattern, the eldest succeeded, the next went into the church - the family living at Forton, the others into the army, the law, the navy and the estate farms. The third son, George Fenton Fletcher Boughey, became a Lt. Col. in the 59th Regiment and died in 1855 on board the "Kohinoor" off Gough's Island on a voyage to Hong Kong. He married Matilda Ottley of Antigua. The seventh son, Major Anchitel Fenton Fletcher Boughey of the 81st Foot died at Umritsar, Lahore, India aged 37. The fourth son, William Fenton Fletcher Boughey was a barrister, Recorder of Shrewsbury, a Stipendiary Magistrate in Wolverhampton, who helped to draw up the Newport Marsh Trust Act of 1854 and acted as auditor for the Trust, starting a dynasty of lawyers, solicitors and judges that continues today, with the same family names! No politics or civil service, no industry or commerce since these did not fit George Boughey's vision of landed gentry.

From 1810 John and his family moved into Aqualate and began to be involved in Newport life. In 1812 he was made a Burgess though he sat infrequently. His sister Anastasia, known as "Aunt Bob" wrote long gossipy letters from Aqualate. Young Thomas [TFF] aged seven, on 21 October 1816 writes in a large childish hand to Francis Twemlow:

> *"Dear Uncle Frank*
> *why can not you come to go hunting with us we have famous*
> *sport and kill a great many we have killed 15 hares 3 rabbits.*
> *23 Oct We have got some hoops I have a very large one I can*
> *drive it from one end of the terrace to the other.*
> *Love to Aunt and cousin Tom*
> *Yours TFF Boughey."*

Staff. R.O. D4216

On the evening of Saturday 17 July 1819 he took his two eldest sons to the theatre in Newport to see Mr Stanton's Company perform "*As you like it*". The building is still there in Upper Bar. Thomas, the eldest was so impressed he kept the poster as a souvenir and wrote on the back *"This was the first play I ever saw. Papa and John were with me."* It is signed TFFB. On the 1 June 1823 eight-year old Richard died. His father rushed back from London had the coffin opened and three weeks later he too died of fever. John Boughey was 39. The entry in the Liddle ledger for 3 July 1823 reads: *"A hearse and four with appendages and mourners coach and four to Forton, £12.12.0."*

> *"Aqualate Hall 3 June 1823.*
>
> *My wife was very unwell in London the evening before and the Monday*
> *morning when I heard of our dear Childs alarming indisposition she*
> *was so unwell as not to be in the room with me at the time but the*
> *strength of her affection has carried her through the infirmities*
> *of constitution. My poor dear boy was dead before the intelligence*
> *of his relapse had reached us – in the account there was a ray of*
> *hope to which I confess I clove till I reached this door – but his*
> *fever had hurried him along beyond all control to a premature*
> *grave. Unavailing regret is all we have left excepting prayer to*
> *Providence to preserve the remainder. I believe if I had been on the*
> *spot nothing more could have been done but there would have been*
> *a melancholy satisfaction to me. He who wishes for long life and honours*
> *knows not what he is wishing for – God preserve me from any more*

such trials and may he enable me to submit to the present – we are really in great sorrow."

Staff. R.O. D4216/E/2/183-255

He goes on to say Anne is unwell and Edward, Anchitel and Robert extremely weak and *"my sweet little Lilla* [Elizabeth] *is now in bed with the same complaint in her throat."*

On 20 June 1823 John Boughey wrote to Francis Twemlow again hoping that they had avoided the dreadful disorder which had caused Aqualate so much anxiety and regret. A week later he was dead.

Home and family occupied much of his time and there is a reasonableness, modesty and caution in his affairs perhaps not surprising in someone coming from a professional and commercial background into a landed estate and charged with fulfilling the social ambitions of his father and George Boughey his benefactor. His household was not large and though he competed politically with the Gowers the family never had aristocratic leanings or appeared overawed by their aristocratic neighbours across the fields at Lilleshall. There were never more than 11 to 15 household servants and household expenditure was hardly lavish and though contributing as an employer and customer to the local economy there was not the patronage and involvement of later generations.

His leisure activities show the same restraint. There was plenty of fishing in the mere and he kept a gamekeeper and helpers and jealously guarded his game but there were not the huge bags of other estates. He bred beagles, a sport because of the nature of the hare, that could be contained in one estate as compared to foxhunting. The Albrighton Hunt drew Aqualate and he enjoyed hunting but further involvement was left to his son TFF. As for gambling and horseracing he does not seem to have had the inclination or finances.

He may not have been an active burgess or JP but he responded to the threat of invasion by becoming a Captain in the Betley and Audley Volunteers and in 1810 was commissioned as a Lt. Col. in the northern regiment of the Staffordshire Militia taking command in 1813. The amount of paperwork indicates this was a demanding and time consuming responsibility.

The purchase of Aqualate had turned an urban family into landed gentry with a large country seat and income. John may have been satisfied, he may have simply been cautious, he may have been restricted by the entailment of his capital, whatever the reason Aqualate remained the core of the estate and though acquisitions were contemplated additions were small, from piecemeal inheritance, his father and mother and cousins, or purchases and exchanges on the edge of the estate mostly by private negotiation. On his death John Boughey had increased his estate from 3940 acres to 7201, including industrial land at Audley. 10,000 acres at that time was reckoned as a base for the great leap forward into the peerage.

The Audley estate brought an industrial element, coalmining. The coal was good, accessible and near to customers. There were four collieries the two principal ones being Ravenslane and Boyls Hall (Audley Colliery). Management was in the hands of tenants and production techniques were simple. In the industrial slump of 1816 John Boughey had to take the administration into his own hands and make decisions on investment and expansion particularly links by rail and canal. Coal mining cost him money though the Audley colliery continued to be profitable into the 20th century.

The difficulty was that Audley was too distant for personal supervision even if John Boughey had the skill and inclination to manage the business. Even in the 1880's Thomas Fletcher Boughey was apologising for his neglect of the Audley property. Aqualate and Audley were too small to justify professional management on the scale of the Gilbert brothers and James

Loch on the Sutherland estates. The Wedges often quoted as agents were in reality little more than errand boys for the decisions of the Boughey owners. This question of scale was never solved.

Thomas Fenton Fletcher Boughey [TFF] was only 14 when he succeeded to the estate his father had created in twenty years. He was a minor so the estate was put in the hands of guardians or trustees. Francis Twemlow (Uncle Frank) was one, Sir John Chetwode (Lady Bougheys' father) another and Lady Boughey suggested her brother and Mr Tollet.

TFF returned to Eton where his letters were soon full of guns and dogs and stuffed birds. On 14 December 1823 he was writing to say his mother had given birth and the boy was well though small. So the last child was born five months after the death of his father. With the Rector unavailable the boy, Charles Fenton Fletcher, was baptised at Aqualate by Mr Meredith, Headmaster of the Grammar School. Typically TFF took him straight out coursing with the dogs for a couple of hours. They caught nothing.

In 1824 there was talk of a rail-road coming through Aqualate. Mrs Borough of Chetwynd was most concerned as to the effect on the estates and drove over to Aqualate to confer with Lady Boughey but she and TFF seemed reluctant to object while the tenants such as the Wedges, were very pro-railway. It did not arrive until 1849.

In November 1824 Lady Boughey consulted Francis Twemlow as to what to do with the boys during the long holidays. She wanted some tuition and was inclined to Mr Meredith of Newport Grammar School:

> *"... a proper person to be with my dear son and he has the manners of a gentleman and I understood was well informed and sensible."*

She also considered Mr Cobb of Newport Grammar who had already taught George and William to read and had not been thought *"objectionable"*. Though respectable in appearance she worried that his manners were those of a writing master and therefore not a person to be a companion to a young gentleman. She enquired of her Aunt Cotes at Woodcote who replied that Saml. Cobb was very capable at teaching arithmetic and the globe though she was not sure of his mathematics but generally he had a very pleasant, clear and intelligible manner of conveying instruction.

By 1827 TFF had followed his father to Christ Church College Oxford relying on the Wedges to manage the property.

On 3 January 1831 he was admitted as a Burgess of Newport.

In 1840 there was great unease in the family when sister Anastasia determined to marry Edward Smythe of Acton Burnell and become a catholic. Several attempts were made to dissuade her and even though her husband died a year later she remained a catholic to the end. The family remained firm protestants.

In 1832, then aged 23, the 3rd Baronet was married at Brewood to Louisa Paulina Giffard of Chillington. Between 1835-50 they had twelve children. A valuation was made of the estate at this time the largest tenants being William Liddle at Sutton farm with 179 acres, Betsey Wedge with 322 acres valued at £437, Francis Wedge, 119 acres at £197 and Thomas Wedge with 451 acres at a value of £523. The estate had property in the town including Banshee House [Rylands 2004] with three acres at a rent of £39 pa.

TFF took every advantage of the golden age of farming. An improving landowner he put in drainage, fencing, built a model farm and water mill at Coley between 1842-50, and new farms at Wilbrighton [1831], obtained by exchange, and Fern Hill. Wilbrighton Hall is a huge house with many bedrooms, now sadly derelict, while Fern Hill is reputed to be a "calendar" house and the largest farmhouse in Staffordshire. He bred Devon cattle. Eventually the estate covered 36 square miles. Through his efforts the new Corn Exchange and livestock market was built in Newport in 1860. He was the first chairman of the Market Company and its principal shareholder with 50 shares at £20 that is £1,000 out of a total cost for the project of £13,000. He carried out other civic obligations being High Steward of the burgesses and giving £500 to the re-paving of the High Street when the markets were moved out.

He was a sportsman, shooting and hunting, his favourite being a pack of harriers he kept from 1840. The English Springer Spaniel was developed at Aqualate. TFF was more active in fox hunting. The Albrighton Hunt became a subscription hunt after 1823 and this helped to share the increasing costs of the sport. The Albrighton included Enville, Shifnal and Woore country so that Aqualate was central. In 1834 TFF was master complaining of tenants who killed foxes. In 1836 he developed Polly Moor House near Gnosall as kennels constructing a purpose built, unique range of buildings with living areas fully roofed some 18 feet high with specialised vents in the ridge tiles. There was a large mounted water tank with a pump and well below and several runs were provided with access through dog doors. It is said that over 100 hounds were housed there in conditions better than their keepers.

TFF built the two lodges to the park in 1835. Amos Jenks a respected worker on the estate lived in one of the lodges well into old age and in 1825 his daughter, Frances Mary, married Charles Gater a tailor from Betley. Soon afterwards they set up business in Newport High Street. Gater had made clothes for the Fletcher/Boughey family in Betley and accounts show he did work for Aqualate. Was this an astute, independent, business move, or part of the Boughey transfer to Aqualate?

A better known servant at the time was Hannah Culwick who appears in the work of A J Munby. She was one in a series of photographs taken by Henry Howle of Newport for Munby in 1872. In *"Hannah's Places"*, she writes how she worked for a lawyer in Newport in 1848 and then in 1850, aged 17, came to Aqualate Hall as an under housemaid. She got on well for eight months:

> *".... but Lady Boughey saw me and another playing as we were cleaning our kettles (we had about 16 to clean, they belonged to the bedrooms) and she gave us both warning. Then I heard a scullion was wanted under a man cook at Woodcote and I went after this place, mind I was dreadfully sorry to leave that splendid park at Aqualate and I was got used to the servants and I felt happy for I had a friend or two and Jim the postillion was such a good looking little fellow and used to take me for a walk in the park with Mary Hart a nice girl and kind to me – so I was vexed to leave and I asked Lady Boughey if she would please forgive me and let me stop but she said "No" very loudly and Id to look out for another place. She gave me a good character to Lady Louisa Cotes and I went there into the scullery it was very different work and a very different place to me after being used to running along the splendid halls and gallery and rooms at Aqualate as a housemaid and I had learnt to make beds and do the rooms there for company………"*

The 1851 census shows Hannah Culwick aged 17 as housemaid born in Shifnal also her friend Mary Hart aged 24 as a "visitor". Mary could have been a servant to Henrietta and Walter Giffard sister and brother-in-law to TFF who were staying at the Hall with their two daughters. Also staying there was his lawyer brother, William.

TFF died on 4 October 1880. His executors were his brother William Fletcher Fenton

Boughey and Thomas Fletcher Twemlow of Betley Court. He left £35,000. Under a Parliamentary Act of 1832 TFF was a "tenant for life" and his meticulous and long will spells the succession out in strict order. He also set up a Trust of £10,000 the income from which was to be shared, as carefully laid out in the will. In a codicil of 1877 he makes special arrangements for the more vulnerable, an £125 annuity for unmarried daughters and the same for his son Francis Boughey if he remained single, which he did.

On 22 July 1881 the executors of TFF under an order of the Chancery Division sold his horses, carriages, saddlery, wines and spirits at Aqualate. There were two horses, "Mercury" and "Ellerton", a Victoria carriage, a coach, a break able to carry ten inside and three out, a phaeton and an invalid carriage. Over 4,000 bottles of port were on offer mostly 1860-70 vintage though there were 4 bottle of 1794, and nearly 500 bottles of sherry and 300 bottles of wine and spirits.

Thomas Fletcher Boughey [TFB] was born 5 April 1836. He was educated at Eton and Christ Church, Oxford. He grew up in the summer of English agriculture and at the peak of British industrial and political power.

A NEW SONG ON THE COMING OF AGE OF SIR THOMAS F. BOUGHEY, ESQ. AQULATE PARK.

Good people all both far and near,
　Come listen for a while,
I'll sing to you a verse or two,
　Will cause you for to smile ;
It is about the merriment,
　The glorious fun and lark,
That will take place upon this day,
　In famous Aqulate Park.

CHORUS.

All you that's fond of fun and glee,
　And wish to have a lark,
Make no delay but haste away,
　To famous Aqulate Park.

To commemorate his age,
　Upon this glorious day,
There'll be a grand procession,
　And the bands will sweetly play ;
From Newport unto Aqulate,
　They'll march in grand array,
And then fat sheep and oxen
　There will be given away.

From Stafford and from Knosall,
　Some thousands they will come,
From Shrewsbury and Wellington,
　With the merry fife and drum ;

From every part both far and near,
　They'll come to see the lark,
And join the grand procession,
　To famous Aqulate Park.

I heard a lass the other day,
　Her name I will not tell,
She says she'll come to Acqualte,
　And cut a pretty swell ;
And there she'll get a sweetheart,
　And off they'll go by gum,
And she stole the bolster of the bed,
　To decorate her bum.

So to conclude and make an end,
　And finish up my song,
Success unto Sir Thomas Boughey,
　And may his days be long ;
So fill your glasses and let it pass,
　And shout three times hurrah !
Think on Sir Thomas Boughey,
　And his glorious birthday.

Then hurrah for Sir Thomas,
　And the goodness he has done,
We'll not forget his kindness,
　At the majority of his son.

PROGRAMME OF PROCESSION,
ON THE ATTAINMENT OF
THE MAJORITY
OF
THOMAS FLETCHER BOUGHEY, ESQ.,
ELDEST SON OF
SIR THOMAS FLETCHER FENTON BOUGHEY, BARONET,
OF AQUALATE,
TO BE FORMED IN THE CHETWYND ROAD,
On the 28th DAY of APRIL, 1857,
AT NINE O'CLOCK IN THE MORNING.

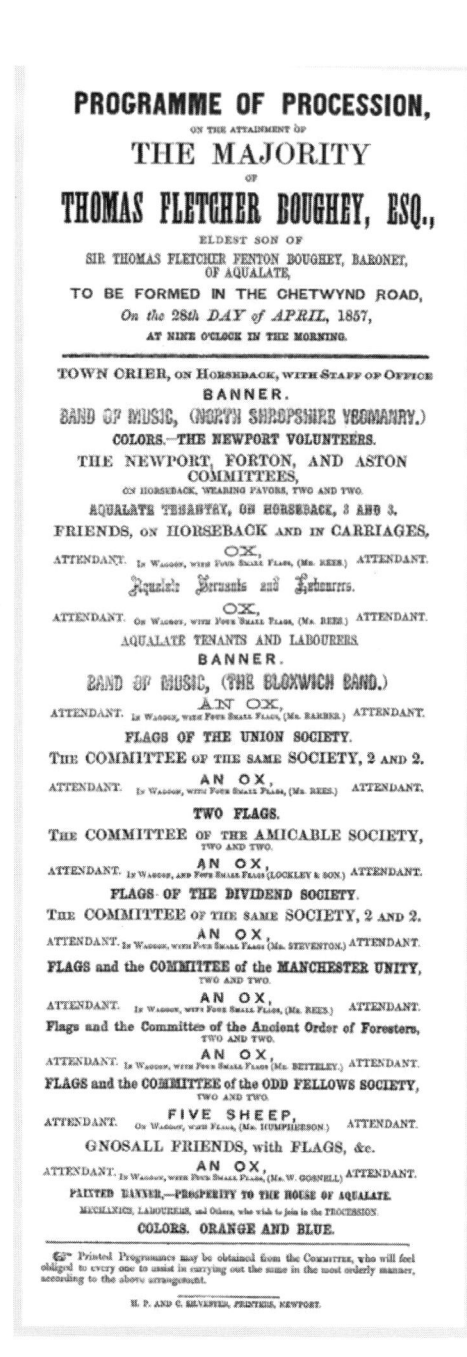

TOWN CRIER, ON HORSEBACK, WITH STAFF OF OFFICE
BANNER.
BAND OF MUSIC, (NORTH SHROPSHIRE YEOMANRY.)
COLORS.—THE NEWPORT VOLUNTEERS.
THE NEWPORT, FORTON, AND ASTON COMMITTEES,
ON HORSEBACK, WEARING FAVORS, TWO AND TWO.
AQUALATE TENANTRY, ON HORSEBACK, 3 AND 3.
FRIENDS, ON HORSEBACK AND IN CARRIAGES.
OX,
ATTENDANT. In Waggon, with Four Small Flags, (Mr. REES.) ATTENDANT.
Aqualate Servants and Labourers.
OX,
ATTENDANT. On Waggon, with Four Small Flags, (Mr. REES.) ATTENDANT.
AQUALATE TENANTS AND LABOURERS.
BANNER.
BAND OF MUSIC, (THE BLOXWICH BAND.)
AN OX,
ATTENDANT. In Waggon, with Four Small Flags, (Mr. BARBER.) ATTENDANT.
FLAGS OF THE UNION SOCIETY.
THE COMMITTEE OF THE SAME SOCIETY, 2 AND 2.
AN OX,
ATTENDANT. In Waggon, with Four Small Flags, (Mr. REES.) ATTENDANT.
TWO FLAGS.
THE COMMITTEE OF THE AMICABLE SOCIETY,
TWO AND TWO.
AN OX,
ATTENDANT. In Waggon, and Four Small Flags (LOCKLEY & SON) ATTENDANT.
FLAGS OF THE DIVIDEND SOCIETY.
THE COMMITTEE OF THE SAME SOCIETY, 2 AND 2.
AN OX,
ATTENDANT. In Waggon, with Four Small Flags (Mr. STEVENTON) ATTENDANT.
FLAGS and the COMMITTEE of the MANCHESTER UNITY,
TWO AND TWO.
AN OX,
ATTENDANT. In Waggon, with Four Small Flags, (Mr. REES.) ATTENDANT.
Flags and the Committee of the Ancient Order of Foresters,
TWO AND TWO.
AN OX,
ATTENDANT. In Waggon, with Four Small Flags (Mr. BETTELEY.) ATTENDANT.
FLAGS and the COMMITTEE of the ODD FELLOWS SOCIETY,
TWO AND TWO.
FIVE SHEEP,
ATTENDANT. On Waggon, with Flags, (Mr. HUMPHERSON.) ATTENDANT.
GNOSALL FRIENDS, with FLAGS, &c.
AN OX,
ATTENDANT. In Waggon, with Four Small Flags, (Mr. W. GORNELL) ATTENDANT.
PAINTED BANNER.—PROSPERITY TO THE HOUSE OF AQUALATE.
MECHANICS, LABOURERS, and Others, who wish to join in the PROCESSION.
COLORS. ORANGE AND BLUE.

☞ Printed Programmes may be obtained from the COMMITTEE, who will feel obliged to every one to assist in carrying out the same in the most orderly manner, according to the above arrangement.

M. P. AND C. SILVESTER, PRINTERS, NEWPORT.

When he returned to Newport in 1857 to celebrate his coming of age he was seeing a town transformed by the same confidence and prosperity. The celebrations were a triumphal exhibition of Victorian society. Paintings and posters record the elaborate arrangements. Committees were set up at Newport, Gnosall and Forton and raised £658 in subscriptions. Tickets were carefully issued for admission to events that began on the 28 April when Thomas returned from Oxford by train to Newport, and continued to 5 May. Nine oxen and five sheep were roasted and were distributed with bread to the poor through numbered "beef tickets". There were street decorations, illuminated arches, for example at the gasworks, and cannons were fired. On Tuesday 28 April there was a large procession which brought spectators in by train. It began at 10am in the Chetwynd Road with the Town Crier on horseback, banners, bands, Newport Volunteers, the various committees on horseback, tenants and workers with friends on horses or in carriages, in total 120 horses and 50 carriages. There were also eight wagons and attendants carrying the oxen, five carrying the sheep followed by groups of mechanics, labourers and others. The parade went around the town and ended at Aqualate. The next day, Wednesday 29 April, there was a ball and supper at Aqualate Hall followed on Thursday by a reception at Aqualate in the huge "Waterloo" tent lent by Lord Hill of Hawkstone. On Friday there was a luncheon, tea and ball at Aqualate and on Saturday a dinner for the labourers on the estate in the "Waterloo" tent.

On the Monday there was a servants' ball in the Hall, on Tuesday a Grand Banquet at the Royal Victoria Hotel, the procession being met at the turnpike gate on the Stafford Road and the young man's carriage being pulled to the town by 24 men. The Royal Victoria was the venue for the final Ball on the Thursday that lasted from 9 till 4.30 next morning. John Cotes presided and there were eighteen toasts proposed and seconded. Expenses for the week totalled £296.15.4 of which £125.10.6 was to Mr Allen of the Royal Victoria Hotel for "collation and wine". Given the number of toasts this huge bill is not surprising. There was a separate item of 5/- for a violinist. The house party included the Wrottesleys, Chetwodes, Twemlows, Giffards, Wicksteds and various uncles.

Thus began the remarkable relationship between Newport and Thomas Fletcher Boughey that continued after his death in 1906.

PUBLIC DINNER

AT THE

ROYAL VICTORIA HOTEL, NEWPORT, ON THE FIFTH MAY, 1857,

TO CELEBRATE THE ATTAINMENT OF THE

MAJORITY OF

THOMAS FLETCHER BOUGHEY, ESQUIRE,

OF AQUALATE.

President.—JOHN COTES, ESQUIRE.

VICE-PRESIDENTS.

Messrs. THOMAS WEDGE,	Messrs. JOHN WEDGE,
HENRY FISHER,	JOHN HOLLAND,
W. E. BADDELEY,	WILLIAM LIDDLE,
GEORGE MASON,	THOMAS LANGLEY.

PROGRAMME OF TOASTS.

The Queen	The PRESIDENT	
Prince Albert and rest of the Royal Family	DITTO	
The Lord Bishop and Clergy of the Diocese	DITTO	REV. F TWEMLOW.
The Army and Navy	DITTO	MAJOR WROTTESLEY.
The Heir of Aqualate	DITTO	T. F. BOUGHEY, Esq.
Sir Thomas Boughey, Bart.	R. M. LEEKE, Esq.	SIR THOMAS BOUGHEY, BART.
Lady Boughey and the Junior Branches of the Aqualate Family	B. BOROUGH, Esq.	MR. GEORGE BOUGHEY.
The Lord Lieutenant and Magistrates of the County	Mr. BADDELEY	
The President	T. F. BOUGHEY, Esq.	J. COTES, Esq.
The Ladies	W. BOUGHEY, Esq.	T. F. BOUGHEY, Esq.
Foxhunting and Hunting in general	R. M. LEEKE, Esq.	
The Members for the County	B. BOROUGH, Esq.	
Mr. Wedge, (Sir Thomas Boughey's Agent)	Mr. MASON	MR. WEDGE.
The Vice Presidents	W. BOUGHEY, Esq.	THE VICE PRESIDENTS.
The Agricultural Interest	Sir THOS. BOUGHEY, Bart.	
The Town and Trade of Newport, not forgetting Chetwynd End	T. H. BURNE, Esq.	MR. HOLLAND AND MR. J. COBB.
The Committees of Management	Sir THOS. BOUGHEY, Bart.	THE HON. SECRETARIES.
The Press	J. COTES, Esq.	THE REPRESENTATIVES PRESENT.

HENRY FISHER, } Hon. Secretaries.
JOHN WEDGE,

AQUALATE TENT, 30th of APRIL, 1857.

A Banquet for Gentlemen,

IN CELEBRATION OF THE ATTAINMENT OF THE

MAJORITY OF THOMAS F. BOUGHEY, ESQ., OF AQUALATE.

MR. WEDGE, CHAIRMAN.

Messrs. HENRY FISHER,	
" W. E. BADDELEY,	} VICE CHAIRMEN.
" GEORGE MASON,	
" JOSEPH JOHNSON,	

Programme of Toasts.

The Queen	The Chairman.	
Prince Albert and the rest of the Royal Family	Ditto.	
The Lord Bishop and Clergy of the Diocese	Ditto.	Rev. F. TWEMLOW.
The Army and Navy	Ditto.	MAJOR WROTTESLEY.
The Heir of Aqualate	Ditto.	THOS. F. BOUGHEY, Esq.
Sir Thomas Boughey	F. Twemlow, Esq.	SIR T. BOUGHEY.
Lady Boughey and the Junior Branches of the Aqualate Family	Rev. F. Twemlow.	Mr. GEO. BOUGHEY.
The Chillington, Wriottesley, and Oakley Families	Mr. Baddeley.	LORD WRIOTTESLEY, Mr. W. GIFFARD, and Sir J. CHETWODE.
The Ladies	Thos. F. Boughey, Esq.	The HON. A. WRIOTTESLEY.
The Lords Lieutenants, and Magistrates of the Counties of Stafford and Salop	Mr. H. Fisher.	F. TWEMLOW, Esq. J. COTES, Esq.
The Chairman	W. Boughey, Esq.	The CHAIRMAN.
The Committee of Management	Sir T. Boughey.	Messrs. H. FISHER and JOHN WEDGE.
The Town and Trade of Newport, not forgetting Chetwynd End.	Ditto.	Messrs. HOLLAND and JOHN COBB.
The Aqualate Tenantry	Mr. Holland.	Mr. MASON.
The Vice-Chairmen	T. F. Boughey, Esq.,	Mr. H. FISHER.
The Press	The Chairman.	The STAFFORDSHIRE ADVERTISER.

HENRY FISHER, } Hon. Secs.
JOHN WEDGE,

In February 1858 he became a JP and deputy Lieutenant of Staffordshire. He was a Captain in the Staffordshire Militia and in 1862 in the Newport Rifle Volunteers.

> *"On Saturday morning, one of the most exciting hunts that it has ever been our pleasure to record took place on the banks of the river flowing through Meretown to Chetwynd. The meet was announced to take place at Meretown, and accordingly a large number of spectators wended their way thither. A beautiful and fine array of dogs, the property of the Hon. Rowland Clegg Hill M.P. were transported to the spot and were ably hunted by T.F. Boughey Esq., in the unavoidable absence of Mr Hill.*
>
> *They traversed the river until they arrived at Chetwynd osiers where they soon found a large dog otter to which they gave chase, which for the space of half an hour was most exciting and amusing, eventually he became a captive and had to appease the anger of the dogs by the sacrifice of his life.*
>
> *The dogs again started afresh, and in a few minutes gave chase to a bitch, which after a very short chase shared the same fate as her partner. Thus, before twelve o'clock, a noble pair of otters weighing respectively 28 lb., and 18 lbs. were securely captured and killed. The party consisted of T.F.Boughey, Rear-Admiral Gawen, Master J.Cotes, Dr Saxton, Rev. W.Elliott, Rev. J.J.Lambert, Dr Codly, H.Fisher Paul Es., Master Goringe, Mr J.Webb, Mr C.Liddle, Mr R.Hearne and several more who then adjourned to the front of Chetwynd Hall and partook of the kind hospitality of its owners Mr Borough's which was most bounteously supplied".*

Eddowes Journal 1860.

On August 25 1864 he married Sarah Annabelle Littledale of Liscard Hall, Wallasey, in the parish church Wallasey; she was the only daughter of Harold Littledale described as a "merchant prince" and "general broker" with, in 1881, a substantial household of eight servants including a butler and footman. As well as his business interests in Littledale and Co., Liverpool, he had a model, scientific, farm at Liscard, and entertained such literary giants as Dickens and Thackeray. Annabelle had a reputation as a brilliant horsewoman. They honeymooned in Italy and went to live at Brewood Hall. Again there were great celebrations at Newport and on the estate, with processions, children's and poor ladies treats, children's games, and a Rifle Corp dinner. He became master of the Albrighton Hunt between 1866-87 and a steward of Newport Races.

Their Silver Wedding in 1889 inspired similar large celebrations in the town. On the Monday deputations from the tenants and workpeople from the different estates and from the town of Newport assembled in the library at Aqualate to make presentations. The ladies gave Lady Boughey a sapphire and diamond ring in a silver box; the Aqualate tenants a silver bowl and two goblets; the Audley tenants a silver gilt loving cup; the Derbyshire, Sterndale, tenants a Derbyshire marble timepiece; Newport an inscribed silver salver; the servants a silver eggstand presented by Mr Cullingford the first servant they had employed on their wedding day; the Literary Institute gave a photograph album. Replying Sir Thomas commented on the good relations between the landlord and tenants and with the town of Newport. He regretted his absence from the Audley estates where he was perfectly content to leave the mining interests in the hands of his agent, and the fact that he had never set foot on the oldest portion of the estate, Sterndale.

On the Tuesday there was a grand ball at Aqualate with trains laid on for the more distant guests. All the rooms were thrown open for dancing with a tent for refreshment and a great display of the presents. The Thursday saw 500 workers and wives sit down to dinner in a marquee in the park while 500 children had tea and entertainment including Professor Golding the ventriloquist, Monsieur Eugene who did contortions on a revolving pedestal, an eccentric performing clown, dogs and Punch and Judy. Each child was given a polished, inscribed box of sweets on leaving. The week ended with a servants' ball in the stables and gardens.

He succeeded to the baronetcy in October 1880 but was still living at Brewood at the time of the 1881 census. Francis (33), Louisa (42), Selina (34) and Anne (46) were still living at Aqualate, all unmarried, all unoccupied, presumably living off the estate.

His patronage expanded. In 1883 he became the founder and first President of the Newport Literary Society a club for middle class men. His generosity to the Society was often overwhelming and long after his death, in 1927, it was the Boughey Trust that bought the present Society's premises. He supported anything that was of recreational benefit to the community including most sports such as cricket and football and just before his death the newly formed Bowling Club. He was associated with the Horticultural Society, the Root Show and Dog Trials. The town abounds with his trophies.

He was the founder and the "heart" of the Newport Agricultural Society in 1889 chairing the inaugural meetings and becoming the first President but only after Burton Borough had declined. He donated £100 and Lady Annabelle £20. The Society was a reaction to the agricultural depression, an attempt to raise morale and encourage good practice and enterprise. In January 1891 there were eight weeks of frost and ice and there was again a Newport Relief Committee for the poor and unemployed as there had been regularly since 1870. Encouraged by Sir Thomas and Lady Boughey hundreds were allowed to skate on Aqualate Mere the money going to the Relief Fund. The depression was biting and in January 1893 Sir Thomas gave a 10% remission of rents, 20% to some tenants.

Skating on The Mere

He had other commercial interests in the town. As well as being a director and principal shareholder of the Market Company he was in 1893 Chairman and shareholder in the Royal Victoria Hotel Management Company and the Newport Brewery (1898). He had leased three properties to the Brewery, the *Plough* at Forton [now part of Newport], the *Swan* at Forton and the *Lion* at Sutton, described as a beer house. He was an executor of the estate of Harper Adams becoming the first Chairman of the Governors of the College set up in 1900.

In politics he was described as a *"broadminded conservative",* who believed property entailed duties as well as rights. For fifteen years he represented Newport on the County Council from its formation in 1888 being Chairman of Weights and Measures. He was elected to Newport Urban District Council when it began in 1894 modestly refusing to become chairman as the chairman of the former District Health Board had more experience. He did serve as Chairman for three years before he retired in 1901. He supported and proposed the schemes for improved water and sewage in the urban area. In January 1906 he chaired the meeting in the Market Hall for the Conservative candidate Kenyon-Slaney and his last public meeting was when he addressed the election crowd from the balcony of the Vine Vaults. Kenyon-Slaney was elected despite the Liberal landslide in the rest of the country.

In 1895 as a Governor of Newport Grammar School he tried to settle the wrangling over the future of the school by offering land in the Wellington Road for a new girls and boys school. It was never taken up. In 1898 he was High Sheriff of Staffordshire.

Otter Hunting

Sir Thomas followed the traditional sports of a country gentleman but not to excess:

> "Sir Thomas's shoots were always managed to perfection. No man knew better than he how ground should be beaten. No one understood more of the habits of birds and animals. So far as he was individually concerned, I don't think he cared whether he fired a shot or not; his one desire was that the friends he had asked out should enjoy themselves, and have a good day………All Sir Thomas's arrangements for the day's sport are always most complete. A cart drawn by a donkey - he had a first-rate one – or pony accompanies the party to carry the hares and ammunition; when the game is put out at lunch-time it is all covered with a light gauze to keep off the flies, and then what a lunch! – not in a marquee erected for the occasion, but under the lee-side of some neighbouring hedge. No champagne or sparkling wine (than which I think there is no greater mistake at a shooting lunch) but the best of beer or whisky and soda, with a glass of brown sherry to finish up with, and then just one good cigar before we again pursue the little brown birds.
> At the end of the day the game is all laid out for inspection – perhaps fifty brace of birds, forty hares, and several rabbits. Then comes the distribution among the tenants and the sportsmen. There is no stint here. Never, I believe, had there been a more liberal man with his game than Sir Thomas. I have often after a big day seen nearly everything given away, and perhaps four or five birds and a brace of hares put into his dog-cart as his sole share of the spoils of the day. There is no wonder, then, that all his estate abounds with game, and that hares are more numerous than in almost any other part. No one of his tenants would ever dream of killing a hare, and I have sometimes seen them running about twenty or thirty in a field".

Tom Collins "School and Sport" 1905.

Sir Thomas was content to find his acquaintances locally, James Paddock who was a tenant at

Aston Manor and then Fernhill, and Sir Thomas were inseparable friends and wherever Sir Thomas went, Paddock would accompany him.

About six hundred yards from the north-west corner of Aqualate Hall, near the Blackwater or "spectacles", two placid dark pools by the mere, stood the giant Aqualate oak. The trunk was 23 feet wide with branches 90 feet across, some, 8 feet 6 inches in circumference. The tree cast a shadow over three quarters of an acre the distance through the tree being 53 yards. At 4.30pm on Wednesday 16 May 1906 it was struck by lightning, the debris covering a wide area. An omen. Sir Thomas was already ill at the beginning of the year and died at 2.30am on 30 August 1906 aged 71, Lady Annabelle having to return hurriedly from Egypt. His obituary in the local paper said he was *"a good old English gentleman of the type which is fast dying out."*

Sir Thomas left property valued at £102,000 paying duty of £10,090 at a rate of 6.10%. His trustees were his wife, the Rev. George Boughey and R P Liddle, a young and influential local solicitor. The Aqualate plate and property stayed in the Trust set up by his father. All the other plate, books, pictures, prints, linen, china, glass, wines. liquors, carriage horses, harness, saddlery and stable furniture in or about the Hall went to Annabelle plus £500pa charged on the estate and the annuity of £500 settled on her at marriage. He wished Lady Annabelle to stay at Aqualate for her life not only for her benefit but because *"I feel sure that under the circumstances such an arrangement would be to the best interest of the estate"*. This is not explained. Other shares and property were to be realised and left in trust to living brothers and sisters except the shares in the Royal Victoria Hotel which his partner in the RVH, Charles Lewis, was given a six month option to purchase.

By a deed of 15 October 1906 the Boughey Trust was set up to receive and hold investments and property for the benefit of the town of Newport. Its first capital came from the sale of the "Barley Mow" Hotel which in a codicil Sir Thomas had specifically left to Annabelle for *"her own absolute use and benefit."* The Trust is still active and influential in financing the recreational activities of the community.

He was generous to retainers. Walter Cullingford received £150, Charles Russell £100, John Thomas Ashlee £100, Harriet Maxwell £100 and Annie Foster £25. Other domestic and outside staff received four weeks wages. William Wedge, the agent, had £200, R P Liddle, his solicitor, £100 and George Webb, managing clerk for Liddle, £50.

Sir. T.F. Boughey Bart J.P.

Sir Thomas was buried at Forton along with all the Bougheys. His brother and successor, the Rev. George Boughey was Rector, but they had for many years preferred to attend Newport Church and on a Sunday morning would arrive in a four wheeled vehicle known as the "Aqualate Hall Bus", with female servants in dark clothing and black bonnets riding on the outside. The horse and bus were left at the "Royal Victoria" opposite the church during the service.

Whatever the family rift Lady Annabelle went to live at Sundorne Castle near Shrewsbury and was buried from there in Newport cemetery in February 1914.

Newport erected a memorial to Sir Thomas, an obelisk with a light on top. After a public meeting a subscription list was opened with a maximum of £2.2.0. The Urban District Council agreed to maintain it. It was erected in 1908 and the lamp lit in January 1909. It remained a feature in the Square until 1955 when it was moved, to make room for the traffic, to the forecourt of the hospital. This aroused opposition but when years later it was moved even further down the road to make a new link road there was no reaction, few appreciating its significance. It now resides in a shrubbed niche in Station Road.

While the first two Aqualate Bougheys produced twenty-five children of whom all but one reached adulthood, of the third generation only the Rev. Sir George Boughey had offspring, four daughters. One by one the elderly brothers followed each other in the baronetcy, set in their ways, not bothering to occupy the Hall. Sir George was educated at Christ Church, Oxford, ordained in 1862, was a curate at Kidderminster and then Rector of Forton from 1863 to 1908, following his uncle, John Boughey. He married Theodosia eldest daughter of the Rev. Charles Smith Royds. His daughters were Ethel, Eva, Dorothy and Mary to whom the estate was entailed though not the title. In March 1909 he sold nine lots of property for freehold building and accommodation land in Stafford Road and Vineyard Road in Newport. In 1910 he had Forton church restored before dying in the August. His wife and daughters stayed on in Aqualate Hall and were there when the fire broke out in the November.

The 6th Baronet was Commander Sir William Fenton Boughey RN. aged 70. He had served in the New Zealand War of 1863 and in Abyssinia. He continued to live at Southend on Sea where he and his wife died in 1912. They are both buried at Forton. He commenced the rebuilding of the Hall. The 7th Baronet was the Rev. Sir Robert Boughey who held the living at Betley for forty-five years. He was a landowner and very much involved in the public affairs of Staffordshire. He stayed at Betley leaving the Hall occupied by Theodosia Lady Boughey who died there aged 82 in 1923. Sir Robert died in 1921. Being single he left £1,500 to his housekeeper. Eva Greene received £1,000 and the other three nieces were left £4,000 in trust. The rest went to Sir Francis Boughey who was the 8th Baronet and the fifth brother to hold the title.

Born in 1848 he had resided at the family estate at Derwen near Oswestry but then farmed at the Guild near Aqualate Hall. On 6 March 1927 he hung himself in an outhouse at Aqualate apparently worried by the illness of his men and agent. His kindness and generosity were proverbial as his will shows. He left his spaniels, his 12 bore shotgun, his motor-car and £400 to his butler William Powell. He left George Knapp, his man, £50 to look after his pet terrier. He was unmarried so that the title went to a first cousin once removed, George Menteth Boughey of Lewes, the son of Colonel George Fletcher Ottley Boughey an engineer who served in India and Afghanistan. The present Baronet lives in Africa.

Lady Annabelle Boughey given the attitude of the day could not follow the same public and political life of her husband but she was just as benevolent and contributed much to the welfare of Newport. She was fond of hunting and appears in a portrait with Sir Thomas and *"Daisy"*, a favourite hound, at the front door of Aqualate Hall presented by the Albrighton Hunt in 1886 when Sir Thomas resigned his mastership. This was left to Newport Market Hall from where it has long since disappeared.

Annabelle travelled to India in November 1902 to see the Durbah.

Annabelle Lady Boughey

Laying of Commemorative Stone, South Porch 1904

She contributed generously to St Nicolas Church, Newport during the restorations of 1880 and 1891; she erected two windows, built the south porch in 1904, contributed to the building of the Parish Room and the restoration of the tower in 1911. She was President of the Newport Agricultural Society in 1910 and of the Shropshire Horticultural Society in 1914 when she lived at Sundorne. She died on the 2 February 1914 at Browns Hotel, Dover Street, London aged 72. She was brought from Sundorne to Newport Church and buried in Newport Cemetery on 21 February 1914 by the central chapel with a monument that pointedly reads *"In loving memory of Annabelle Sarah Lady Boughey of Sundorne Castle"*.

> *"By the death of this lady the town has lost a truly generous friend and the Church a most loyal and faithful member. The funeral service was conducted in Newport Church on Saturday 21st and was the most striking proof of the esteem in which the Lady Annabelle Boughey was held not only in the town and neighbouring districts but in the counties as well. The procession from the Church to the cemetery was such as Newport had never seen before. The Vicar of St Chad's Shrewsbury preached the sermon the following Sunday when he said, the best memorial to Lady Annabelle Boughey was the Church itself. She contributed to the restoration carried out under the supervision of the late Rector, Prebendary Burgess [sic] she paid for the building of the South Porch, and contributed to the Church Wall. She placed the beautiful stained glass window in the South Chapel in memory of her husband and paid off the debt on the restoration of the Church Tower."*

Newport Advertiser 21 February 1914.

Funeral of Annabelle Lady Boughey Feb 21 1914

She left £15,000 for a Cottage Hospital, £5,000 to be spent on the fabric and £10,000 to provide working revenue; £5,000 went to Newport Parish Church, £500 in trust to the Parish Room, £1,000 to the Agricultural Society and £200 to the Literary Society. £50,000 went to William Alfred Littledale Fletcher, Oxford Blue and oarsman in the winning crews of 1890-94. In June 1907 Christies had sold her collection of eighteenth and nineteenth century silver and now they sold the collection of porcelain she had bequeathed to Fletcher. This was a collection formed originally by John Bolton of Storrs Hall Windermere, bequeathed to the Rev.T. Staniforth and then Lady Boughey. Furniture, books and paintings were also sold, some by Murillo fetching £10,000. The total sum in her will was £274,048. Her household at her death consisted of a housekeeper, maid, gardener, chauffeur, bailiff, stableman, footman and usher.

To return to the female line, to the daughters of Sir George Boughey; Ethel was born on 4 February 1876. She spent her childhood at Forton Rectory and then at Aqualate with her mother until her marriage in 1919 returning to the Hall in 1930. She was at the Hall in 1910 when it burned down and she records all these events in her diaries. These are full of the commonplace incidents in the life of an unoccupied, well-off young lady, the weather, the seasons, visits, visitors, sickness - everyone had the measles in 1896 including Lady Annabelle. There are endless descriptions of the meets of the Albrighton Hunt that she seems to have followed on foot or bicycle.

Family gathering with Ethel Morris against pillar on left

On the 26 January 1898 at the age of 22 she went to the Newport Ball at the Market Hall:

> *"A most enjoyable ball. I danced everything straight from 1 to 20, with only one exception. About 150 people. Very pretty, but not quite so smart as last year, but the flowers and supper were even better and the Duchess of Sutherland came, but did not bring a party. The company was not quite so rackety this year. There was no mixing the drink, or shieing things about. We danced Sir Roger de Coverly for a supper dance. Altogether it was a great success and the best possible fun. About 30 came from Aqualate and the Victoria. Wore pink."*

There were other celebrations; the silver wedding of her parents in May 1900 with meals for everyone and dancing on Forton cricket ground; hardly a dozen people in the parish, she said, did not come; in June 1902 over 1,200 people were fed and entertained for the coronation even though it had been postponed. On the 7 August she watched the delayed coronation from in front of Westminster Abbey.

On the other hand she never shirked reporting the horrors of the Boer War and both world wars.

In 1919 at the age of 45 she married John Robert Morris of Wood Eaton Manor near Stafford quietly at Forton. No invitations were issued. The Morris family were originally solicitors who became neighbours at Calvington. John Morris succeeded to the Dol-llys estates in Montgomeryshire and his first wife, Margaret Clegg, who died in 1918, brought him Horsley Hall near Eccleshall. He died in 1936. There were no children from his second marriage.

On the 27 March 1928 the Aqualate Estate Company was set up to acquire the life interest of Mrs Morris. Share capital was £25,000 in £1 shares. This was a private company in agreement with Mrs Morris who was the "governing director" for life and able to exercise alone all powers. There were to be five directors but only two were named, Mrs Morris and her husband, John Morris.

In March 1929 Mrs Morris put up 1,500 acres for sale in Gnosall, Norbury and Forton including six farms such as Plough Farm. Several of the farms such as Coton Bank Farm, were withdrawn when they failed to reach the reserve. Extensive alterations and extensions were begun on the Hall. The Jacobean part left after the fire was rebuilt by W. D. Caroe the architect who was working at the time at Betley Court for George Fletcher Twemlow. The original rose-coloured bricks were revealed and the house was reduced from three to two storeys. The oak panelling came from one of the old estate farmhouses. The brick, stone mullioned and gabled house came to look very much as it had been three hundred years before.

In 1927 before the house was altered an inventory was taken of household furniture and effects to determine what constituted *"heirlooms"* as instructed in the will of Sir Francis. The contents would take too long to record but the list of rooms show an extensive building with entrance hall and passage, a long gallery with balcony, the "New" Drawing Room, dining room, Wainscote Room, another drawing room and a spiral staircase hall. Upstairs there was Sir Francis` bedroom and 13 others and thirteen attics. There was a bathroom and two men's *"Boffeys"*. Servants quarters contained a butlers pantry, still room, housekeepers room, kitchen, pantry room, salting house, scullery, lamp room and servants hall. The New Drawing Room contained the *"Halston heirlooms"* and there was a long list of silver and plate as well as linen.

In 1927 when Mrs Morris took over there was an overdraft of nearly £8,000, farms and cottages were in a bad state and every ditch and brook choked while there was hardly any timber worth cutting. Every gate and gatepost had to be replaced. The estate repair book from 1929 shows forty properties to be maintained as well as forty-one cottages attached to farms. From 1933 often under plans from the Chief Agricultural Officer buildings were repaired and re-painted, cowsheds, dairies and fold yards were improved as were toilets, drains, sewers and water supplies. There were new cottages at Coton Bank and Watton Grange, two at Forton while at Islington two cottages were turned into one. The Estate maintained the Forton school and schoolhouse at a cost of £346 in 1937. In 1936 the farm at the Swan Inn, Forton, was removed and the house leased to W. Butler & Co, Wolverhampton.

Every penny from the estate had to be spent on the estate and it was not until March 1943 that the account was balanced and the overdraft worked off. It had taken sixteen years and improvements only stopped with the war.

In the Second World War the house was occupied by Dr Barnardos whose orphanage had been bombed. There were at times forty-two children with about a dozen nurses and staff. They left in August 1945 before their time was up. The matron became a firm friend and Mrs Morris worried about the children when the army came.

There were army exercises in January 1942 with mock attacks involving six hundred men and seventy RASC vehicles. Mrs Morris was shown how to use a Tommy gun! In March there were similar manoeuvres involving Belgian troops but it was in July 1942 when Mr Liddle the family solicitor rang up to say the War Office had requisitioned the whole of the parks for a motor transport depot for 1,000 vehicles and the castle for repair shops, and intended to erect huts for three hundred men. Soldiers arrived and cleared out the stables and the coach house and removed the estate fire engine. By September 1943 there were between 4,000 and 5,000 vehicles parked in lines and squares linked by tarmac and concrete roads. There was a NAAFI often used by civilians. More huts were erected when fifty more ATS joined the existing one hundred. While the men were quiet Mrs Morris thought the girls *"idle undisciplined and quite useless."* This was mild compared to her opinion of Americans:

> *".... look as fat as pigs and look as soft as butter and push civilians off the footpaths and populate the whole country with dagoes".*

While the army was accepted – *"Hitler would be worse"* – there were real problems. The area available for the deer shrank, fences were broken and gates left open so that the deer escaped and did damage on neighbouring farms leading to quite expensive claims. From over 100 the number of deer went down to 70. For eighteen months the whole army was supplied with light from the oil engines which served the house, similarly with water, all for nothing.

At the beginning of the war a boom had been put across the mere using logs of wood and a wire hawser and over time the timber broke away and damaged the drainage around the mere. With a lack of men and materials by the end of the war the whole drainage system had broken down. To make things worse the War Department had used the mere boat the "Belerophen" to erect the boom and had badly damaged it.

Farming was controlled during the war by local Agricultural Executive Committees who often irritated with their suggestions one being to lower the level of the mere to provide more land and the ploughing of light sandy soils which tended to blow away. Double summer time Mrs Morris regarded as simply silly for agriculture and gardening with people leaving work at 5pm which was really 3pm and the hottest part of the day, while people were going to bed at 10.30 which was really 8.30 with the sun still shining.

But not all her grumbles were selfish; she thought rationing unfair to country folk who often got into town to find everything gone while the 1 cwt of coal a week was fine except that merchants would not deliver such small amounts to country customers because of the cost of transport and petrol. The farm labourer too had a tough time with little food, long hours, heavy work in all weathers and not even a thermos to keep his tea warm. This is why she refused to sell the Red Lion at Sutton even though the £2,000 would have been useful to the estate, because it was the only recreation of the farm worker during the war. It was eventually sold by the estate to the Wolverhampton and Dudley Brewery in 1952.

The entry at the end of hostilities is a perfect summary:

> *"There is no blackout, no search light, no sirens, no HG,*
> *no CD, the signposts are all restored, trains, stations and*
> *streets lighted and German prisoners are breaking up*
> *the concrete roadblocks and barbed wire entanglements*
> *which were put up "to be ready when the Germans came"*
> *and now the Germans are here but not as they expected."*

2 May 1945.

Throughout the war Mrs Morris continued hunting and there were frequent shooting parties despite the petrol restrictions on travel. There were no restrictions for saving foxes and pheasants. Mrs Morris had been made President of Newport Agricultural Society in 1939, its Jubilee Year. There had been no shows since 1931 but she, and a few others, kept the idea of the Society alive during the war years. Still President in 1946 it was decided to buy Mere Field, on the Forton Road, off the Aqualate Estate, 16 acres for £1,250, ironically paid for by £1,000 from the Boughey Memorial Fund (set up in 1935 with monies left by the Boughey`s and the sale of fixtures) and £250 from the Boughey Trust. Mrs Morris also purchased one of the wartime nissan huts on the Estate and gave it to the Society to erect on the showground.

In 1954 it was reported to the Urban District Council that because of the housing shortage, sixty families were living in damp and derelict conditions in the former ATS huts in Castlefields, in the grounds of Aqualate Hall. In the copse by the Newport Lodge can still be seen the foundations of these wartime Nissan huts.

Photograph Courtesy of Jany Graef

The 1930's were not good for farming, the depression that had begun in the 1870's returned with force. In 1934 Edward Watson Jones rented Whitley Ford from the Estate, 171 acres, for £320 pa. In 1939 he rented Fernhill, 208 acres, from Mrs Clegg Hill. She had it on lease and from 1956 was prepared to sublet the buildings and land for 25/- per acre (£1.25). Edward moved in his son and the farm was improved as a residence:

> *".... but the difficulty was Mrs Clegg Hill wanted to keep in hand 40 acres of good land. The farm was in a very run out condition and was notorious in the locality for the poor crop and bad farming".*

P Watson Jones, "The Jones Collections".

The Paddock Family at Fernhill 1905

Eventually in 1976 the Watson Jones organisation purchased the freehold of Fernhill and Whitley Ford from Aqualate, the landed estate epitomised by the Bougheys was out, *"agri-business"*, as practiced by the Watson Jones`, was in.

On 30 July 1912 Eva Boughey married John Wollaston Greene of Bury St Edmunds at Forton Church. This was the first wedding from Aqualate for 100 years. They were cousins through their mothers. They had one child who died in infancy. John Greene was a solicitor, clerk, coroner and registrar of Bury St Edmunds. Mrs Greene was a public figure, councillor and mayor in 1928 and 1931, the first lady councillor and mayor, as well as a Suffolk County Councillor. She was Chairman of Education and Health. She succeeded Mrs Morris on her death in 1956.

Dorothy the third daughter married Gerald Spencer Clegg-Hill youngest son of Viscount Hill of Hawkstone at Forton on 3 April 1907. Lady Annabelle did not attend. He was described as a keen agriculturist, poultry in particular, ducks being a speciality. After their marriage they lived at Hinstock where they were engaged in market gardening. Later they farmed at Fernhill until his death at the age of 51 in April 1930. Dorothy then managed the farm on her own until after the war when she moved to London to reside with her daughter Selina. She was 94 when her daughter Selina succeeded Mrs Greene.

Selina Juhre was born at Hinstock in February 1915. She was a keen horsewoman and rode with the Albrighton and also the North Shropshire hounds. Selina served in the WRNS during the War and worked for the Polish Government in exile as an interpreter, secretary and social worker. She continued to take an active part in the Polish community and in April 1947 at Westminster Cathedral she married 2nd Lieutenant Janusz Juhre a civil engineer then serving in the Polish Army. This was her second marriage. They had three daughters and a son.

However this was not the end envisaged for Aqualate. The picture of a generation of old ladies clinging on is not true. In 1945 at the end of the war Ethel Morris was 69 and began negotiations with Sir Richard Boughey to take over her interest in the estate and that of her sister Eva Greene. It would she said mean everything to the estate to be owned by a young, vigorous male with money to back him rather than two poor old ladies. It would also have the advantage of uniting the title and the name of Boughey with Aqualate they having come adrift as an unforeseen result of the 1832 Act. Unfortunately agreement could not be reached with the younger sister Dorothy and her daughter Selina so the arrangement was never completed. Relationships became uneasy, contents were dispersed, instead of unity and consolidation there was disintegration and there the matter rests.

Mrs Morris died on 16 December 1956. A grant of probate on settled land valued at £168,300 was added to unsettled estate valued at £36,768 giving a total of £205,069. On the 15 November 1957 outlying portions of the estate around Gnosall were offered for sale consisting of eight dairy and mixed farms ranging from 57 acres to 345 acres, six smallholdings with houses and buildings and 84 acres of accommodation and farm land, all subject to existing tenancies. There was also 49 acres of woodland. Rents were described as moderate bringing in £3,980 per annum for 1,853 acres. When offered as a whole bidding only reached £80,000 at which it was withdrawn all but three of the fifteen lots then being sold separately to tenants. The largest farm was Beffcote at Gnosall 337 acres going for over £16,500.

The *"Aqualate Diamonds"* were also sold and the collection of silver went under the hammer at Christies on 4 July 1958 again on the instruction of the Trustees of the Boughey Settled Estates.

Mrs Greene was 96 when she died and left Aqualate to be buried in Thurston, Suffolk. Dorothy was 95 when she took her place at Aqualate the estate and Hall reverting to her only daughter Selina. A combined birthday and welcome home party was held during which a tree was planted on behalf of Mrs Clegg-Hill by her grand-daughter Miss Zofia Juhre. Another cedar tree was planted by Mrs Juhre watched by tenants and staff. The Rev. J.C.Hill, Rector of Newport and a cousin, proposed the toast and gave the guests the family background. It is not recorded what he said.

Aqualate Hall and Stables c1925
Courtesy Mrs. Joan Vijups

Estate Workers c 1925
Courtesy Mrs. Joan Vijups

NOTES.

Two. The Bougheys of Aqualate

1. Twemlow, Francis, *Manor of Mere,* (1916), Staffordshire and Stoke on Trent Archive Service and the William Salt Library. [SSTAS].
2. Twemlow, Francis, *Twemlow Wives and Women, SSTAS.*
3. Morris, Mrs John, *Aqualate and the Manor of Mere,* Staffordshire Life, Vol. 2., December 1948.
4. Yale, Don, *The Landscaping Of Aqualate Park 1805-1813,* Staffordshire Studies, Vol. 6, 1994.
5. *Victoria County History, Stafford, Vol. 6*, Forton, pp. 103-111.
6. *Shropshire Family History Journal,* September 1998, for the Gater family.
7. NMDA, 1855 onwards, for details of family participation in public affairs, obituaries, accounts of the Coming of Age, 1857 and the Fire of 1910.
8. SSTAS. Acknowledgement must be made for the assistance given in using the vast amount of archive material particularly on the building of the hall and park, correspondence, drawings, accounts, conveyances, valuations and wills. Acknowledgement is made in the text where relevant.
9. Boughey, Clare and William. Grateful acknowledgement for permission to use photographs, to quote from the Ethel Morris diary and for generous help with all enquiries.
10. Robinson, D H, *The Sleepy Meese,* Chap. 7, 1988.
11. Watson Jones. P. *The Jones Collection,* privately published.
12. Adams.D.R.B. *The History of Newport and District Agricultural Society,* 1989.

Postscript.

Who loved Annabelle?

The obituary of Annabelle Lady Boughey could not be more overflowing; generous, loyal and faithful she was held in high esteem throughout the county not just Newport. She was the lady bountiful during her life and after her death. She contributed generously to the restoration of Newport Church; erected windows and the south porch; restored the tower. A bequest on her death in 1914 led to the building of Newport Cottage Hospital. The surplus from this fund and money from her housing fund is still used to provide accommodation for the elderly in Newport. After the funeral service at Newport Church hundreds lined the High Street as the cortege moved to Newport cemetery where there is a large monument inscribed to Annabelle Sarah Lady Boughey not of Newport but Sundorne. For years Thomas and Annabelle Boughey had been coming to Newport Church on a Sunday with their servants in a four wheeled carriage described as the "Aqualate Bus".

Yet Forton Church was in their gift and the living held by members of the Boughey family, at this time George Boughey the next baronet. This allegiance to Newport struck a bit odd. Why not be buried with the family? Why the deliberate choice of "Sundorne" on the monument when she had only lived there six years after twenty six as the Lady of Aqualate?

Behind the bountiful façade what was the relationship between Sir Thomas Boughey and his wife, more important what was the relationship between her and her husbands family?

In his will Sir Thomas had made the specific request that Annabelle stay on at Aqualate Hall after his death. Was this the cause of any friction? It was always thought that soon after his death she moved out to live at Sundorne Castle near Shrewsbury shaking off the dust of the Bougheys. The opposite now appears to be the case. She lingered on.

Was there a deeper rooted antipathy over the treatment of "Tom" by his wife? Was it her character? There were no children in a family that was prolific. Can we read anything into that? Was it a sore point? Sir Thomas Boughey died in August 1906 and there has always been some doubt as to what happened within the family after that.

Ethel Boughey [Morris] was the elder daughter of the Rev George Boughey Rector of Forton. She kept a diary. In 1896 there are entries telling how Aunt Annabelle called twice, how they had dinner at Aqualate Hall and garden parties, walked around the gardens and picked flowers for the church. There was certainly regular contact.

Before the death of Sir Thomas in 1906 there are other entries which say that nobody liked Annabelle though she does not say why presumably because everyone connected with the diary knew why. The indication is from the diaries and conversations with later Bougheys that she ruled "Tom" with a rod of iron and was pretty "ghastly".

The diary in August and September indicates that Thomas was very ill and recounts his death and the confusion at Aqualate.

The funeral was a big affair with an enormous crowd mainly women and children. The tenants from Aqualate and Audley turned out and there were numerous deputation's and guards of honour, though, the diary records not many of the family or friends. "The coffin was oak, grown on the estate and was brought on his timber wagon, with his own team of horses. Great numbers of wreaths. Everything went off very well."

There is no further mention of Aqualate or Annabelle until November 1906 when there was a sale at Aqualate of his private things. There is no mention of either throughout the 1907 diary the regular previous social intercourse had completely dried up.

Friday 24th January 1908: "Annabelle Lady Boughey left Aqualate yesterday. Servants leave tomorrow. Good riddance." Wednesday 29th January 1908: "Annabelle Lady Boughey has left Aqualate today for good." Was this just frustration on the part of Ethel and her family at having to wait sixteen months to move into the Hall as the successors or was it a deeper dislike?
Certainly when they did enter Aqualate Hall it was very empty and "very small and queer."

Sales went on from February 8 to the 12 and Ethel's family had to compete and buy what they could. They did manage to get some furniture. They then had to spend time painting and seeing to carpets, curtains and décor. They had to completely refurbish Aqualate as a home. This situation was difficult and frustrating and could lead to friction but was normal at such times. It was not until Monday 29th June 1908 that Ethel and her father moved into their inheritance shorn as it was. Nearly two years late. Lady Boughey had hung on selling all Toms possessions. Was this revenge for asking her to leave despite the request of Sir Thomas? Was it just a result of the hatred she had for Tom's brothers and the hatred they had for her?

In April 1907 Dorothy Boughey married Gerald Clegg-Hill but from Forton Rectory not Aqualate Hall which she would have done if they had been in occupation. Lady Boughey did not attend the wedding.

Lady Boughey died in a hotel in London on 2 February 1914.

The Bougheys of Aqualate

Sir Thomas Fletcher, Betley Court, Stafford, created Baronet 1798, d 1812. Wife Anne Fenton of Newcastle under Lyme.

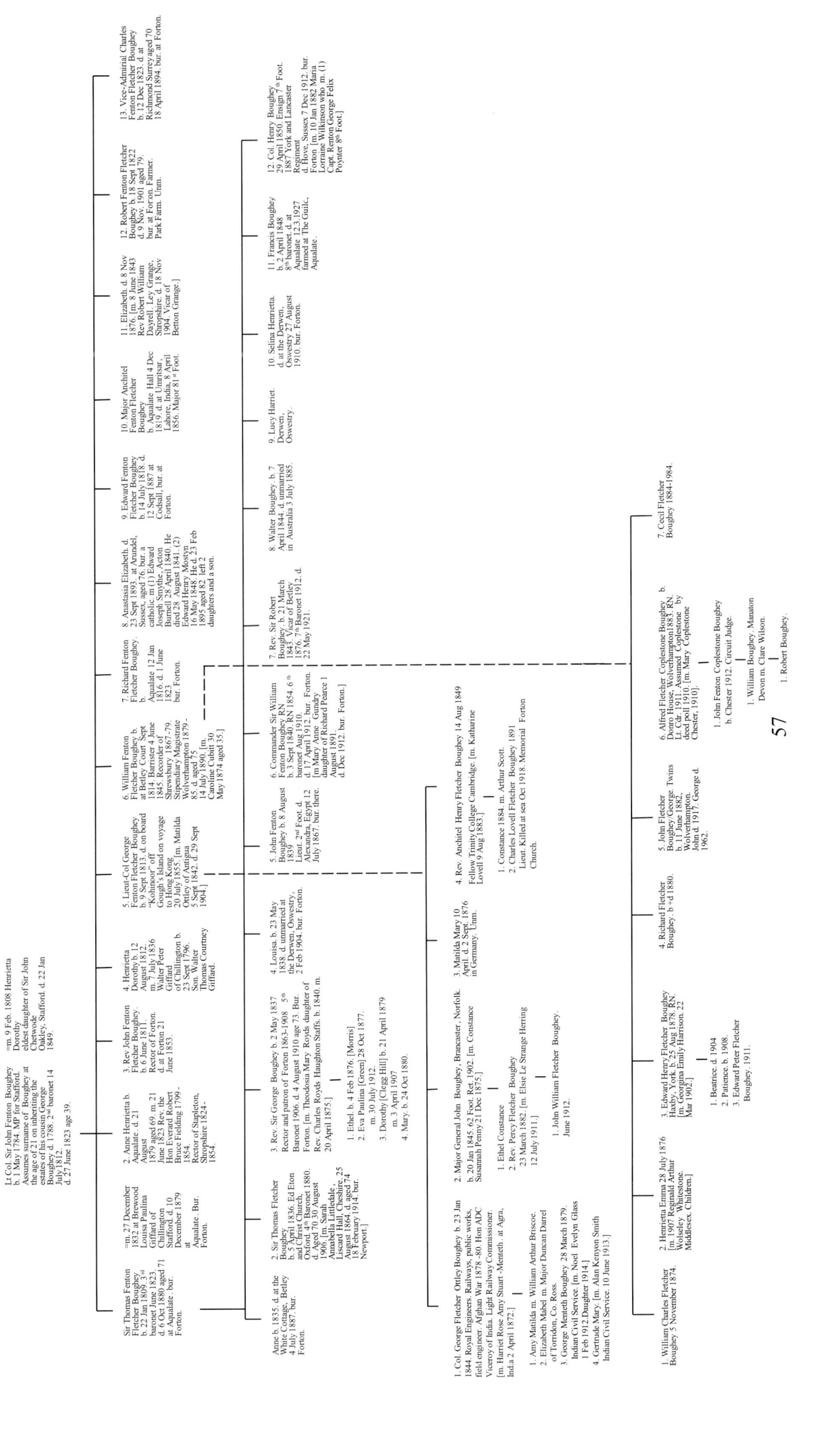

Lt Col. Sir John Fenton Boughey b. 1 May 1784. MP for Stafford. Assumes surname of Boughey at the age of 21 on inheriting the estates of his cousin George Boughey d. 1788. 2nd baronet 14 July 1812. d. 27 June 1823 age 39. =m. 9 Feb. 1808 Henrietta Dorothy eldest daughter of Sir John Chetwode Oakley, Stafford. d. 22 Jan 1849.

Sir Thomas Fenton Fletcher Boughey b. 22 Jan 1809. 3rd baronet June 1823. d. 6 Oct 1880 aged 71 at Aqualate. bur. Forton. =m. 27 December 1832 at Brewood Louisa Paulina Giffard of Chillington Stafford. d. 10 December 1879 at Aqualate. Bur. Forton.

2. Anne Henrietta b. Aqualate. d. 21 August 1879 aged 69. m. 21 June 1823 Rev. the Hon Everard Robert Bruce Fielding 1799-1854. Rector of Stapleton, Shropshire 1824-1854.

3. Rev. John Fenton Fletcher Boughey. b. 6 June 1811. Rector of Forton. d. at Forton 21 June 1853.

4. Henrietta Dorothy b. 12 August 1812. m. 7 July 1836 Walter Peter Giffard of Chillington b. 23 Sept 1796. Son. Walter Thomas Courtney Giffard.

5. Lieut-Col George Fenton Fletcher Boughey b. 9 Sept 1813. d. on board "Kohinoor" off Gough's Island on voyage to Hong Kong 20 July 1855. [m. Matilda Ortley of Antigua 5 Sept 1842. d. 29 Sept 1904.]

6. William Fenton Fletcher Boughey b. at Betley Court Sept 1814. Barrister 4 June 1845. Recorder of Shrewsbury 1867-79. Stipendiary Magistrate Wolverhampton 1879-85. d. aged 75 14 July 1890. [m. Caroline Cubitt 30 May 1874 aged 35.]

7. Richard Fenton Fletcher Boughey. b. Aqualate 12 Jan 1816. d. 1 June 1823 bur. Forton.

8. Anastasia Elizabeth. d. 23 Sept 1893. at Arundel, Sussex, aged 76. bur. a catholic. m (1) Edward Joseph Smythe, Acton Burnell 28 April 1840. He died 28 August 1841. (2) Edward Henry Mostyn 16 May 1848. He d. 23 Feb 1895 aged 82. left 2 daughters and a son.

9. Edward Fenton Fletcher Boughey. b. 14 July 1818. d. 12 Sept 1887 at Codsall, bur. at Forton.

10. Major Anchitel Fenton Fletcher Boughey b. Aqualate Hall 4 Dec 1819. d. at Umritsar, Lahore, India, 8 April 1856. Major 81st Foot.

11. Elizabeth. d. 8 Nov 1876. [m. 8 June 1843 Rev. Robert William Dayrell, Ley Grange, Shropshire. d. 18 Nov 1904, Vicar of Betton Grange.]

12. Robert Fenton Fletcher Boughey b. 18 Sept 1822. d. 9 Nov. 1901 aged 79. bur. at Forton. Farmer. Park Farm. Unm.

13. Vice-Admiral Charles Fenton Fletcher Boughey b. 12 Dec 1823. d at Richmond Surrey aged 70 18 April 1894. bur. at Forton.

Anne b. 1835, d. at the White Cottage, Betley 4 July 1887. bur. Forton.

2. Sir Thomas Fletcher Boughey. b. 5 April 1836. Ed Eton and Christ Church, Oxford. 4th Baronet 1880. d. Aged 70 30 August 1906, [m. Sarah Annabella Littedale, Liscard Hall, Cheshire. 25 August 1864. d. aged 74 18 February 1914. bur. Newport.]

3. Rev. Sir George Boughey b. 2 May 1837 Rector and patron of Forton 1863-1908. 5th Baronet 1906. d. 4 August 1910 age 73. Bur. Forton. [m. Theodosia Mary Royds daughter of Rev. Charles Royds Haughton Staffs. b. 1840. m. 20 April 1875.]

4. Louisa. b. 23 May 1838. d. unmarried at the Derwen, Oswestry. 2 Feb 1904. bur. Forton.

5. John Fenton Boughey b. 8 August 1839 Lieut. 2nd Foot. d. 17 April 1912. bur. Forton. [m Mary Anne Gundry daughter of Richard Pearce 1 August 1891. d. Dec 1912. bur. Forton.]

6. Commander Sir William Fenton Boughey RN b. 3 Sept 1840. RN 1854. 6th baronet Aug 1910.

7. Rev. Sir Robert Boughey. b. 21 March 1843. Vicar of Betley 1876. 7th Baronet 1912. d. 22 May 1921.

8. Walter Boughey b. 7 April 1844. d. unmarried in Australia 3 July 1885.

9. Lucy Harriet. Derwen, Oswestry.

10. Selina Henrietta. d. at the Derwen, Oswestry 27 August 1910. bur. Forton.

11. Francis Boughey b. 2 April 1848 8th baronet. d. at Aqualate 12.3.1927 farmed at The Guild, Aqualate.

12. Col. Henry Boughey 29 April 1850, Ensign 7th Foot. 1887 York and Lancaster Regiment d. Hove, Sussex 7 Dec 1912. bur. Forton. [m. 10 Jan 1882 Maria Lorraine Wilkinson who m. (1) Capt. Kenton George Felix Poynter 8th Foot.]

---

1. Col. George Fletcher Ottley Boughey b. 23 Jan 1844. Royal Engineers. Railways, public works, field engineer. Afghan War 1878–80. Hon ADC Viceroy of India. Light Railway Commissioner. [m. Harriet Rose Amy Stuart-Menteth. at Agra, India 2 April 1872.]

1. Amy Matilda m. William Arthur Briscoe.
2. Elizabeth Mabel m. Major Duncan Darrel of Torridon, Co. Ross.
3. George Menteth Boughey 28 March 1879. Indian Civil Service. [m. Noel Evelyn Glass 1 Feb 1912. Daughter 1914.]
4. Gertrude Mary. [m. Alan Kenyon Smith Indian Civil Service. 10 June 1913.]

2. Major General John Boughey, Brancaster, Norfolk. b. 20 Jan 1845. 62 Foot. Ret. 1902. [m. Constance Susannah Penny 21 Dec 1875.]

1. Ethel Constance
2. Rev. Percy Fletcher Boughey 23 March 1882. [m. Elsie Le Strange Herring 12 July 1911.]
  1. John William Fletcher Boughey. June 1912.

3. Matilda Mary 10 April. d. 2 Sept. 1876 in Germany. Unm.

4. Rev. Anchitel Henry Fletcher Boughey 14 Aug 1849 Fellow Trinity College Cambridge. [m. Katharine Lovell 9 Aug 1883.]

1. Constance 1884 m. Arthur Scott.
2. Charles Lovell Fletcher Boughey 1891 Lieut. Killed at sea Oct 1918. Memorial Forton Church.

5. John Fletcher Boughey/George. Twins b. 11 June 1882, Wolverhampton. John d. 1917. George d. 1962.

6. Alfred Fletcher Coplestone Boughey b. Donro House, Wolverhampton 1883. RN. Lt. Cdr. 1911. Assumed Coplestone by deed poll 1910. [m. Mary Coplestone Chester, 1910.]

1. John Fenton Coplestone Boughey b. Chester 1912. Circuit Judge.
  1. William Boughey. Manaton Devon m. Clare Wilson.
    1. Robert Boughey.

7. Cecil Fletcher Boughey 1884-1984.

---

1. William Charles Fletcher Boughey 5 November 1874.

2. Henrietta Emma 28 July 1876 [m. 1907 Reginald Arthur Wolseley Whitestone. Middlesex. Children.]

3. Edward Henry Fletcher Boughey. Haxby, York b. 25 Aug 1878. RN. [m. Georgina Emily Harrison. 22 Mar 1902.]

1. Beatrice. d. 1904
2. Patience. b. 1908.
3. Edward Peter Fletcher Boughey. 1911.

4. Richard Fletcher Boughey. b *d 1880.

"Aqualate Was Burnt Down."

The diary of Ethel Boughey

Monday 28th November 1910.

W to N. White frost. A beautiful sunny day. Aqualate was burnt down. The fire was discovered by the housemaid when she went to open the shutters about 6.30. I got down soon after. The gallery was then full of smoke but not dense and the fire was in the library by the small window opposite the door, between the pillars and the door into the old billiard room. The servants were carrying buckets of water and working the little handpump inside the room. I went to get some clothes on and walking through the north door I saw that the whole of no. 13 was in flames. When I got down at 9 I found that the servants had got the small manual engine out and fixed on the water main and the end on the green walk. I shut the doors into the gallery all round and we broke in the windows and the 4 maids worked the engine while the Butler and Albert held the hose. I went to the yard and rang the fire bell and sent Williams to Newport for fire engines and help. The woodmen and gardeners hearing the bell and Forrestry and Stacy came about 9.30 and S J got the big engine out. By that time the fire had spread to the Drawing Room and no. 14 and the roof had caught and there was a strong, steady wind from W to NW, the worst quarter possible. By 9 the engines began to come and a lot of people but by the time they got to work the whole of the south tower was on fire and the gateway was a sheet of flames upstairs and the lead roof of the gallery had caught. Colonel Fitzherbert and Captain Fitzherbert motored up and took mother away at 10 o`clock and afterwards Mrs Sykes took her to Longford. Dorothy and Gerald arrived at 10.30 and the gallery roof and both the domes went in just after they got into the yard. It was too late to save anything out of the house, by the time the people came. By 9.30 the smoke made it impossible to get inside the rooms, and we had no hands to work before, else we could have saved the furniture in the gallery and drawing room if we had any help in time. The dining room furniture and the picture of Sir John and Dame Henrietta Dorothy were the only things saved. All the other family portraits and all the china, Queen Anne chairs, miniatures and snuff boxes were burnt. By middle day the whole of the new part of the house built by Sir John Boughey in 1808 was entirely destroyed, only the walls left, but the firemen had succeeded in cutting the roof and saving the old seventeenth century house but the roof over that was badly damaged and the whole house saturated with water. We got all the furniture and clothes out of our own and the library bedrooms which were all in the old part of the house and the plate and papers out of the business room and safes. But everything else is gone. I went to Meretown, Dorothy and mother to Longford and Gerald and Uncle Francis stayed at Aqualate as the fire was still burning in several places. There were five fire engines, Newport, Stafford, Wellington, Eccleshall and our own two and crowds of people. Some of the tenants came quite early and they and the tradesmen from Newport worked hard. There were all our own people and hundreds of the roughest people from all over the County but they worked well, only one man was hurt but not badly and was taken to Stafford Infirmary. The place is a ruin and the whole thing is too awful. Thank god father is dead.

Tuesday 29th. N. Hard frost, foggy early. Sunny later. V cold. Went to Aqualate to try and get things straight. All the things saved and packed no how into the stables. Several of the neighbours came to see us again with offers of help and they and relatives have offered to take us in. We got most of the servants off except the ones who have to stay to cook for the Watchers. Gangs of men have to be on duty all night as the fire is still burning in the library and dining room and keeps breaking out. The fire engines are all gone but Newport.

Wednesday 30th. NE. Vy hard frost and thick fog all night. Dull and very cold. Went to Aqualate again and did more tidying up. Walter Vernon motored over and Uncle William and his sons and Uncle Robert came and went to the Victoria. They were all drunk as owls. Got Gerald away to Longford. Neither he nor Uncle Francis have had their clothes off since they came over on Sunday or have had any sleep and Gerald fell on the ice in the dark and broke a bone in his wrist.

Thursday 1st December. Vy cold. Rained all day. Went back to Aqualate. The Uncles etc were all there. Eva came back from London. Mrs Sykes spent the day helping us to pack up the plate for the bank and to sort out furniture. Uncle Walter Greene and Lady Boughton motored over from Grove and went on to tea at Longford to see mother. Freda Radcliffe left and the Fitzherberts went to Walton for the Stafford Ball.

Friday 2nd. .... There are tremendous floods out hundreds of acres under water. The snow had hardly melted when the rain came and the rivers were too full before that.

Saturday 3rd. Rained all night and all day. V dark and cold. Spent the day at Aqualate. The fire is still smouldering in the library and dining room and there have been several outbreaks. Uncle William and his sons and Uncle Robert went home. The rain has got in through the damaged roofs and done no end of mischief to the rooms inside. They have begun to wash them out. The Fitzherberts came back and Miss Worthington.

Sunday 4th. 2nd in Advent. SE. rained in the night. Dark and cold with fog and showers. Walked to Aqualate with Col Fitzherbert PM and had tea with Uncle Francis and Mr Webster. There have been crowds of people trying to get in to see the place but we have had the gates locked and the keepers on duty to stop them.

Thursday 8th. SE. cold and dark. Uncle Francis came to tea and to talk business. They will not rebuild the house.

Sunday 25th. Christmas Day. The first Christmas we have ever spent apart and not in Forton parish. Now mother and Eva are at Peatwood, Mary at the Derwen and I am here. Father is dead, the only one left at Forton.

Mr. Morrey, estate employee inspects rebuilding of the hall c1928
Courtesy Mrs. Joan Vijups

Edgmond Workhouse January 1825.

Whereas it hath been duly certified to this Court by Thomas Leeke Esquire, one of his Majesty`s Justices of the Peace acting for and resident within the Newport Division of the Hundred of Bradford in the said County of Salop, that he did on the 9th day of January in the year of our Lord one thousand eight hundred and twenty-five visit the Parish Workhouse kept or provided for the Maintenance of the Poor of the Parish of Edgmond in the said Division and County, and that he did examine into the state and Conditions of the Poor people therein, and the food, clothing and bedding of such poor people and the State and Condition of such house. And that upon such visitation he did then and there find just cause of complaint, inasmuch as the Said house was in very bad repair, the Roof in several places admitting the rain into the wretched Bedrooms under it, the windows in want of Glass, the door Cases in holes so as to admit the wind and rain, and in one room the wall was so defective as to let in the wet through it; That in one bedroom the floor was one half deprived of boards the rain penetrating in various parts of the roof, and that a young woman who had been sickly for some months was destined to sleep in this upon Straw without Bedsteads and with only one sheet and Blanket. That this wretched house was inhabited by 20 persons, 9 of whom were children, with their parents. That they were allowed certain sums weekly and provide themselves with food, fuel and clothing. That no Superintendent lives in the house. That the Overseer who accompanied Mr Leeke had not been there for 3 weeks, nor had any other Parish officer. That the whole establishment is shamefully neglected and the inmates filthy, badly clothed, and the greater part idle. That there was no work whatever going on in the house. That the family of Kaye, his wife and 5 young children, an old widow and her grandchild, occupy one apartment of the House, consisting of a ground floor and a room upstairs. That in this one Bedroom the roof of which has a large hole in it admitting wind and rain, all these person sleep being nine in number. That the two Bedsteads belonging to the Kayes, in which repose a man and his wife and 5 children, have only two ragged worn out blankets between them, one on each bedstead. One sheet only on one bedstead and no sheet on the other. Some matted straw all to pieces over Some Cord which supports it on the Bedsteads, the ticking being all gone. That the 5 children have no clothes but what they wear, and no change of linen. That one little girl has not even a flannel petticoat. That they are ragged, starved and filthy. That a widow and her sick daughter in another department of the house have only one thin blanket and a sheet in holes allowed them. That many of the panes of Glass are out of the window in their Kitchen, and that the wind and the rain have also admission through the roof. That the Clothing of the Poor and the Bedding is disgracefully scanty in the house, and that the weekly allowance is not sufficient to enable the inmates to purchase Blankets or a change of sheets, or a change of Garments. That the Overseer appears very much to neglect the Conduct of the inmates, their wants, and the Condition of the house. That the house is as filthy without as within. And whereas Andrew Moore and Robert Goodall overseers of the Poor of the said parish of Edgmond were duly summoned and did appear at this Court of General Quarter Sessions of the Peace to answer such Complaint. And upon reading the said Certificate and hearing what *could be said by all parties the Court hath thought fit and doth hereby order for the removing of such complaint, and the Said Overseers of the Poor of the said Parish of Edgmond do immediately after the receipt of this order, cause the said Workhouse or Poorhouse to be thoroughly repaired, and rendered warm, dry and cleanly. That the wall through which the wet penetrates in the apartment occupied by Barber and others be repaired. That the roof in Kaye's apartment be thoroughly repaired. That the outer Door-frame in Bold's dwelling be repaired. That the roof over the room occupied by Sarah Martin be repaired and the floor made perfect. That the manure and filth lying about the Said Workhouse or Poorhouse be removed, and the precints of the Same be kept clean and in order. That panes of Glass be placed in the windows where they are wanting. And it is further ordered that the 5 children of Kaye be supplied with Clothing as follows viz, each Girl with two linen Shifts, a flannel petticoat and frock; and each boy with 2 linen shirts, a coarse cloth jacket, waistcoat, and trousers and that all the inmates of the Said Workhouse or poorhouse who have not a change of linen be supplied with the Same and never be without it. It is also ordered that a Bedstead be immediately supplied to the bed occupied by the daughter of Barber, and another to the Bed occupied by Sarah Martin. And that the Besteads upon which Kaye and his family sleep be repaired, and that 3 sound Blankets and 2 sheets be given to each of their Bedsteads, and that a chaff bed, 3 blankets and 2 sheets be attached to every bedstead in the Said Workhouse or Poorhouse. And it is also further ordered by this Court that the Acting Overseer of the Poor for the time being of the Said Parish of Edgmond do at least once in every week inspect the Said Workhouse or poorhouse, and enquire into the State of the inmates and their wants, and it is hereby ordered accordingly.*

Transactions of the Shropshire Archaeological and Natural History Society 1878.

3. The Poor of Newport.

On the 15 November 1836 the newly appointed Relieving Officer of the Newport Union reported to the Guardians that he had been violently assaulted by William Adams of Lilleshall, who had scaled the walls and broken open the doors of the workhouse. The problems of the Newport Board of Guardians appointed under the 1834 Poor Law Amendment Act had begun.

The first meeting of the *"Board"* had been a month earlier at the Workhouse in Workhouse Lane, now called Vineyard Road. They found that the workhouse had no proper accommodation for a meeting and adjourned to the Town Hall. Being a brand new authority the Board, which was elected, had attracted the highest in the area, Mr Cotes of Woodcote being elected Chairman and Sir Thomas Boughey, of Aqualate, Vice-chairman. They had the task of adapting a system of poor relief, which had lasted nearly 250 years, to a new, radical, rational, centralised organisation with a rigid philosophy.

Traditionally the poor, as with other things such as highways, had been dealt with by the parish, a unit of government recognisable and manageable. The elected overseers of the parish would raise money through a rate on property to support the poor whatever the cause of that poverty, such as age, sickness or unemployment. The genuine or *"deserving"* poor could be helped in kind or money paid to them in their own homes, called *"out relief"*, while malingerers could go to work houses where they were put to work to pay for their keep. By the 1830's a system had grown up of linking payments to the price of bread but with rising prices during the Napoleonic wars the cost of poor relief had become enormous. At the same time population had doubled and the industrial changes had caused the growth of towns, swamping the parish system which was a rural concept. It was impossible to send thousands of urban poor back to their original parish to get help.

There had always been a fear of poverty leading to crime and disorder, as illustrated in the nursery rhyme *" Hark, Hark the dogs do bark the beggars are coming to town"*, to this was now added the belief that poverty was the result of idleness and that paying the poor reduced their independence and made them shiftless and lazy. To enforce this view a structure would be put in place that would get rid of all the old traditional, sentimental attitudes and would impose the same standards throughout the country. It would also have the advantage of being cheaper and independent of the government. A Poor Law Board was set up in London headed by three Commissioners with assistant Commissioners in the provinces and officers at the local level responsible to Boards of Guardians elected by ratepayers.

Under the 1834 Act, Guardians were elected by all rate-paying occupiers and all owners of land and buildings within the Union without distinction of sex. There was plural voting where occupiers and owners had a number of votes in proportion to the rental value of their property. This lasted until 1894 when it became one vote per ratepayer. By this time working men had got the vote anyway. This was the year when District Councils, Urban and Rural, were created. To be nominated as a Guardian you had to have a rateable value of £25. Elections were annual and to avoid *"mob pressure"* voting papers were delivered and collected from the homes of the electors. Proxies were allowed. This voting system was advertised in the Newport Advertiser every year. The same system as postal voting today [2004]. Parishes were united irrespective of county and traditional boundaries into *"Unions"* of parishes a word that came to represent the workhouse itself. While the genuine poor would still be given payment in their own homes the able-bodied would have to go into the workhouse where conditions were deliberately made worse, or less attractive, than outside. This was known as *"less eligibility"*. Workhouses once seen as places of refuge were now places of punishment and degradation. This hatred and fear caused them to be called

"Bastilles" and lead to rioting and bloodshed in the north. This loathing lives forever in *"Oliver Twist"*, and is still remembered by the elderly today [2004]. For the next hundred years regulations poured from the centre to be interpreted by gentlemen guardians not all in the Dickensian mould and not all acquiescent to central authority.

The strict, harsh discipline of a *"well-regulated"* workhouse produced many rules; the separation of men and women; prevention of visitors; no smoking or drinking; unattractive work; provision of only the necessities of life, that is a basic diet. It was envisaged that there would be a workhouse for each category of poor, the elderly, children, able bodied men and women, but in reality cost led eventually to one central Union workhouse.

The Newport Union, true to the central policy, was formed on the new concepts of efficiency and utility so that the Union stretched from East Shropshire into Staffordshire as far as Gnosall, the historical boundaries being ignored. The parishes were divided into three districts (1) Newport, Chetwynd, Forton, Adbaston, High Offley and Weston Jones; (2) Gnosall, Norbury, Stockton, Woodcote and Chetwynd Aston; (3) Edgmond, Lilleshall, Longford, Church Aston, Tibberton and Cherrington. Newport was the focal point. The Guardians inherited accommodation or "work" houses in the parishes certainly those at Newport, Lilleshall, Chetwynd, Gnosall and High Offley are mentioned in the first minute book.

The first meeting on 6 October 1836 appointed a clerk, Henry Heane, at £50 pa. It discussed the terms of a workhouse governor and his wife who was to act as matron or schoolmistress whichever was required. Salary was £50 pa with *"allowances"* per week of, 14lbs of raw meat, 14lbs of bread, 1½ of cheese, 2lbs of butter, 4 quarts of milk and 1 peck of potatoes. At the November meeting they retired to the comfort of the Union Hotel where they discussed the property they had inherited and for which they were now responsible, the rentals they would have to pay to the overseers of each parish, any repairs, and the valuation of the furniture. They appointed Mr and Mrs Pritchard governor of the Newport workhouse. They also appointed Relieving Officers for each district to sort out the applicants and to pay outdoor relief.

Supplies to the workhouses were to be by tender and contract for everything from food and coal to coffins.

They faced ticklish interpretations; was the husband of a woman who had a bastard before marriage and who was married to her before the passing of the Poor Law Act [1834] bound to maintain the child? The Commissioners had allowed the concession of tea, butter and sugar to be substituted for gruel for older people. Newport asked permission to do this.

The Guardians gave outdoor relief where possible allowing people to stay in their own homes. This relief was preferably in kind; an allowance to purchase calico and flannel to make petticoats and shirts; providing blankets during illness; to facilitate this they set up depots in the villages. They also gave loans.

> *"Maria Holding be allowed some clothes to enable her*
> *to remain in her service with Mr West, Chetwynd Parish".*
>
> *"Mr Pritchard do obtain what articles may be necessary*
> *for the women who are expected to lie in and do also employ*
> *the able bodied in his workhouse in making clothes for the*
> *establishment till other employment can be obtained."*

Union Minutes. January 1837.

In August 1837 it was ordered that men and women were to have an additional suit of clothes so that the washing could be done every fortnight. The clothes were the property of the workhouse and in February 1840 Harriet Dyke was prosecuted for absconding with her workhouse dress and also the gown, shawl and bonnet belonging to another pauper.

Though harshness was the policy towards the able bodied, children were innocent and deserving. The Commissioners wished them to be maintained separately and Newport did this keeping the Gnosall workhouse as a "Poorhouse" for children, while Newport was defined as a *"Workhouse"* set aside for the able bodied. Parents, and in particular fathers, were pursued for desertion and prosecuted for maintenance even for bastard children and where possible paupers were maintained outside the workhouse or sent back to their original parish. Ellen Boss was paid 1/3 a week because her husband had left her and later 2/6 was allowed to transport her back to Derby. With Julia Harris it was the other way, £2.10.06 being paid to convey her and her children from Macclesfield to Newport workhouse. With a lack of appropriate accommodation families were split, Mary Barnett in February 1837 had three children sent to Newport while the other three children went to Lilleshall workhouse. In April 1839 the Master`s wife had been employed as either a matron or a schoolmistress but the Board changed its mind and decided that children in the workhouse and the poorhouse should not be taught reading or writing. Five years later they changed their minds and were buying spelling books for the Gnosall children.

The difficulty of not distinguishing between the causes of poverty meant that the fit and well were mixed with the physically and mentally sick. Newport recognised this; lunatics were paid out relief or sent to private asylums. In December 1841 it was:

> *"Ordered that a nurse be provided for the Newport workhouse*
> *to attend to the women who have fits and that they be kept*
> *separate from the others."*

Like Oliver Twist children were apprenticed out:

> *"That James Heath a pauper in the Newport workhouse*
> *be bound to John Ashley Bates of Ironbridge, taylor, at*
> *the next meeting at the expense of the parish of Adbaston."*

Union Minutes. June 1841.

Yet we find the guardians in 1842 objecting to certain clauses in Lord Ashley`s Bill against the employment of boys under the age of 13. Children at work were not a burden on the poor rates.

The moral welfare of the inmates was paramount after all poverty was a sign of moral degradation. The Commissioners ordered that each workhouse should have a chaplain. Newport demurred. The guardians pointed out that Newport workhouse was for the able bodied and that they did not need a chaplain as they could walk to church. At Gnosall the Rector was willing to act for nothing. However they did pay £4.10.00 for religious books from the Society for the Propagation of Christian Knowledge. In the end the Commissioners ordered them to have a chaplain so they appointed the Rev.W Sandford, Second Master at the Grammar School, Curate at Newport and a Guardian, at £20 pa.

Physical welfare was often a question of diet and the Commissioners were always enquiring as to the least an inmate could eat while staying fit. This was a matter of cost and also *"less eligibility"* the principle that conditions inside the workhouse should be less acceptable, less attractive, than those outside. Poor food was one way of keeping the poor out. In January 1837 the guardians reduced the allowance of meal and increased that of potatoes in order to make savings. At the same time they increased the salary of Mr Heane from £50 to £80 pa.

Adulterated food provided on contract to the lowest tender could be a problem and in April 1840 the guardians ordered Mrs Belcher to appear before them to answer complaints of bad meat and improper pieces.

Concern over food costs and the desire not to make the workhouse too attractive led to detailed instructions from the Poor Law Board as to what proportion of a meat allowance could be classified as *"waste"* including bone. They said 25%, Newport insisted on 33%. The weekly diet for the workhouse had to be calculated by the medical officers and approved by the Poor Law Board so that provisions could be costed and bought accordingly. In November 1857, as an example, men (women) on a Monday had 6 (5) ounces of bread and 2 (1½.) pints of gruel for breakfast; 16 (12) ounces of suet pudding for dinner; 6 (5) ounces of bread and ½ (½) ounce of cheese for supper.

Spiritual matters took precedence over the stomach:

> *"That the suet pudding day at Gnosall Poor House be on*
> *Sundays instead of Friday so that the Poor thereby may*
> *be the better enabled to attend church and that the meal*
> *day be on Friday instead of Sunday."*

The Commissioners of the Poor Law Board continually issued instructions on the most minute matters such as appointments, purchases, allowances, contracts, as did the Board of Health, irritating the Newport Guardians who complained that they and their officers were doing the job well and at great cost in time and labour. The main irritant was Edwin Chadwick one of the three Poor Law Commissioners and later Head of the Public Health Board until in the end he upset too many and was pensioned of in 1858 for the rest of his long life.

The Newport Union inherited property from the individual parishes for which they had to pay rent to the owners mostly the parish overseers, and to maintain them. At the same time the Commissioners were requiring the provision of separate accommodation for different categories of poor. The difficulty was how to reconcile this and reduce the poor rate. Within the first year they tried to rid themselves of the Lilleshall workhouse and therefore the Lilleshall relieving officer but the guardians were never unanimous and decisions were postponed. They did manage to move the Lilleshall children to Gnosall. In Lilleshall the workhouse was the gift of the Duke of Sutherland who owned most of the rateable property anyway. They were paying him rent. In June 1840 the guardians wanted to *"consolidate"* the *"two receptacles"*, meaning Newport and Gnosall, for the destitute poor, into one establishment and had invited Mr Day of the Poor Law Commission to come down and discuss the matter even though they were not unanimous. Unfortunately the visit coincided with Newport Races:

> *"That in consequence of the Newport Races happening on*
> *the next Board the Clerk do write to Mr Day and inform*
> *him thereof and that he had better postpone his visit."*

Union Minutes. June 1840.

They did close the High Offley Poor House and sold it to John Talbot.

The repairs to these old buildings and the alterations required to fit the national directives, were a concern from the beginning, plus the need to find accommodation for the board meetings and central offices for the increasing work of the relieving officers. A building was found in Lower Bar, Newport, to serve as a Register Office and Board Room. It was purchased from Thomas Parsons and £500 was borrowed privately at 5%. They met there for the first time in March 1838 and continued to meet conscientiously and weekly for many years. In May 1884 it was rebuilt by Muirheads for £445 and it is this building that is now [2004] owned by the Boughey Trust and used by Longford Playgroup and others.

The Newport workhouse needed frequent repair and in January 1848 the Commissioners were asking for it to be enlarged. Improvements were made by John Cobb, particularly the cellars, and in 1849 loan sanction was granted for £380.

> *"Newport, under the new Poor Law, is the centre of a Union, comprising sixteen parishes; and a new and commodious workhouse has been erected."*
>
> Slater`s Directory. 1849.

By 1850 the guardians had acquired other duties with the realisation that there was no one cause of poverty and these other causes required specific remedies. The Poor Law itself threw up masses of information and statistics on these problems, problems that the money from the poor rate was insufficient to tackle. The Poor Law also needed information if it was to do its job. It needed to know about births, deaths and marriages. The guardians became responsible for the 1836 Registration Act under which all births, deaths and marriages had to be registered. The Union was divided into two districts for this, Newport and Gnosall, and the Register Office was opened in Lower Bar.

In 1840 they accepted the provisions of the Vaccination Act which followed from the work of Edward Jenner, who proved that an injection of cowpox gave immunity against smallpox - *vaccus* meaning a cow. There was a serious smallpox epidemic in 1837-40 which led to permissive legislation in 1840 authorising vaccination at public expense. Poor Law Authorities were given the duty of carrying it out. The guardians were given free vaccine and so they became the first public vaccinators but it was not compulsory until 1853 for children and many parents opposed it until 1871 when there was a fresh outbreak and fines were imposed. Many resented not the vaccination but being bullied into health. Vaccination remained one of the major jobs of the medical officers, and one of the major costs, to such an extent that payment to the doctors was increased in July 1850 from 1/- to 1/6 per vaccination:

> *".... hopefully vaccinators will use their best endeavours in seeing that all poor persons be properly vaccinated in their respective districts."*

Smallpox had virtually disappeared by the end of the century though there was an outbreak in the workhouse as late as 1928.

They also became responsible for the *"Nuisances Removal and Disease Prevention Act"* of 1848 and had to instruct their medical officers of health, of which there was one for each District, to survey any such nuisances in their area. This act arose from the creation of a national Board of Health which in turn arose from the cholera epidemic which swept Europe that year. It again raised the problem of how a group of local men elected to deal with local poverty could tackle a national epidemic? Some people saw their chance Mr W Liddle and Mr W Griffiths petitioning the guardians in July 1849 to proceed against the owners of Bellmans Yard to abate the "nuisances". This yard was notorious for filth and overcrowding. Officers of the Union were ordered to inspect and a committee was set up with powers to act. Later they ordered all poor persons who may be attacked with the *"bowel complaint"*, their description of cholera, to apply to the medical officers for *"such remedies as the case may require."*

Advertisements were taken out in 1853 warning residents about accumulating any refuse or filth near their dwellings and informing the public that the guardians were now responsible for the Commons Lodging House Act and that they intended to enforce it. Lodging houses accommodated a particularly mobile and unhealthy section of the community and there were several in Newport in Marsh Lane and Bellmans Yard.

In September 1849 the Union was paying £129 for the County Police rate though they were not happy with having to collect money levied by someone else, so much so that in 1851 the Newport guardians set up a committee and raised subscriptions to petition Parliament about having to levy a rate imposed by *"irresponsible parties"*, not controlled by the ratepayers. It was, they said, taxation without representation.

So the guardians were accumulating duties simply because they were the only elected local authority capable of administering them.

The Poor Law may have been a modern, efficient, system of administration but its money came from the ancient parish. The guardians worked out what was needed for all their operations then sent the bill to the parish overseers to levy on property owners based on the value of their property. The overseers were voluntary, though often not volunteers, elected at a Vestry meeting and confirmed by the local Justices of the Peace. In normal times a group of well-intentioned men could do the job but by 1840 times were not normal, England had become an urban nation. Up to 1850 the guardians were constantly threatening the overseers in the different parishes for non-collection of rates. In 1843 for example, Gnosall faced a bill of £1,000 which it had difficulty collecting. The overseers were summoned to appear to compel payment of £964 outstanding. In 1862 the Guardians took over rate assessment making valuations fairer between each of their constituent parishes and in 1866 the cost of the Union came out of the general fund for the whole Union rather than the individual parishes being charged for the actual costs they incurred, that is a standard rate for the whole area. In 1869 a permanent assistant paid overseer was appointed to collect the rates. His job was to make out and collect and lay the charges before the guardians. For this he received an annual salary of £25 and had to give a bond of £300. His name was John Humphreys. This avoided the frequent confrontations with the overseers.

The half-year payments due from the overseers in June 1853 included Newport £347, Chetwynd £102, Edgmond £54, Church Aston £86, Lilleshall £307, Forton £260, Gnosall £296 and High Offley £168. The half-year total from all the parishes was £1,925 (£3,850 for the year).

The 1830's was a decade of political unrest over parliamentary reform and unrest in agricultural areas with violence and rick-burning and the Tolpuddle Martyrs. The 1840's, *"the hungry forties"*, were times of industrial depression, unemployment, declining wages and high corn prices. Down the road in the East Shropshire coalfield 1842 saw strikes and violence with the miners fighting the newly formed police and Yeomanry. The Newport workhouse was full and the guardians had to rent a cottage to house the overflow at 2/- a week. In 1843 they were instructing the Clerk to write to the Commissioners informing them that the local nature and character of the area made it utterly impossible for them to find work for the unemployed. They did write to the Duke of Sutherland asking for twenty acres of land to be let to the guardians for tender to parishioners and able bodied paupers now unemployed at Lilleshall. They also wrote to the Lilleshall Company to obtain Cinder Hill where the unemployed could be put to work breaking stones. They appointed a superintendent of pauper labour. The guardians had made conditions hard ordering oakum for picking by the able bodied, which they sold to the Lilleshall Co., regulating hours of work and breaks, but the extreme conditions of 1842 and 1847-8 swamped the system.

Prosperity in farming and industry returned from 1850 but coming down the A41, as they always had done every harvest, were the Irish, but this time in their thousands, driven by the potato famine and here to stay.

Mr Pritchard died in February 1845 and his wife immediately lost her job and home. Samuel and Mary Binnell were appointed on the same terms as 1836. In 1841 there had been 29 inmates, in 1851, 34, of these 10 were children under the age of 10 belonging to four unmarried mothers:

> *"The Newport Union House, situated in Workhouse Lane, is a plain brick structure which will accommodate about 60 inmates; the aged, infirm and the older children are sent to the Union House at Gnosall, in Staffordshire, which is connected to the Newport Union, and this house is for the reception of the able bodied poor and very young children. The several places comprised in the Union in the County are Newport, Chetwynd, Chetwynd Aston, Church Aston, Cherrington and Edgmond. The townships and places in Staffordshire are Adbaston, Forton, Gnosall, High Offley, Norbury and Weston Jones. Chairman to the Guardians, John Cotes esq, Clerk, Henry Heane, Chaplain Rev William Sandford; Surgeons Mr William Lindop, Mr Godby and Mr John Green. Relieving Officer, Mr Benjamin Rees, Master Samuel Binnell, Matron, Emma Wellings."*

Bagshaw's Directory. 1851.

The census of 1851 shows the yards of Newport such as Cock Yard and Bellmans Yard crowded with Irish, fourteen or fifteen to a one bed-roomed cottage. Many had been there since 1847. There were complaints about these yards harbouring such great numbers of Irish, mostly agricultural labourers or tinkers, and of drunkenness, fighting, blockage of pavements and general disorder until in August 1858 there were reports of over fifty fighting on a Sunday night. In September 1858 there were said to be over 200 Irish fighting in the main street with pokers, stones and missiles. Yet given the misery and poverty which had driven them from Ireland there is not one Irish person in the Newport workhouse in 1851 and only three in 1861. They are not mentioned in the Union minutes except for one terse statement that provides the answer:

> *".... ordered that the Clerk do take what steps he considers advisable toward stopping as far as possible application for relief made to this Board by the Irish."*

Union Minutes. August, 1853.

As late as January 1882 the Irish fought the police in the High Street when they were taking prisoners convicted of drunkenness at the Christmas Gawby Market to the railway station. The fighting began at Bellmans Yard, continued to the station and involved the deputy Chief Constable of Shropshire. In 1881 there were only six Irish in the workhouse out of 99 inmates. In 1901 there were five Irish, four of them well over 70. If they were a problem it does not seem to have affected the poor rates.

In July 1851 the guardians were considering consolidating all the establishments at Newport though the vice-chairman, Mr Boultbee, protested that it was not the time for such expenditure with agriculture labouring under great depression because of low prices for their products. The proposal went through. At the same time they appointed Benjamin Rees to be relieving officer for both Newport and Gnosall – he got an extra £30 but had to agree to keep a horse – owing to the decrease in pauperism in the Gnosall district. The Poor Law Board questioned this while urging the building of a central workhouse rather than spending money on the existing buildings. One suggestion was to purchase the *Royal Victoria Hotel,* at the time the newest and most prestigious building in the town, for conversion into a workhouse. This was thought to be *"not proper"*. Sir T.F.F. Boughey moved the building of a new workhouse and they bought three acres, three roods and fifteen perches of land in Audley Avenue from the Marsh Trust for £160 an acre, a total of £615. The land was conveyed on 14 April 1856. The contract for the building was given to John Cobb of Newport and they agreed to borrow £615 for the land and £2,995 for the building. Here again the Poor Law Board raised difficulties refusing to loan the money and telling the guardians they should look elsewhere. They were furious replying that they had so tried but as it was the idea of the Poor Law Board to build a new workhouse they should have found a source to finance it! In the end they borrowed the money, £3,610, from the Metropolitan Life Assurance Society over twenty years at 5%.

During 1855 while the building was being erected the Board tidied up the system, giving notice to the overseers at Newport and to Mr Tildesley whose cottage they had used as a tramps room. They told the officers at Gnosall they were vacating the premises there and made arrangements for the children to go to Stafford.

The master of the workhouse died in February 1856. His wife had died in 1850 and been replaced by her niece Emma Wellings at £20 pa plus rations which consisted of 7lbs of raw meat, 7lbs of bread, 2 quarts of milk and half a peck of potatoes. The Board was now able to use the *"Newport Advertiser"* to advertise for a new master who was required to give a surety of £100. In May 1856, they appointed Lewis James as Master, he having married Emma Wellings. Lewis had previously been a draper with a shop on what became the Vine Vaults. He was paid £50 pa and rations.

The old workhouse in Workhouse Lane was advertised for sale by auction in March 1857 and again in September 1858. It was described as being on an eminence with a fine view and recently substantially erected. There was a Governors house in the centre with rooms and chambers either side for the able-bodied men and women. There was a wash house and bake house. It was suggested that the building would make good cottages which it now is. The Girls National School was probably in the workhouse and certainly was in the old workhouse building by 1865 and 1869.

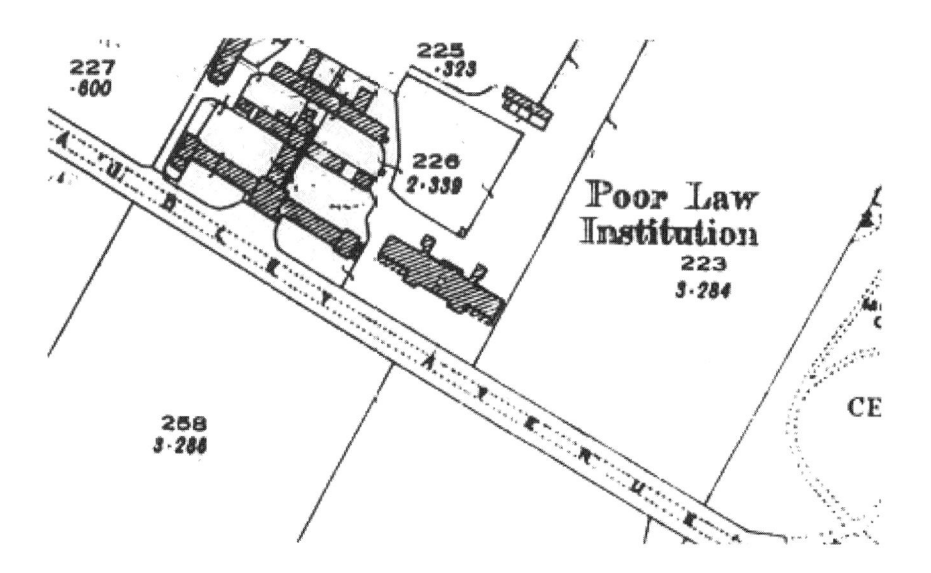

The new house had a sick bay and the old folk's room had special low tables to eat off and forms with backs to sit on. By 1858 extensions were being made including a nursery.

When talking of conditions in the workhouse it has to be remembered that the Master and Matron were dealing with a vast age range and a variety of problems and that many of the inmates came from the least civilised and illiterate sections of the community. James Talbot and Thomas Hains acted obscenely in the workhouse and were punished by confinement in a separate room with an alteration of diet, *"similar in kind and duration"*, namely 48 hours. At Gnosall in 1852 two paupers were beaten and confined in the *"dead house"*; the master and matron were reported to the Poor Law Board; in July 1854 the master and matron at Gnosall were repeatedly guilty of punishing children contrary to the rules, one lad, named Brayne, having his head cut open with a stick. They were reported and proceedings taken for assault. Sarah Plant a *"refractory pauper"* was given twenty-four hours in the *"refractory cell"* and a special punishment diet.

John Miles` wife who had died of typhus was buried at the expense of the guardians and in 1858 we find them negotiating with the new Burial Board at Newport on terms for burying paupers in the new cemetery just down the road. Coffins were interred on top of each other quite close to the surface. There were other medical difficulties a father with the *"itch"* and a son with smallpox were removed in October 1853. Workhouses could spread infection and in 1857 there was widespread ophthalmia, an inflammation of the eye, and the Newport Board gave a £3.03. 00 (£3.15) subscription to the Royal London Ophthalmia Hospital.

A particular problem, were the *"ins and outs"*, families who came in for a short time for varying reasons such as debt or seasonal unemployment or family troubles. Edwin Lloyd in June 1853 deserted his wife and two children leaving them on the *"parish"*. The Newport guardians advertised his desertion in the national gazette issued by the Poor Law Board a kind of *"wanted"* list for absconding parents. In the end Edwin's father turned up took over the family and paid any charges.

Dealing with children was the most sensitive area for guardians with on the one hand the Christian ethic of protecting the innocent and on the other the desire not to give too much care and relieve parents of their responsibilities. Nationally youngsters comprised a third of the pauper population dealt with by the Poor Law four fifths of these were dealt with by *"out relief"* about 200,000 a year. Children in the workhouse were a minority of inmates and this was true in Newport. Where possible they were kept as family units, usually young unmarried mothers with illegitimate children. Older youngsters needed some education but the dilemma here was should the Union pay for pauper education while working parents outside had to pay their own school fees? The Newport guardians did set up an Industrial School at Gnosall with a paid superintendent and where there were National Schools as at Moreton, Lilleshall and Donnington Wood they paid the fees of pauper children on out relief. This was a policy copied by many other Unions in the 1870`s. Later they sent about 25 indoor children to Quatt industrial school:

"The Guardians of the above Union have at the Industrial School, Quatt, 12 girls aged 13-15, for whom they are desirous of obtaining situations. B Rees, Relieving Officer."

Newport Advertiser. 18 April 1863.

Union Minutes November 1857 Diet

		Breakfast			Dinner						Supper			
		Bread	Gruel	Milk Porridge	Cooked Meat or Bacon	Cooked Vegetables	Pea Soup	Suet Pudding	Bread	Cheese	Bread	Cheese	Butter	Broth
		oz	pts	pts	oz	oz	pts	oz	oz	oz	oz	oz	oz	oz
Sun	Men	6	2					16			6	½		
	Women	5	1½					12			5		½	
Mon	Men	6		2					6	1½	6	1½		
	Women	5		1½					6	1½	5		½	
Tues	Men	6	2	2	3	16					6			2
	Women	5			3	16					3			1½
Wed	Men	6		2			2				6	1½		
	Women	5		1½			1½				5		½	
Thurs	Men	6	2		3	16					6			2
	Women	5	1½		3	16					5			1½
Fri	Men	6		2				2			6	1½		
	Women	5		½				1½			5		½	
Sat	Men	6	2		3	16					6			2
	Women	5	½		3	16					5			½

In 1851 there were 32 in the old workhouse, 12 male and 20 female, of these 10 were under the age of ten; in 1861 in the new centralised Newport house there were 83 inmates of whom 36 were male and 47 female, 19 under the age of ten and 23 over sixty; there were five unmarried mothers with fifteen children and two widows with six children; of the men 26 (66%) were agricultural labourers. Well over half the adults were unmarried (33). 23 were from outside the Union area, from as far away as Guernsey, Warwick, Cheadle, Edgbaston, Wolverhampton and three from Ireland.

The Poor Law from the 1860's settled into a quiet bureaucratic routine. Time silenced the most zealous opponents and the system was not seriously disturbed until after 1900. People were no longer shocked by the cost of the poor, indeed with the working vote and the rise of trade unions many advocated more expenditure on social welfare but directly by the State. In 1871 Gladstone amalgamated the Poor Law and the Public Health Boards into the Local Government Board thus tacitly recognising the interconnection between all three strands. In November 1872 the Newport Guardians advertised for an Inspector of Nuisances at £3.3.0 a week to carry out the duties laid down by the Local Government Board, these included making a complete sanitary survey of the town by 1 March 1873. Mr John Cobb, the builder of the workhouse, who had gone bankrupt, was appointed. Tenders were invited to build an infants school at the workhouse but the cost of £1,000 put them off. The next year tenders were sought for building a casual ward. *"Tramping"* was becoming a problem.

Statistics at the time, 1871, show the Newport union covered 16 parishes with a population of 15,839. Paupers relieved up to 1 July 1871 were 874, expenditure £6,036; the proportion of paupers to the population was 5%. In 1874 *"In"* maintenance was £485, out relief £1,138. 1 in 35 was receiving outdoor relief. People preferred to be helped in the community and so did the Newport Guardians.

> ***Newport Guardians.*** *- at the ordinary fortnightly meeting of the above Board, at the Victoria Hotel, on Monday morning, there were present:- R W Ralph, Esq. (chairman); Revs J Rogerson, and R Jackson; Messrs. W. Massey, J. B. Ball, G. Ingram, M. Thompson, C.Greene, W.D.Turner, J.Pearce, G. Hammonds, R.N.Heane (clerk), and J.Crickmer (relieving officer). – The Clerk read an extract from the "Master's Journal," which stated that he (the Master of the Workhouse), had to report that Elizabeth Fox had given notice of her intention of leaving the Workhouse. She had a boy at Quatt School, who would be 14 years of age next June. He now applied for an order to fetch the boy. – The Board accordingly made an order to that effect. – The Clerk reported that the following parishes were in arrears with the call due on the 2nd February, and was instructed to write to the Overseers: - Cherrington, Newport, Church Aston, Tibberton, and High Offley.*
>
> Newport Advertiser. 8 March 1884.

Mr. & Mrs. Buck - Master and Matron 1912

Tramps were a problem hence the casual wards, and in October 1889 172 tramps were relieved in a fortnight, 143 in the workhouse and 29 in other accommodation. In September

1893 stone breaking cells were installed since many tramps used Newport because, allegedly, the work was easy. In the first five months of 1904 over 1,000 men, 473 women and 76 children passed through the vagrant wards at Newport. In addition between June 1903 and June 1904 1,823 people were given tickets for 4d to go to common lodging houses in town because there was no room at the workhouse. They therefore avoided work at the house such as breaking stone and pumping water and were known as *"able bodied dodgers"*. In 1907 Guardians were still alarmed at the number of vagrants who were *"a serious menace to the peace and well-being of this country."* They thought labour colonies should be set up to deal with the problem on a national scale. The tramp wards had beds and hot water for delousing. At the time they were breaking so much stone that the Marsh Trust complained that the weight of the wagons were destroying their road to the workhouse, while no one wanted to buy the stone.

Workhouse Group c.1912

Replying to fears that tramps were overfed Mr Buck revealed that rather than being a burden the workhouse would not function without the labour of the vagrants:

"Vagrants Dietary.

> *In reply to your enquiries of the 13th inst., I beg to state that in the strict sense of the word I do not depart from the Dietary in any case – in dealing with the vagrants at this workhouse where there is little or no able bodied help in the Home I submit there is special circumstances with regard to the men kept for a day, which as a general rule, number four, and out of whom we are bound to get a pretty solid days work from 7 am to 4.30 PM; their duties are wood sawing from 7 till 3 and from 3 to 4.30 pumping water – we get no difficulty in obtaining men voluntarily to stay – there are always some who are very willing to be off the roads for a day to get a little change in the shape of warm food and a rest for their feet – but our aim naturally is to choose the best and most able men among these volunteers. As a rule I find the majority are very poorly clad and suffering more or less from the pangs of hunger their food being principally bread and water. We have in the House Dietary Tables one soup dinner one broth dinner and one meat stew dinner*

*during the week and from these is generally some leavings, but
not to any great extent, which cannot be used again in the House
and these are all collected and if there is sufficient with a little
water added it is given to the detained tramps at dinner time and
although I have very little sympathy with the tramping class –
being as we find them very dissatisfied and abusive generally –
I cannot help thinking that where a man has to do a decent days
work he is better fitted to do it after a warm dinner of soup than
a cold one consisting of bread and cheese only. Further I do not
keep or detain them as a deterrent, but under existing arrangements
as useful and necessary to the general management as without
them we should be without water and without a wood chopping
business- useful and although not large still a profit bearing
employment for the majority of the male inmates who are unable
to perform work of a laborious character. In the garden also I
am to a great extent dependent on them. If the Board are of the
opinion that this practice should be discontinued I am of course
in their hands and must abide by their decision.
In conclusion I beg to emphatically state that there is no food
given to vagrants that could be possibly used up for the inmates of
the House."*

Union Minutes 23 April 1909.

An Inspector in November 1920 complained that rain leaked through into the tramps wards and the slates were repaired at a cost of £7.7.6. [£7.37]. The Grammar School were playing cricket in the next field and the guardians sent them the bill alleging that the damage was caused by cricket balls being hit on the roof. Mr Finnis, a master at the school wrote back refuting the claim and two years later the school bought the field for £350, known as the *"Shuker Field",* built a pavilion and went on playing cricket there until the 1970's.

In 1925 the Casual Poor Relief Order said tramps had to be held for two days but there was little work to do as there was no pumping since the workhouse was by then on the mains and stone breaking had been abandoned. There was no room or disinfecting apparatus to detain so many. However they adopted the Order. Next year they were instructed to keep them for three days but how, by fences? W Latham the first working class guardian objected that workhouses were becoming prisons. The difficulty of cleansing in the casual wards was highlighted in February 1928 when a case of smallpox was found. Many refused to be vaccinated and as by law they could only be detained two days there was no means of isolation. The guardians had to pay for all vagrants to be inspected and if necessary treated for many days.

If anything the problem got worse in the depression of the 1930's as men took to their feet, if not their bikes, to find work. In 1929 over £800 had to be spent improving the casual wards. W Latham opposed the expenditure as he disliked the treatment of vagrants by the Poor Law and also because the workhouse was soon to be abolished anyway. When chided he snapped back:

> *"Well at any rate the Board would not put these people up at the Victoria Hotel – though they were as worthy as many of the men who went there, he was sure!"*

Here was an example of a social problem for which the poor law had not been designed.

> *"The spike consisted simply of a bathroom and lavatory, and, for the rest, long double rows of stone cells, perhaps a hundred cells in all. It was a bare, gloomy place of stone and whitewash, unwillingly clean, with a smell which, somehow, I had foreseen from its appearance; a smell of soft soap, Jeyes' fluid and latrines…"*

> *Down and Out in Paris and London.* George Orwell. 1933.

Lewis James master of the workhouse died aged 75 in 1888. Mr and Mrs Ide were appointed at a salary of £45 and £25 for the matron plus rations, washing and a furnished apartment. They had to be under fifty years of age and give a bond of £100.

In 1890 came diet improvements; tea four times a week with an allowance of butter and sugar; 4oz instead of 3oz of corned meat three times a week; lobscouse stew [a stew or hash with vegetables or biscuit, a sea dish; origin obscure] one day per week instead of gruel; more rice instead of suet; half pint per head of milk per day.

In February 1890 Dr C. E. Baddeley, the medical officer reported on the condition of the workhouse. The general plan and construction he thought was good though the ventilation and sanitary and drainage were poor. The privies emptied into nearby cesspools and polluted the wells from which the water supply was pumped. The local Marsh Brook was also polluted causing complaints from Newport and even Longford over a mile away. The accommodation for the infirm and sick was insufficient since they made up the vast majority of the inmates, 58 out of an average weekly number of 74. The master and matron, he felt, could not attend the sick and do other duties. Separate wards and attendants were needed. The report was allowed to lie on the table. However in May they did advertise for a nurse between 35-45 at £18 pa with washing, rations and laundry.

By 1891 the guardians were having to deal with problems unimagined by the 1834 Act, also the poor rate was having to cover at least a dozen other expenses not only relief of the poor but County and police rates, the registration of births and deaths, vaccination, parliamentary registration (1845), highways (1865), rural sanitary affairs (1873), school attendance (1878) and others.

The old Board of Guardians met for the last time in December 1894 as changes came in with a new Act. There were now two Boards one for the rural area of Shropshire and one for the rural area of Staffordshire, meeting twice a month each section staying on after one of the meetings for their own meeting.

Another first was the election of the first woman guardian, Miss Roddam.

A Local Government Board circular of 1895 stressed a more humane, neighbourly approach to the guardians duties; while the able-bodied were the main problem the administration was still one of deterrence but now the sick, aged and infirm were preponderant and a new spirit of administration was required. The Newport Guardians were ordered to carry out improvements to the insanitary condition of the workhouse pointed out by Dr Baddeley six years earlier. To be fair they had hesitated not knowing whether the poor law would be divided between Staffordshire and Shropshire as had the rural sanitary authorities. Now they acted borrowing £1,000 at 3.5% for fifteen years.

Dr Baddeley persisted: *"a complete reorganisation of the workhouse is imperative"*; there was no distinction between classes of inmates, the sick were treated in the general wards, imbeciles mixed with the ordinary inmates, boys with adults. He was supported by the Duchess of Sutherland who after a visit to the workhouse in 1900 commented that it was completely out of date and the infirmary was insanitary.

There had been a tremendous decrease in numbers by 1900 compared to (1872); 1900 indoor paupers 79 (127); outdoor 237 (723); total 316 (850). The cost per head of poor relief in Newport in 1900 was 1/5 [7½] this was above average for the district.

"Christmas day at the Workhouse"

> *Christmas Day is one that is eagerly looked forward to by the inmates, for on that joyous occasion, discipline is relaxed, and innocent enjoyment reigns. And although this year Christmas Day fell on a Sunday, yet the festivities were not therefore forgotten, but simply deferred to the next day – Boxing Day. The dinner itself, as ordered by the Guardians, was served on the set day, and consisted of roast beef, mashed potatoes and parsnips, with plum puddings. For breakfast the inmates had coffee and buns, the gift of Miss MEAKIN`s and bread and butter. Miss Meakin also gave a Christmas letter to each inmate. For tea there was cake and bread and butter. The Chaplain held service in the afternoon. Boxing Day was considered half--holiday and after tea the hall was cleared for the evening`s amusement which comprised dancing, singing, musical chairs etc., in which all those who were able joined, thoroughly enjoying themselves without the slightest hitch or unpleasant incident. The dining hall was tastefully decorated, the evergreens, as usual, being kindly given from the cemetery. The gifts were: Miss Meakin, coffee and buns and Christmas letters; Mr J C BROWN, oranges and tobacco; Mr E ELKES, cakes, crackers and sweets; Mr BATT, tobacco; Mr DOUTHWAITE, oranges; Mr NEWBOLD, oranges, sweets, nuts and tobacco; A friend, oranges, and, as on previous years, 1/- to each of the old inmates, from their anonymous friend."*

Newport Advertiser. 31 December 1898.

The 1901 census shows Mr and Mrs Ide as master and matron with two infirmary nurses. There were 81 inmates made up of 43 male and 38 female; 41 were over 60 and 9 under the age of ten. 19 of the men gave their occupations as *"labourers"*. None of the women were listed as having *"occupations"*. There was one *"blind"*, 3 feeble minded, 5 imbeciles and 4 *"imbeciles from birth"* bearing out Dr Baddeley's complaint of 1896. There were ten casuals (not vagrants) from as far away as London, Holyhead, Tunbridge Wells and Newcastle on Tyne.

One immediate change to make the system more humane was to start calling the workhouse *"Audley House"*.

The Local Government Board continued to press for a new infirmary at Newport and with Mr and Mrs Ide retiring the time was opportune. They were replaced by Mr and Mrs Buck from Cannock. The Marsh Trust again supplied the land for £150 and the cost of £3,765 was approved and £4,000 borrowed. G. I. Muirhead got the contract for £3,100 and work commenced in 1907. Unfortunately Muirhead went bankrupt leaving complications over payments and unfinished work. Eventually in 1908 the Infirmary was opened by Miss Roddam supported by the Duchess of Sutherland. Miss Roddam had lost her seat as a Guardian in March 1907.

Matron and nursing staff taking tea outside the infirmary
c.1920

It was proposed that the old infirmary rooms be equipped with baths and used as receiving wards as people coming into the workhouse were frequently in a dirty and verminous condition and had to be cleansed before they could mix with the other inmates. In 1909 there was only one bath in the workhouse, which had to be used for male and female inmates and by applicants on their first admission, this was why reception wards were necessary

In 1887 the workhouse was still lit by candles as they had refused to pay the cost of a gas main. In 1907 they had advanced to oil lamps but it was not until April 1912 that tenders were received for gas lighting for the workhouse, the infirmary and casual wards. The work went to W Bromfield for £36.15.00. [£36.75]. In 1905 no agreement had been reached over provision of a water supply by the Urban District Council and the workhouse still relied on a pump. This meant there was no fire protection or proper sanitation. The Board did decide to provide water for the new infirmary but it was not until 1925 that the workhouse was joined to the town supply. A telephone was installed in January 1926.

Local boards had always sought ways of removing children by fostering or *"apprenticeships"* or emigration. The latter had flourished in the 1880's but it had been impossible to check the welfare of the children in their new homes. James King an orphan who had been deserted was sent to Canada in May 1907 by the Newport Board under the auspices of the Catholic

Emigration Society. The cost was estimated at £15.18.04. They did receive reports back about his progress. In 1908 aged 14 he was working on a farm and in the house for board and clothing only. The Emigration Society said he should be paid but his employers refused until the Society demanded he be paid $2 a month and clothes or be returned!

In September 1920 James Pascall was placed on a farm in Ontario by the immigration branch of the National Children's Home and Orphanage.

Children were offered for employment. Mr J. N. Warrender a blacksmith from Sheriffhales answering an advertisement in the Newport Advertiser in February 1909 for a boy said he would be treated as one of the family and they would *"do what we could to learn him a good trade."* In 1920 Sarah Buttery was found a place as scullery maid with Mr Talbot of Edgmond Rectory, the guardians paying £6.10.00 for her outfit.

Legislation in 1888 and 1889 allowed Guardians to *"adopt"* children up to the age of 18. Frank Howells was adopted in 1909 and boarded in a suitable home at 4/- a week and right at the end, in 1929, three children named Forrester were adopted by the Newport Board and boarded out by the National Children's Home.

Another option was to send boys into the services, the army and navy and even the fishing fleets. Ernest and Frank Adderley were sent to the training ship *"Mercury"* at Southampton on the understanding that at the age sixteen they would enter directly into the Royal Navy.

A blind girl from Lilleshall was sent to the School for Indigent Blind at Liverpool. A report was made in September 1907 on the three women imbeciles who had been in the workhouse for many years. They were found to be usefully employed in the laundry and the house; they were tidy and contented with good beds and clean dormitories and a large garden to walk in; it was felt the new infirmary would improve their accommodation.

In 1909 the Guardians finally closed the boys home at Gnosall, this was a home for boys whose parents were in the workhouse, an attempt to free them of the workhouse *"taint"*. The reality was it was expensive and they were going for the cheaper option of boarding out except no one would board out such boys. It took a long time to convince the Local Government Board but the final straw was the death of the matron in the May, Mr Buck from Newport having to go to Gnosall to make emergency arrangements to look after the boys, to complete the planting of the garden and the feeding and cleaning of the pigs. The former Matron's husband removed and sold all the furniture and cutlery, even the bed, from the living quarters.

In many areas workhouses were used as places of detention for delinquent children and Newport agreed, after all it was 5/- a week. Fortunately the Local Government Board ruled that Newport was unsuitable.

Diets in the workhouses were determined nationally this was partly to control cost but also part of the rule that conditions in the houses should not be better than those outside; inmates must not be seen to be pampered. This was one of the principles of the 1834 Act. We have seen complaints about the feeding of vagrants. There were similar complaints about the feeding of inmates and officers. Whenever W Latham tried to improve rations and salaries for staff he was defeated.

In February 1909 Mr Buck the master was questioned about eggs. Provisions were supplied by contract so variations had to be explained. He had to give a detailed account, including a chart endorsed by the Medical Officer, of the consumption of eggs for the four weeks in February and why 80 eggs, then 80 eggs had risen to 88 then 92? He had to explain that he had had to go out and buy extra eggs because they had been prescribed by the medical officer for a new inmate and that the nurses had extra eggs in lieu of their cheese ration which was allowed by the regulations.

The next year an outside report discussed the wastage of meat, not a new topic, and explained that it was because the matron had to do the cooking as well as her other duties and was constantly called away from the kitchen. Without her supervision wastage took place. The master and matron were the only people in charge of 77 inmates the guardians having got rid of the porter or labour master and his wife. The scrubbing of the building was actually done by the male tramps the female tramps being judged to be too filthy! Mr and Mrs Buck, the inspector recorded, could never take a holiday and had also been looking after the Gnosall house. No wonder, he concluded, the cooking was not economical.

The guardians agreed to re-appoint a Labour Master and wife at £20 pa with accommodation and rations.

In 1921 the food bill was still under scrutiny and it was decided to substitute corned beef – apparently the inmates loved it – for mutton, on the grounds of cost.

At last in 1914 it was ordered that children between the ages of 3 and 16 must be provided for elsewhere than in a workhouse. The Newport Junior School logbook shows one of the difficulties:

> *"Have been informed that Philip Barker, a child living at the workhouse will not be able to attend school again as he is to be transferred to a home for Feeble-minded Boys."*

Newport Junior School Logbook. 13 September 1918.

Here are two little tales of children caught in the system, one from 1916 the other from 1919. Samuel Felton from Church Aston had been an inmate for nearly 50 years. Weakly at birth he had been admitted to the workhouse when it was in Workhouse Lane [Vineyard Road], transferred to Audley House when it was built, become blind and had been able to do little but knit. He died on 3 August 1916 aged 69.

Emma Scragg died aged 74 in March 1919. Her mother had died when she was two months old and her father, who was a sailor, set off to take the child to friends. He walked and put up at the workhouse in Workhouse Lane where he was taken ill and died; with the exception of two or three weeks at long intervals Emma remained in the workhouse all her life. Dickens could not have written this.

Many people around Newport were trying to improve pauper conditions within the system, people like the local doctors, Baddeley and Elkington and Miss Roddam, not just by changing the poor law but through wider changes in living conditions and local initiatives. Many remain unremembered.

William Latham was one such person. He was the son of Joseph Latham of Donnington who was closely associated with the Salvation Army at Oakengates. He influenced his son over trade unions and working and living conditions. At the age of eleven William was working in the Lilleshall Company pits and stayed there until he became a full time official and agent of the Shropshire Mining Federation a position he held until his death. A member of the Labour party, a Primitive Methodist local preacher and Sunday School superintendent, he was elected to Newport Rural District Council and was the first working man on Shropshire County Council and eventually one of its oldest members, and a popular Alderman in Council despite his ardent socialist and nonconformist principles. A fierce propagandist and champion of the working class he was involved in many controversies but was not to be underestimated as a man of considerable ability. He was totally against the poor law system believing it was for the State to provide for its needy. It was not just the poor law he was thinking of when he said in 1909.

> *".... if there was one place in the world where light was needed it was Newport. They wanted to send a searchlight and remove the shame and disgrace of that town. They all knew what the morality of Newport was...."*

With the abolition of the property qualification for guardians working men like William Latham could get on the Boards and soon made themselves felt. He opposed the "prison" conditions for vagrants and was angry that any child, no matter the reason, should enter a workhouse. As late as 1927 when the County Council proposed to house mentally defective children in Newport he strenuously objected to any child being in an institution. In 1908 before State pensions were introduced, he was proposing that paupers over the age of 70 should get 5/- per week out relief. It was defeated.

At national level attitudes were changing. The Royal Commission on the Poor Law reported in 1909 and though the findings were not unanimous, there was a general feeling the Guardians should go. The minority report advocated the abolition of the Poor Law and the taking over of its duties by committees of the County Councils such as the Local Education Committee taking over everything to do with children. Other aspects of their work were removed by the Liberal Government from 1906. In January 1909 over 70`s got a State pension of 5/- per week unless they were on poor relief. Labour exchanges were set up and national insurance schemes alleviated unemployment and sickness though they did not cover wives and children. Lloyd George called it an implacable war against poverty and squalor.

The Newport Guardians objected to the findings of the Poor Law Commission of 1909 believing the abolition of Guardians and Unions would lose the *"personal interest and care now bestowed by Guardians both for the Poor and the ratepayers."* Sambrook Burne, chairman for 22 years, went so far as to resign as he was *"unable to adapt myself to the new manner and methods which are being introduced."*

A Ministry of Labour was created in 1916 and a Ministry of Health in 1919 thus ending the Local Government Board but the guardians were reprieved to face unprecedented problems between the wars.

While before 1914 300,000 applicants for relief was considered high by 1922 2,000,000 were seeking help despite unemployment insurance. Poor rates went through the roof and guardians went broke. With unemployment increasing outdoor relief payments were cut in 1924 to 7/6 for adults, 12/6 for couples, first child 5/- and others 2/6. W Latham objected. The cost of out relief doubled in 1926 because of the miners strike. In 1925 it had been £203 for 205 recipients in 1926 it was £440 for 685. Relief was mainly paid in kind but it was still estimated that the strike cost the ratepayer £70 a week. In 1928 the Newport Board was still facing increased out relief because of the high unemployment in the industrial areas of the Union as mining and other basic industries declined and unemployment benefits were paid late. The Poor rate levy that year on the constituent authorities was Newport UDC, £582, Newport Rural District Council, £799, and Gnosall RDC, £808. The total levy was £2,398.

Though shorn of many of their duties the Newport Guardians went on; the laundry room had to be improved in 1923 as temperatures rose to as much as 104 degrees. A sliding horse on cast iron rails was installed for drying and airing, heated by hot air. It was still there at demolition in 1983.

Cast Iron Sliding Laundry Rails

Arthur Edwin Jordan, the master, died in November 1926 aged 47 he had been master for fifteen years, after 12 years in the navy. He had seen many improvements, the laundry, kitchen, casual wards and had converted an old institution into a modern one. He had organised the Christmas treats. His successor was Lester Titley a local man who had been Poor Law Clerk at Liddle and Heane.

From 1929 the government handed over the workhouses to the County Councils and Shropshire proposed to use the space in Newport - there were only 40 inmates in space for 100 - for child mental defectives, twelve children with three nurses. The alterations would be paid for by the County Council. Improvements continued to be made to bring conditions up to twentieth century standards with new heating apparatus, a new boiler house and hot water:

> *"The dining room and front of the building were at present entirely devoid of heat and were consequently damp, causing the ironwork and bedsteads to rust."*

Newport Advertiser. September 1928.

The last meeting of the Newport Guardians took place on the 17 March 1930. It was a plain business meeting, no comments, no speeches, no farewells. The minutes were signed on the 31 of March and that was the end.

Some traditions continued. In 1930 there was a surplus on pigs of £27, on the garden £49 and on firewood, £12.

A new phrase *"public assistance"* replaced the *"workhouse"*. In 1930 workhouses were centralised under the Public Assistance Committee of Shropshire County Council but still with a local clerk, R. P. Liddle and relieving officer, G Crickmer. Newport became part of the Wellington Guardians Committee. By February 1931 there were only 31 inmates and it was again proposed to use the spare capacity for twenty insane young women. As in the past charity provided extra comforts Miss M Elkes, a Guardian, raising money to install a wireless.

The Infirmary, a separate building built in 1908, was adapted and opened as a Childrens' Home in May 1935 with 30 children up to the age of 5. It was now known as The Newport Public Assistance Institution.

The *"Institution"* did not escape the war as it was in a direct line across the fields from where a V1 flying bomb landed; the Master noted in his report of 11 January 1945:

*"The blast from a flying bomb broke 11 panes of
glass in the institution on December 24 and the cost
of repairs was £3 6s 8d."*

From 1945 and the huge social changes of the Labour Government the move was from workhouse to welfare but even though things improved Audley House was still run on workhouse lines into the 1950`s. There were notable physical changes the large seven foot wall between the House and the Avenue was lowered by two feet; the tall chimneys were dismantled to roof level; and the whole place was wired for electricity, lighting and power. The slowness of change was often masked by changes in terminology; Master became Superintendent then Principal Officer; Workhouse became Institution then Home.

In workhouse days the interior was not at all impressive. The floors were mainly brick or had tiles, smaller rooms and those upstairs had stained wooden floors and there was very little matting to be seen anywhere, if there was any it was of the coarse, hard wearing type. The walls were roughly finished, in some rooms there was just the bare brick painted over. The colours throughout were dull and dark shades of brown or green for the lower half of the walls in particular, with a lighter shade for the upper half. Beds were the heavy iron type with strong mattresses and flock mattresses on top. Sheets were strong twill and the blankets were rough, all seem to have been chosen for durability rather than comfort but then workhouses were not meant to be a luxury only to provide the bare necessities of life. The day rooms were not very cheerful places either. There were armchairs and ordinary chairs around the rooms and a table in the centre with very little else in the way of furniture. The women`s rooms had very little to be cheerful about the outlook at the front was a high wall and the other side was a yard and laundry building. There was very little difference between the men`s and ladies rooms. The dining room had a red tile floor with a mat running down the centre and either side were long wooden tables with bench type seats each side of them. The kitchen was very spacious, a large gas cooker stood against one wall and a small cooker stood nearby, a fish fryer was in one corner and there was a boiler near the far wall and a long table in the centre. A door led to a pantry on one side. There were pipes everywhere, for gas, hot and cold water, steam, running along the walls all exposed. The laundry was another dismal place, brick walls were whitewashed, there were several long tables and a boiler for boiling the clothes. The washing was done by hand and clothes dried outside on lines stretched across the yard from the laundry wall to the wall of the opposite building. Ironing was done with flat-irons. Apart from the small staff bathroom there were two large ones each containing two baths, one was in the left wing of the building for the women and the other in the right wing for the men. Situated at the extreme right of the building were the mens washbasins and toilets, five of the latter side by side each one very narrow. The building had four sets of stairs, three being stone and one wooden. The toilet block for the women was opposite to the mens but in the same pattern. Each wing had an additional small toilet upstairs. At the far end of the kitchen was a building that housed the main boiler that supplied hot water throughout. Coal was the fuel used and it had to be fed by hand. Next to this was a smaller building with a smaller boiler; this took care of the central heating. The number of radiators in the building was barely adequate. Adjacent to the main day room but a separate building was the food store.

At the far end on the right but separated from it by a driveway was a much more modern building, the 1908 Infirmary, that became the Childrens Home, accommodating young children up to the age of five years. Some were orphans and some were placed there by the courts. These were looked after by trained staff assisted by trainees. In 1954 Mrs M Talbot was employed as childrens nurse and this is her summary of what it was like:

*"The Childrens Home accommodated 25 children usually aged
between two and five years. Mr and Mrs Gidman were Master and
Matron and Miss Pickering was deputy of the childrens section.
Mr Scarrow who was deputy of the elderly section had no*

official role to play with children but they adored him. On Sundays if he was off duty he would take several children together with a nurse, out for a drive and always buy tea for everyone in a café. This was very enjoyable for the children as it was something different from their daily routine. The nurses uniforms were a pretty floral dress in various colours which made us look more homely. Life was not always easy looking after a cross section of various temper--aments but on the whole they were happy. They tended to be very possessive on any personal belongings such as a toy given to them by their parents, that is those who were lucky enough to have parents to visit them. It was quite heartbreaking to hear a child fantasising that their mum or dad would be coming to see them today when you knew they had no-one to visit them. Another problem was the attention seeking child often doing damage to the others toys or being cruel to children they felt had more in life. However we tried to give them all equal love and attention even though some were more loveable than others.

The day began at 7.30 and often after breakfast on weekdays a nursery teacher came and kept them occupied in the schoolroom until lunchtime. Following lunch the children had a rest then they were split into groups two nurses to each group. We would please ourselves what we did until teatime either go for a walk or play in the playground. One of the old men, Mr Landon, who we all called the "donkey man", looked after the childrens donkey. It was familiar sight in Newport to see him and his donkey with a cart full of children going through the town. The children really enjoyed this. The townspeople, particularly shopkeepers, were very kindly to us and used to give the children sweets and fruit. A visit to Moreton's hairdressers always ended with sweets all round. After tea was bath time which was always a lively affair with a lot of laughter and noise. When they were all clean and in their night clothes they would all be encouraged to sit quietly then have a drink of milk and biscuits. A bedtime story would be read to them. All tucking up in their beds was done personally and with a bit of loving they always looked like little angels.

Their bedrooms were decorated and hand painted with nursery rhyme murals painted by Mr Don Oakley, the handyman. We all had to do our share of night duty so that there was 24 hour cover. These children always appeared to be happy but later on the Childrens Home closed, about 1956. Then Cottage Homes were introduced and it was wonderful to see the small family groups. These homes created much more of a real atmosphere, like a real home, than the large establishments. Today the childrens home is the female block of Audley House a far cry from the days of little children running along the corridors."

Tommy the donkey died amidst great sorrow in 1951.

The workhouse had a master and matron in charge living in a flat upstairs in the main building above the hallway and offices. Helping them were another married couple known as the assistant matron and assistant master. The wife also worked as a cook while the husband was in charge of the stores and helped out in the office. They had a small living room off the hallway and a bedroom above it. The other staff comprised male and female general assistants, three of these were residents, handy man, cleaners, laundry workers, assistant cook and night attendant. The female assistants including the assistant matron had uniforms similar to nurses and the men had a navy blue melton [strong cloth for overcoats as in Melton Mowbray] suit. The residents or inmates were mainly elderly and most of them were fragile physically and mentally, others had slightly minor disabilities or mental disorders which required some supervision but all inmates were able to undress, dress and do basic things for themselves. All were in fairly good health though none were on regular medication, in fact the only medication kept on the premises were such things as aspirin, cough mixture and indigestion mixture. If any inmate did become ill and had to stay in bed more than three days they were transferred to hospital. Most of the inmates were permanent, but a few, mainly men, used to come in for the winter and discharge themselves and take to the roads for the summer. Quite a few did jobs around the place, some worked in the garden, some did odd jobs such as sweeping up, while one man was in charge of the boiler and spent most of his time in the boiler house, being allowed a ration of tea, sugar and milk for a brew up. Another peeled the potatoes every day. The men were given a packet of cigarettes, the ladies sweets, each weekend. The workers received no pay but an extra ration of cigarettes or sweets and food. The women also worked making beds each morning, cleaning floors and the younger ones helped in the laundry. In all there were 50 to 60 residents, numbers fluctuating because of those who only came in for a short period. The food was plain but no one complained, as it varied from day to day. For breakfast the men were given two thick slices of bread, a small piece of margarine and a spoonful of marmalade which was placed on each plate as there were no dishes on the table for them to help themselves. There was porridge and a pint mug of tea. The women had thinner slices of bread and a smaller cup of tea. For dinner it was meat on Monday and occasionally one other day, fish on Friday and sausage, or a stew or tinned meat the other days. There were two vegetables these being supplied from the large garden at the back, and a sweet to follow, the favourite being rice pudding. Sunday was a special day when there was always a large joint with enough left over for Monday. For breakfast this day there would be fried egg or sometimes bacon. Tea on weekdays meant the usual two slices of bread, margarine and jam, a cup of tea or perhaps a slice of tinned meat. On Sunday there was the added luxury of a piece of cake. For supper they had a mug of cocoa.

There was little in the way of entertainment apart from the radio. There was little time though for entertainment in the evenings as the inmates had to go to bed at 7pm in the winter and 8pm in the summer, the exception being when the master periodically gave a film show. He had his own small projector and hired the films, mainly comedies. On rare occasions the inmates were invited to a show given by a local amateur concert party.

After the war the House was wired for electricity and in the 50`s Audley House became a "Welfare Home" for old people with a Superintendent. Later a house was built on the site of the old tennis court and the matron and superintendent moved in, the deputies taking over the flat in the main building.

The main bedroom at the far end of the right wing was changed to a day room the larger of the two former day rooms being converted to a clothing store and the smaller one to a sewing room. A seamstress was employed to check clothes after they had been laundered and issue new clothes when necessary. New chairs were provided for all day rooms, all floors were covered except the kitchen and mats were laid in the day rooms and bedrooms. Walls were re-plastered where necessary and the place was decorated throughout. The iron beds were replaced by wooden ones and the old mattresses by spring ones though this was done over a period of time. New bedclothes were also provided. In the dining room the long wooden tables and seats were replaced with smaller tables and chairs making four to each table. In the kitchen the gas cooker was replaced by a coke-burning stove though some years later these were replaced by two, large modern gas cookers, then when electricity was laid on more labour saving equipment such as a slicing machine and a combined mixer were provided. Otherwise little change was made. Food became more plentiful, there was greater variety and more cooked meals. Residents were given a cup of tea in bed in the early morning.

The laundry was provided with two new washing machines and a drier. Larger items, such as sheets and blankets where necessary were sent to an outside laundry. There was also a new electric iron. In the bathrooms a partition was placed between the baths to give more privacy. Apart from the wards being repainted there were no other changes. There were no changes either to the toilets, the old stone steps that were very worn on the edges and dangerous were built up and covered. A few years later fluorescent lighting was installed in all rooms but the bedrooms. After the women had moved to the old Childrens Home there were vacancies on both blocks and new residents began to come in. These were of a lower standard both mentally and physically, some required a lot of help dressing and undressing. Some of the mentally ill had to be taken meals and put to bed at night. They had to be watched as they were liable to wander off. There was a shortage of hospital beds so residents who became ill had to remain at the Home and be looked after, only in an emergency was a resident admitted to hospital. The majority of inmates were on some kind of regular medication which had to be given three times a day and sleeping tablets at night. At times the place was more like a hospital than a Home.

However there were a few who were more agile and sensible and some of these liked to do odd jobs to help the staff who at times were hard pressed. Nor did the standard improve over the years. The residents enjoyed greater freedom after it became a WelfareHome, they were allowed to go out and return freely and there was no longer a specific bedtime. Later the Home was reclassified as a residential home which meant it was not limited to old people. Several young "sub-normals" were admitted but were later found places that catered for "that type of person" though some remained in the ladies block. The Superintendent became the *"Principal Officer"* with a deputy and two senior care assistant one for the mens block and one for the women, the other attendants being called care assistants.

In 1981 a new one storey block was built on to the womens block. Eight men and eight women were moved in. They had individual bedrooms and were allowed to mix in the two lounges. They also had their meals there. Adjoining each lounge was a small kitchen but these were more for the purpose of washing up and making drinks since the food was supplied by the main kitchen. Everything was modern and the residents were very comfortable. One of the day rooms, or lounge as they were now called, had been converted in 1982 into a kitchen on the ladies block and fitted with all modern equipment. This took the place of the old kitchen in the mens block. Changes were also taking place in the mens block, new floors were put in all the upstairs rooms. These and other rooms were covered in vinyl floor covering, the lounge was fitted with carpets and the place was redecorated throughout. By now all the residents had divan beds but the change had been gradual. The number of beds in the large rooms was reduced to six and every resident was provided with a wardrobe and a small chest of drawers. A new fire alarm system was fitted throughout with smoke detectors in each room the system connected direct to the fire station. Also a new call system was installed throughout all blocks on all sides with this a resident could call a care assistant who was on duty from any part of the building by just pressing a button. The care assistants carried bleepers that provided a noise or signal stating by how many bleeps where the care assistant had to go.

So apart from the new block the Home had been greatly improved over the years and had many modern facilities and features. With such an old building there was a limit to what could be done so it did not compare with the recently built county homes.

There were two main outbuildings at the rear of Audley House. A short distance to the rear of the left wing with its end facing the road was a long one-storey building. This was the casual ward or the tramps ward as some called it. It provided a night shelter for the tramps. They were not allowed in before evening and could stay one night only. There were casual wards at other workhouses such as Market Drayton, Bridgnorth, Ludlow and Bishops Castle and many of these tramps travelled round from one to another. When a tramp arrived he was booked in giving his name, where he had come from and where he intended to go next day. This information was useful to the police.

The building had rough whitewashed walls inside, two baths and a toilet. After being given a bath the tramp was provided with his supper, two thick slices of bread and a piece of margarine and a piece of cheese and allocated a cell for the night. After being given breakfast next morning he had to do one or two hours work to pay for his lodging perhaps in the garden or sweeping the yard or chopping sticks for bundles of fire lighting which were sold locally.

The number of tramps taking advantage of this service gradually dwindled so that the casual wards and boiler room were closed and by the end of the 1939-45 war they were being used to store vegetables. Many years later the casual wards were converted into accommodation for homeless families, divided into several bedsits with a large common room at the end. Bathrooms and toilets were built. Only women with their children were allowed to live there, husbands could only visit. At first they had to collect their meals from the kitchen but later were provided with electric cookers. When the District Councils became responsible for the homeless the place was closed down and became derelict. To the right of the casual ward were storerooms including the soap store, the clothing store where the inmates' clothes were kept to be returned when they left. Another room housed the donkey and the cart provided by the County Council.

In a corner of the large garden was the pigsty. Small pigs were bought, fattened and sold at a profit fed by the workhouse scraps. They were looked after by one of the inmates. In 1951 three pigs were sold to the Ministry of Food for £72 having been bought in the July for £7 each. Three more were bought in for £7 each. This all came to an end in the early `60`s and the sty became a ruin.

By the 1980's there was more entertainment, each lounge having a colour television. Local organisations such as the Round Table took an interest in the Home and organised outings and gifts at Christmas. There was also a League of Friends that gave a trip every weekend during the summer, a party and presents at Christmas. Even the local children brought gifts and adopted the Home. It had its own Comforts Fund which provided extras and outings.

It was planned to close the older buildings at Audley House and to this end the former 1908 infirmary was again remodelled and re-furnished with new extensions giving single bedrooms. Here was a comfortable bed, continental quilts, matching bed linen, curtains, lampshades, wardrobes and lockable drawers. There were bleepers to bring help. There were cosy and homely lounges and dining rooms shared by men and women. Catering was excellent with three good meals a day. Visitors could come and stay as long as they wanted and residents could visit and stay with relatives when they wished.

The taste of the poor law may have been eradicated but the buildings were harder to remove. Despite noble attempts to reconstruct and reclassify them as hospitals, homes or even maternity units the workhouse looked what it was.

There was a campaign by Staff and supporters to keep the Home open as a caring, essential service but by 1984 it was to close.

When the site was sold for redevelopment the laundry with its iron drying racks, the casual wards, the communal dining room, the workhouse bell on the roof, were still there after 150 years. The bell was never recovered. Audley House became apartments and the outer buildings were demolished for other private housing. The infirmary was sold to a national charity, Combat Stress.

Workhouse Bell

In 2004 the Newport Workhouse still peeps through, grim and foreboding, like the many others scattered around Shropshire, monuments to an attitude that saw poverty as at best a weakness at worst a crime to be treated by the application of firm and rational principles.

The Old Infirmary – now Combat Stress

Audley House – now converted into apartments

Audley House Mews

Duties of the Nurses

The Committee appointed to consider the duties of the nurses at the Workhouse beg to recommend the Guardians to adopt the following rules as to the duties of the nurses.

1. The Day Nurse to commence her duties at 8 a.m. and go off duty at 8 p.m. but not to leave before relieved
2. Night Nurses to commence duty at 8 p.m. and go off duty at 8 a.m. but not to leave until relieved.
3. The turn of duty to be changed fortnightly viz. on alternate Sundays at 2 p.m.
4. The Nurse off duty not to leave the house without permission of the Master or Matron and to be allowed one day's leave of absence every fortnight.
5. The Day Nurse on duty to be allowed half a day's leave of absence a week providing she makes arrangements for her duties to be carried out during her absence.
6. If possible both nurse's to be allowed 14 days annual holiday
7. To attend to all the sick in the Workhouse and to all the inmates of the Sick and Lying-in wards under the orders of the Medical Officer.
8. To take charge of the domestic arrangements of the Sick and Lying-in wards under the general supervision of the Matron.
9. To attend at the Bath room during the bathing of the Female Inmates and children and to see that their heads are kept combed and cleaned.
10. When on duty to wear the uniform provided.
11. To obey all the orders of the Guardians and the Master and Matron applicable to her office.
12. To perform all duties laid down by the Local Government Board.

S.T.H.Burne, Chairman of Committee, 20th December 1897.

SRO. PL 11/155

NOTES.

Three. The Poor of Newport.

1. Horn, Pamela, *The Victorian Town Child,* Sutton publishing, (1997)
2. J.J and A.J. Bagley, *The English Poor Law,* Sources of History, MacMillan, (1966).
3. Cox, D.C., *Shropshire County Council Centenary History,* (1989).
4. Orwell, George, *Down and out in Paris and London,* Penguin, (1963)
5. Hill, Karen, unpublished project for In Service course at Telford College of Arts and Technology.
6. SRRC. Minute Books of Newport Poor Law Guardians PL11/4-PL11/35, particularly 1836-58, 1906-09; and 1927-30; Pl1/111-148 letter books particularly 1920-21; PL11/106 Building Committee 1882-84.
7. NMDA. From 1855: Reports on meetings, accounts, rates, tenders, elections, obituaries, buildings, conditions and Tommy the donkey.

4. The Newport Patrole.

On the 11 April 1814 Napoleon Bonaparte abdicated and was exiled to the island of Elba retaining his title of Emperor. Newport in Shropshire where the news of the abdication took many days to arrive, was not convinced, after all they had had twenty years of fighting the French under one guise or another. In November 1814 they bought a new patrole book, they were not going to be caught off guard. Of course they were right for in February 1815 Napoleon escaped from Elba and for one hundred days became once more Emperor of France. It was not until 18 June 1815 that he was defeated at the battle of Waterloo and sent to St Helena.

Even then the patrole did not disband for the entries in the patrole book continue until 1817. The Duke of Wellington remarked after the battle that there was only one thing worse than losing a war and that was winning one and for many years after 1815 there was great distress, unemployment and social disorder as men returned from the wars and industries collapsed while at the same time the price of bread rose. There were riots in Spa Fields in London, and in Nottingham; in 1817 there was the march of the blanketeers from Manchester and in 1819 several people were killed by the military in a peaceful demonstration in that city known sarcastically as "Peterloo".

Locally the years 1815-22 were ones of profound social crisis with depression in the iron trade just down the road in east Shropshire and wage reductions. In 1817 and 1820 there were strikes of colliers and ironworkers. In 1821 fighting on the cinderhills and spoil-heaps at Old Park saw two men killed by troops. In such dangerous times and with no police force Newport felt it wise to watch the town at night. Extra vigilance and protection was necessary in addition to that provided by the Parish Constables, men willing or unwilling, elected annually since the middle ages at the vestry meeting in the church, equipped with decorated staffs and led by the Headborough a kind of chief constable.

One incident recalled by Mr Thomas W. Picken caused no little excitement and was the talk of Newport for years. In 1823 a young man by the name of Richard Smith part of a larger gang was arrested in Newport on the 27 May the night before the May fair. Mr Cureton a plumber was a parish constable of the town and had to make the rounds of the lodging houses the night before the fair in search of suspicious and bad characters who frequented such fairs and the crowds they attracted. Knocking on a door he recognised one of the gang and placing his back against the door insisted on searching a bundle he had with him. Richard Smith, who it proved to be, put his hand in his breast coat pocket and drew out a pistol that luckily misfired through a flash in the pan. After a tremendous struggle Cureton overpowered Smith and had him lodged in the Town Hall crib where on his bundle being opened it was found to contain the plate that had been recently stolen from Sheriffhales church. Smith was tried and executed, sacrilege carrying the death penalty then. He was buried at Sheriffhales where there is an entry in the register:

> "Richard Smith Shrewsbury gaol April 18th 1824 by
> Robert Dean, curate."

It was said that the main hiding place of the plunder was under the stage of Stantons Theatre which was then in Upper Bar, Newport, later a Methodist chapel. Another member of the gang was transported and the pistol was still in Newport around 1900.

Enforcement of minor offences consisted of a whipping post near the former market hall which stood on the Square, and stocks which were placed at the south end of the market hall and stayed there until the roads were improved in 1857. They were then converted into moveable ones with four iron wheels going from place to place to *"encourage"* the inhabitants of the town. Into the 1860's the standard punishment for drunkenness was six hours in the stocks. The lock-up was also in the market hall and was known as the *"crib"*. It was replaced in 1847 by the lock-up and police station in Stafford Road when the Shropshire police force was created. Parish Constables were still being appointed by the courts in the 1890's; service was compulsory but there appeared to be no lack of people to serve as there was a salary of £4 pa. Police constables at that time were still carrying cutlasses when on night duty.

Information on the patrol book comes from four letters written to the Newport Advertiser in 1884 by W. W. Cobb of Atherstone a member of an old Newport family. T.W.Picken, the local chemist and friend of Cobb also saw the book and made notes under the heading of the *"Old Patrole Book of 1814"*.

On 16 August 1884 W.Cobb wrote: *'I have in my possession an old book bearing on the history of Newport and I think a few extracts from its pages may be interesting to your readers. The title page is printed and runs thus: "Newport Patrole. By Order of the Magistrates, from November 12th 1814 to May 1st 1815, to be on duty from 10 0'clock at night until 5 o'clock in the morning. Silvester, Printer, Newport, Salop"*.

It was a strongly bound and parchment covered book with leaves of very strong hand made paper ruled throughout in five columns with printed headings as follows: Names; Present or absent; Hours (10,11,12,1,2,3,4,5.); In or out; Reports. It is the last column which was the most interesting with hand written entries made by the sergeant on duty for the night or in some cases by the patrol. The spelling is original.

The guardroom was in Middle Row which in Mr Picken's time was the shop of Mr Adderley the hairdresser and remained in their family until the 1950's, and then became various cafes and restaurants and is today [2004] an Indian takeaway

"Mr Adderleys shop was the guardroom of the Newport Patrol in the early Nineteenth century. The Patrol consisted of twelve members who patrolled the town nightly – four in a gang of a four hour watch."

Shropshire Magazine. February 1951

Taking the average of attendance in the minute book the patrol seems to have been as a rule composed of eight members. They patrolled the town two and two alternately throughout the night and morning with one set of four in and one set of four out. The first name on the list of attendance for the night seems to have been made the Captain and to have written the remarks and signed the reports. Members of the patrol received 2/- [10p] per night.

The members comprised the leading influential men and tradesmen of the town with several ladies such as Miss Clegg, Miss Bentley, Miss Swan, Miss Williams, Mrs Newark, Mrs Boultbee and Mrs Burden. These ladies were included as householders and ratepayers and though their names do appear as attending some of the meetings of the patrol mostly men substitutes were sent, on several occasions for example Richard Roberts appeared for Mrs Burden and Edward Maddox for Miss Bentley. There were other representatives. Miss Elizabeth Bentley, High Street, had a good business as a milliner and straw hat and bonnet maker and TWP`s mother had been her apprentice.

> *Saturday 12 November 1814. Present James Baddeley,*
> *Edw Beech, Robt Birch, Richd Allman, T B Baddeley,*
> *Sml Cobb, R Bott.*

From 10 to 4 o`clock the entries are *"All Well"*, for each hour and at 5 o`clock we find *"All going home"*.

> *Wednesday 16 November 1814. Present Mr Parsons,*
> *Jno Roper, M M Silvester, John Gosling 11.15 and out,*
> *Joseph Bates 11.15 and out, Isac Lea, James Shotten, Rev*
> *Joseph Scott, Richard Williams 2.15 and out, Joseph*
> *Whitehouse, William Griffiths. Signed John Langley.*

Edward Beech was a tailor, Robert Birch a basket maker, Samuel Cobb a writing master at the Grammar School and Richard Bott a tailor also a constable and a staymaker the last of his trade in Newport.

John Langley who signed the second page in the book was the Rev John Langley church minister and second master or usher at the Grammar School from 1801. He was soon in dispute with the school and later with the town over his riotous and public quarrels with his wife, his debts and his misuse of public money so that in 1818 when he was appointed headmaster the managers and towns people physically prevented him from entering the school. He left the area leaving several large bills for drink. Moses Mark Silvester was the opposite of John Langley, a strict Congregationalist, merchant and carrier and the brother of Henry Price Silvester who also appears in the book and who was a printer and postmaster whose family founded the Newport Advertiser. Joseph Whitehouse was a cabinet maker. The Rev Joseph Scott was headmaster at the Grammar School and was 70 years old retiring in 1818.

Mr Picken lists other notables whose names appear on the rolls but whether they ever attended or whether they sent substitutes is not clear. There were the surgeons Robert Higgins and T. B. Baddeley the latter gets his own eulogy: *"a gentleman of great public spirit to whom the town was at that time indebted for its increased supply of water from the formation of the Baddleys wells."* Ambrose Brooke was a solicitor and deputy steward to the Burgesses and Thomas Dickenson was the managing clerk to Mr Charles Morris, solicitor, and later set up on his own. Thomas Parsons (either senior or junior) was a banker in the High Street until 1834. Earlier he had been a timber merchant but Mr Picken says he was also the inventor of a patent lock *"that was a great success."*

John (James?) Massey was a millwright responsible for several water mills and windmills at work in the neighbourhood. *"A good millwright"* Mr Picken says, *"at that period was like our handy man in the Navy could turn his hand to any kind of work."* The Massey's remained in business until the 20th Century. Another handy man was G. B. Brown the plumber and pump maker whose family had built the town's fire engine in 1776. John Griffin the tailor was another practical man known as the *"London Tailor"* because after finishing his apprenticeship in Newport he had worked as a journeyman in London before returning to set up his own business:

> *"He was a talented person educated at the Grammar
> School. His knowledge of mathematical science
> obtained there proved afterwards of great service as
> he perfected a principle of the greatest use to him in
> his business."*

There is no evidence of this useful *"principle"*.

Two others mentioned and put together because of size were Mr Adderley the barber and hairdresser whose descendants are still in Newport today [2004]. He was a tall man of a fine portly appearance as was Charles Simpson a watch and clockmaker from Middle Row. Mr Picken describes him as Town Crier and Headborough to the Burgesses wearing their dress of a blue frock coat and yellow breeches and a tall silk hat with a brass armlet with the three fishes in relief upon it. In processions he would carry a handsome pole signifying his office. Unfortunately Mr Pickens memory seems faulty for Charles Simpson was town crier between 1844-56 and if he was a member of the patrol, he would have been only twenty. William Underhill, another clockmaker, was also a member.

> *Saturday 29 November 1814. I see very great danger in
> leaving the house with a fire lighted and so small a fender.
> I saw red hot coles fall on the floor 3 times.*

The signatures are illegible. The next report of any interest is a list of those on duty:

> *19 December 1814. On duty Richard Blakemore, John
> Hawkins, substitute William Wild, John Hawkins,
> substitute Arthur Mountford, John Smith substitute.*

At 10 o'clock that evening when members reported for duty it was found:

> *In except for Thos Arrowsmith or substitute. Thos B-
> substitute for Arrowsmith arrives at half past ten, in
> Liquor, incapable of going his round, sent him home.
> H P Silvester*

Being drunk would have horrified Henry Price Silvester a pillar of the Congregational Church, teetotaller and solid businessman, printer, bookseller, stationer and commissioner for taking special bail. He was also the postmaster.

> *22 December 1814. One man absent, but donte no our it is.
> R Beeston.*

On the fly leaf of the book is the signature *"John Snow 4th Battalion. Royal Artillery, Newport"*. Many of the reports are signed by him and he appears to have shared the responsibility with Richard Bott who was probably a sergeant also. John Snow had seen active service abroad and had risen to the rank of sergeant and his leading part in the patrol was because of his experience as a soldier. His writing and remarks suggest a man of some education.

12 January 1815. On duty Wm Whittingham, Thos Griffiths, Rich Hammond for J Meecher, Joseph James, Geo Brayne. One abstant but don't knowe hoe he his but I think it is Mr Lees the skinner.

Thomas Lees was a skinner from St Marys Street.

1 October 1815. From this night the men Recd only Eighteen pence instead of Two Shillings allowed before.

15 October 1815. At half past 12 o'clock some person in the neighbourhood of Mr Morris's whistled repeatedly – as was reported to me by Thos Whiston and John Williams – John Snow.

17 October 1815. Quarter before 2 o'clock heard a whistling several times when in the Back House Lane. Came to the top and Lisned herd it a gain in the Market Hall persued and found it to be thomas the fool at Mr Morrises. Richard Bott.

Back House Lane was "Bakehouse Lane" now Stafford Street.

23 October 1815. At quarter past 11 o'clock met a man with a bag on his back on asking who he was and Where he was going and What he had got, he cryed Murder 3 thimes Very Loud it proved to be Maddox of Church Aston fatching a batch from the mill – Richd Bott.

Tuesday 23 September 1816. On duty Rchard Bott, James Shotton, Charles Simpson, and John Moreton. At a quarter before 12 o'clock found Sarah S- and Susannah R- and put them in the crib both being drunk.

Thursday 25 September 1816. On duty Edward Howell, John Snow, Thomas Cropp, William Hughes, William Griffiths. At half past 10 o'clock was called out to quite a row between W- and H- when we took Elizabeth H- and her husband to their home in a wounded state. At half past two went our rounds when we were insulted by Wm W- and took him into custody. A number of people having collected about him he escaped from us. Thos Bently was observed by us among the crowd and following Wm W- apparently with an intention of rescuing him and taken prisoner and confined in the Lock-up House. Took up two people a man and a woman who either could not or would not give an account of themselves. On returning to endeavour to retake Wm W- we found him in the street brandishing a stick and putting me and my assistants at defiance – we attempted to take him and were assaulted by his family and himself with sticks and a large kitchen poker and received some contusions and bruises – he was again rescued by a number of people when on the way to the lock-up House. At half past 12o'clock released Thos Bently on his fathers stating that he was in an ill-state of health and undertaking of his future appearance if called for.

The next night things had calmed down and the report says *" nothing extraordinary during the night"*, signed by John Snow using an expression that appears some thirty times in the book. Thomas Cropp was master at the workhouse and William Hughes a smith.

Taverns, public houses and drunks feature often in the book as is to be expected at that time of night. There do not appear to be any publicans as members of the patrol.

> *8 November 1816. Patrol consisted of Anthony Pooler, Wm Adderley, Wm Powell for Mark ?, Geo Jarvis for Jno Jarvis. All well at 12 o'clock except at the Bear refused to let us in – Geo Jarvis*

> *18 November 1816. At quarter past one o'clock when on the Round met Wm P- drunk and without any words struck Chas Simpson owing as they thought from his words, from putting Jno Partridge into the Cribb on Sattarday night. Thos Whiston.*

> *1 December 1816. On duty Fras Beetlestone for H P Silvester, John Roberts, and Thos Wedge. John Lane absent on Sunday he caled at My House to say he was lame it was past time to summond one in his place Richd Bott.*

> *6 December 1816. There are only Two rattles and no Staffs in the Watch House; Nothing else to report – John Snow.*

> *7 December 1816. Thos Plowman was served with a notice but absented himself. Wm Heatley volunteerd to send a Man for himself. Jno Snow.*

1817 began quietly with nothing to report signed alternately by John Snow and Richard Bott who now describe themselves as constables.

> *25 January 1817. There is an impudent fellow by the name of Cross, who frequently troubled the patrol. The above Cross lodges at Mrs Shepherds.*

> *2 February 1817. There was noisy company at the Fox at eleven o'clock this being Sunday night.*

The Fox and Grapes was near the corner of Stafford Street and was demolished in 1860 to build the market hall.

> *6 February 1817. At 3 o'clock in the morning we discovered a chimney on fire in a house adjoining the bridge occupied by a woman by the name of Williams, which at first assumed an alarming appearance, upon giving the alarm we were promptly assisted by Mr G Brown and others and succeeded about half past 3 in extinguishing it.*

> *Query -would it not be proper to keep the Key of the engine house in the Watch House.*

We find Richard Bott complaining about the absence of William Pugh:

> *11 February 1817. Sent to me about 7 o'clock last night to ask if a child he as apprentice Would do to Come on the patrole My answer was not. Nothing further to report.*

> *20 February 1817. 8 on patrol. Thos Cartwright, Charles Foray (?), John Woolridge, Richard Shaw for William Pugh, Thomas Whistans, Francis Beetlestone, James Shotton, and Edward Maddox – Sergeants Bott and Snow. The patrole was doubled this night in consequence of some men of suspicious appearance and conduct having been observed in the town during the day. We visited the different publick and lodging houses from ten to eleven o'clock without discovering anything extraordinary. After a vigorous search during the remainder of the night we found all well.*

By 1817 the enthusiasm for the patrole seems to be fading. None of the town notables indicated on the original roll seem to be taking an active part and much relies on the work of the two semi-professional officers John Snow and Richard Bott and substitutes who may or may not turn up, plus the halt and the lame. John Snow complains about the effectiveness of the patrol:

> 16 March 1817. *NB the frequency of people absenting themselves from the patrole causes the town to be but imperfectly watched.*
> 20 March 1817. *Mr John Barber absent. Mr William Bayley sent Joseph Hodson a lame man as a substitute who I sent back he being unfit for the duties of a watchman.*

Increasingly substitutes were sent until it was decided to ask the magistrates to summons absentees:

> *23 March 1817. Ordered that Rd Bott Constable do apply to the magistrates for a Summons for such persons as absent themselves from the Patrol.*

This was signed by John Langley the permanent curate and Usher at the Grammar School; Joseph Icke a malster in the High Street; J E Stanion; Geo B Brown plumber, painter and glazier and James Icke a druggist. The outcome is not known for the last entry is dated 3 April 1817 and the next page in the book is full of memoranda and Newport names.

The streets at night reverted to the old watchman with his wooden rattle calling the hour and the state of the weather as he passed up and down the street. The curfew bell also tolled from the church tower at 8pm and 6am until the 1880's. The peace of the town was in the hands of the elected constables until the first policeman was stationed in Newport in 1841. He lodged with Mr Whistan the watchmaker in Middle Row next door to Thomas W.Picken who was a boy of 5 at the time. He could remember John Davy aged 25, a tall man in a blue suit with a long swallow tailed coat in the hind pockets of which he kept his manacles, handcuffs and staff. He had a way of his own, Mr Picken said, of dealing with the intoxicated taking them home for a shilling or issuing a summons to appear before the magistrates. Another police officer 30 year old William Jones lodged at the Kings Arms in the High Street.

TWP concluded with thankfulness that he lived under the beneficent reign of *"Victoria the*

Good" and that lives and property and security and freedom were under the guardianship of Sergeant Waterson and his well trained and steady men compared to that of the old patrol.

Since the Newport patrol had stood guard against Napoleon Great Britain had become the strongest and wealthiest country on earth. Mr Picken had every reason to feel confident and safe.

NOTES.

Four. The Newport Patrole.

1. Newport and District History Society archives for notes by T.W.Picken on the Newport Patrol.
2. NMDA., letters from W.W.Cobb, Atherstone Grammar School, 16 August 1884, 30 August, 1884, 13 September 1884 and 11 October 1884.
3. Both were quoting from the original which I have not located.
4. Trinder, Barrie, *The Industrial Revolution in Shropshire*, p. 382 for details of the social unrest in East Shropshire at this time.
5. Elliott,D.J., *Policing Shropshire 1836-67*, Phillimore, (1984).

5. The Chetwynd Estate.

The Chetwynd Estate lies in the gap north of Newport where the road, having crossed the marshland, clings to the steep slope of the Scaur above the meadowlands of the River Meese where it meets the Lonco Brook before widening out into the north Shropshire plain. The Hall and Park lay across this route and used the water-power of the river, as did many other small industrial undertakings producing corn, iron and paper. The parish itself came right to the doors of Newport as does the ecclesiastical parish today. There was even an attempt to exploit the commercial advantages of the location when on the 17 July 1318 Sir John de Chetwynd was granted the right to hold a market and a three day Fair on All Souls Day, 2 November.

> *".... profits to be derived from the droves of cattle which came that way out of Wales to relieve the famine which was then desolating a great part of England; and both would be glad to set up a rival to Newport which was fast becoming a thriving town".*

> Eyton, "Antiquities" VIII p 88.

It did not succeed though in an odd way Sir John got his revenge for the Newport Agricultural Show, the nearest we have to a Fair, is now held in Chetwynd Park.

The Chetwynd Estate was only one of several in what is now the civil parish of Chetwynd which includes settlements such as Chetwynd, Puleston (Pilson), Pickstock, Howle and Sambrook. By 1800 these settlements had passed through several hands, the main families being the Chetwynds and the Pigotts. From this date the story is one of consolidation of property by one family until by 1900 the *"Estate"* roughly coincided with that of the civil parish. While Longford had been resuscitated by *"new"* wealth from the colonies, Chetwynd, and also Aqualate were created by an infusion of new money from industry and commerce generated by the Industrial Revolution.

The Pigott family were at Chetwynd for eleven generations ebbing and flowing in status like most minor gentry, acquiring land by marriage, even illegitimate heiresses, then rising to host Charles I in 1645. They stayed Jacobites like many small country squires, such as Fieldings' Squire Western, resenting the Hanoverians and flirting with treason and the Pretenders. However the last Pigott, Robert, was infected with gambling, mortgaging then selling his estates to pay his debts. Having lost his status he tended to equality and, adopting reform and revolution, died in France in 1794. The estate was sold in September 1779 to investors such as William Waller and the Rev. William Lloyd, and passed through several hands with the house and park being leased. It was offered for sale three times between July 1801 and May 1802 before being sold by private treaty. It amounted to 1670 acres almost all held by the purchaser.

The purchaser was Thomas Borrow of Derby, a barrister whose wealth came from industry and property though they aspired to a more genteel lineage which they retained by including the name Burton through every generation. Originating from Leicester and Nottingham the family had achieved legal distinction as barristers and recorders and received municipal honours as Mayors and Sheriffs. Like the Sutherlands they had shown great discrimination in taking heiresses as wives. Thomas was the son of Thomas Borrow of Castlefields, recorder of Derby who died in 1786 shortly after rebuilding the family house at Hulland an estate they had purchased in 1690. They held the Hulland estate to the end. This Thomas was the son of Isaac Borrow of Hulland Hall by his second wife Honora, daughter of Thomas Burton of Surrey, hence *"Burton"*. It was Isaacs father John Borrow who bought the Derbyshire estates and became High Sheriff in 1688. As the city expanded and railways came in the family were able to sell their central property and fund their purchases of land in the 1800's at very reasonable prices. There are still streets in Derby named after the family, Borough Walk, Chetwynd Street and Hulland Street.

When Thomas Borrow came in 1803 the Estate was centred around the Hall sheltered by the steep, wooded, Scaur. The road separated the Hall from the walled deer-park and the deep, hidden, Chetwynd Pool with its ghostly memories of Madame Pigott.

> *".... although covering about 40 acres, it is fed by trickling streams from springs so insignificant that if the pool were let out, it would take three years, it is said, to fill it again. It is a beautiful spot, where the park deer come down to drink, and quite one of the features of the place, both on account of its surroundings and from its being well stocked with fish.."*

The Hall and the estate buildings were carefully sited at the confluence of the Meese and the Lonco which provided the water power. The Church completed a compact settlement dependent on water even at Domesday which records a mill with two fisheries paying 5 shillings and "64 sticks of eels" that is 1,600 eels. The road of that time probably went through the middle of the complex but was moved to the base of the Scaur to improve the Hall.

Like his successors Thomas Borrow was very fond of mechanical work and spent a lot of his time in the workshops turning wood. In this he was accompanied by Silas Griffin who had secured the carpentry work on the Chetwynd estate. Silas had come from Frampton on Severn to work as foreman on the building of Longford Hall and when this was finished set up on his own in Newport. They built a summer house in the middle of the Scaur. In the huge tannery fire in Newport in 1791 it was Silas who was active in using gunpowder to blow up houses to stop the fire spreading.

Over the century an integrated estate yard was developed constructed of brick, tile and iron. There was an estate office, a school room, laundry developed from a previous seventeenth century mill, cowshed (dated 1816), a half-timbered barn, sawmill, metalwork shop and covered stockyards and a series of foldyards. There was also a Georgian stableblock. All these eventually became listed buildings. Over the years water power was supplemented by steam. A Robey and Co. mobile steam engine in 1881 was used to pump water anywhere on the estate but was mostly used in the laundry. There was a Blackstone oil engine to power sharpening tools and lathes and a variety of other agricultural equipment such as coracle bellows and grinding mills.

Besides the building work there was a programme of landscaping and also an expansion in land when the opportunity arose. The first was in 1825 when they purchased the Sambrook estate of the Anson family who became the Earls of Lichfield. The 380 acres were scattered across the area among the old open fields, and the family continued to pick up such pieces of land with purchases in 1848, 1872, 1874 and 1886. By then they held almost all of Sambrook which was the only part of the estate to have a distinct village community with shops, post office and public houses, though no separate parish or parish church.

In 1866 they purchased most of Puleston and Standford from the descendants of Mrs Sarah Dalton who was formerly a widow in the Bayley-Marsh family. In 1851 Pickstock was still a small township in the parish of Edgmond but detached and separated by the parish of Chetwynd. The principal landowner was Robert Gardner of Sansaw much of it copyhold land scattered around the village. In 1875 he sold to the Borough family who continued to add the smaller plots until by 1910 they had 1079 acres.

The Boroughs had property in Edgmond that came with the original purchase in 1803 but over the years they purchased land when in came on the market particularly if it fringed their Chetwynd estates. Given the historic nature of landholding in the village this was often small, scattered pockets of land belonging to original copyholders. In 1840 they owned 373 acres and in 1910, 507 acres. One property included the present *Lamb Inn* on the main Shrewsbury road. On quarter days this hosted the Rent Day Dinners when estate tenants assembled to pay their rents. In 1872 plans were drawn up for extensive alterations to include a new sign bearing the Borough coat of arms and motto *"Virtute et Robore"*.

Mabel Wheat recalls the rent dinners which the Borough family gave to their tenants twice a year at the *Lamb*. The first day all farmers attended and after paying their rent a meal was provided with plenty of drinks of all kinds. The Squire or his agent always presided. George Ingram, father and son, were the agents for most of the years of J.C.B. Borough. Afterwards as many as could, sang, recited, or told tales; tea was served and a happy afternoon and evening were spent. The next afternoon the smallholders and cottagers had their rent dinner on the same lines. These dinners were abandoned when the *Lamb* was sold in the 1920's.

By 1870 the *"Golden Age"* of farming was over, cereal prices slumped except for barley, and for those with capital, land was cheap. In 1883 they had over 7000 acres of which nearly 5000 were at Chetwynd. It was in these depressed years that estates of between 3000-6000 acres brought some stability and confidence to agriculture particularly in Shropshire.

Improved farming required improved communications particularly to the market town of Newport. In 1802 Standford bridge on the present A41 was rebuilt and lasted until 1956. This may have inspired Richard Whitmore of Batchacre Hall to get similar improvements from his side of the river to Newport. The existing road past Chetwynd Hall and across the Meese to Pulestone was either over an impassable bridge for carriages, or across a ford up a steep hill to the settlement which was then under the hill. After acrimonious correspondence the County built the present bridge in 1812, straightened the road, and the settlement moved to the present *T* junction. It is unclear whether Thomas Borrow was active in this for Richard Whitmore had been straightening and improving roads on his estate for a long time. Having bought the Sambrook land and built a new church a bridge was built across the Showell Brook in 1856 at the bottom of Church Bank, Sambrook. This was a co-operative effort between John Charles Burton Borough [1810-1894. (JCB)] and the main landowner at Pickstock, Robert Gardner, with several of the tenants carrying materials.

As land came into the estate, fields and common were enclosed and holdings combined. Cottages and farms, as around Pickstock Common, disappeared. New, straight roads were put in when the family enclosed the common after the purchase of the Batchacre and Flashbrook property leading to the assumption that these were *"Roman"* roads. Streams were also straightened and weirs removed which damaged the ancient eel fishing.

The prosperity of the 1850's and 60's saw more aesthetic improvements to fit the style of a country seat. The visual aspect was improved with tree planting and the building of two lodges approaching the Hall and a keeper's lodge in the Deer Park. A new church was built at Chetwynd, again partly for aesthetic reasons, and at Sambrook, here creating a new ecclesiastical parish.

CHETWYND LODGE

The lodges were picturesque rather than practical. There were only four rooms, no water or drainage and certainly no gas or electricity. Water came from a hand pump 100 yards away while the earth toilet was in the wood and incorporated a pigsty, bake oven and duck pen. Nature was very close as was the main road with its traffic and tramps. Chetwynd Lodge and Keepers Cottage have been refurbished but Middle Lodge is still a problem. This is better than the Aqualate Estate where all the lodges are in ruins.

While the Borough family were unifying the Estate, the parochial system was diverse. Some parts were in Chetwynd while Pickstock, as we have seen was in Edgmond and Sambrook was part of Cheswardine. In 1856 an order was made creating Sambrook a separate ecclesiastical Parish. The impetus came from the difficulty people had in travelling several miles for weddings and christenings even though a chapel had been opened at Sambrook in 1838. There was also the need for a proper school. The moving force was J.C.B.Borough who in 1850 gathered a committee to see to the work and obtain subscriptions. He gave the land, most of the money and pledged the endowment. The object was to build a church, vicarage, school and school-house on one site. It was a well motivated community effort which would have brought tears to the eyes of the numerous rural agencies today [2004]. Mr Borough provided a quarry, Mr Gardner the bricks from Well Bank Farm and twenty-five residents carried the materials. Mr Heane of Newport did the legal work for nothing. The church was consecrated on 2 October 1856 and the school and school house opened in 1857. Cost was £3,724 with over 200 subscribers.

> *The new district church of Sambrook, in the Parish of Cheswardine, was consecrated by the Lord Bishop of Lichfield on Thursday last, October 2nd. The want of accommodation in such a large area, containing a population of about 600 souls, has long been felt to be a serious evil, aggravated by the limited sittings at Chetwynd, as well as by its distance, and that of the Parish of Edgmond Church, from the homesteads of several of the parishioners. This state of comparative spiritual destitution which was temporarily remedied by the erection of*

a small chapel and by the ministrations of a resident clergyman, whose stipend was furnished by Mr J.C.B.Borough of Chetwynd Park, is now entirely ended by the erection of a structure in the Early English style of architecture, containing upwards of 200 free sittings and supplied with schools and residence for the incumbent, and another residence for a school-master. The difficulties which have been met, step by step, and the strong determination which has been necessary to surmount them, are known only to a few, and it must be very gratifying to Mr J.C.B.Borough, the promoter of the good work, to see that his zealous labours have led to a practical result, which will prove an incalculable blessing for years to come. The Church and Vicarage were out of the contractors hands on Monday last, and the schools and master's house will be ready in November. The estimated cost of the buildings is about £3,724, and we trust that we shall be able in our next issue to announce the present deficit of £370 as existing no longer. The district embraces 253 inhabitants of Chetwynd, 153 of Cheswardine, and 151 of Edgmond whose Rector, the Rev J.C.Pigott, provides an endowment of £15 per annum, and the Patron of Chetwynd providing an annual sum of £105 during the lifetime of the Rev. T. Whateley, and a further increase upon his retiring from the living of Chetwynd. The Clergy were invited to meet the Bishop at the Vicarage at 10-30 a.m., and about 20 to 27, wearing gowns attended the summons. The Laity present included Mr and Mrs. J.C.B Borough, Rear-admiral Roberts Gawen, Mr A Roberts, V Vickers and party, R Masefield and party, Hon.R.H.Herbert, Capt and Mrs Hill, Mr H Heane and party, Misses Burne, Mr T Rylands, Dr. Godby, Mrs Liddle, Mr and Mrs Derrington and party, Mrs Smith, Mrs Holland, and party, Mr Cobb and party, Mr and Mrs Underhill, Mr Ford, Mrs Pickworth, Miss Pooler and many parishioners. The office of consecration used on the occasion was that usually adopted in the Diocese of Lichfield. Prayers were read by the Incumbent, Rev S Clarke, the Lessons by Rev Harding of Cheswardine, and Rev A Burn of Kynnersley and Rural Dean, and the Gospel by Archdeacon Allen. The Bishop gave a very good address. The ceremony of consecration was proceeded with, after which the Holy Communion was administered. The musical service was very steady and effective, and the collection amounted to £64 10s.4d. At the conclusion of the ceremony the visitors enjoyed an excellent cold collation at the Vicarage. The workmen who had been employed on the edifice were also regaled. Nor were the children attending the Sunday School, who mustered in neat dress and with flags flying, and the older portion of the parishioners, forgotten in the festivities. Triumphal arches were erected, nor was anything spared to give the district the air of a fete day, and it truly was, in a high and holy sense. Now through the liberal contributions of Mr Borough, his friends, and the parishioners, the public services of the Church and the blessings of Pastoral visitation are offered to the people of the district who have long been in want of such aid. Particularly those living in Howle. We understand that if the site chosen by Archdeacon Allen, on the Chetwynd Glebe, had been granted, the donations already received and promised would easily have covered the outlay".

Newport and Market Drayton Advertiser.

In May 1865 a meeting was called with the intention of rebuilding Chetwynd church on a new site along with a school and school-house and rectory. The original church was on the doorstep of the Hall and indeed the original graveyard is still consecrated and still there along with the Borough vault last used for John Sydney Burton Borough [1852-1924 (JSB)] in 1924. Many practical reasons were given for rebuilding but *"No doubt its being so close to the Hall interfered with the privacy of the owners"*. The accommodation was poor, attendance was increasing, and the school was two miles down the road in Chetwynd End. In an age when the Church and education were indivisible it was convenient and sensible to have both on one site. The new rectory on the Edgmond road would also allow the building of the Church (Chetwynd) Lodge.

J.C.B.Borough gave land, sandstone from the Standford Bridge quarry and £3,000 of the total cost of £3,675. As at Sambrook much of the carting was done by local farmers. Material was recycled from the old church as well as the organ and bells. The church was dedicated in April 1867 Mr Borough providing lunch at the Hall. Here he said the church was large enough to seat 260, *130 of these being free.* He also stated the principle, apparently learned at his mothers knee, that property had its rights but also its duties. The Squire was about to be challenged and tested.

The first challenge came from the newly appointed Rector over the patron's interference in church affairs. Letters were exchanged, the law invoked and the Rev Young did not attend the consecration of his own church. He only vacated the Rectory at his death in 1872, his wife and three children being forced to leave. His replacement was the Rev. H.G.Jebb of Firbeck Hall, Yorkshire whose daughter Edith married John Sydney Burton Borough.

Pew seats were allocated to property which reflected the social rankings. The poor were put in the gallery, or on benches at the back while traditionally the very poor and sick were consigned to a stone shelf around the outside, hence the phrase *"going to the wall"*. JCB insisted his family sat in the chancel and to ensure this kept the key to the chancel door and on another occasion placed his servants in the choir stall guarded by a policeman. It was decided to re-allocate the pews and also to charge for those who wished to use them. Church rates were no longer compulsory after 1868 and this "pew tax" would replace them. Unfortunately the proposals infuriated the Chetwynd parishioners who were excluded from the allocation and others who believed the church should be free. More unfortunate for Mr Borough it aroused the fury of Brooke Hector Smallwood a Newport solicitor and champion of the underdog who lived in the parish at Chetwynd End. A man wonderfully strong in invective, a rapid issuer of writs and prolific writer to the Press, in May 1867 he attacked Mr Borough over his "arrogant and illegal" distribution of pews. His anger knew no bounds when in 1870 he found Mr Borough had been appointed by the diocese as a Commissioner to re-allocate the Newport pews. He objected to the appointment of a man who in his opinion had made such a mess of his own, Chetwynd, allocation. In the end the allotment was abandoned, the choir sat in the chancel and the family in the front two pews in the nave. JCB must have been shocked to see his philanthropy so rewarded.

The Borough family always showed an interest in education the first Mrs Borough having a school probably in the estate buildings in 1806. Later they supported the National School near the Blue House Farm, Chetwynd End.

> *"The National School is situated about midway between Newport and Chetwynd Church; there is a residence for the teacher, and the number of scholars that attend average about seventy."*
>
> Bagshaw Directory 1851.

They supported the early school at Sambrook and its replacement in 1857. This in turn was replaced by a Board School in 1880 with new buildings. The original Church School is now the Village Hall.

> *"Board School, erected in 1880, with residence for master, for 80 children; average attendance, 58; William Arthur Ruck, master; Miss Mary Ruck, mistress."*
>
> Kelly's Directory 1891.

The new Chetwynd School opened in 1867 and closed in 1959 when the property reverted to the Estate and was sold in 1988 for housing. The first Headmaster was Isaac Ashmore who after seventeen years, in 1885, took over a private school at Rosemont in Chetwynd End. This also was estate property. The estate had other property in Newport such as 88 High Street, which they sold in 1887 for £1,500.

How much the school relied on the Squire can be seen from this letter:

> *Chetwynd School*
> *19 April 1882.*
>
> "Sir
>
> *I beg to say that at meeting held last night in the Schoolroom, it was unanimously resolved "That J C Burton Borough Esq be asked to kindly grant permission for the use of the Cricket ground for the season: and, if permission be granted to kindly name when Cricket may be begun."*
>
> *I am Sir*
> *Yours faithfully*
> *I Ashmore*
>
> J C Burton Borough Esq."

In 1869 a committee was formed in Newport to build a National School and thus pre-empt the possibility of a Board School. Who better to turn to than the man who had already built two church schools. So on the 14 September 1869 the first fundraising event was held in

Chetwynd Park the main feature being Blondin crossing Chetwynd Pool upon a rope. The wind being too high and the rope too slack the conqueror of Niagara never made the walk but the committee made £113. A contemporary pamphlet describes the day:

> *"Tha good Squire from Chetwin gid the fokes lafe ta*
> *hav a da`s fun in the Parke. There were two chaps sellin*
> *tickets out a two big boxes and tha fokes pusht in like*
> *stame..........*
> *Sumboddy toud me as ow oud Orn waz guin in a belewn*
> *up in tha ar ta luk at tha mon on tha tite roap.*
> *Thay sen az hou he cum from Hostraylia a purpus ta*
> *walk on it – the roap wonna tite, but ould Orn sed that*
> *sum a tha fokes was tite.*
> *So Blond-hin didna risk is nek, nor ould Orrn go in tha*
> *belewne on tha Chewsday. Cob`s chaps puld like oud*
> *bricks ta get tha roap tite, but cudna do it; our gaffers*
> *chem would a farmed it."*

The wind that stopped Blondin walking also blew down the walls at Mr Underhill's new factory in Avenue Road. The problem was the Committee had borrowed the scaffolding holding up the wall to erect the rope in the Park. Mr Underhill was never slow in invoking the law and the ensuing court case was the sensation of the time. Chetwynd Park continued to host entertainment's and pageants until the 1920`s.

On the 24 May 1872 Elizabeth Charlotte Borough, wife of JCB laid the foundation stone. Her husband returning thanks said;

> *"They had long been residents in the neighbourhood, and*
> *had always received from the town of Newport the utmost*
> *attention and kindness, and it would be monstrous if they*
> *did not feel the greatest possible interest in an undertaking*
> *of such vital importance to the town as these new National*
> *Schools".*

Considering the acrimony over the pew sittings this was a generous speech. Thanking Mrs Borough, who had requested a simple ceremony, Mr Chalmers, the chemist, waxed lyrical:

> *"I am sure that I am only the mouthpiece of those around me*
> *when I pray that Heaven`s best and choicest gifts may rest and*
> *descend upon each individual member of the house of Chetwynd".*

In 1874 Mr Borough made up the final deficit of £127.

The objectives had been achieved, that is to keep education in the hands of the Church, to do it cheaply and off the rates.

The interest in education continued when in 1957 Newport Secondary Modern was opened by Col. John George Burton Borough [1890-1960] who was the first Chairman of Governors. Later, when the school became semi-comprehensive it was renamed the Burton Borough School.

Thomas Borrow died in 1838. By this time he had not only changed his residence but also his name to *"Borough"*. Accounts with local tradesmen show the name-change. Between 1811 and 1816 his account for the hire of horses with William Liddle of the *Red Lion* is headed *"Thos Borrow Esq"*, by the 1820`s it is Thos Borough of Chetwynd and by 1831 *"Burton Borough"*. He appears to hire a pair of horses about five times a month mainly for social visiting. In 1816 he hired for fifteen journeys at a cost of £14.60. Most local gentry did this - using their own carriages? His inventory of that year made by John Holland, estate agent of Newport, values his furniture, plate, linen, china, books, pictures, wearing apparel and ornaments at £1836.75; his wine and other liquors at £206.65; his horses and carriages, farming stock and implements of husbandry at £1469. 35 a grand total of £3512.75. The wine cellar contained 44 dozen bottles of port, 2 dozen of sherry, 15 dozen of claret, 8 dozen madeira, 14 dozen of hock and 4 dozen bottles of champagne; there were 4.5 hogsheads of ale. This was for entertainment none of the local gentry attempting to rival Squire Western. Mrs Borough`s bedroom in 1838 contained a mahogany four post bedstead with crimson moreen [stout corded woollen or cotton] hangings; feather bed bolster pillow and two wool mattresses; three blankets and a quilt; carpet and rug. Other furniture included an easy chair, mahogany wardrobe, fender, coal urn and fire screen; an oak pillar and claw table and stools; a double mahogany chest of drawers and dressing cabinet; a bracket clock, press and a white table with white ware foot pan and jug. There were muslin and moreen curtains and blinds and a bidet.

The property was about 1,800 acres. This included the walled Deer Park, a wildlife sanctuary for over two hundred years, with a large arable field of twenty acres but mainly open grassland with ancient woodland covering the height of the Scaur and surrounding the large mere at the base. It is said that Thomas Borrow brought the deer from Castlefields in Derby and the present herd of about 75 fallow deer are descended from these.

> *"The park comprises about 300 acres of land, and is situated on the west side of the turnpike road leading from Newport to Market Drayton. It has a bold undulating surface, well timbered and stocked with about 200 head of deer; a fine sheet of water covers about thirty acres."*

Bagshaws Directory 1851.

By 1899 the mere is quoted as 18 acres in extent.

Captain Thomas Borough (Borrow) of Castlefields and Chetwynd Park married Jane the only surviving daughter of William Smithson of Ledstone Park, Yorkshire. They had two sons, John Charles dying in infancy and Lt. John Charles Burton Borough (1810-1894) who married Elizabeth Charlotte daughter of Rear-Admiral Roberts-Gawen RN. Their were three sisters, Anne and Honora died young, while Jane in 1832 married Captain George Hill son of Sir Robert Hill of Prees Hall dying in 1894, the same year as her brother.

J.C.B. Borough realised substantial funds from urban development in Derby, Leeds and Wakefield and carried out the improvements and extensions of the estate as we have seen. He was helped by the prosperity of the Golden Age of agriculture in the 1850`s, following the repeal of the Corn Laws, and even the depression of the 1870`s when landowners with capital could pick up land cheaply in what had become a buyers market. By the 1880`s there was an estate of 6,000 acres. JCB also inherited, and reunited the Castlefield and Hulland estates when he succeeded to Hulland and other Derbyshire property from John Borrow (Borough) who died childless and who in turn had inherited the large estates of his uncle John Tempest-Borrowe (1702-1781).

JCB was only 28 when his elderly father died and was to run the estate for 56 years. Not as active in local affairs as some other local gentry he played his part while being committed totally to his estate. Perhaps in this commitment we can see the beginning of that eccentricity that became more apparent in his son and grandson. The disputes with the vicar and other parishioners over the pews and other affairs in the new Chetwynd church have a touch of farce with a policeman on guard in the chancel during a service in July 1867. Mr Talbot being killed by a fall from the spire while advising on the building was not a good omen.

The 1881 and 1891 Census show a household with twelve domestic staff including a housekeeper, cook, butler, valet, ladies maid, dairymaid and coachman. There were outside staff like Arthur Mills, head gardener, with his own house on the Pulestone Road, the Garden House, supplying vegetables and fruit to the Hall; William Turner was the deer-keeper and John Bradley was farm bailiff living at the Pool Lodge. There were numerous employees housed in cottages or the estate yard including farriers, clerks, stable men, cowmen and women in the laundry. Tenants in bad times were found work around the estate. People worked there for generations, grandparents, brothers and uncles.

Having said this, an account book beginning 1869 shows a high turnover in gamekeepers. In that year Ronald Kynaston, under keeper, entered the service of JCB at the rate of 15/- per week payable on the first day of each month. In June 1870 Edward Whitton became under keeper at 18/- less repayment of an advance of 30/-. He signs with his mark "X". He left in February 1872 to be replaced by Wm Griffiths then, in April 1873 by James Pryce and in March 1875 Edward Smith at £60 pa only to be taken ill and sent to Bicton Asylum. The Squire advanced £1.75 for the fare of his wife and goods to Stourport. On 30 June 1875 John Loveday was taken on at 20/- per week and his rail fare of 19/8 and the 4/- expense of moving his goods to the railway station were also paid. On 6 August 1875 John Hay came at 20/- per week but left in August 1877.

In 1887 the butler to JCB was 26 year old John Carrier Brown from Radford. The next year he married a schoolmistress and moved to the *Pheasant* in Newport, and then, for twenty-one years, the *Shakespeare*. This was a familiar route for butlers. He became a public figure, Councillor, Freemason, builder of the Granville Villas and the Newport bowling green.

John Charles Burton Borough of Chetwynd Park and Hulland Hall, Derby, died on 27 November 1894 aged 84. The gross value of his estate for probate was £38,114. He left three sons the eldest John Sydney Burton Borough, then Dr. Thomas George Borough of Hulland and Sharnbrook House, Bedford who died in January 1937 unmarried, leaving £59,877; Charles Gawen Borough who assumed the name Roberts-Gawen, married Florence the daughter of General Percy Hill. He was left £5000 by his father and an annuity of £100. There was also a daughter, Jane Charlotte who became Mrs Bowles.

The eulogy for J.C.B. Borough was unknowingly given by Mr Heane, the Newport solicitor, at the celebrations for the wedding in 1889 of his son, J.S.B.Borough. The changes in the estate over the last thirty years were, he said, amazing. Property had been improved, the land made more fertile and the estate extended. Where there was once common grew splendid crops; there were good and beautiful cottages where once stood hovels; there were now schools and churches. The tenants, labourers and community had reaped the fruits of it.

> *"Most freely has he spent his income on permanent improvements,*
> *such as reclamation drainage, fencing, and in altering or erecting*
> *farmhouses and buildings and cottage accommodation."*

Newport Advertiser. 27 April 1889.

John Sydney Burton Borough, born 1852, did all the proper things, Eton, Christchurch Oxford, JP., High Sheriff and Deputy Lieutenant. He married Edith second daughter of the Rev. Gladwyn Jebb of Firbeck Hall, Yorkshire in 1889 and before succeeding lived at Chetwynd Knoll on the Edgmond Road. Her father had been Rector of Chetwynd from 1872 to 1878. At Chetwynd the wedding was celebrated on the day by a luncheon in a marquee at the Kings Head with tea for wives and children and games in the park. There was then a supper in the marquee including cottagers and employees and residents of Chetwynd.

"The well-to-do farmer, the brawny smith, the waggoner, and ploughman, and shepherd, and cowman and stockman were all represented at that festal board, besides a host of others, and like a crew well piloted, they set to work in good earnest, and the joints quickly disappeared."

Newport Advertiser. Ibid.

In the evening the park was turned over to numerous pleasures. Walking in the woods, fishing in Chetwynd Pool, a band, dancing and balloons and childrens amusements. Mr Borough who had been too ill to attend the meals walked around the park in the afternoon.

Their return from their honeymoon abroad was celebrated in the usual style at Firbeck Hall with the family and tenantry, over 100, sitting down to dinner in a marquee erected in the courtyard while the children were given tea later. Their arrival was greeted with cannon, the horses unhitched and the carriage drawn by estate workmen to the Hall: *"the evening was spent in dancing, concluding with cordial expressions of appreciation of the liberality of Mr and Mrs Jebb".*

J.S.B. Borough, B.A., D.L., J.P.

JSB was notorious in not having the church clock altered for summer time but in this he was no different than George V! Tenants recalled him riding around the estate on a penny farthing bicycle with solid tyres with an oil can in his pocket hooting and yelling at anyone in his path. He never dressed up for church and with his goatee, overalls and hobnailed boots he must have been quite a sight. It is also said that when hunting deer in Chetwynd Park he used a bow and arrow. Nevertheless he was ahead of his time having one of the finest blacksmithing workshops repairing all the tractors and machinery at Chetwynd. He was also a fish farmer

"The old squire was a law unto himself he was the fellow that rode his penny farthing bicycle to Sambrook everyday to count his fish in the Sambrook millpond. An eccentric old buffer really but he had a son who was much more civilised and daughters which were equally civilised. The son gave his name to the Burton Borough school at Newport and I think he was quite a good cricketer so you can forgive him for anything. He also drove a Morris Cowley car. The girls used to ride a horse, an Arab horse which was rather a good looker."

Interview with Alf Dillamore, March 1999.

John Sydney Burton Borough had been a magistrate, Deputy Lieutenant for the County and High Sheriff as well as holding local offices, but ill health had caused him to retire from public life for many years and devote himself to his estate. His main hobby had been engineering and though self-taught he had a gift in practical mechanics. His biographical entry read *"chiefly interested in mechanical pursuits."*

Colonel John George Burton Borough took over on the death of his father in 1924. In 1923 the estate had become a limited company Chetwynd Park Estate Ltd. The "Colonel" or the "Squire" managed it himself. Wartime inflation and shortages had brought some prosperity but after 1920 imports pushed down prices and the depression was as bad as pre-1914. Rents stood still or fell, there was no investment or modernisation and farms fell into disrepair. Chetwynd like many medium sized estates hung on. In 1934 the Colonel invited Edward Watson Jones to take over the Home Farm 171 acres at 30/- [£1.50] per acre.

Things improved during and after the Second World war only for a costly family settlement in 1953 which led to the sale of 1475 acres in the northern part of the estate including 8 farms, 5 smallholdings and Sambrook Mill; the purchaser was Col. Lowe but by 1956 he had died and the land was sold to sitting tenants for instance Pickstock Manor Farm, 229 acres, going for £11,250 to Edward Watson Jones. Soon the Watson Jones' would have over 2,000 acres while by 1960, when the Colonel died childless, his estate was scarcely 3,000 acres.

Colonel Borough was born in 1890 the eldest son of JSB and was educated at Charterhouse School and Christ Church, Oxford where he graduated M.A. He also studied estate management at Wye College. He grew up in the halcyon, rose-tinted Edwardian days before 1914. An outstanding sportsman he played football and cricket at Oxford and for Free Foresters and Corinthian Casuals. In 1914 he played soccer on tour in Berlin and Moscow. At home he played football for Newport FC and cricket for Newport over a period of many years serving in every office up to President. His mother and father both served as president of the cricket club. He was also President of Shropshire Cricket Association.

"Mr J G Borough has taken part in the last few matches and has shewn good form behind the sticks with the gloves".

Newport Advertiser 14 August 1909.

In 1911 he joined the Staffordshire Yeomanry and served in Egypt and Palestine in 1914-18 and remained as Colonel in command until 1937. His younger brother Lt Alaric Charles Henry Borough was killed in action in 1917. There were two sisters, Elisabeth (d.1956) and Cynthia (d. 1974), both unmarried. There was no one to succeed to the estate.

Elisabeth Borough died aged 60 in Kenya. In her younger days she had become an accomplished musician and singer and inaugurated and led musical, choral and dramatic efforts in the Newport area before she left for London and Jersey. Her sister Cynthia was a librarian in the Bodleian Library, Oxford.

The Colonel was active in local affairs. He was a County Councillor from 1922 and an Alderman in 1949 serving on the Education, and Roads Committees. He was a Poor Law Guardian, Governor of Harper Adams College and Adams Grammar School as well as an active magistrate cycling to court in an old coat tied with binder twine. He took a great interest in the Royal British Legion

The Colonel on the left of
Walter Wheat, in 1935.

On the 9 January 1942 he announced his engagement to Mary Belcher only daughter of J Morris Belcher of Tibberton Manor the well-known breeder and judge of shire horses. He was 52 and she 38, an avid rider with the Albrighton Hunt, and a hockey and tennis player. A *"fashionable wedding"* followed on Wednesday 15 April at Tibberton Church. The church may have been full of the right people but the reality was it was 1942 with rationing and shortages so that the bride wore a dark blue suit and hat carried a bouquet of carnations while clothing coupons did not run to bridesmaids. The reception was held in a small tent with a war-time tea and a cake with no icing. Curiously for those days there was not a man or woman in uniform.

Fashion was not a word associated with the Squire who was known locally as "barbed wire Jack" from the tattered state of his clothes. He wore shorts even at respectable funerals causing resentful comment.

Mrs Edith Borough (Jebb) died aged 84 on 8 August 1942 at Chetwynd Park where she had continued to reside with her son. For over fifty years she had worked closely with Miss Roddam on district nursing and the Nurses Home. She had been a governor of the Girls High School and through her son a cricket enthusiast, being President of the Newport club. She supported the work of Chetwynd church donating the organ and the lectern. At the funeral there were no flowers donations instead to the Newport Cottage Hospital.

When Colonel Borough died in 1960 probate was settled on an estate of scarcely 3,000 acres. At the dedication of a stained glass window erected in his memory by Mrs Mary Borough in May 1963 the story was told of the Hulland estate that one year, allowing for repairs and improvements, it made only £12, from the rents of 1,000 acres. The Colonel decided to give £2 to Derbyshire County Cricket Club and £10 to the Derby diocesan funds!

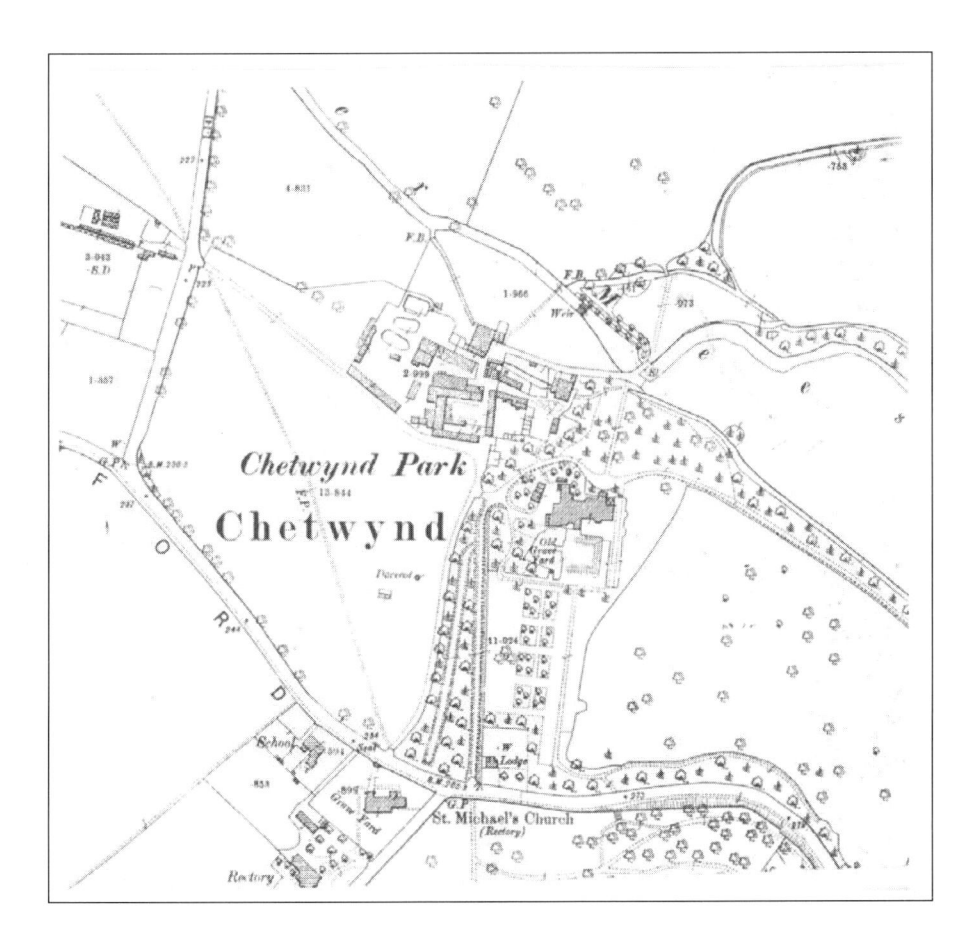

At his death a number of tenanted farms and cottages were sold as they became vacant and a large portfolio of investments accumulated. For 28 years the Park was administered by Trustees on behalf of Charterhouse and Christ Church to whom the bulk of the estate had been left as he had died without issue. Mrs Mary Borough remained as life tenant until her death on the 6 April 1987. At this point there were about 1,600 acres. The estate was valued at £193,000 for probate.

Mrs Borough, a local girl, was devoted to charitable work, WRVS, Women's Royal British Legion, Newport Cricket Club, Agricultural Society, Girl Guides and many others. She was buried in the new church she loved along with her husband.

The *"trust for sale"* now had to be realised and difficulties were envisaged with sitting tenants in the farms and residential property, while there was little commercial timber and no historic mansion.

The Hall had been on the site for centuries and by the time of the Borrows was part timbered with brick and roughcast and covered with ivy. The Church was on the side and the estate yards down the lane. The large pigeon cote remains in the Cordy Croft. Entrances have changed over the years and additions made. In 1645 it was described as a pretty house with glass in the windows depicting the coats of arms of those families connected with the Hall. King Charles stayed three nights on his way to Naseby and the room over the drawing room was known as the King's Room.

*"The Hall is an ancient structure near the east end of the church,
which appears to have been built at different periods;
in the lowgrounds in front of the Hall, the river Meese,
an inconsiderable stream, takes its course".*

Bagshaw 1851.

In 1871 it is described as *"a handsome and spacious building".*

*"You may count seven or eight lofty sharp-pointed gables
on the side where the church once stood,
everyone mantled from bottom to top with a dense growth of ivy."*

The Hall was demolished in 1964 and replaced with the existing modern structure though the closed graveyard and the old ice house are nearby and in front the ha-ha keeping out the deer.

In the end the farms and cottages were offered to the tenants and the woodland sold by private treaty. The main house was sold and the deer-park purchased by Newport Agricultural Society for a new showground having sold the Forton site to developers. 476 acres including the demesne lands and the estate yard went for £1.5 million. The watermill, though probably just a laundry, cowsheds, stableblock, barns, former school and estate office have all been sympathetically re-developed for housing with property retaining the name of the original usage. The final sum for the Trust was about £3.5 million.

The more sentimental sale was that of the farm effects and equipment described by the agent as a time capsule, some dating back 200 years.

A four wheel harvest wagon marked J S B Borough in excellent condition dated about 1890.
A tipping cart, with J G Borough markings, on iron-rimmed five feet diameter wheels.
A milk float, a governess cart, and what could either be a game cart or fodder cart, even a dog cart.
One of two timber drags, which appeared until quite regularly on the Chetwynd Park Estate's stand at the Newport Show.
The mechanical piece de resistance is the mobile Robey and Co steam engine used to pump water anywhere on the estate, but mainly used for the estate laundry
There is a Blackstone oil engine used to power such items as a saw sharpener, a mechanical hacksaw and a lathe.
There is a huge variety of smaller agricultural equipment, including several coracle bellows and grinding mills, one of which is by Corbett and Son.
And as if to represent the end of a pre-mechanisation era, there is a coffin bier…hand-drawn of course.

Newport Advertiser 10 June 1988.

Today the ancestors of the original deer look out from the park over the modern highway that cuts between them and the house that was once the centre of a unique working, self contained, agricultural estate.

Principle Structure

1. Watermill and Laundry –
   Two storey brickbuilt structure under tiled roof, incorporating early paddle wheel.
2. Estate Office –
   Split-level brick and tile building..
3. Schoolroom –
   single sotrey structure of stuccoed brickwork with slate roof
4. Cowshed and Slaughterhouse –
   sandstone building under slate roof.
5. Stableblock –
   brickbuilt, two storey structure with slate roof.
6. Barn –
   brick and slate building on two floors.
7. Cartshed –
   with brick pillars and tiled roof
8. Iron Store –
   brick and tile structure on two floors.
9. Cart Shed –
   with brick pillars and tiled roof.
10. Barn –
    timber framed structure with stone foundations, brickwork panels and tiled roof
11. Sawmill –
    timber and corrugated iron building housing traditional sawmill machinery
12. Cartshed and Garages –
    open fronted range with stone walling, oak pillars and corrugated iron roof.
13. Metalwork Shop –
    detached, two storey building of brick under corrugated iron roof.
14. Stockyards –
    brickwork structures with corrugated iron and tiled roofs.
15. Cartsheds and Stores –
    open fronted range of brick and stone with corrugated iron roof.

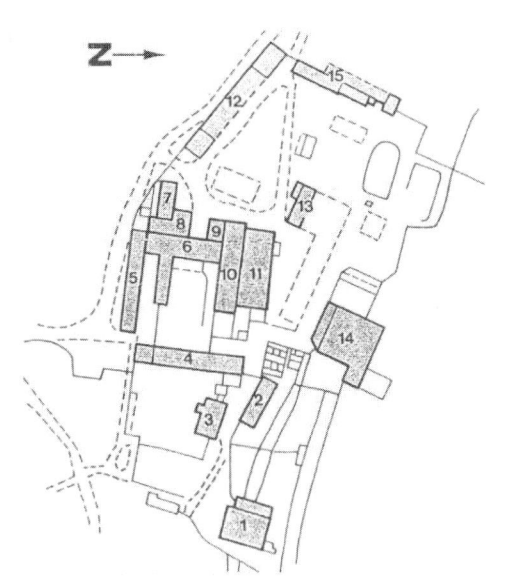

NOTES.

Five. Chetwynd and the Burton Boroughs.

1. Leach, Francis, *The County Seats of Shropshire,* Shrewsbury, (1891)
2. Wheat, Mabel, *A Story About Sambrook Parish,* (1954).
3. Wheat, Mabel, *Chetwynd Salop,* (1958).
4. Watson Jones, Peter, *Chetwynd And The Parish Church,* (1988).
5. Craven, M, *Derbyshire Families,* unpublished, Derbyshire Record Office. [DRO]
6. Craven, M, *Derbyshire County Homes,* (1984) DRO.
7. DRO, for assistance with other biographical details.
8. Byrne, Nicholas, *Chetwynd Park Epitaph for a Country Estate,* Shropshire Magazine, September 1988.
9. NMDA, for information on the Lamb at Edgmond, Chetwynd Park Fete 1864, obituaries, reminiscences, the 1988 estate sale and the redevelopment of 1990.
10. Ruscoe, Anthony, *Landed Estates and the Gentry,* Vol., Four, Weald Moors and Newport Areas, (2000).
11. SRRC, *Liddle and Heane Collection,* 3670/61. Borough Collection 1696.
12. Robinson, D. H, *The Sleepy Meese,* Chap. 7. (1988).

Chetwynd 1891.

Chetwynd is a picturesque many-gabled mansion, the principal portion of which is in the same structural condition as when, in 1645, Charles I. was entertained here by the loyal Walter Pigott. Successive additions to the structure have produced the long, irregular pile which, closely covered with ivy and embosomed in the midst of a pretty park, forms an interesting specimen of a mansion of the olden time, carefully retained in the condition of its pristine beauty. The ancient church which formerly adjoined the mansion, by reason of successive alterations had become an ordinary specimen of the "churchwarden" style of architectural restoration, and was taken down about a quarter of a century ago, when a handsome edifice was erected in its stead on the main road near the park gates. The site of the old church now forms the handsome terraced lawn at the rear of the mansion. One portion of it, marking the situation of the ancient "God`s Acre," is preserved with scrupulous care, and, almost beneath the windows of the residence, still bears its old memorial stones and one or two altar stones in situ. Beyond is a splendid prospect across the park with well-timbered glades reaching to undulating hill country in the distance. The residence is approached by two carriage drives - one leaving the Birmingham and Chester road, opposite the new church; the other entering the grounds from the same road nearer Newport. A curious feature which Chetwynd shares with Loton and other places is that the ancient park of about 210 acres is divided from the house and grounds by the high road already mentioned. Near the house is a magnificent arboretum, with cuttings from which Mr Borough has had planted the whole of the new church drive. Symonds, the diarist of the Civil war, several times mentions both the house and the church in his records. "In the parlour windows of this pretty howse of Mr. Pigott`s," he saw a shield above which was inscribed "former quarterings," and which bore the arms of Pigott, Leveson, "and many more." On May 19, 1645, he records that "His Majesty lay at Mr Pigott`s, at Chetwynd, one myle beyond Newport; and the troops advanced May 20." In the old church, Symonds states, was a south window with armorial bearings and the inscription, "Orate pro Sta`u Joh`is Pigot de Chatwyn Ar. Qui hanc fenestram....An`o D`ni 1501." The Pigott arms were also in the east window, and an ancient recumbent statue was near, which "they call the monument of Chetwyn ante Conq."

The King`s room is a spacious cheerful apartment at the head of the staircase on the first floor, panelled in oak, and lighted by three windows overlooking a delightful prospect. Elegantly furnished in modern style, it is now Mrs Borough`s boudoir, and contains, among a large number of choice paintings, a contemporary portrait of King Charles. Most of the other principal rooms in this charming residence have been modernised in aspect, but the arrangements are practically those of the original 16th century mansion. The entrance hall is an elaborately appointed apartment containing some family portraits, including those of Thomas Borrow and also of his wife, both by Wright, of Derby; Isaac Borrowe, Honor (nee Burton), his wife, and John Borrowe all by Kneller; and Thomas Borough and Jane, his wife, both by Keeling. The hall gives access to the conservatory and the suite of apartments on the ground floor. The morning-room opening from the hall, is fitted with low open bookcases, with numerous paintings above and a valuable collection of china. The paintings include several copies of old masters by the late Mr Borough and his daughter. Thence opens the drawing-room, an elegant apartment panelled in white and gold, with a deep bay window overlooking the lawn, the site of the old church, and the uplands beyond. The ceiling of this room is one of remarkable beauty, and indeed is the most attractive feature of the interior of the house. It is entirely hand-modelled by Italian artists, and is of great antiquity. Among the paintings here are landscapes by Van der Heyden, and a subject picture, "Joseph and his Brethren," by De Witt. The dining-room adjoins, and is a spacious apartment, with a handsome moulded ceiling, and lighted by three windows. Two richly-worked fire-screens bear the heraldic quarterings of the family; above the fire-place hangs a large portrait in oils of Admiral Gawen, by Maddox, of Bath; and on the east wall one of Robert Burton, by Kneller. On the remaining wall space are, among others, a landscape, by Claude; one with bathers in the foreground, by Salvator Rosa; two landscapes and two paintings of the Coloseum, by Wright, of Derby. The same painter, of whose pictures the late Mr Borough formed a good collection, is further represented by "The Indian Widow" and "The Anatomist," the latter a very fine work.

Francis Leach, "The County Seats of Shropshire", 1891.

6. LONGFORD AND THE LEEKES.

In September 1988 a notice appeared announcing that the remains of the Leeke family would be reburied in concrete in the vault of their own church at Longford which had been deconsecrated eight years earlier and purchased for conversion into a private house. Wellington businessman and licensee Mr. Anthony Thacker discovered he had not only purchased a 19th Century sandstone church but also a vault containing brick shelves or niches in which the coffins of the Leekes had been laid since the church was built in 1806. In all there were thirteen coffins, nine identified. These were Dorothy Thursby (1806), Egerton Leeke (1806), Ralph Leeke (1829), Thomas Leeke (1836), Ralph Harvey Leeke (1849), Augusta Leeke (1855), Ralph Merrick Leeke (1882), Honoria Frances Leeke (1887) and Hester Urania Leeke (1887). A disturbing, if not undignified, end to a landed estate.

In reality the end had come in 1935 when Colonel Ralph Leeke had put the Longford Hall Estate up for sale. It covered 1,635 acres and comprised Longford Hall, gardens and pool, seven productive farms ranging from 58 to 271 acres, smallholdings, a secondary residence, 100 acres of woodland and numerous cottages. It contained several settlements to the west of Newport, such as Longford, Brockton, Cheswall, Vauxhall, and parts of the parish of Church Aston and Pitchcroft. To the west it was bounded by the natural feature of the Strine and the Shropshire Union canal and in the east, Church Easton or Aston, by the LMS railway. A moderate estate for a gentleman of comfortable if modest means pinched between Newport and its powerful neighbour at Lilleshall which it survived by twenty years. The later sale of the Longford estate was due to the great age of Col. Leeke and the lack of heirs, for most estates of similar size had long since gone, 80,000 acres in Shropshire between 1918 and 1923, as landed families sought less expensive surroundings.

On the Lilleshall side bounded on the north by the Strine are several long, narrow enclosures at right angles to the stream and used as pasture. These are the *"Moors"* formerly part of the Weald Moors which the estate seems to have acquired in the draining of the wetlands without the disputes that affected much of the clearance or any formal enclosure. They could have been part of the Adeney estate. The 619 acres of the Adeney estate were bought by Ralph Merrick Leeke in 1876 and Col. Leeke owned the whole of Adeney in 1910 but by 1934 it had been bought by the occupiers John and William Edwards, though it must be admitted that in those hard times occupiers were often unwilling to own land preferring the shelter of larger landlords. On this side also were the mixed arable and pasture farms of Longford Mill (131 acres), Cheswell Manor (271), Brockton Manor (206) and Brockton House (167). In the middle on the traditional crossroads site of the Longford and Edgmond roads was the blacksmith's shop run by the Peaceful family who also held the office of Parish Clerk.

Church Aston was a medieval open village of three large fields an outpost of Edgmond until it came into possession of the Talbots. Because of the nature of open field farming ownership was scattered and the Estate seems to have only owned half of the parish, most in the south and west in small holdings and cottages linked to the industrial working of the lime. This was true at Pitchcroft, Blackberry Bank and in the miners' rows such as Slate Row and Well Row joined by a network of paths across the fields, to the pits and kilns and the canal. The *Last Inn* is traditionally so called because the inquests on miners were held here. The Longford Estate had many aspects, in miniature, of its Lilleshall neighbour with clearances from the waste, good farming on the glacial clays and gravels and exploitation of the mineral resources.

Longford was there at Domesday and its name suggests an ancient crossing of the marshland to the high ridge of Edgmond to the north-west pre-dating Newport. For most of its life it was in the hands of the Talbots a branch of the Earls of Shrewsbury. The Talbot Chapel remains in the grounds of Longford Church with a monument to Thomas Talbot 1686 and his wife, 1706, and their tenacious faith survives in the Roman Catholic Church at Salters Hall in Longford Road, Newport. They built the first Hall and Park. A map of 1682 shows that the parkland was still functional and utilitarian the sophistication of the eighteenth century was still to come. The landscaping was limited to a small area of formal gardens in front of the house with avenues of trees leading from the house which did not interfere with the grazing. Medieval fishponds had become ornamental pools and the church remained isolated to the north in what had once been the village.

When the Talbot line ceased the estate passed back to the Earl of Shrewsbury. In 1788 Charles, Earl of Shrewsbury, nephew of the former Earl, had the Estate valued and the next year sold it to Ralph Leeke then living a Haughton near Shifnal.

The Leekes were an old Shropshire family a son of Ralph Leeke of Ludlow in 1334 marrying into the Mydlletons of Chirk Castle. Four generations later they married into the Ottleys of Pitchford Hall and during the Commonwealth a Leeke was a Baron of the Exchequor. They appear as Burgesses of Newport in 1714 and 1763.

> "30th Nov. 1714 they elected Ralph Leeke gent`, High Steward to retrieve their affairs, as all neighbouring Gentlemen of note refused to fill the office till he has effected that design".

By the early 1700's Thomas Leeke was living at the Vineyard, Wellington. In 1780 his will records that he gave Ralph, his second son, £400 when he went to India where he was paymaster of Islamhabad and Resident at Tipperah under the Honourable East India Company. In 1785 Ralph was asking the Governor if he could return to England. In 1786 he came home to look for a wife and an estate which he found at Longford and Church Aston. This was unusual, for that period in India, between 1770 and 1830, was one of wholesale interracial mix and widespread assimilation, virtually all Englishman, away from the coast, Indianised themselves, dressed Indian, had Indian wives and harems and adopted Muslim codes and native masters whether high civil servants, mercenaries or adventurers. The English mem-sahibs isolated in their cantonments despising Indian society were well in the future.

On 10 December 1787 he made a marriage settlement of £10,000 on Honoria Frances Thursby daughter of Walter Harvey Thursby of Shrewsbury, money which was immediately lent back to Ralph on security of the property at Longford. The estate was valued at £40,125. In January 1789 he is admitted as a Burgess of Newport and in 1792 he is leasing coal and ironstone mines in Muxton. In February 1798 we find him appealing against the land tax because Shrewsbury being a Catholic had had to pay double the ordinary rate. Much to his chagrin he was told any reduction on land tax on the house would have to be made up by increased tax on the rest of the property.

Ralph was at this time, 1794-97, involved in considerable expense in rebuilding the Hall to a very personal design of J Bonomi. The original Hall had faced west now it was turned through a right angle to face south with a ha-ha separating the park. Pevsner describes it as built of:

> "....*square stone blocks, seven by four bays, two storeys high,*
> *with continuous giant pilasters and a consciously heavy,*
> *Etruscan porte-cochere of four big Tuscan columns with pediment".*

Longford Hall 1935

Over the door is the Leeke coat of arms and their logo, "a leg" can be found in plaster. The hall frieze is a copy of the Parthenon and beyond the hall is a bronze staircase with a well leading up to a lantern roof. On the left the drawing room has double doors with two keyholes, one false. The outbuildings such as the coach house remained with a dovecote and two sundials dated 1680. The kitchen wing was a later addition. The Domesday village removed to enhance the perspective from the Hall had a new church in 1806 built by John Cobb of Newport. This view was still protected in 1935 for the sale of land to the south carried restrictions on development except with the permission of the owners of the Hall. In 1935 the Hall was lit by acetylene gas generated on the premises while water came from a well pumped from a separate engine house. It did have central heating and domestic hot water. The prospect was also enhanced by the construction of a picturesque lake of 6.5 acres fed by watercourses off the estate under agreement in 1814 with John Cotes of Woodcote and in 1842 with the Duke of Sutherland.

The Kitchen Garden

Ralph appears quite determined in his building for the parish register of 6 October 1790 records:

> *"Memorandum. The first load of stone (in all, 30 loads) towards the erecting of a new church on the eminence in the field call'd the Windmill Field was carried by my team this day. Robert Outlaw, Rector. Mr Leeke of Longford Hall, afterwards changed his mind, and carried the stone from this spot to the lodges leading to the hall which was employed in the building of the lodges".*

Ralph played the role of country gentleman being elected a burgess in 1789 and becoming High Steward of Newport in 1812 while his son Thomas was admitted a Burgess in 1813. His younger son, Rev. Ralph Harvey Leeke, was also a Burgess and was in the deputation that met Princess Victoria when she visited the town in October 1832. Ralph Harvey filled the family living at Longford from 1825-1844, as did Thomas Newton Leeke, 1880-1883, and William Leeke, 1892-1899.

The Liddle ledgers show Ralph using the *Red Lion* at Newport in 1811 for the carriage of portmanteau and boxes to London and Chester and for the carriage of pheasants, hare and other game as far as Birmingham and London. He frequently hired a chaise and horses for local journeys. On rent days he paid for dinner and ale for 16 to 20 people. He was a subscriber to the Coffee Room at the Inn. His son Thomas was living at Aston Hall between 1812-27 and 5 November, 1819, finds him buying 98 teas at 7.5p each and paying for wine at coursing meetings in 1821. Miss Leeke of Longford in 1822 was hiring a carriage off William Liddle at £6 per month even paying £5.5.0 for damage. An early case of women drivers! Hirings indicate the social round of Aqualate, Woodcote and Shifnal.

This was the time of the French Revolution and Napoleonic threats, and Ralph with other prominent gentlemen, took the lead in raising the Newport Volunteers, consisting of 443 men in 1803, and drilling them in *"Soldiers Piece"* a field on the estate at Vauxhall, a short walk from the town. Ralph acted as Commandant with the rank of Lieutenant Colonel. On 24 April 1804, Mrs Leeke presented them with Colours which were laid up in the Hall when they disbanded in 1816.

> *"1806. Memorandum. On the 11th of September, 1806, His Royal Highness George, Prince of Wales, accompanied by his brother, His Royal Highness the Duke of Clarence, arrived in Newport at 10 a.m. They were received with every demonstration of loyalty and respect by the inhabitants, and Ralph Leeke, of Longford Hall, Esqr., High Steward of the Corporation of Newport, and Lt Colonel commandant of the regiment of Newport Volunteers, received them at the head of his Corps, as they drove into town, and fired three vollies upon their leaving it. The above was transcribed by the earnest desire of the above named Ralph Leeke, Esqr., by John James, sworn Clerk of the Parish and Parish Church of Newport, in the county of Salop, in the year of our Lord 1826, June 1st."*

Parish Register.

Ralph died on 30 September 1829 and was succeeded by his son Thomas, a confirmed invalid. His first wife, Louisa Shaw died in 1811 and he was married a second time in 1822 to

Ann Shaw Plunkett of Dublin. He died in 1836. His son, Ralph Merrick Leeke was ill for years and frequently absent from Longford. He married Lady Hestor Fellowes daughter of the Earl of Portsmouth. He exchanged and consolidated holdings for example with Rosa Fleming Washbourne in May 1858. It was he who purchased the Adeney estate in 1871 which brought in brick and tile works.

For over twenty years before his death in 1882, Ralph Merrick Leake had been compelled to spend longer and longer periods of time away from Longford, including several years in Madeira, because of asthma. He managed to return in March 1871 to celebrate the coming of age of his son Ralph but his short and modest speeches reflected his problems:

"As a country gentleman, I know I have done very little to deserve such great kindness; and any popularity which attaches to me and my family, has descended from my father and grandfather".

"I can only say I regret having been an absentee for so long, but thank God I am now very much better."

He survived another twelve years dying on 26 November 1882. His contribution to the welfare of the town had been that of a lively interest rather than active participation. He was a magistrate who sat little; an ex officio on public bodies such as the guardians and highways authority; he provided the cricket ground but the town was most indebted for his liberal supply of town water that originated on his land.

His funeral was quiet with an absence of any display except the *"cheerful modern fashion"* of covering the coffin with wreaths. The town of Newport partly closed its shops, drew the blinds and rang a muffled peal.

Colonel Ralph Leeke, born on Christmas Day 1849, was the eldest son of Ralph Merrick Leeke. He went to Harrow and Christ Church, Oxford. On the 10 March 1870 he purchased an Ensigncy and Lieutenancy in the Grenadier Guards paying a deposit of £1,200. This must have been one of the last purchases since the purchasing of promotions and commissions in the army was abolished under the Cardwell reforms of 1870 during the Gladstone government. His brother, Thomas Newton Leeke, was Rector of Longford 1880-83. A third son, Henry Leeke RN, of *HMS Stork*, died aged 26, just after his father in August 1883, being drowned off the coast of Africa. He is buried in Church Aston. The youngest son was the Rev. William Leeke, Rector of Longford 1892-99, a missionary in Queensland and Vicar of Holy Cross, Shrewsbury and then Lydbury North.

Ralph Leeke celebrated his coming of age on Wednesday 12 April 1871, the celebrations lasting several days, the highlight being a procession nearly a mile in length, starting from Newport and passing through Church Aston and Brockton to the Hall. Nine wagons containing 6,000lbs of beef and £50 worth of bread, to be distributed to the poor, took part in the procession. A congratulatory address was read to the young Squire on the lawn at Longford, in the presence of a large and influential company. Later in the day a banquet was given in the Royal Victoria Hotel.

Col. Ralph Leeke

The family continued to lease out the Hall. In 1883 it was rented to Daniel Adamson the promoter of the Manchester Ship Canal. In the First World War it was, like many other large houses, a hospital, with a VAD convalescent wing with twenty men. Between 1903 and 1935 Col. H.P.Sykes resided there on his retirement from the army. His second wife was Winifred Charlotte Jane Wellesley, great-grand-daughter of the Duke of Wellington. Col. Leeke made his home at the Dower House, Aston Hall, Church Aston.

Longford Hall – Military Hospital 1917

Aston Hall had been erected in 1815 as the dower house for Longford and Col. Ralph Leeke lived there until 1943. In 1947 it was bought as a boarding house for Adams' Grammar School by the Chairman of Governors, T. C. Ward, who feared that co-education threatened by the 1944 Education Act would *"produce conscientious objectors"* and sons who would be unfit to fight in the next Battle of Britain. A description of the Hall in that year shows that the sanitary and toilet arrangements were rather sketchy for such an imposing building. There were two wings with stables and outhouses for numerous domestic animals and paddocks for pigs and cattle as well as lawns and domestic gardens and two tennis courts. The drawing room still retained the fifty-year old French wallpaper. The Grammar School retained the gardens and the gardeners and housed up to forty boarders until the property was sold in 1967 ironically to help purchase Longford Hall. Today it is the Pinewoods housing estate with some remnants of the garden wall, the original trees with the noisy rookery and Dog Bank Cottage.

Colonel Leeke did what was expected of minor gentry being a deputy Lieutenant of the County, a magistrate, a County Councillor for sixteen years, a Commissioner for Land Tax and Chairman of Newport Savings Bank. He shot, rode with the Albrighton Hounds and motored, with a chauffeur, until he was ninety. He had married in 1881 Mary Theresa Manners, a daughter of the second Baron Manners. They had two sons, Ralph Henry, born 1883 and Charles, born 1887. They did the social rounds in those Edwardian summers, dances, hunting, croquet, cricket, hockey before taking up the career for most sons of the lower gentry, the army:

> *"Ralph Leeke came to tea and played bridge. He came to*
> *say goodbye before joining his regiment in Cairo".*
>
> Ethel Boughey [Morris] 19 November 1902.

He was 19. She was 24. The war was unkind to the landed gentry, it was brutal to Col. Leeke, both sons being killed, both unmarried. In May 1923 the east window in Longford Church was erected by their mother and dedicated to their memory. As if to compensate, the fourth generation all lived to a great age. Col. Leeke died aged 93 in 1943, his wife also aged 93, in 1947. His sister, Miss Hester Leeke, of Ivy Cottage, Edgmond, died aged 100 in January 1949. A remarkable woman with her carriage, music and hunting and an esteem in the village, amounting to reverence.

The Estate was offered for sale in 1935 and again in 1937 after much of the timber had been felled. The Hall was eventually sold to Mr R.H. Davies who died there from the result of accidental food poisoning.

```
SHROPSHIRE
On the outskirts of the busy Market Town of Newport, 6 miles from Wellington (fast trains to London),
18 miles from the County Town of Shrewsbury.

FOR SALE IN LOTS

The Highly Attractive Freehold
Residential, Agricultural and Sporting Property

The Longford Hall Estate
Near Newport,
of
1,635 Acres
comprising—
LONGFORD HALL
(with 88 or 146 Acres upwards), a Handsome Georgian Residence, containing Halls, Billiard
and 4 Reception Rooms, 9 Principal Bed and Dressing Rooms, 4 Bathrooms, 8 Secondary and
Servants' Bedrooms, etc.
Excellent Water Supply, Central Heating, Modern Drainage, Acetylene Gas Lighting, Main Electricity
nearby. Ample Garages and Stabling.
LOVELY GARDENS and Grounds with fine WALLED KITCHEN GARDEN,
SPLENDIDLY TIMBERED PARK with LAKE.

Seven Productive Mixed Farms
from 58 to 271 Acres, all well maintained and with good homesteads.
Accommodation Lands.   Building Sites.   Co's E.L. and Water.
Small Holdings.        Secondary Residence.
Over
100 Acres of Valuable Woodlands
and a
Large Number of Cottages
The whole for Sale by Private Treaty by
MESSRS.

CONSTABLE & MAUDE
AND
JOHN D. WOOD & CO.
(acting in conjunction).
Solicitors: Messrs. HUNT & STURTON, The Old Post Office, Northallerton; Auctioneers:
Messrs. CONSTABLE & MAUDE, 42, Castle Street, Shrewsbury (Phone 2891, Shrewsbury), Head Office;
2, Mount Street, London, W.1), and Messrs. JOHN D. WOOD & CO., 23, Berkeley Square, London,
W.1. (Mayfair 6341—10 lines).
```

Sale Catalogue of 1935

Mr Patrick Davies recalls walking along the Longford Road in 1934 which was then an avenue thick with overhanging trees. His own firm, Davies, White and Perry sold the estate to a developer who stripped all the trees except those down to the church. During the Second World War it was used by the Royal Artillery as storage and the Hall itself became little more than a cattle shed with animals drifting in and out of the house.

Later the Hall was bought by Mrs Hall from Broughton Hall near Eccleshall who began its restoration. She was followed by her son, Mr Patrick Hall, who was head of the British Reinforced Concrete Co. Ltd. of Stafford and Hall Engineering Co Ltd Shrewsbury and other undertakings. He brought the Hall back to life. While there he was involved in many benevolent objects including the redecoration of Longford Church which was absorbed into Newport in 1923 and made redundant in 1987, and the restoration of the Talbot Chapel. In 1966 at the age of fifty he *"retired"* to Switzerland. The Hall and Park was bought by the Haberdashers Company in 1967 for use as junior boarding accommodation for Adams Grammar School for the nominal sum of £40,000. The land and farms were sold to the Prudential Insurance Company. The church went into decline.

The Talbot and Shrewsbury names are now preserved as street names on the large housing development that has edged westwards from Newport over the Longford fields. The threads of history remain.

Meanwhile at Longford Hall the dovecote yard and the gardens have been developed as exclusive housing to provide a fund to maintain and develop the Grammar School.

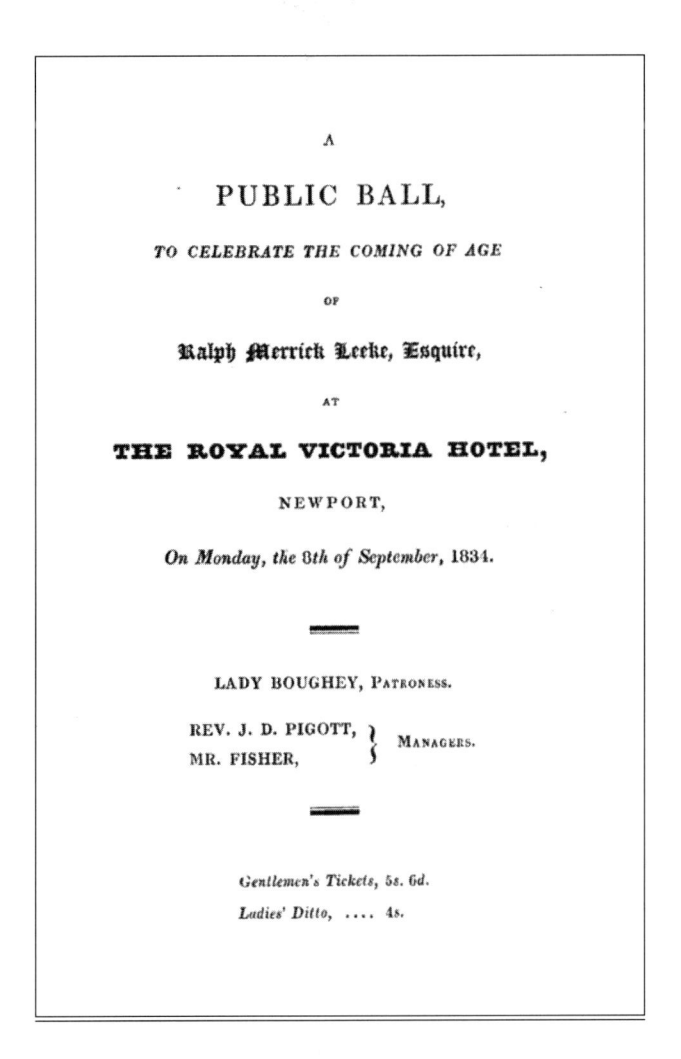

>
> A
>
> PUBLIC BALL,
>
> TO CELEBRATE THE COMING OF AGE
>
> OF
>
> Ralph Merrick Leeke, Esquire,
>
> AT
>
> **THE ROYAL VICTORIA HOTEL,**
>
> NEWPORT,
>
> On Monday, the 8th of September, 1834.
>
> LADY BOUGHEY, Patroness.
>
> REV. J. D. PIGOTT, } MANAGERS.
> MR. FISHER,
>
> Gentlemen's Tickets, 5s. 6d.
> Ladies' Ditto, ... 4s.

NOTES.

Six. Longford and the Leekes.

1. Pevsner, N., *The Buildings of England – Shropshire,* (1958), p. 172.
2. Rowley, Trevor, *Shropshire Landscape,* (1972)
3. Ruscoe, Anthony, *Landed Estates And The Gentry,* Vol., Four, (2000).
4. Longford Estate sale catalogue 1935.
5. SRRC, Leeke Collection 81; Liddle and Heane Collection, 3670/62
6. NMDA, various articles and reports on Longford Church, Patrick Hall and obituaries of 1943, 1947 and 1948.
7. Dalrymple, William, *White Mughals,* Harper Collins, (2002).

7. THE HARROP DIARIES.

John Harrop`s diaries had not really been lost they had been in the possession of the Addington family in Elham near Canterbury ever since they had taken over the large house next door in 1972. Time moved on and by 1987 members of the Addington family were living in Newport, Shropshire and re-reading the diaries on a visit home realised the connection with Newport. In the first diary of 1861 John Harrop was living at Edgmond Hall and in 1868, the second diary, he had moved to Broughton Hall near Eccleshall in Staffordshire. It was clear in both diaries that his life revolved around Newport so they were brought back for investigation. Who was John Harrop, why was he in Newport and why were the diaries in Kent?

The diaries showed John Harrop to be the guardian of four grandchildren named Wilcox and that the two boys went to Rossall School near Fleetwood, a public school founded in 1844 that still exists. A letter to the Headmaster brought details from the registers of 1860 and 61. The Headmaster of the school between 1849 and 1869 was the Rev. W. A. Osborne who is mentioned in the diaries. They showed Charles Walford Wilcox, Magdalen College Cambridge, and The Manor House, Wolston, Coventry. The 1861 register also listed a brother Henry Augustus Mortimer Wilcox, who had been two years at the school then at Jesus College, Cambridge; he graduated B.A. in 1871, and in 1876 was ordained became vicar of Wolston, Coventry and died in 1909. A letter addressed simply to *"The Vicar of Wolston, Coventry"* brought all the answers. Firstly came a family tree from a local historian and then Mrs Betty Gillan who lived nearby at Frog Hall revealed that she was the great, great, granddaughter of John Harrop and had the other diaries. She also had a photograph of John Harrop taken by Henry Howle of Newport on 8 December 1866 and an *" in memoriam"* card on his death at Broughton on 29 August 1869 aged 79. He had been buried at the next village, Croxton. Frog Hall had originally been an Inn and it was here that William Wilcox had first met Frances Elizabeth Harrop the daughter of John Harrop of the diaries.

Mrs Gillans mother had lived in Eltham until 1972, when aged 86, she had left to live with her daughter in Warwickshire. In the confusion of moving the diaries had been mislaid and in the mass of family documents had not been missed. Now they have returned but not before giving us a glimpse of a small portion of Victorian Newport. The *"Kent mystery"* was solved.

It was clear that John was a Manchester man. He still travelled by train to the city where he had an aged aunt and his eldest daughter, Maria, was married to Richard Milne Redhead. Mr Redhead sent John two volumes of the Manchester Grammar School Registers in September 1868 and John, in October sent Mr Redhead *"a copy of my Grandfathers newspaper "The Manchester Mercury" no. 423 Tuesday April 22nd 1760"*. The 1861 census finds John at Edgmond Hall, aged 69, occupation *"mortgagee"* and born in Manchester; his wife Sarah was 50 from Saltney, Flintshire. Manchester Central Library provided extracts from *"Manchester Streets and Manchester Men"* and the *"Manchester School Register"*.

It was no insignificant man who had retired to Shropshire for his grandfather was Joseph Harrop, a printer, who was responsible for the longest existing newspaper in Manchester - 78 years. Joseph launched his weekly newspaper on 3 March 1752 under various titles ending as *"The Manchester Mercury, and Tuesday`s General Advertiser"* and costing 1½.d and then 7d as stamp duty increased. Foreign and London news depended on meeting the mail coach at Derby two days earlier. He was a rabid government supporter and his intolerant language led to more liberal papers overtaking him though the Mercury had the field to itself for thirty years. He retired in 1788 leaving the business to his son James who died in 1823 passing the newspaper to his son John. He had also been Postmaster at Salford. The last edition was 28 December 1830 when the Mercury had long been overtaken.

There is no entry for John Harrop in the Manchester School register nor do we know when and why he retired to become a country gentleman.

Incidentally one *"aged aunt"* he mentions was his father's sister Mary who was a renowned beauty, even in old age, so much so that she is said to have refused all proposals even from an Earl! Aunt Sarah was 83 in 1861.

Who are the family members who appear in the diaries? They are John Harrop (b.1792), Sarah Harrop (b.1798), Maria Redhead (daughter b.1825), Georgiana Pechel (daughter b.1828), Richard Redhead (son-in-law b.1828) and Aunt Sarah (b.1778). His daughter Frances and her husband William Wilcox both died in 1853 and John became guardian to their four children. William was Lord of the Manor of Wolston. The grand-children were William Wilcox who died aged two in October 1845; Charles Walford Wilcox 1847-1926, who in turn became Lord of the Manor of Wolston and had the right of advowsen so that his brother Henry Augustus Mortimer Wilcox became Vicar of Wolston in 1876. There were two Wilcox daughters, Frances Eliza and Clara Isabella. Charles had seven children only one daughter surviving, she marrying a Danish barrister Eric Alfred Hoffgaard. It was this lady who left the diaries at Elham.

The other grandchildren were William Charles Mortimer Pechell (b1850) and Mary Georgiana Harrop Milner Redhead (b 1860). John Harrop had a son not listed in the diary, Henry Vernon Harrop, who had a daughter Fanny Vernon who came to stay with her grandfather in April 1868 coming with her cousin Clara from school.

The diaries were produced by Mansfields of London, cloth bound priced 2/6. They were for business people and like today contained information considered essential for the age. There were interest tables, lists of London and country banks, members of parliament, stamp duties and taxation. Income tax in 1861 was 10d in the pound and in 1868 it was down to 4d. There was a tax of £1.25 on menservants over eighteen years of age and of £1.17 on persons using hair powder. John added his own information on the flyleaf. His name; details of his gold lever stopwatch: *"double cased large gold lever stop watch, no 2092 makers name Samuel Brothers and Coy, Liverpool"*. He recorded the weights of his grandchildren in lbs. (Clara in 1861 aged 10 was 68lbs); their birthdays; his dog licences and a useful calculation: *"to value calves multiply the weight by 50 divide the product by 8"*. At the back of each diary are meticulous, monthly details of personal and household expenditure. Entries are brief, abbreviated and factual. Working diaries.

Edgmond Hall
Once the home of John Harrop is now owned by Sandwell Corporation

What the diaries do reveal to our home-owning democracy is the standard practice of renting at every income level. John paid Mrs Hill £47.17.6 half yearly for Edgmond Hall and Sir H. de. Broughton £66.10.00 half yearly for Broughton Hall. Edgmond Hall was the home of the Bayley family from Stamford who had property in Newport. It was known as *"The New House"* when John Bayley died there in 1833 and his wife and two daughters left to live at the Bayley-Hill farm nearby in 1842. It was unoccupied in 1851. Anne Bayley married John Cooke Hill and it was she who was renting it to John Harrop possibly as early as 1853. On 24 September 1868 he notes the wedding of Miss Hill *"married to a man named John Bodenham"*. Bodenham was a bank manager in Newport.

In 1868 John Harrop is at Broughton Hall and was visited in April by relatives of Sir Henry Broughton. Broughton Hall is a fine timbered house on the Market Drayton - Eccleshall road made notorious in the 1930's when the family were involved in a murder in Kenya. The Hall was rented out for many years being sold after the First World War to the Hall family, rich industrialists from the Potteries. Tragedy accounted for the father and two sons and the widow left the Hall in the fifties to a religious order and came to live at Longford Hall, Newport.

The diaries show how self-contained a country house was as late as the 1860's. Crops were produced from gardens, fields and orchards. Horses, cows and pigs were bought and bred; there were chickens and geese; vegetables, potatoes, strawberries and flowers; mowing and haymaking were important events. In March 1861 he went to Wellington to see a bull, *"quite a monster"* he comments; in April he sent the *"Red cow to Dukes bull"* at a cost of 5/-; in October he bought an Alderney cow for £6.7.6 and a heifer for £7.0.0 at Hodnet; in November he sent the cow *"to bull"*. Also in November he bought a Welsh cow and calf at Shrewsbury for £10-5-0. In March he went to Shifnal to see a stallion *"Knights of Wars"* and dined there; the next month he went *"...with Blake to Wellington to see stallion "Hunting Horn"."* It cost 16/- to go. Later on in the month he was there again *"...with servant Stockton to see Hughes grey mare covered by Wadlows brown brood horse "Hunting Horn" – two leaps"*. He paid the groom 2/- presumably not for the two leaps! In May the grey mare was covered by his own yearling colt *"Master Tatton"*. In November he was killing fat pigs and his old Spanish Cock drowned to be replaced a few days later by a Black Spanish Cock from Bailey of London for £1.15.3. Mr Wedge the agent at Aqualate sent him two white wild ducks but sadly *"one flew away"*. On the 2 October he went next door *"...to see working of Mrs Hills new machinery"*.

At Broughton in 1868 he was selling individual animals to butchers such as Shropshire's and

Bridgewood's of Newport. Thompson the Newport fishmonger and greengrocer took surplus game and cucumbers. Bridgewood paid £14.13.0 for a cow. He had a calf and a heifer die. These were the years of the *"Cattle Plague"*. He bought a bloodhound, *"a fine, noble dog"*, from Tamworth, three and a half years old. He called it *"Marmion"*. In 1861 he had bought a cat and sent for certificates for Birmingham Cat and Dog Show. On the 30 November he entered *"Marmion"* in the Dog Show at Birmingham but *"there was no chance of a prize"*.

There were 18 acres of meadow to mow at 6/- per acre. He employed six women for six days at 9/- (£2.14.00) and three men at 9/-. By 6 July the hay was stacked and on the 16th he gave supper to 23 people, nine of his own men with wives, four mowers, three carters, six women haymakers and one parker, [park keeper?]. He bought a chestnut gelding called *"Robin"* for £12. He improved the garden by building a *"hanging garden"*, dried dahlias, and fought rabbits, squirrels and rooks.

His social life consisted mainly of local business people around Newport. His neighbours, the Hills, Mr and Mrs Fisher, solicitors, Harry Allen from the Royal Victoria Hotel where he often dined and stayed late; Edward Jones from Jones and Aston in town. He went coursing at Longford and Mucklestone with Allen. He dines with Mr Masefield at Ellerton Hall *"a pretty and complete place, had a delightful day"*. In 1868 Charles Wilcox attended a Ball at Ellerton and went hunting for which he bought a chestnut hunter from Allen for 30 guineas. John Harrop took Mrs H – he always refers to her as "Mrs H" – and the grandchildren to a Rifle Volunteers Review at Hawkstone in a fly provided by Allen at a cost of £1.07.02. He took a party to Woodcote gardens and went to the Franklin Wake dinner, Mr Franklin being the landlord at the *Kings Head* in Chetwynd End. On one day in May he walked with Mrs H. to Longford by the brook and back home over the bridge a walk still possible today. This is surprising because when the diary opens in January 1861 he is very unwell with gout and had not been able to put his *"gouty shoes"* on since December. Right until the end of the year he is often in bed with gout in his knee and unable to get out. Is this because of his extended visits to the *"Vic"* and his large drink bills, or is this being unkind?

He visited the *Lamb* at Edgmond, the Royal Victoria Hotel, as we have seen, and sent an empty porter barrel back to Morgans of Stafford. George Doody of the *Raven and Bell* in the High Street, Newport, delivered two dozen rum at 18/- and one dozen Scotch Whisky at 21/-. [£1.5p]

He shopped in Newport. He went with his wife and granddaughter to the most fashionable milliners and dressmaker in Newport, The Hon Catherine Belcher, paying accounts at times of £20. He used Edward Peplow for his own coats and the boys` suits. This came to £24.06.00. In January 1868 he bought a velvet jacket and a silk velvet waistcoat with a silk under waistcoat. You can follow his purchases down the High Street, Huxley the grocer at Lower Bar, two bags of wheat, which were returned as musty; T.G. Icke the bookseller, for magazines; a large grass roller from Underhills the ironmongers; grain from Parton at the "Old Crow"; oil-cake from Jones and Aston; an alarm clock from Northwood for 4 guineas; he took a gun by Hollis of Cheltenham, to Tipping the gunsmith, to be sold. His newspapers came from Silvester and Horne. He went further afield for specialities buying a piano from Wrights of Stafford while his phaeton was sent by rail to Leamington to be repaired. In 1868 John was thinking of buying a double-seated Brougham for £60, from Birmingham.

He used the railways frequently since by 1861 the main rail network was nearly complete. He went to Manchester to see his aunts and his daughter Maria Redhead often dropping Mrs H at Chester at her relatives. He was met at Ordsall station in the centre of Manchester. In November 1868 he was met by Redhead's eldest son with the carriage. He had dinner at the Quadrilateral Society then went with Mrs H to the Cathedral. At Broughton the nearest station was Whitmore a two hour journey from Chester. He would go by train to Rugby to see the Wilcox' at Wolston one trip being bitterly cold so that he was ill, and to make things worse he left his blue ring on the train. A typical journey would be to leave Newport at 1.10 arrive at Stafford at 1.45 then to Wolston at Rugby for 5.30. He had his own horse and carriage for local trips though he would use the omnibus on occasion from Newport. Road travel could be dangerous with accidents as frequent as today. On 28 August 1861 he records Harry Wiggin aged 31 being thrown from a trap and killed at Chetwynd End while coming from Newport Races. In January 1868 Dr. Swift broke his neck at Adbaston. In April Stockton, his servant, and Fanny had a trap turn over on the New Inn bank at Newport and in December grandson Charles was thrown out when brushed by a farm cart and the horses bolted against an iron lamp-post smashing the trap to atoms. Charles was badly bruised and *"sulphurous acid in a lotion"* was applied.

Young Victorian servants were not the pliant, docile people one would imagine. Take the 1861 Edgmond servants, Norman Huntbach from Croxton, was engaged in February for no wages only clothes and boots, the next week he was measured by Peplow the draper. On 22 May he was found tipsy in Newport on gin and water. John complained to the boy's father about his drunkenness, lying and inattention and a weeks holiday followed but in November the boy was sent home and replaced by Thomas Marsh of Edgmond on the same terms. Adverts were placed in Newport, Stafford and Wrexham papers but no girl seemed to stay long, Emma Plant, engaged in March, soon gave notice for Christmas. In 1868 at Broughton eight young servants came and went. In March John Swinnerton was replaced by John Tyldesly, who received livery, hat and boots and a common suit in his first year. On Boxing Day he left along with Sarah and Emma Moulston. Emma, said John, was a *"good girl"*, John and Sarah, *"good for nothing"*. John was replaced by James Griffiths on the usual terms no wage, two suits of clothes and shoes. The diary tells how James` sister aged five died when pushed into the fire-grate by an eight-year old boy. It is difficult to say how many servants there were but the weekly wage bill was £3.16.00., there was certainly a housekeeper, a gamekeeper called Talbot and a cowman, Levi Dodd, who in 1868 asked for a character to become a warder at Stafford prison. In March 1861 old Joe Heaton gave notice, changed his mind, asked for a pay rise and was told to go. After advertising, Joseph Stockton and his family came from Wolverhampton for 15/- then 16/- per week, a cottage rented from Mrs Hodson for £5 pa and a pint of skimmed milk each morning. Stockton was lent £5 to fetch his family and goods from Wolverhampton to be repaid at 2/- weekly. Stockton was still there in 1868 as coachman, handy man and friend. That Christmas he got a present of £1 and his grandchildren 5/-

John Harrop was fond of his grandchildren and for many years guardian to several of them when his daughter and son-in-law died in the same year. We see him settling their estate: *"affidavit from Mr Baker about Mr Wilcox`s personalty"* and as late as 1868 writing for a copy of their marriage and birth certificates. The diaries show how John saw his grandchildren through school, consoled them with letters, sent them parcels, notes, pocket money, gifts, paid their train fares and met them at the station. He gave grandson Charles a musical box costing £24.06.00. He sent 10/- each to Charles, Fanny, Clara and Henry on Henry's birthday. He paid fees of £64.00.05 for Charles and Henry at Paddons School in Preston and £35.11.01 plus £2 pocket money for Charles at Rossall and £26.17.00 and £1.10.00 pocket money for Henry. On Good Friday 1861 the Rev. Osborne, Headmaster at Rossall, sent Charles his Easter exam and in August the Reverend wrote to John requesting no more parcels be sent or taken by the boys to school. One wonders why? Charles caught mumps and in November and December scarlet fever was so bad the pupils were sent home. The boys had seven weeks holiday in the summer and five weeks at Christmas. At the end of August 1861 John forgot and sent the boys back to school a day late. Henry was still at Rossall in 1868 when the fees were £49.16.05. Clara was with her cousin at a Ladies School in Vineyard Road, Wellington, kept by Miss Davies and Miss Gerecke. He paid the fare to school of £1.10.00 and the fee of £26.15.08. He notes that he had sent Fanny and Clara their half-yearly money of £120. On 29 June 1868 Charles Wilcox now 21 years old, assumed the guardianship of Henry, Fanny and Clara and they went to live with him at Wolston Manor

House in Warwickshire. By now there were four additional Redhead grandchildren.

John Harrop was now 78 years old, increasingly ill and gouty reflected in his shaky handwriting. Sometimes entries are in another hand. In February he buys a bath chair for £19.10.00. He comes to Newport often, driven by Joseph Stockton. He has his interests attending sales and buying furniture and antiques from places such as Eccleshall Castle and Doddington Park. He is active in the elections of that year attending Conservative meetings at the Northern Railway Inn, Stafford and Conservative dinners chaired by Captain Boughey.

There was sadness. Harry Allen and his family from the Royal Victoria Hotel had become very close and his bankruptcy in May 1868 and his death at Bournemouth in July came hard: *"Poor Harry Allen aged 44 (?) buried at the Newport Cemetery a very sad and melancholy end of a dear friend"*. Even more painful, in September, he voted for Jane Ellen Allen, daughter of Harry Allen, to be admitted to the Wolverhampton Orphanage to which he had previously sent a donation.

A man of kindness and charity on Christmas Day 1868 he gave £4.10.00 in Christmas boxes and lists special gifts: *"Wilcox (3) 15/-; Redheads (5) £1-5-0; Pechell 5/-; Holbrook 5/-; Shuffer 5/-; Talbot 5/-; Randall 5/-; Chalkill 1/-; Herbert Holmes 2/-; Vernon 5/-; Fair Oak 2/-; Joseph £1-5-0"*.

John Harrop died at Broughton Hall on 24 August 1869 aged 79 years and was interred in the little church at Croxton which still retains its high-backed, enclosed pews and looks out over the beautiful Shropshire and Staffordshire countryside, a far cry from the grime of industrial Manchester where the Harrops made their fortune.

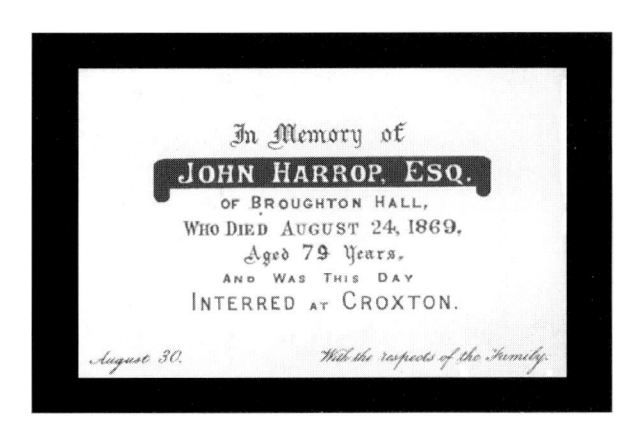

NOTES.

Seven. The Harrop Diaries.

1. Rossall School, Fleetwood, Lancashire for information from the Rossall registers of 1860-61.
2. Manchester Central Library, for extracts from *Manchester Streets and Manchester Men,* and the *Manchester School Register.*
3. Miles, Malcolm, *The Harrop Diaries,* Shropshire Magazine, May 1988.
4. Correspondence with Mrs Betty Gillan, great, great, great granddaughter of John Harrop who now has all the diaries and who kindly provided information, photographs and memorial cards.

8. William John Fieldhouse

By 1988 the organ of St Nicolas` Church, Newport, had developed qualities unthought of by the builders, and notes were heard not apparent in the music. Time and mice had combined to bring an element of surprise to services, as the organ went off into spontaneous and unrehearsed arrangements. Such happenings, though enjoyable, did not add to the formalised worship of the Church of England. The Congregation was faced with the massive task of fundraising for a replacement….or a wealthy benefactor! Impossible? A close look at the organ would have found a dedication dated 17 December 1917:

*"In grateful and affectionate remembrance of Seymour,
son of William and Lucy Fieldhouse of Austey Manor,
Wootton Wawen, Warwickshire, who passed out of this life on
January 4th 1907 through a riding accident in Ceylon
and was laid to rest there in the English Cemetery
in his 20th year".*

The Rev Budgen recorded the gift in the Parish Register for 1917:

*"The present organ, the gift of John and Lucy Fieldhouse
of Austey Manor, Wootton Wawen, Warwickshire, in memory
of their son Seymour Fieldhouse, was placed in the church in
1917, and built by Messrs Brindley and Foster of Sheffield.*

*Mr Fieldhouse was born in Newport and educated at the
Grammar School.*
            Wm Budgen, Rector.

John Fieldhouse was a Newport boy who became a rich industrialist and never forgot his home-town, though perhaps the town forgot him. Local boy makes good is a familiar story and most people have heard of the 17th Century William Adams because of the survival of Newport Grammar School which he founded and is still supported by the Haberdashers Company of London of which Adams was a member. William Adams went to London John Fieldhouse went to Victorian Birmingham which does not have the same romantic aura. But in the 1880`s Birmingham was the place to be, a centre of the new technology, transformed and rebuilt, and a model of municipal government. Ideal conditions for an enterprising lad.

By 1800 the Fieldhouses were long established on the Shropshire-Staffordshire border as grocers, farmers, butchers, malsters and blacksmiths. Many lie buried in Forton churchyard. They owned property and often made claims to gentility with Scottish Lords, Irish nobility, the local Tayleurs and Beaumonts, and even an Indian Princess popping up in their pedigree and numerous coats of arms.

Notable connections often meant notable gentlemen who married Fieldhouse women for their money, a practise not uncommon then or now. This is important, for John Fieldhouse had a great yearning to prove his lineage like many nouveau riche.

19th Century Newport is full of Fieldhouses all appearing to be named Thomas, William or John. At the beginning is a John Fieldhouse a blacksmith in St Marys Street and the High Street. He did a lot of shoeing of coach horses for Mr Liddle at the *Red Lion*. He was deceased by 1836. On the 27 January 1841 John Fieldhouse, a farmer from Forton, purchased the premises of the former Red Lion, now Barclays Bank, and turned them into three shops using one himself as a grocers and the other two being occupied by Mr. Pember, a boot and shoe maker, and Mr. Franklin a printer, stationer and bookbinder. Down the yard were stables, piggeries, a tea warehouse, malthouse, a candle manufactory and even reading rooms. These rooms had formerly been the Mechanics Institute of which William Fieldhouse had been librarian. These can still be seen. He had two sons Thomas and William. William, the younger, stayed in the business as grocer and tea dealer and though living at Forton, actually died at Buxton in July 1890 aged 76. He had confined himself to his own business and took little part in town affairs. His son, also William, predeceased him in 1881 as did his wife and they are all buried in Forton churchyard. The older brother Thomas (1811-1875) left to become an auctioneer and malster living at 97 then 61 and 21 High Street where we find him in 1861 with a daughter Matilda (9), Thomas (6) and William John (3). Thomas had married Anne Hall listed as born in Fair Oak, on the Shropshire-Staffordshire border, in January 1850. Son Thomas became a chemist and is possibly the Thomas who moved into the empty factory of William Underhill in St Marys Street in June 1873 and set up "*St Marys Pork, Bacon, and steam sausage factory*", taken over in November 1873 by Isiah Shutt. This son died in 1887 aged 33.

To return to Thomas the father. In 1871 he is a retired auctioneer while his wife Anne has a millinery business employing five female assistants. Between 1881 and 1883 she is recorded as still in business but now also in Birmingham. In 1883 she moved to Birmingham. William John Fieldhouse would have been 25. Is this the Birmingham connection?

William John Fieldhouse JP, CBE, FSA was born in Newport, Shropshire on 19 January 1858. He entered business in Birmingham. He was a partner with Mr G. H. C. Hughes in the St Stephens Wheel Works in the city, the firm being known as *"Geo H Hughes"*. Mr Fielding acquired a major interest when Mr Hughes died in 1906. A lady who worked there from 1919 to 1937 recalls Fielding:

> *"....was a good man (or gentleman), also a magistrate and used to attend at the Birmingham Law Courts every Wednesday, apart from that he was at the office always driven by his chauffeur from Wootton Wawen".*

He was also connected with the Griffin Foundry in Browning Street, Edgbaston. This made kitchen ranges, cast iron grates, fireplaces and sanitary fittings. Writing in 1966 the "Griffin Group" knew little of its history except that it was formed originally by a partnership of Mr Fieldhouse and Mr Moore. They did not even know their Christian names. They quote the beginning of the company as 1839 this is patently untrue and must mean 1889. Oddly the telegraph address in 1966 was still *"Moorfield"* an amalgam of the names of the two founders. Since the 1930`s the firm had moved into merchanting that is selling fireplaces and kitchen suites and this was acknowledged in its new name *"Griffin Sales"* and a move to Shirley. By 1973 it had become part of the PWA group, Parker Winder and Achurch Ltd, architectural and builder ironmongers with very little knowledge of their original founders or products.

In 1882 at the age of 24 John Fielding married Lucy, daughter of Abraham Wood and had two sons, Ernest Francis and Seymour who died in Ceylon. He also had a daughter Olive Nancy who married Major C. W. Barnard. In 1903 business success allowed them to move from the city to the village of Wootton Wawen two and a half miles from Henley in Arden. He now began the role of country gentleman, philanthropist, archaeologist and collector, at first in a house made from two cottages but then *"The Priory"* a house opposite Wootton Mill. In 1912 he built at the top of Navigation Hill, Austey Manor, in the style of a Cotswold manor house. At the same time he purchased part of the Wootton Hall Estate and from his sixty acres, with swimming pool, nine hole golf course, staff bungalow, pasture, paddocks and woodland he could command a fine and extensive view of the Warwickshire countryside.

In 1914 he purchased the manorial rights of Henley and so became Lord of the Manor, revived the Court Leet and presented a handsome chain and appropriate robes for the use of the High Bailiff. He also restored the Gild Hall and had prepared a copy, on vellum, of all the extant records of the manor.

In 1922 he was elected a Fellow of the Society of Antiquaries and his interests ranged from archaeological digs on Stratford golf course to collecting leather jacks and bottles, carved coffers and dower chests and paying for expensive monographs on the subjects as well as the restoration of local buildings. Like many self-made men he was determined to prove his place in the past and constructed a coat of arms and these are emblazoned on his tomb in Wootton churchyard with mantling, crest, badge and motto *"Infirmis opitulare"*.

But this idiosyncrasy was outweighed by his extensive charity. During the Boer War, along with Sir John Furley, he designed and supervised the construction and equipment of the first hospital-train to be used in South Africa. In August 1914 they again undertook the provision for the Red Cross Society, of portable hut hospitals and later on in France, they improvised an ambulance train out of French rolling stock. He also erected and maintained a hospital-hut at Wootton for wounded soldiers, of which his daughter, Mrs Barnard, acted as sister-in-charge. For this work he was awarded the CBE in 1918.

In 1919 he built almshouses in the village to the memory of his son Seymour and in 1925 he erected a nurses' home in memory of his wife Lucy who died in 1921. He was also a generous donor to Stratford-upon-Avon hospital and the local church.

By now he was a retired *"celebrated local resident"*. He died, aged 71 on the 28 October 1928 and is buried at Wootton Wawen. He left £291,000. Among his numerous bequests was £500 to the Newport Rector and Churchwardens to found the *"Lucy Fieldhouse Charity"* to provide bread and meat on Christmas Day to poor, aged persons in the parish of Newport. There is also the W. J. Fieldhouse Trust invested in £6,240 Consols to provide £26 a year at 50p a week, for six people resident within three miles of Newport. He left the residue to his son and daughter exhorting them *"..to be always charitably and benevolently disposed towards the deserving poor, and in all cases of distress and poverty and within their power and means to subscribe liberally to charitable institutions and so maintain the escutcheon of my house, and if they have ever seen anything in my life that is honest and good that they will for my sake strive to copy it tenfold, and if anything that is evil that they will shun it as they would a serpent"*.

Only one person from Newport attended the funeral. There is no Fieldhouse at Wootton Wawen yet every Christmas a wreath appears on the family tomb. In Newport nobody remembers the local lad who for seventy years brought deep, sweet music to their devotions.

NOTES.

Eight. William John Fieldhouse.

1. Victoria County History of Warwickshire, Vol., 3, (1965)
2. *Wootten Wawen Its History And Records*, courtesy Warwick Library.
3. Information from Mr.C.J.Fieldhouse, Market Drayton, December 1982.
4. Information from Mrs.C. Dipple, Westwood Hoe, North Devon.
5. Information from Mr.R.Simpson, Wotten Wawen, Solihull.
6. Solihull Libraries and Arts Department, local studies collection.
7. City of Birmingham Public Libraries, local studies, for obituaries from Birmingham Post and Birmingham Mail.
8. Correspondence with Parker, Winder and Achurch Ltd., Camp Hill, Birmingham.
9. Newport parish register extract for 1917.

9. The Surgeons of Newport.

The Baddeley family served the medical needs of Newport for over two hundred years. They were here before our starting point of 1795, for the "Newport Advertiser" in December 1905 states the family was:

> *".... one of the oldest and most highly respected families in Newport; a family upon whom William Adams conferred a unique privilege in connection with the Grammar School when he founded and endowed that establishment."*

These Baddeleys were nephews of William Adams and the privilege was that the family of John Baddeley (Badulie), and other named families, should have "priority of admission" over the eighty free scholars specified in the constitution of the Grammar School.

It was not just a family but a social and professional network based on a common code, values and skills and above the pressures of politics, class or money. This enabled them in later years to adopt and apply the work of Pasteur and to advocate changes in public health despite the opposition of a wide range of townspeople. It was a family and professional network that gave them security, independence and integrity. The closeness of the ties lead to family names becoming perpetuated as Christian names and cousins often marrying cousins.

The century from 1795 saw vast improvements in medicine and surgery beginning with Edward Jenner`s smallpox vaccine in 1798, chloroform in 1847, Lister`s antiseptic surgery in 1865, Pasteur's germ theory in 1878, Roentgen and X-rays, through to the age of antibiotics, with Fleming`s discovery of penicillin in 1928.

Newport, being in the countryside and with a long established supply of clean water, did not have the scale of the public health problems of the Victorian industrial cities but superstition, guesswork and sheer prejudice saw malnutrition, high infant mortality and a lack of public administration persist. Burial records in Newport for 1856 and 1860 show high levels of infant mortality and these were prosperous years:

	1856	1860
Total recorded burials	60	55
Under the age of one year	25%	34%
Under the age of 5	35%	43%
Under the age of 10	35%	49%

Smallpox may have been eradicated but before and after the First World War Newport schools could still be closed for weeks and deaths ensue because of measles, mumps and whooping cough. There was no local hospital and only a basic system of district nursing thanks to Mary Roddam.

In a will of 1749 we find William Baddeley, Gent, of Smethwick in the County of Stafford, leaving £200 on trust to his father Jno Baddeley and his mother-in-law Mary Adams for his wife Elizabeth and, after her death, to his son Thomas, to be used for his maintenance and education until he reached the age of 21. Elizabeth Baddeley died aged 27 in 1852 when Thomas was only two.

Thomas Baddeley, described as surgeon of Newport, married Martha, second daughter of Bernard Holland, described as Bernard of the Rea, at Highley on 3 January 1777. A branch of the Hollands were prominent in Newport affairs throughout the 19th Century. Bernard had married Catherine daughter of a Mr Holmes of Stamford Hall near Newport. Her brother Thomas was for a time a draper in Newport. Her other brother married Mary Holmes, a cousin, from Walsall. Her elder sister married a Mr S. Monger. There were also Hollands at Burwarton, one, Thomas, having three sons the two eldest dying at Newport Grammar School of fever. The third son reputedly became a recluse and a miser!

In 1781 we find Thomas Baddeley, surgeon, selling property in the tanyard and on 14 December 1795 Thomas signed a co-partnership agreement, with bond, with Robert Higgins another Newport surgeon. In 1804 we find him a Lieutenant, then in 1805 a Captain, in the Loyal Newport Corp of Volunteers. By 1812 he was a Burgess as was his son TBB and grandson WEB. In the same year six bells of St Nicholas' Church were recast the second being paid for by a subscription raised by Thomas Baddeley. 8 June 1796 we find him writing from London to his daughter Mary Anne:

> *"My Dear Mary, our hasty journey to this great place, deprives*
> *us the pleasures of receiving and answering your letters, which,*
> *we suppose, may fix the times for our sending for you to*
> *Newport, with the consent of your good Uncle and Aunt Monger.*
> *We would come through Ludlow, if we had hopes, that, our*
> *Brothers and Sisters would accompany us home; and, at*
> *present, intend leaving here, about the end of this week, or the*
> *beginning of next; loath to decide our intentions for a day or*
> *two. We unite in love to all, with our blessing to yourself.*
> *Your affectionate father (in haste), Thos Baddeley."*

Thomas Baddeley died in August 1828 by which time he had been joined by his son Thomas Bernard Baddeley. In 1811 we find accounts of TBB for the hire of gigs, as a member of the Oyster Club and the Coffee Room at the *Red Lion* and ordering wine for a coursing meeting. In 1814 he was a member of the Newport Patrol which kept watch at night during the Napoleonic Wars. By 1838 he was a Burgess and a Bailiff. On 10 August 1809 at the age of 24 and newly qualified, he married Isabella Hornblower a widow, and daughter of Edward Holmes a lawyer at Walsall, a marriage within the family.

The family lived in a large town house *The Limes,* now 10 High Street next to Baddeley Court. With them was Robert Kyffin a surgeons' assistant who moved next door to number 12 after his marriage. Robert was a man of property and kept his own servants. In 1846 he bought the former *White Horse Inn* for £1,250 and in 1859 sold it to the new Market Company for £1,400 for demolition to build the Market Hall. When he died in 1877 aged 77 he had just under £1,000, a tidy next egg.

Thomas Baddeley had six other children besides TBB. The eldest was Catherine Martha born in 1779 who married John Clarke of Peatling Hall, Leicestershire in 1810. He died in 1818 and between the age of 31 to 35 she had five children, the eldest Sarah Catherine married Marston Buzzard a surgeon from Lutterworth. Years later we find a grand niece, Eliza Catherine Buzzard, in Newport, acting as a trustee to her Great Aunts, Mary Anne Cooper and Elizabeth Adams Baddeley, the second sister, at the Old Hall [now Linden Hall a doctors' surgery]. Mary Anne is listed as a proprietor of houses and was lending money to local businesses. In 1812 she married John Cooper of High Offley, Staffordshire, as his second wife. He already had six children and was to have six more before his death in 1819 at the age of 44. The two eldest boys of Mary Anne both became surgeons. Henry Ralph Cooper (1813-1864) who died at Ixworth in Suffolk also had a son Charles Baddeley Cooper who died a surgeon, in 1883, in Canada. Frederick Thomas Cooper (1814-1875) was a surgeon in Tunstall, Staffordshire. Mary Anne's third son, Charles Alfred was a clergyman who died in 1853 aged 34 in Kingston, Jamaica, of yellow fever. His son from his second marriage, also

Charles Alfred, also became a surgeon and died young in 1884 at Ilkeston, Derbyshire.

The second son of Thomas Baddeley and brother of TBB, was William Holmes Baddeley who became a soldier in the Indian army and died in 1818 aged 30 in Hyderabad. He was unmarried. The third brother, Charles Holland Baddeley, was also a soldier in the Honourable East India Company but survived to die in Lancashire aged 72. He owned what is now Station House in Station Road, Newport, then apparently known as Aston Terrace, which was occupied by his sister Mary Anne Cooper until on 19 January 1849 he sold the house and the adjoining fields to the Shropshire Union Railway and Canal Company. The house had a pew in Church Aston Church. Charles Holland Baddeley married into the Clarke family of Leicester and had a son Edward Adams Baddeley (b.1850). He lived at Wigston Hall, Leicester for many years. Charles James Baddeley, his nephew, was a farmer at Wigston, and acted as executor for William Edward Baddeley (1816-68), his brother, and held shares in Newport Market Company.

The last son of Thomas Baddeley, Edward Monger Baddeley was a surgeon as well but died aged 25 in 1820. He is buried in Holborn, London.

Thomas Bernard Baddeley had eight surviving children but it appears his first child, Isabella born in 1810 died young and the Isabella who died aged 67 in 1889 was named after her deceased elder sister which was usual at that time. She lived at Church Aston, near Newport, with her two other unmarried sisters, Elizabeth Holmes Baddeley (d.1869) and Catherine Baddeley (d.1877). It was often difficult for so many daughters of this class to find husbands in small rural communities. The eldest son was also Thomas Bernard Baddeley and became a solicitor practising in Newport. His office was sold and demolished when the Market Hall was built in 1860. He lived for many years, unmarried, next to the former *Plume of Feathers* at the end of St Mary`s Street. He died in September 1882 while returning from Newport railway station and is buried in Newport next to his brother George Augustus Baddeley (1823-83) a surgeon at Gnosall. Charles James Baddeley was, as we have seen above, a farmer at Wigston in Leicestershire. Herbert Hancox Baddeley, the youngest, born in 1831, became a sailor and settled and married in Victoria, Australia in 1851, and had five children the last one dying unmarried in 1939.

TBB died in June 1846 and is buried in the family tomb, which is still retained in Newport Churchyard. He was succeeded by his son William Edward Baddeley who had qualified in Edinburgh and in 1850 described himself as general practitioner. In that year he married Sarah Webb aged 19, from Church Eaton in Staffordshire. Sarah died at *The Limes* in 1922 aged 91.

Medicine has its own momentum and some of the 19th Century changes, such as chloroform, vaccination and antiseptic surgery have been mentioned and these no doubt affected the practice of the Newport doctors. But health is determined by wider factors as the Victorians discovered, these include poverty, malnutrition and living conditions, put simply, air, water and sewage. By 1851 half the population lived in the urban areas and though the scale of problems was low compared to these areas Newport could not ignore the consequences of cholera and typhoid, overcrowding, poor housing, poverty and problems of sanitation. The connection between dirt and disease was known and though we did not have the *"Great Stink"* of London in the 1860`s, or require the massive sewage construction of Bazalgette, the Marsh Brook and the Strine to the east and north of the town were open sewers, which the prosperous townsfolk of the 1850`s found offensive and embarrassing.

Before we start on the career of WEB perhaps we can look at Newport in 1850, the year he married and when he had succeeded his father. Historians have said that if you could choose the best decade to have lived in it would be the 1850`s. Certainly in Newport there was a new vigour and determination to improve. It was the decade of agricultural prosperity known as the *"Golden Age"* of farming. The High Street was completely re-paved with granite setts, by public subscription. As it would have been ridiculous to have returned the livestock markets back to the open street, a new Market Hall and livestock market was constructed (1860) under Act of Parliament paid for by shares all raised locally. The old market hall and butter cross were demolished. New roads were constructed such as Stafford Street, Avenue Road and New Street. These opened up the town, particularly the Marsh, to developments such as the cemetery, opened in 1859, and the new workhouse in 1855. This optimism reflected the national confidence epitomised by the Great Exhibition of 1851. The nation had emerged from the *"Hungry Forties"*, from social discontent, possible revolution, mass movements like Chartism, strikes and riots, several on the Coalbrookdale coalfield just down the road. Newport too suffered riots with the huge influx of Irish into the town after the Irish Famine. The Irish were also crammed into the most overcrowded and insanitary yards off the High Street. The 1840`s were years of industrial and agricultural depression and saw the return of cholera in 1848. These years focussed minds on the need for reform. The progressive men in Newport particularly the doctors, were listening.

Even so change did not come overnight and it is typical that the best description of conditions before 1850 comes from Dr. C.E. Baddeley addressing a public meeting on the *"water question"* in January 1889. Since the Middle Ages, he said, water had been supplied free from wells near Church Aston known as the Wells or Walls Head. It had then been conveyed by 2" pipes to four cisterns at Upper Bar, Market Square, the Church and Church Square, opposite the Grammar School. These cisterns or tanks were frequently the receptacles for dead kittens and dogs and the water was unwholesome, and discharged so slowly from small lead pipes that people had to wait to get their share of water. Only one house in the town had its own supply. High Street properties had their own wells but since Newport is on sand and gravel these were polluted by effluent and waste of all kinds. About 1840 the Burgesses, the traditional administrators of *"Nova Burga"*, used money from the sale of land to the canal to improve the mains, to construct a reservoir [Millwood Mere] and put in free hydrants, or stand pipes, at various points around the town.

A summary of the water history in the *"Newport Advertiser"* of 20 February 1909 points out that the *"free"* water supply was a privilege conferred by the Burgesses and paid for out of land rents. It also states how this free access had been abused and the cisterns polluted. The Burgesses had covered over the cisterns and between 1815-20, with the financial assistance of Thomas Jukes Collier, a local coal and iron master, had fitted them with gas lamps. A wise precaution when the Parish Register of 1665 records that Anne Brooks actually drowned in the Talbot Cistern when she slipped off the steps going down to it. They offered a private supply to houses for 15/- pa in 1817.

> *"This water is conveyed into large open cisterns placed almost in the centre of the streets, and these, independent of being ill adapted for the convenience for those who have not pumps, are in dark nights very dangerous, especially to strangers. It is singular that these cisterns are suffered to remain in there present state, and that more convenient devices have not been adopted to answer the same purpose."*

Preface to "Silvesters Housekeepers Pocket Book" 1801.

This account says that in 1843 the Burgesses set up a Committee of Inquiry under the High Steward, Sir Thomas Fletcher Fenton Boughey, which recommended that an increased supply of water and a new scheme of distribution was necessary, as the cisterns were a *"nuisance, dangerous to the public health"*. Mr William Massey was instructed to sink new artesian wells, appropriately called *"Baddeleys wells"*, and construct a reservoir for fire extinguishing, all on Col. Leeke`s land at Church Aston. They are still there. The cost was £1,000 met from the sale of land to the canal company. This extension brought more private customers and increased rents so that expenses were met from revenue.

Baddeley's Wells – near Millwood Mere

Henry Fisher, a local solicitor, and former deputy steward to the Burgesses, at an enquiry in June 1885 said:

> *"The inhabitants generally, rich and poor, formerly took*
> *water out of certain cisterns. Into these dead dogs and cats*
> *were often flung and they also contained putrid matter.*
> *These were closed and hydrants erected, the inhabitants*
> *drawing the water gratuitously."*

"Putrid matter" included all kinds of *"nuisances"*, the mess from the cattle markets in the streets and the unhealthy smells from an overcrowded churchyard and burials within the church. A budding poet in April 1856 waxed lyrical on the problems;

> *"And when the prime fatstock is shown*
> *Thy balmy gales we sniff, Cologne,*
> *Nor long to drink thy perfumed air,*
> *Where Fair is foul and foul is Fair.*
> *Here from the turf in mouldering heap,*
> *Unhealthy exhalations creep.*
> *And mingle with the air we draw,*
> *In spite of sanitary law."*

To be fair he did look forward ten years when:

> *"An extra-mural market then*
> *Shall claim its cattle, sheep and men,*
> *The Churchyard Turf shall hallowed be*
> *And death shall have his cemetery."*

The water improvements were limited. Since the hydrants were fed by gravity there was never enough pressure to serve the higher districts such as Upper Bar. There was never enough water to flush sewers. When fire broke out valves had to be closed at the waterworks and water fed from the reservoir. This gave two problems, one, the pressure was never enough to reach the tallest buildings and secondly the water-pipes were polluted for days afterwards.
This deficiency is illustrated by the fire reported on 13 August 1870 when the top half of the new Market Hall was destroyed:

> *"It was so difficult to maintain a supply of water, however, that neither of these last engines* [from Lilleshall Hall and The Lilleshall Company] *could be employed at the fire and all that the Aqualate engine used was carried by hand from pumps around. Of course this scarcity arose in part from the long drought; but the ordinary supply is sadly deficient for ordinary purposes, and therefore cannot be expected adequately to meet any emergency like this."*

The name of William Edward Baddeley does not appear in the petition to remove the cattle markets from the High Street but in 1859 he did purchase 10 shares (£200) in the new Market Company. By 1861 he was living comfortably with his wife and three children at 10 High Street, with a groom, cook, two female servants and a seventeen-year-old nurse. He had built up an extensive country practice but by 1866 was ill. He took as an assistant and later partner the twenty-three year old Dr. Richard M Hickman. A year later this young man had the whole weight of the practice: *"He was in the saddle or the gig from morning till night."* A pleasant, amiable and respected man he was killed on the 27 October 1872 when his horse bolted at Donnington while returning to Newport. He was buried at Shrewsbury.

WEB died aged 51 on the 2 October 1868 and was buried in Newport churchyard. It appears the intention was for Dr. Hickman to run the practice until Charles Edward Baddeley, son of WEB, had qualified but in 1872 he was only seventeen. It was in these tragic circumstances that Dr. Ernest Alfred Elkington came to Newport in 1872 to take over a practice created by the Baddeley family in the 1780's. He was born on the 21 December 1848, a year of revolutions, the son of Dr George Elkington of Edgbaston, Birmingham. Elkington, a name familiar in Birmingham, was to become as influential in Newport, for only a year earlier, Tom Collins, Headmaster of the Grammar School, had married a Minnie Elkington, also from Birmingham.

Ernest Elkington attended King Edwards' School, where Tom Collins was teaching at the time, Masons College, and gained his MB at London. He continued his studies at Edinburgh University where he formed a close friendship with Lister of antiseptic surgery fame. He went to Paris where he got caught up in the Franco-Prussian War of 1870 leading to the siege and occupation of Paris by the Prussians, and the French surrender. In March 1871 there was a radical rebellion by the Paris Commune which was savagely put down by French troops while the Prussians watched. During these stirring events Pasteur was at the Ecole Normale in Paris developing his germ theory which was to profoundly influence Elkington and the world. It was from such a background that this young man came to take over a quiet, rural practice.

E.A. Ernest Elkington, M.B., M.R.C.S.

Ernest had a brother, Dr George Elkington of Birmingham and a sister, Charlotte, who was a nurse, matron at St Thomas' Hospital, London and Queens Hospital, Birmingham and a personal friend of Florence Nightingale. She died aged 94 in January 1947 at Gable End, Granville Avenue, Newport, the home of her two nieces. She is buried at Llwyngwril, North Wales.

However from a medical point of view Newport was no picturesque country town. Despite the improvements of the 1850's Ernest found a community with no sewage system, people crowded into courts or yards using cesspits, ashpits or night emptying of privies, euphemistically known as *"night soil"*. Some houses as in Stafford Street did not even have space for privies. On the west side of the town sewage ran into open cesspits then into the Strine at four points; on the east side the Marsh Brook was an open sewer draining the railway, the workhouse and the tannery, then discharging into the Strine which was so offensive by the time it reached Longford, a mile to the west, it brought loud protests from the Leeke family, who lived at Longford Hall. In a letter to the *"Advertiser"* Ralph Leeke explains how he has the right to divert water to his millpool and waterwheel but these were silted up with foul sewage while the wells were polluted, and there were offensive smells and cases of fever in the cottages near Longford Church. The whole watercourse was choked with reeds through sewage.

Identifying and persuading people of the problem was one thing, finding a system to produce the changes required was another, at national and local level. The Victorians tended to produce specific remedies for specific needs, the *"ad hoc"* approach, such as Health Boards for health, Guardians for the poor, Highway Boards, Sanitary Authorities while underneath was a whole warren of medieval institutions such as Vestries and Burgesses. These overlapped, competed and conflicted and frequently consisted of the same group of gentleman anxious about the costs on the rates. These problems often had a common cause so that poor sanitation and water led to ill health that led to poverty and the workhouse. While Dr Elkington and Dr. Baddeley fought the cause locally the national politicians struggled to find a system of local government which would provide a comprehensive, acceptable and funded answer to these social needs.

In 1872 Dr Elkington found the medieval Burgesses still providing the water supply, paid for out of the rents of land within the town. Often they had not met for decades and, through inheritance many Burgesses were remote and the work was left to local men as deputy stewards and bailiffs. At this time the deputy-steward was Henry Fisher a local solicitor. In 1854 a new Act had set up the Marsh Trust to manage the marsh property enclosed in 1764. It was the duty of the Marsh Trustees to use their income to improve the town. We must remember at this time the *"town"* began and ended at the canal bridge and Upper Bar. This Act recognised that the Burgesses owned certain cisterns, mains and service pipes but gave the Marsh Trustees the right of access to the waterworks and to make new works, and to lay down conditions as regards digging up the streets, replacing excavation, and clearing rubbish. The Trustees had the right to repair watercourses and charge the Burgesses if they should fail in their duties. There is an obvious clash of interests here as the *"Advertiser"* noted in April 1856:

> *".... we are glad to hear the Burgesses have resolved to remove the water supply from the centre of the street, and that Mr Massey has undertaken the work…because of the cost the Burgesses have been forced to adopt a water rate increasing payments to better off property, nearly the same for second class property, and 5/- pa for cottages. It is hoped the Marsh Trustees will lose no time in commencing repairs [new granite setts in the High Street] and in making their approach to the Marsh. [Avenue Road]"*

There was also the Vestry meeting with various duties as regards parish roads and appointing overseers to collect the rates for the other bodies such as the Guardians. The Guardians had been created by the Poor Law Act of 1834 a logical, utilitarian approach to poverty which paid no heed to traditional boundaries so that the Newport Union and Workhouse stretched from Donnington in Shropshire to Gnosall in Staffordshire. As the link between poverty and living conditions was recognised, Guardians became rural and urban sanitary authorities as well. It was from these bodies that the system of elected Urban and Rural Sanitary Boards came into being in 1875, known as District Boards, to become Urban and Rural District Councils from 1894. District Boards took over highways and streets from the Highway Board and the Marsh Trust; water supply from the Burgesses; sanitary duties from the Guardians and the Fire Brigade and street lighting. In 1886 the Burgesses were abolished though the Marsh Trust lingered on until an Act of Parliament in 1930 absorbed it into Newport Urban District Council.

The District or Local Boards of 1875 were the authorities created by the Local Government Act of 1872 and the Public Health Act of 1872 under the centralised Local Government Board. They combined multifarious duties including a variety of sanitary measures dealing with sewage, scavenging and cleansing, the supply of water, cellar dwellings and lodging houses, infected meat, infectious diseases and hospitals, epidemics, mortuaries, the making and repair of highways, street lighting, recreation and slaughter houses. More important they had powers to make bye-laws, to levy rates and borrow money. Fifty-four Newport gentlemen were nominated for the twelve seats but forty-two kindly withdrew. Even more important the District Boards provided the first effective framework for reform. At first the medical men stayed clear but in May 1883 Dr. Elkington was co-opted and in March 1886 all four local doctors - Baddeley, Brereton, Davies and Elkington - were on the Board.

Lets see how things developed from 12 January 1856 when Mr Holland advertised the sale of the sweepings of Newport street manure at the rear of the gas works – in seven lots!

In August 1866 came the Report of a Sub-Committee of the Board of Guardians into the health of the town after the cholera outbreak of 1865-6. It found the sewers *"satisfactory"* and water *"adequate"* though there were problems in the courts and yards. The worst offence was the Marsh Brook with:

> *"Bleak slimy banks which lie reeking under a hot sun,*
> *giving forth those poisonous exhalations which are*
> *so injurious to the human system."*

In November the Guardians appointed an Inspector of Nuisances and in December 1872 the Burgesses were urging townsfolk to link their premises to the main pipe in the High Street.

In March 1873 the Guardians commissioned another report by Mr J.F.Cobb. This revealed that the drainage was almost universally carried into the town sewers running down the main street and then into the Strine. If house drains were properly constructed and trapped there was little nuisance but in the yards and alleys such as *"Watkins` Yard"*, *"Bellmans Yard"* and *"Cock Yard"* conditions were not good with refuse, ashes, slops and filth of all kinds thrown near the houses causing fever and disease. Street gratings were *"offensive"* but the most offensive was still the Marsh Brook. The Strine near the canal wharf was taking half the filth and sewage, including the contents of 60-70 water closets from Chetwynd End which by now was a better-off suburb. Water supply was good but new pipes, pumps and taps were needed. It was the question of the town sewage that needed settling.

In June 1875 came another survey this time by Dr. W.N.Thursfield the Medical Officer of Health for the County. This can be said to be more professional, thorough and unbiased. Commissioned by the Guardians it would have to be put into effect by the new District Board. In 1875 Newport had a population of 3,500 people overlapping three parishes. Its main problem, he concluded, lay in the half dozen courts or yards where surface water could not escape and because of the *"dirty habits"* of the people living there. They needed *"educating"*. He makes the distinction between surface drainage and sewage disposal of waste. The two had become confused and dangerous. Regarding excrement removal, the existing drainage was of the old brick construction and was a dry system, that is, unflushed, and was no problem while people had gardens to take and bury the waste. But there were already 60 water closets so that a mixed system of "dry" and flushing sewers was required, a dry system in the courts *on account of the difficulty of keeping water latrines in good order in poor neighbourhoods.",* where there should be watertight cesspits separate from land drainage and surface water.

Water closets, though a private boon, were a public menace, particularly when discharged into square, brick drains meant for storm and surface water, which would not take a flow and frequently leaked. On the Wellington side of the town three of them emptied into open cess pools, visible and offensive, and then into the Strine. On the east side of Newport the Marsh Brook was the common sewer. Dr. Thursfield proposed culverting the brook which ran openly from behind the workhouse and the cemetery, under a bridge at what is now Meadow Road, behind the rows of poor cottages in Marsh Lane and Underhills factory, then through the tannery at Tan Bank and into the Strine. He suggested intercepting sewers to divert the seven outfalls into the Strine into filtration and treatment beds to the west of the town.

As for water supply, since Newport stood on sand and gravel and was closely populated, well and pump water should not be used for drinking. There was a good supply of public water though more standpipes were needed.

He identified four *"noxious"* trades. The tannery, though no real problem despite complaints; fishcuring where new drains were needed to take the overflow of waste salt water; fat-boiling which had been *"much-complained of"* but where he found no nuisance; tripe-boiling which he found *"clean and reasonable".*

His one fear was sewer gas so he recommended that all waste pipes should be trapped, soil pipes should be at a certain height outside the house, and there should be no drains under houses.

The Burgesses, near to death, had a burst of life in August 1880, receiving a report from Henry J. Martin a London engineer who suggested deepening Baddeley's wells, erecting a 70` high tower, and a reservoir on the hill behind the Wheatsheaf at Chetwynd Aston. This would give an increased supply and enough pressure for hydrants to reach the top of the highest buildings without fire engines. They argued about this all through 1881, but at least in 1882 they stirred themselves to extend the mains into New Street, Beaumaris Road, Wellington Road and Avenue Road with seven additional hydrants and stop valves.

Meanwhile what of the Baddeleys? Charles Edward Baddeley was born in 1855 the eldest son of W.E. Baddeley. When his father died in 1868 he was only a teenager but in 1881 he was qualified and joined Dr. Elkington as a partner in Baddeley, Elkington and Morgan. He had been educated at the Grammar School and then King`s College, London where he studied medicine. He obtained the Diploma of the Society of Apothecaries in 1878, and held the resident appointment of Assistant and House Physician at King`s College Hospital in 1878-9. In 1880 he took the membership of the Royal College of Surgeons (England) and the degree of Bachelor of Medicine at the University of London, with Honours in Medicine. In 1881 he was resident medical officer at Queen Charlotte`s Hospital, London. After his partnership he resided at Gnosall where his uncle, George Augustus Baddeley was a surgeon and medical officer. Charles in turn became registrar of births and deaths, public vaccinator and medical officer at Gnosall. His uncle George died in September 1883 and in 1885 Charles resigned and removed to Newport where he became medical officer for the district and the workhouse, an appointment he held for thirteen years. He became highly popular with his patients and soon was one of the dominant figures in the area. He had a surgery in St Marys Street until 1887 and in 1890 was resident at Weston House, High Street [ex-Masons, butchers 2004], where a son was born in 1896.

Meanwhile E.A. Elkington had married Maria Eliza Derington daughter of Thomas Derington of Chetwynd Villa, Chetwynd. She was an invalid and died in June 1885. In June 1888 he married, very quietly, Anne Isabella Baddeley, the eldest daughter and fourth child of W.E. Baddeley. The medical partnership was sealed by marriage.

The second son of WEB was Thomas Webb Baddeley, M.A. Cantab, a solicitor who died in 1896 aged 39. William Edward Baddeley, (1860-1931), the third son, was M.A. from Christ Church, Oxford and a solicitor with W.M. How of Shrewsbury, but was long retired with his mother at The Limes, then at Gower House next door. Keen on football, cricket and bowls, he seems never to have played preferring chess at the Literary Institute, where he was president *" of a retiring and somewhat reserved disposition, Mr Baddeley was one of the most generous of men and performed numerous acts of benevolence in an unostentatious manner"*. He is said to have gone poaching and gave things away with abandon. He was known affectionately as "Trot". Genial, quiet and unostentatious were terms used about the other brother George Herbert Adams Baddeley who also died at The Limes, the home of his mother. He was an auctioneer at Stafford and died aged 42 in 1905. The youngest daughter of WEB. Charlotte Evelyn (1864-1931) died soon after her brother and sister, at Gower House. She too was described as benevolent and unostentatious. She was an active sportswoman, fishing, walking in Switzerland and keen on dogs. She did the things familiar to a spinster daughter, the Parish Church, Nursing Association and the Choral Society.

In the 1880's Newport now had two doctors partners by profession, by family and in their reforming zeal. There was also for the first time a local government structure that would allow these changes to come about and the realisation that changes could not be paid by levying charges on the users but would need a general rate to which all contributed equally. As early as 1876 the Surveyor for the Board, George Hammond, was reporting on the state of the town in much the same language as previous reports. In May 1885 he published a more detailed account for the Board. He pointed out that the original *"sewers"* were designed for carrying house slops and storm water and the outfall for these were spread around the town as owners of land used them for irrigation. It has to be remembered that these deposits were then not so offensive as there were no water closets. In fact J.H. Adams of Adams House in the High Street objected to a new sewer and the diversion of sewage *"which has been used for irrigation by Mr Adams and his predecessors in title from time immemorial."* The type of sewer varied from 2" to 7" made of uncemented brick or plain pipes or rubble. Some sewage went direct into surface drains. Below the church the sewers were self cleansing but in other parts were so shallow *"that offensive deposits have accumulated, undermined by rats, percolating into surrounding soil; no ventilation."* He lists nine outfalls. (1) through land from Wellington Road belonging to B.H. Smallwood, a local solicitor, and J.H. Adams to the Strine taking from Upper Bar, Station Road, Marsh Road and Wellington Road. (2). Through J.H. Adams' property from High Street opposite Mrs Baddeley's, the Raven and Bell, National Provincial Bank and Smallwood's. [Smallwood Lodge]. (3). From Chalmers, [now Boot's Chemist], Raven and Bell, across the road through Cock Yard to a huge cesspool on the land of J.H. Adams then through gutters to the Strine. (4) (5) and (6) went along Salters Lane to the Strine; (7) served Bridge Terrace; (8). From Addisons [67 High Street] through Lower bar and St Marys Street; (9). The Marsh Brook.

Mr Hammond recommended nearly four miles of new sewers using the old ones as storm drains. These should consist of 9"- 18" glazed, socket pipes with adequate gradients to one outfall works. And so appears the glazed sewer pipe that probably did as much for health as penicillin!

In January 1881 a public meeting was held in the Catholic School on the water question. Dr C.E. Baddeley outlined the history and the proposals of the Board which were in essence to purchase the works off the Burgesses and carry out improvements. Such improvements and any deficit would have to be met from the rates. (Cries of "no, no".) Objectors wanted things to simply remain as they were; they claimed that wastage was the problem and that if people wanted taps higher up their property they should pay. Dr Baddeley, exasperated, said the free hydrants would remain, but did they want a voluntary scheme or a compulsory one from the Local Government Board?

The District Board soldiered on despite the overseer running off with the funds and charges of corruption in the elections. In January 1891 an enquiry was held in the Marsh Trust Room in the Market Hall, which few people attended given all the fuss. This was on an application by the Board for a loan of £1,000 to purchase the freehold of Baddeley's Wells and the reservoir, and construct a new main and tank. In January 1893 the opponents of the scheme held a public meeting in the Market Hall under the slogan *"the voice of the people should govern the town"*. It passed a resolution against the *"uncalled for and unprincipled and ridiculous water scheme"*. The election of March 1893 was fought on two issues, the "water question" (that is the expense) and the extension of the sanitary area to include places such as Chetwynd End and Church Aston. The sound-bites rang out: *"protect ancient rights"*; *"free water"* and *"no water required."* The latter was on a large sign in Stafford Street one of the dirtiest areas. The Advertiser sarcastically commented *"no water required has been the motto for a long time of many of the people living there"*. In the end two "anti" and two "pro" were elected. Mr W.Hayward, the local grocer believed that

> *".... water closets were all very well in large towns but in a place like Newport there was nothing like the old fashioned way of having them at the top of the garden."*

R.R.Pearce, the Primitive Methodist, owner of the Tanyard dramatically concluded

> *"Depend upon it we shall not be blessed by the inhabitants of Newport in the present and in the near future if we carry out this scheme at enormous expense."*

On the 5 August 1893 Major General Henry Darley Crozier RE carried out a local enquiry on the application by the Newport Urban Sanitary Authority to borrow £2,400 to improve the water supply. It reviewed the history, all the previous reports and outlined the needs and the proposals which were, to provide toilets, to flush sewers, to include new areas, to provide fire hydrants, to replace polluted wells and prevent soil being permeated with filth. The Inspector had no doubts:

> *" The local Board have decided to make this application, and I don't pay much attention to any defeated party. Of course you can produce your evidence and I will report it to the Board. [The Local Government Board]. I think this scheme seems to be a proper one. What does the Local Government Board exist for, but to press on these authorities that they will incur a grave responsibility if they fail to produce an adequate water supply. The Board is most anxious that these things should be done. It is for the good of the town. People will not come to this place unless there is a good supply of water and proper sewerage"*.

The work of Elkington and Baddeley was endorsed, the opposition had no future, neither had the District Board. From 9 January 1895 it was replaced by Newport Urban District Council which included all the urban areas of the adjacent parishes. Drs Elkington and Baddeley transferred from one to the other. They found an ally in Sir Thomas Boughey who believed landowners had duties as well as rights and in 1896, on his proposition, it was moved that there should be a committee to start improving the sewage of Newport in every way. It was, he said, no use having water conveniences if there was no sewage system. There were murmurs of dissent on cost, all of them from shopkeepers, but he persisted:

> *".... they had good town water and it was the duty of that Council to put on that water and so save the town from disease and the lives of the many of the inhabitants from danger".*

By now Baddeley had had enough and was removed from the Council in 1896 for non-attendance. He wrote to the newspaper decrying the opposition, that is the four men who had opposed everything and had rendered progress difficult by long and acrimonious discussion on things decided already in Committee. He blamed the weak Chairman and the lack of rules of procedure. He was premature, for in November 1897 the Sanitary Committee after what was described as the most arduous task in time and future cost any committee had ever taken, produced a comprehensive scheme of drainage for the town including the purchase of over 14 acres of land in Mill Lane [Broomfield Road] for treatment works. It was to add 30-40% to the rates. It was supported by Dr Elkington and Sir Thomas Boughey with even a fervent opponent agreeing *"it should be proceeded with as soon as possible"*. It was carried "nem con".

The Advertiser called it *"the approaching triumph."* The Council had now spent over £4,000 and was committed to a further £7,000 exclusive of the purchase of land. Dr Elkington cut the first sod of the sewerage works in 1901; by 1902 most property was connected to the main sewers and on 23 March 1904 Dr Elkington formally opened the new sewage works. The Advertiser praised:

> *"Dr Elkington, who has safely piloted the scheme through the midst of many dangers and difficulties, at an expenditure of time and energy very few men would care to give to such a task."*

However a surprising new opponent appeared. Tom Collins the former Headmaster of the Grammar School was elected in 1903. He had a romantic view of the working man and had designated himself his protector. For example he supported the *"working mans right"* to the free water from the street hydrants, forgetting it was the hydrants that encouraged property owners not to connect to the mains and led to enormous costs in scavenging and cleansing and to a huge wastage of water. Enlightened in many things educational, Collins had little vision in social matters. He attacked Elkington in his autobiography, pouring scorn on the lack of social status of small town Councillors and on the unnecessary and costly scheme. Elkington admitted that £15,200 was a lot for a town of 3,200 people but much of the increase had been brought about by the high standards required by central government and the cost of land. Collins washed his hands: *"he was truly thankful that he had not got it on his conscience that he had taken any part in it."* In November 1907 when the UDC sought powers to force the conversion of privies to water closets Collins objected on the grounds that cottage rents would go up, workers would freeze and *"nothing could be more sanitary than the old style of privy, if it were properly looked after"*.

In June 1906 Dr Elkington gave up the chairmanship of the Sanitary Committee of the UDC which he had held since its formation in 1894:

> *"His education and his scientific attainments, coupled with his assiduity and zeal have rendered him a valuable voluntary worker in the best interests of his fellow townsmen".*

There is no doubt that it was the force of his argument and his sincerity, which pushed through views ahead of his time, in the teeth of opposition. He did not seek re-election in 1907.

He lived at Smallwood Lodge which in August 1891 was connected by telephone to his surgery on the other side of the High Street at Gower House.

He later lived at 47 Upper Bar at the side of Smallwood Lodge where his initials, and those of his wife, and the date 1891, can still be seen above the window. This was a very comfortable house with stables, a large garden and five acres of grass extending as far as the Gravelly Walks, yet all on the High Street.

He was a small, robust man, who rode to hounds and could cover, on his rounds, a hundred miles a day needing four horses. It had its dangers. In December 1902, accompanied by his page, he was driving along High Street when the wheel came off his gig. The doctor and the boy just retained their seats. Sartorially he had a goatee beard, frock coat and always wore a bowler hat. People remembered he could be quite sharp and meticulous always paying his accounts on time, always on the same day. After Dr C.E. Baddeley left in 1898 he had other partners Drs Hedges, Cuthbert and Evans, until he was joined by his son *"Dr George"* on January 18 1921. The surgery was at Gower House, 12 High Street. He had the reputation of being very skilled in childbirth rarely losing a mother or a baby. He had nine children himself.

He was involved in many other things in the town, the Burial Board, medical officer to the Workhouse and the local Friendly Societies. He was a Governor of Adams Grammar School and Churchwarden between 1886-1890. He helped establish the Literary Institute.

Dr E.A.Elkington retired in 1932 and went to live at Gable End in Granville Avenue, where he died aged 87 on 17 November 1936. Mrs Elkington nee Baddeley, had died in 1930 but his nine children survived him. There was Dr "George", Captain Frank Elkington, Major E.B.Elkington RE and Dr John St Clare Elkington a physician at St Thomas' hospital and a Cambridge Fellow. Of the five girls Miss I.M. and Miss A.M. were at Gable End in 1947, Alice Margaret having worked in the Food Office in Newport during the war. Miss D.L.

taught violin and piano at Shrewsbury Girls High School; Miss E.H. was in South Africa doing orthopaedic work having trained under Agnes Hunt. Margery Elkington married Dr Richard Harper in 1931 having obtained a B.A. Oxon and a doctorate at the University of Paris.

Dr C.E. Baddeley continued in the town until 1898. If Dr Elkington was the heart of reform, Dr Baddeley provided the brain. It was his profound knowledge that provided the efficient high pressure water service and an up-to-date scientific system of sewers and sewage disposal. In 1889 he gained an M.D. at the University of London one of the highest qualifications in sanitary science. He had a profound knowledge of the causation and prevention of the communicable diseases and the general application of bacteriology to the work of public health. In 1898 he moved to Stafford where after practising for a while he went to Belvedere in Kent where he resided the rest of his life. He was a founder of the Old Novaportan Club [Adams Grammar School] and its President in 1912. He died in December of that year aged 57. His stepson Rear Admiral H.G.Wilson, ex-AGS, who had served in the Boxer rebellion and the Battle of the Falklands died aged 73 in 1947.

George Ernest Elkington was the eldest son of Ernest Elkington and was born on the 20 March 1889. He attended Adams Grammar School and graduated in medicine at Birmingham University in 1912. After qualifying he worked as a house surgeon at the General Hospital in Birmingham. Within a week of the war starting in 1914 he was with the army in France and stayed in the RAMC to the end reaching the rank of temporary captain. He also received the Military Cross. In 1921 he joined his father in Elkington, Evans and Elkington. Over the next 38 years there were various partners, Dr J.R. Pooler, Dr Sowerbutts and Dr Neville. He gradually took over his father's professional appointments. In April 1931 he married Kathleen Mary Budgen second daughter of the Rev. Preb. Budgen former Rector of Newport. This was very quietly in the Lady Chapel of Lichfield Cathedral Mrs Elkington, his mother, having recently died. After his father's retirement they went to live at 47 Upper Bar, Smallwood House. The Budgens were a remarkable family with nine children also, who all married into a tight network of local professional, middle class, families. Dr George died in Newport aged 97 in May 1986. His funeral was attended by his three sons, Stephen, Julian and Andrew, who all followed their father into the medical profession though, alas, not in Newport so ending a medical dynasty of 200 years.

He had lived through a period of social change as dramatic as the medical revolution experienced by his father and had maintained the moral sense of duty and standards of his father and that Victorian age. The crucial principle was the sense of duty to the community, a principle that inspired their family for two centuries.

The Baddeleys

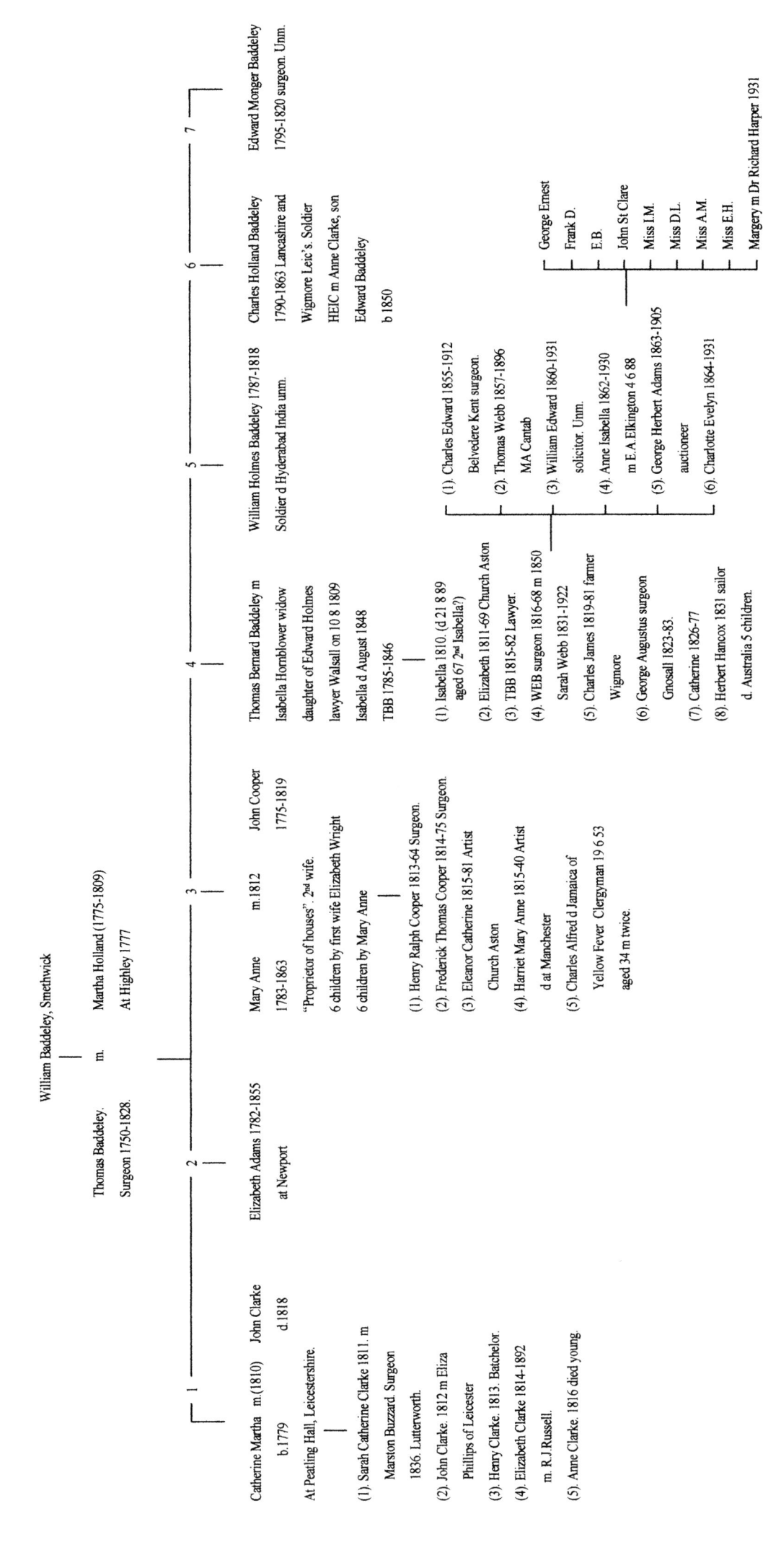

William Baddeley, Smethwick m. Martha Holland (1775-1809) At Highley 1777

1. Thomas Baddeley. Surgeon 1750-1828.

2. Elizabeth Adams 1782-1855 at Newport

3. Mary Anne 1783-1863 m.1812 **John Cooper 1775-1819**
"Proprietor of houses". 2nd wife.
6 children by first wife Elizabeth Wright
6 children by Mary Anne

(1). Henry Ralph Cooper 1813-64 Surgeon.
(2). Frederick Thomas Cooper 1814-75 Surgeon.
(3). Eleanor Catherine 1815-81 Artist Church Aston
(4). Harriet Mary Anne 1815-40 Artist d at Manchester
(5). Charles Alfred d Jamaica of Yellow Fever Clergyman 19 6 53 aged 34 m twice.

4. Thomas Bernard Baddeley m **Isabella Hornblower widow** daughter of Edward Holmes lawyer Walsall on 10 8 1809
Isabella d August 1848
TBB 1785-1846

(1). Isabella 1810. (d 21 8 89 aged 67 2nd Isabella?)
(2). Elizabeth 1811-69 Church Aston
(3). TBB 1815-82 Lawyer.
(4). WEB surgeon 1816-68 m 1850 Sarah Webb 1831-1922
(5). Charles James 1819-81 farmer Wigmore
(6). George Augustus surgeon Gnosall 1823-83.
(7). Catherine 1826-77
(8). Herbert Hancox 1831 sailor d. Australia 5 children.

5. William Holmes Baddeley 1787-1818 Soldier d Hyderabad India unm.

6. Charles Holland Baddeley 1790-1863 Lancashire and Wigmore Leic's. Soldier HEIC m Anne Clarke, son Edward Baddeley b 1850

7. Edward Monger Baddeley 1795-1820 surgeon. Unm.

Catherine Martha m(1810) **John Clarke** b.1779 d.1818
At Peatling Hall, Leicestershire.

(1). Sarah Catherine Clarke 1811. m Marston Buzzard Surgeon 1836. Lutterworth.
(2). John Clarke. 1812 m Eliza Phillips of Leicester
(3). Henry Clarke. 1813. Batchelor.
(4). Elizabeth Clarke 1814-1892 m. R.J.Russell.
(5). Anne Clarke. 1816 died young.

From WEB/Sarah Webb:

(1). Charles Edward 1855-1912 Belvedere Kent surgeon.
(2). Thomas Webb 1857-1896 MA Cantab
(3). William Edward 1860-1931 solicitor. Unm.
(4). Anne Isabella 1862-1930 m E.A Elkington 4 6 88
(5). George Herbert Adams 1863-1905 auctioneer
(6). Charlotte Evelyn 1864-1931

George Ernest
Frank D.
E.B.
John St Clare
Miss I.M.
Miss D.L.
Miss A.M.
Miss E.H.
Margery m Dr Richard Harper 1931

NOTES.

Nine. The Surgeons of Newport.

1. Miles, Malcolm, *Doctors 30-Year Fight For Water And Sewerage,* NMDA 2 November 1984.
2. Interview with Dr George Elkington, 5 May 1981.
3. *Dr George Elkington Man Of Principle,* NMDA 11 July, 1986.
4. Mate, C.H., *Shropshire, Historical,* (1906).
5. Biographical information courtesy of John Cooper, Auckland, New Zealand.
6. Elliott, D.J., *Shropshire Watch and Clockmakers,* Phillimore, (1979)
7. NMDA: accounts of the debates on water and sewerage; obituaries 1868, 1912, 1922, 1931 and 1936.
8. Minutes of District Board from 1875.
9. Reports of Newport Urban District Council from 1894 in NMDA
10. Minutes of Marsh Trustees on water question.

10. Mary Roddam and District Nursing.

As everyone knows Florence Nightingale created modern nursing out of the bloodshed of the Crimean war. Yet it had become obvious to many by the 1880`s that her trained, disciplined, hospitalised nurses left the great core of sickness in the country untouched. Through practical experience or sheer instinct they saw the greatest need for nursing lay in the homes of the poor, particularly for childbirth and child welfare. One answer was a system of visiting nurses paid for by donations and small subscriptions that even the poorest could afford. The founder of District Nursing, as it became known, was an Edgmond woman, Mary Selina Roddam. This is not to decry the *"untrained"* country midwives who were not all *"Sairey Gamps"* but clean, knowledgeable old women who took a pride in their office and saved country doctors long rides over bad country roads at night. Many villages, as Flora Thompson describes in *"Lark Rise to Candleford"* in the 1880`s had the use of the Rectory Box often supervised by the clergyman's daughter and available for every pregnancy with *"half a dozen of everything – tiny shirts, swathes, long flannel barrows*, [a long sleeveless, flannel garment for infants] *nighties and napkins, made, kept in repair and lent for every confinement"*. Often including packets of tea and sugar and a tin of groats for gruel.

Mary Roddam was the second daughter of William Roddam of Roddam Hall, Northumberland. He was formerly Mr Spencer Stanhope being a member of a well known north country family whose seat was at Cannon Hall, Yorkshire, but he assumed the name of Roddam on inheriting the property of his kinsman, Admiral Roddam. Her mother was Selina Henrietta Cotes third daughter of John Cotes of Woodcote Hall, Newport, and Lady Maria Cotes. After her fathers death Miss Roddam resided with her mother at Rugeley but in the 1870`s came to Summerhill, Edgmond, where both lived the remainder of their lives. Mrs Roddam died in January 1893 and is commemorated by a memorial pulpit in the parish church, erected by her daughter. That year her daughter began her great social work. She was a woman of independent mind and independent means, which allowed a substantial household and a wide margin for benevolence. She kept her own brougham and waggonette, a top-hatted coachman and later a chauffeur. At her death she left property and gifts to her many servants.

Her church work led her to active involvement in the Girls Friendly Society as far back as 1881. This was an organisation to train and find employment for young working class girls. She held many of the leading posts of the Society both in regard to the Lichfield Diocese and her own local branch. From at least 1885 to her death she was a member of the diocesan

149

council of the Society when she represented the Edgmond Rural Deanery branch being at one time a Vice-President of that Council for the Archdeaconry of Salop. She was also formerly Hon Secretary of the Society in the Edgmond Deanery and used to frequently entertain members at Summerhill.

Summerhill – Edgmond

In 1895 Miss Roddam became the first elected, women Guardian. This was possible because though women did not have the parliamentary vote, women ratepayers had since 1834 been allowed to vote for the Guardians and even stand as candidates. Also in 1895 under a new Act the local Board had been divided into two sections, one for the Newport rural area and one for the Staffordshire portion of the Union. The Local Government Board had issued instructions for a more humane view of duties since the sick and the aged were now the main problem.

A distinction was made between inmates and a separation begun, boys from the men, imbeciles from the normal, the sick in separate wards. The Guardians sought permission to borrow £1,000 to improve the sanitation of the workhouse. Miss Roddam was one of the earliest to realise the value of removing the children of inmates of Poor Law Institutions into more suitable and congenial surroundings. For three years she had a home at Chetwynd End for homeless girls mostly from Newport workhouse and in 1898 she built and equipped at her own expense the Edgmond Girls Home in Newport Road, Edgmond, now known as *Moorfield.* Here girls from the workhouse and other girls in humble circumstances were taken in and brought up in a happy atmosphere under a *"motherly-hearted matron"*. On leaving school they were trained in domestic duties and then placed in service. Although some public funds were received towards the expenses of the home the bulk of these were met by Miss Roddam. In 1922 the Home was closed as the need declined or was served in other ways. In 1907 Miss Roddam lost her seat but her work was remembered in 1908 when she opened the workhouse infirmary in the presence of the Duchess of Sutherland who in1903 had described the workhouse as *"completely out of date"*.

Miss Roddam was for many years a manager of both Edgmond and Newport C E schools appointed by the new Local Education Authority, Shropshire County Council.

> *"Miss Roddam came in to see the children. I questioned them for a short time on their scripture and she was very pleased with the way they answered – she promised to come and see them again some day".*

Newport Infants School 15 March 1905.

Newport People

In 1914 when soft toys ceased to be imported from Germany because of the war Miss Roddam started an industry in Newport, then later in Edgmond, for the manufacture of toys, employing a large number of women and girls. Many large orders were secured from London firms and it proved the first of other industries of a similar nature in the country. It ceased with the return of foreign toys after the war.

"The Shropshire Toy Industry which was initiated by Miss Roddam of Summerhill, Newport some twelve months ago has made wonderful progress since it was started and may now be said on the highway to success. The original idea of the founder was to find profitable employment for young people in the town and villages, especially in the making of the best style of soft toys. With that object in view she secured the services of a competent instructress, enlisted a bevy of workers and rented a room in which the necessary operations could be carried out. At the outset the venture was confronted by the inevitable difficulties but those were eventually overcome. The young women proved to be apt pupils, who quickly realised the necessity of the cooperation of brains, hands and eyes with the result that they may now be said to be skilled workers. Some time ago the original section was transferred from Newport to Edgmond where the work is carried on under ideal conditions and in picturesque surroundings. Fourteen girls are employed with Miss Gorst as manageress and Miss Asterley in charge of clerical work. A section with six workers has been started in Market Drayton and we understand that the initiation of additional centres in other parts of the country is contemplated.

An exhibition of the work that is being done was held at Edgmond on Thursday afternoon and was largely attended. Having been in a position to watch the project from its inception, we write authoritatively when we say the progress accomplished has been wonderful. The exhibits might be equalled but they could not be excelled elsewhere, either in freshness of design or in excellence of workmanship. There was nothing shoddy or shabby, the ideal of excellence had been aimed at and was attained. Want of space prevents our detailing all the toys on view but we may say that among the most notable were flocks of farmyard fowl, in form and colour true to life, rabbits both life-like and tricked out in the fantastic disguises so dear to the children; crows and rooks which might have come from the neighbouring landscapes and flown in through the open windows, dogs of almost every conceivable kind, the bull type being especially noticeable, teddy bears innumerable, golliwogs many and Humpty-Dumpties in many a quaint device. One of the last was the original design of one of the Edgmond workers and the same young lady had also produced a perfect little model of a fantail pigeon.

..One interesting fact was that Miss Roddam and others were trying to do was to find work for women, a necessity which would be more pressing after the war."

Newport and Market Drayton Advertiser 2 October 1915

Her prime concern was still childbirth and welfare in the poorer homes. The workhouse had shown her that the main cause of poverty was sickness and age. In 1893 she founded the Newport Benefit Nursing Association for general and maternity nursing of women in their own homes. She had trained at Plaistow, at her own expense, two young women, Nurses Willet and Bradford for Edgmond, with Mrs Lawton for Newport. The first meeting was in July 1894 and her private venture became the Newport and District Nursing Association and for thirty-five years Miss Roddam was secretary and treasurer with Mrs Leeke as President until 1944. There were two *"cottage"* nurses and two joined later. The aim was *"to help people help themselves and not depend upon charity"*. In the first year they dealt with 64 cases. Class 1 subscriptions were 2/- pa (78 subscribers) and Class 2, 3/- pa (44). In 1899/1900 as the work grew Miss Roddam bought a house in Newport to turn into a home for the nurses and matron and later bought an adjoining house to enlarge the home. This became what most people remember as the Mary Roddam Nursing Home.

Mary Roddam

In 1902 Miss Roddam met the deficit of £247 on the Nurses Home. In September 1904 at a Tea meeting in the Town Hall to obtain support, it was emphasised that the Nurses Home was strictly a private venture subsidised by Miss Roddam while the Nursing Association was run by a committee financed by donations and subscriptions but based at the Home. However the two worked closely together and became inseparable in most peoples' eyes. In 1904 subscriptions were 2/-, 3/- and 5/- and there were 480 benefit members with the training of the nurses the biggest expense (£30).

In 1900 Miss Kate Nicholls was matron and in 1905-11 The Hon Miss Edith Walsh, who was also the County Superintendent for Shropshire, based in Newport, supervising 44 nurses in 100 federated associations in the County.

In 1907 the Association affiliated to the Queen Victoria Jubilee Institute ("Jubilee Nurses") set up out of £70,000 donated by women on the occasion of the 1887 Jubilee, for the education of nurses to tend the sick in their own homes.

The work of the Association increased as the depth of Edwardian poverty was revealed while finance based on donations and subscriptions was always weak. In 1909 Miss Roddam gave £200, in 1921, £115 and even then there was a deficit of £212. In 1911 4,692 visits had been made and nurses had worked 62 nights. In 1921, when there was no balance sheet, 4,300 visits had been made. In 1919 an infant welfare and maternity centre had been set up at the Home and the standard and scope of work was expanding. Progress was not without difficulty and even opposition, particularly as regards money. Income came from subscriptions, from parishes, donations and fundraising such as the Hospital Sunday Committee and in June 1926, Harper Adams' Rag Day. Subscribers had free nursing for twelve months; if not it was 6d [2.5p] a visit. There were charges for confinements. In 1921 it was reported that some parishes were dropping out while others were not giving an adequate quota according to population e.g. Edgmond with 913 people gave £28 while Newport with 2,800 gave only £35. Different classes of subscription with differing benefits gave rise to suspicion one speaker in 1921 emphasising that cottagers should be shown the benefit of nursing not just depend on charity or feel the Association was for the *"toffs"*; better collectors were needed to collect the subscriptions in pennies or half pennies since 4/6 was a lot in one go. This working class theme had been raised in 1904 and was repeated in 1922 when it was felt there should be a working woman from every parish on the committee.

By 1922 there were maternity beds at the Home, infant welfare facilities, a dental clinic for children referred from schools and an eye clinic that saved many journeys to Shrewsbury. School nursing brought a great deal of work. In September 1923 a new welfare wing opened at the rear of the building. In 1925 there were 36 cases in the Home mainly working class mothers; an infant welfare room; school clinic every morning; a dental clinic and orthopaedic after care. That year at the Annual General Meeting Dr Pooler outlined the history of the Association. The Association, he said, had been begun by Miss Roddam to provide general and maternity nursing of women in their own homes. She had trained the nurses and provided a home for them at her own expense with two rooms for abnormal and accident cases. There had been a fully trained superintendent or matron. They had eventually enlarged the house to provide two wards and six cubicles for the nurses, bathrooms and a sitting room. Miss Roddam bore the whole expense of the Home. It had become the base for the Shropshire Federation. It became impossible to take in-patients, except for some out-patient dressings, because of the pressure of outside work. Major surgical cases and operations were carried out but these became incompatible with midwifery. It evolved into a maternity home pure and simple, that is a home for nurses with mothers admitted for a fee. By 1925 the Home was carrying out maternity, ante-natal, child welfare, school visits and daily treatment and after care for the County Council. The nurses also had a car.

By 1939 there were two cars costing £100 pa and Shropshire County Council had taken over school nursing and visiting. It now began to advertise as a Nursing Home and a Maternity Home and from 1940 birth announcements appeared regularly in the Newport Advertiser.

Roddam House

Miss Roddam retired as secretary and treasurer in March 1928 with heart trouble. In the Association's report for the year ending 31 March 1928, her successor in the secretaryship, Mr C. W. Smallman, wrote of her *"..we are very grateful to her for the good work which she has carried on for the past 35 years and deplore the circumstances in which she has found it necessary to hand her life's work to others to carry on. Her name will always be associated with the alleviation of sickness and suffering, will be a sweet savour not only to those living in the district, but to the whole County".*

Miss Roddam died on Tuesday 28 April 1931 aged 80, at Summerhill. She was described as the pioneer of district nursing who *"..took the keenest interest in all matters appertaining to the social and moral welfare of the inhabitants and numerous charitable causes as well as individuals, benefited through her generosity".* She was survived by two nephews, Mr Thomas Craister of Craister, Northumberland and Mr W. S. Craister of Salisbury, Southern

Rhodesia; also by a niece Miss Craister and a cousin Miss Pulleine, who had resided with her for thirteen years.

On the Wednesday the body was conveyed from Summerhill to Edgmond Parish Church where it remained until the funeral, covered with a white and purple pall.

In her will published in August 1931 Miss Roddam left £6,000 and premises in High Street, Newport, to Newport District Nursing Association, the money to be invested to provide an annual gift to the Home. She also left £300 to Miss Jane Brazendale, superintendent and matron of the Nurses Home; "Moorfield" House and £200 was left to her chauffeur, William Lewis; £200 to her former coachman Albert Nelmes of High Street, Edgmond. She left wages to all her servants.

By 1939 the Association as we have seen had become overloaded with duties devolved from the County Council through national legislation. It was already beginning to revert to its core work of maternity care. Also local authorities increasingly began to set up their own welfare systems while in 1948 came the comprehensive, free care of the National Health Service. In 1943 when the Association celebrated its jubilee it had an income of £2,070 and expenditure of £2,051. There was also the investment of £6,550. The year before they had rented Gower House [John Henshall Insurance] as a nurses home and sublet part of it. In 1944 Miss M Hall was matron and nurses salaries had increased 50% with government aid. There had been 14 medical and 98 maternity case, 466 antenatal visits while District Nurses had dealt with 385 cases totalling nearly 5,000 visits. In 1946 there was deficit of £139 on expenditure of £2,250; a new nurses' car was required and £400 of investments had had to be realised to repay the bank overdraft.

In July 1948 came the last meeting of the District Nursing Association after 56 years. The Chairman was the Rev. Bradley and the secretary Mrs Stephens. The work had been extensive. 144 medical; 63 surgical; 37 midwifery; 17 maternity; 2,473 general visits, 338 midwifery, 209 casual, 1,204 health, 47 antenatal. The Home had dealt with 80 maternity, 26 midwifery, 13 medical and 510 antenatal examinations. There were assets of £6,478 and an endowment of £6,000 plus an overdraft of £361. They were still hopeful of continuing the Home through the endowment and the Boughey Trust.

This expectation was quickly dashed for a public notice of the same date announced "..*owing to the revolutionary effects financial and otherwise of the National Service Act which came into force in the 5th inst, the District Nursing Association can no longer function. Consequently it has been decided to close the Home on or before the 30th September next. By order of the Committee July 1948"*.

The sale of 127 High Street was advertised on 13 August 1948. The building included an entrance hall, 3 reception rooms, 6 bedrooms and dressing rooms, 4 staff bedrooms, 3 baths and lavatories, kitchens and Aga; there was a side entrance and detached buildings which could convert into cottages. It was sold privately to Shropshire County Council to provide clinic facilities and for public health purposes. The contents were sold on 30 September including surgical equipment and linen. It was eventually purchased as a boarding house for Adams Grammar School for £3,500 in 1953 when the Welfare Centre in Beaumaris Road was opened.

A Testimonial Fund was set up for Miss Hall and Mrs Meredith and Miss Morgan.

Why the quick demise? The changes in health provision after 1945 made the Nursing Association unnecessary and the Maternity Home could not exist on its own, the fees and the endowment being inadequate. The Charity Commissioners would not allow trust money to subsidise the Home since all expectant mothers could now get free treatment.

R. P. Liddle of Liddle and Heane, solicitors, had a genius for acquiring trust moneys and by 1950 he had succeeded Mrs Stephens and controlled the funds which since 1948 had been lying in abeyance in Consols bringing in £200 pa. There were two sources of money the Mary Roddam Trust Fund and the £6,000 legacy left to the Nursing Association. This was to be used for sick people in the area but when the Urban District Council submitted names for wheelchairs, Liddle, by phone, demanded that applicants should pay half!

In 1952 after four years of wrangling the Mary Selina Roddam Aid Sickness Fund was set up as a registered charity with £4,475 in Commonwealth of Australia Registered Stock. The money was to cover the poor in the parishes of Newport, Church and Chetwynd Aston, Woodcote, Edgmond, Longford and Forton. It could supply special food and medicines to the sick poor, medical comfort, bedding, fuel, medical and surgical appliances, provision of domestic help, grants of money for defraying the expenses of convalescence or in things of a manner the Trustees thought fit. Various trustees were appointed with R. P. Liddle a trustee for life.

In November 1984 it was combined with the Annabelle Lady Boughey Charity to form the Lady Annabelle Boughey and Mary Roddam Housing Trust, which has built old peoples' bungalows at Longford Road, Roddam Court and Havisham Court.

So the work of this Victorian pioneer continues with the same kindness and sympathy and in her own unostentatious and devoted manner.

NOTES.

Ten. Mary Roddam.

1. NMDA., has provided much of the information particularly reports on the work of the Benefit Nursing Association. Obituary 1 May 1931.
2. Reminiscences of Mr and Mrs W.Lewis, Newport, who provided photographs.
3. SRRC., Liddle and Heane Collection 3670/NA/1-7.

N/A Friday May 1st 1931.

Death of Miss M S Roddam prominent social worker, founder of Newport Nursing Home.

Shropshire is the poorer for the passing of Miss Mary Selina Roddam one of the most prominent and active social workers in the County who passed away at her residence, Summerhill, Edgmond, on Tuesday morning after being an invalid for the past three and a half years. During that period she had had to abstain from all active work owing to heart trouble. The deceased lady who was in her 80th year was the second daughter of the late Mr William Roddam of Roddam Hall, Northumberland. He was formerly Mr Spencer Stanhope being a member of a well known north country family whose seat was in Cannon Hall, Yorkshire, but he assumed the name of Roddam on inheriting the property of Roddam from his kinsman, Admiral Roddam. His wife, the mother of Miss Roddam, was Miss Selina Henrietta Cotes daughter of the late Mr John Cotes of Woodcote Hall, Newport. At her fathers death Miss Roddam resided for a time near Rugeley, during the 70`s they came to Summerhill where both lived for the remainder of their lives. Mrs Roddam, who died many years ago, is commemorated by a memorial pulpit in the Parish Church, erected by her daughter. Throughout her long residence in the Newport district Miss Roddam took the keenest interest in all matters appertaining to the social and moral welfare of the inhabitants and numerous charitable causes as well as individuals, benefited through her generosity.

Her sympathy and kindness of heart were well known and may truly be said to have in an unostentatious manner devoted herself to the service of the county, especially those of the Edgmond and Newport district

One of the organisations for which she accomplished a considerable amount of good work was the Girls Friendly Society her connection with which dates back as far as 1881. She held many of the leading posts of the Society both in regard to the Lichfield Diocese and her own local branch. From at least 1885 to her death she was a member of the diocesan council of the Society when she represented the Edgmond Rural Deanery branch being at one time a Vice-president of that Council for the Archdeaconry of Salop. She was also formerly Hon Secretary of the Society in the Edgmond Deanery and used frequently to entertain the members at Summerhill.

For many years a member of Newport Board of Guardians, Miss Roddam was one of the earliest to realise the value of removing the children of inmates of Poor Law Institutions into more suitable and congenial surroundings and in order to forward that object about 1891, she built and equipped, at her own expense, the Edgmond Girls Home now known as "Moorfield". Here girls from Poor Law Institutions and other girls in humble circumstances were received and brought up in a happy home atmosphere under a motherly-hearted matron and on leaving school were first trained in domestic duties and then found places of service. Although some contributions from public funds were received towards the expense of the home the bulk of these were borne by Miss Roddam. A few years after the war [1914-18] this excellent institution came to an end owing principally to the fact with the advance of humanitarian work there was no longer the same need for it as formerly.

During the war when soft toys ceased to be imported from Germany Miss Roddam inaugurated an industry at Edgmond for the manufacture of these employing a large number of women and girls. Many large orders from London firms were secured and excellent articles were turned out the undertaking proving the pioneer of other industries of a similar nature in this country. It however came to an end after the war with the return of foreign toys.

What however may have been described as her life work was what she accomplished for nursing in Shropshire especially that in connection with the Newport Nursing Association which she founded in 1893 establishing its headquarters together with a home for the matron and nurses at a house in Newport owned by her. For 35 years she acted as the first secretary and treasurer only resigning in March 1928 on account of ill health. From its foundation to the end of her life she gave to the Association and its work most generous financial support also working hard for it in other ways as long as she was able to do so. She lived to see a remarkable extension and development of its labours notably in relation to maternity, aftercare and child welfare. In the Associations` report for the year ending March 31st 1928 her successor in the secretaryship and treasureship, Mr C W Smallman wrote of her " we are very grateful to her for the good work which she has carried on for the past 35 years and deplore the circumstances in which she has found it necessary to hand her life's` work to others to carry on. Her name will always be associated with the alleviation of sickness and suffering, will be a sweet savour not only to those living in this district, but to the whole County", words that will find an echo today in the hearts of the many friends in all classes of the community by whom she was loved and esteemed. In the early years the work of the Newport Nursing Association aroused considerable interest in the county with the result that similar associations were formed in many other places. Miss Roddam thus became the pioneer of District Nursing in Shropshire and the instigator and one of the principal founders of the Shropshire Nursing Federation which now contains upwards of 100 Associations. Her work in this connection cannot be too highly praised.

Miss Roddam was for many years a manager of both Edgmond and Newport C E schools an associate of the Edgmond branch of the Mothers Union and the founder of Edgmond Women's Institute of which she was made a Vice-President for life

Miss Roddam is survived by two nephews Mr Thomas W Craister of Craister, Northumberland, and Mr W S Craister of Salisbury, Southern Rhodesia; by a niece Miss Craister and a cousin Miss Pulleine who has resided with her for nearly 13 years.

On Wednesday evening the body was conveyed from Summerhill to Edgmond Parish Church where it remained until the funeral yesterday afternoon, the coffin being covered with a purple and white pall. The funeral ceremony, which was choral, was attended by a large congregation representative of the many activities and organisations with which the deceased lady had been connected.

11. Tom Collins.

"In 1870 being engaged to be married and desirous of settling down as soon as possible, I went in for the Headmastership of Newport, Salop, Grammar School".

T. Collins M.A.

Thus began the association between Newport and Tom Collins which lasted until his death at the age of 93 on 16 March 1934. He was appointed to a school founded in 1656 by a local boy William Adams with a comfortable endowment of £1,200 a year from estates at Woodseaves near Market Drayton, Shropshire and Knighton in Staffordshire. It was a Grammar School *"free for 80 scholars within 3 or 5 miles"*. Adams had made a fortune as a haberdasher in London and the school, along with other bequests such as almshouses, was under the authority of the Worshipful Company of Haberdashers where his portrait still hangs in the Livery Hall.

Tom Collins was born in 1841 at Warwick where his grandfather and great-grandfather had been members of Parliament. When County Courts were set up in 1847 his father became Registrar of the Courts around the area of Bury St Edmunds in Suffolk. A quiet enough town except for the rowdyism, corruption and bribery that was standard at election time. At an early age he went to a dame's school and then was entered at Bury Grammar school where the masters were clergyman scholars of Greek and Latin, often above the heads of their pupils, controlled by harsh discipline and bullying. In return the boys behaved as *"foolish barbarians"*. In 1859 he obtained an exhibition at the school and tried for Cambridge colleges and succeeded at Christ's. Lectures were a farce, if students liked they could go and if they preferred to stay away they could do so. College Fellows were curious individuals often more devoted to Bacchus than Minerva, the goddess of wisdom.

For a young man with money and the physical attributes of an athlete life for three years was an idle round of cricket, fives, racquets, billiards and shooting. Classics were ignored and tradesman's bills avoided.

During the whole time he was up at Cambridge Collins captained the College cricket Xl. They played on Parker's Piece which had the advantage of no boundaries so it was possible, if the ball was not "lost", to run a seven or an eight. He knew the great cricketers of the day because before the arrival of the County Championship, Cambridgeshire was a force in the cricket world with leading professionals such as Tom Hayward, Robert Carpenter, who hit the first ever six at Lords and George Tarrant an intimidating, round-arm fast bowler. Collins used to pay the professional 2/6 an hour to bowl at him in the nets at Fenners, they being wily enough to allow him to hit them all over the ground so that they could rest while the ball was returned. He knew the leading University players of the time most going on to be the leading amateur *"Gentleman"* of the day. He met other great players including T Lockyer the wicket-keeper:

*"His hands were a sight. The palms were driven in and the
backs were convex from the constant impact of the ball".*

In the long vacations he played for Suffolk and against teams such as Newmarket, Stowmarket and Ickworth. Games began at eleven with a cold lunch at two and a finish at 6.30. Later like most sportsmen he lamented these days past:

*"Now in the country these whole day matches seem
to have died out. Why is it? Is it that people are busier
now than then, and cannot spare the time, or do a
different class of people play country cricket now?"*

In the season of 1862 Collins was ill with typhoid but the following year he played for Cambridge against Oxford at Lords a game they were expected to win as they had easily beaten Surrey a few days earlier. His experience in this game helped to change the Law in June 1864 when a bowler was allowed to deliver the ball from above the height of his shoulder. Until then only round arm bowling was legal. Collins took the wickets of R.D. Walker and R.A.H. Mitchell and was then *"no-balled"* five times for delivering the ball above the shoulder. This spoiled him for the match. He did not get another wicket and scored only nought and one. The *"Sunday Times"* in 1930 described him as the oldest living *"Blue"*, a dangerous bat when settled and a fair bowler.

His other passion was billiards especially when it was too wet for cricket. It was a game frowned on for many years:

*"Years ago billiards was supposed to be rather a low game,
fit for sharpers and gamblers only. Times have changed,
and nearly every large house now has its billiard table
to amuse its owners guests". [1905]*

In 1883 when he helped form the Newport Literary Institute and which he attended every day until old age, the game became one of the main features now replaced by snooker.

After three years he was struck by remorse and the realisation that his father, not a rich man, had made considerable sacrifices to keep him at University. Constant idleness ensured that he knew next to nothing and strong coffee and cold towels around the head brought only a second class degree in 1863.

This disappointment did not prevent him in the August joining [Sir] Walter Greene on a sporting trip to Norway with provisions from Fortnum and Masons. Muzzle loading guns brought at least twelve brace a day including capercailzie [a grouse the size of a turkey] and ryper [ptarmigan]. They managed to assault one of the locals and only left the country after a visiting aristocrat paid their fine.

He now needed a job and answered an advertisement for a classics master at King Edward's School in Birmingham. He was successful he believed because he had a Blue and they wanted to promote athletics. He was a qualified barrister yet found himself at the age of 22 teaching a class of over forty boys in a school of 650 pupils. King Edward's was a conservative institution in a liberal, radical, nonconformist city. A strong - he was over fifteen stone - young man found life congenial. There was plenty of shooting, cricket and fishing, dances and dinner-parties, few evenings were spent alone and late nights were frequent. He discovered new pastimes including Bridge which was to become a life-long passion, and golf which like rowing he never really mastered, and joined Clubs, the Union, naturally, and the Edgbaston Quoits and Bowls Club which dispensed hospitality, gambling and late nights. For seven years he led the life of a bachelor gay.

In 1869 it was said that that the William Adams Foundation had more money than it knew what to do with. The school may not have been poor financially but it was in many other ways and when Collins stated *"the School when I took it over was in a most unsatisfactory condition"*, he was only repeating what the townspeople had been saying for years. He should have added that this was precisely the reason why he had been appointed, he was young, impressive in appearance and personality, a barrister rather than the traditional clergyman. It was believed he would be the man to break the mould.

The complaints had been many throughout the 1860`s, mainly along the lines that a classical education was not suited to the needs or character of the boys in a rural community. A wider more commercial syllabus was required. This was not just talk, numbers averaged only 46 in a school endowed for eighty and many parents paid for their sons to attend the commercial schools of Mr Picken at the Old Hall in Station Road, and that of Mr Ashmore at Rosemont, Chetwynd End, even after Collins arrived.

Much of the blame was put on his predecessor, the Rev. C.W. Saxton, a man fonder of studying than of teaching, who had been there twenty-four years, was ill and disabled and his marriage was in trouble. In 1871, a rare event, he and his wife agreed to separate. Sir Oliver Lodge, famous scientist and Old Boy, describing the school in Saxton`s time, recalled how he sat in a box in the corner of the room using his cane as a walking stick while the writing master kept his down his shoe known as a *"Blucher"*. Latin, Greek and mathematics, he said, might have been easier with a little more humane assistance. The *"box"* was in fact a specially constructed wire chair from which Saxton rarely rose because of his operation. The contrast with the youth and vigour of Collins is obvious.

Collins' impressions were of boys who had been caned morning and afternoon so that most of them would lie continuously to get out of trouble. Intellectually he found them inferior to his Birmingham pupils; many Newport pupils he alleged came to the school aged fourteen knowing nothing and the average stay was only two and a half years. In 1873 he was still complaining of the *"deplorable state of ignorance of the boys when first put into our hands"*. This was despite the fact that in 1879 the entrance examination was:

> *"....of the usual easy character, just sufficing to show that*
> *the boys have learnt to read and write and the merest*
> *elements of arithmetic and geography".*

The 1665 Orders of William Adams were still being complied with, for instance two poor boys were still paid 20 shillings a year to sweep out the school each day and they also rang the school bell. There was no fire until 5 November and no lights, lessons simply stopped when it got dark

Collins did some very simple things first. He appointed a porter at £30 pa, partly his own servant, to look after the school. This man stayed with him twenty-six years and accompanied him on all his sporting trips. All but the poorer boys had to find their own books and thus, hopefully, treat them with respect. He also began to take boarders in his own house.

> *1871 Census.*
> *Thomas Collins. 30. Barrister at Law. MA. Warwick. Unm*
> *Albert.H. Brother. 15. Scholar. Bury St Edmunds.*
>
> *There were 3 female servants and 4 boarders including*
> *Leigh.H. Elkington 14. Birmingham.* [Was he his fiancées brother?]

By May 1871 he had introduced athletics and appointed a fourth master.

> *"Forty years ago many schools had no athletic sports at all,
> now they are almost universal, and are looked forward to by
> the town and neighbourhood where the school is situated
> as an annual institution. Thirty-four years ago there were
> none at Newport School. I started them and they have gone
> on every year since with increasing eclat".*

He played cricket for the school against the Old Boys and usually paid for the teas. He captained Newport Cricket Club for twenty years. He founded the school magazine the *"Novaportan"*, which reported despondently in the 1880`s on the shirking of cricket practice and an absence of *"esprit de corp"* in games. This seemed to coincide with a decline in numbers.

Another innovation typical of Collins and combining several elements of his character was the Annual Dinner to herald the midsummer vacation. It was first held, rather hurriedly, in July 1874 and was preceded by a cricket match between past and present in which Collins scored 60 including two sixes and four fours though the old boys under J.S. Underhill could only muster ten men. The dinner followed at the Royal Victoria Hotel where 40 sat down to salmon and duck under the chairmanship of the headmaster. It was, he said, very pleasing to see so many former pupils, many who had never been taught by the present staff, rallying round and supporting the school, for after a master had taken pains with the boys, had learnt to respect them and feel affection for them and to admire them, it was hard to think that they would never see them again. Speakers commented on the much better condition of the school since the arrival of Tom Collins, the improvement in respect, the concern for the welfare of the boys, the emphasis on the teaching of English and the importance of outdoor, physical pursuits. In comparing past and present the advantages and benefits lay with the present pupils under Tom Collins.

At the same time he made the school a centre for the Cambridge Local Examinations and in fact supplied most of the candidates for years. This had its problems one examiner, a clergyman, quite rightly seeing Newport as a quiet, secluded spot, brought down his mistress passing her off as his disabled sister. When her husband rode over from Stafford to fetch her back Collins` reaction was livid but typical:

> *"Examiners might bring down a harem each as far as I
> was concerned, but I would not submit to their introducing
> the ladies, who accompanied them, to my wife as their
> sisters".*

The competitive element of games and examinations was significant but he was continually frustrated by the limits of the original constitution and by the quarrels it engendered. Also by the size and condition of the buildings and the limited catchment area and ability of the pupils. The last problem eased considerably with the introduction of elementary education in the town after 1873 but the first problem, the constitution, was never settled to his liking and the buildings were only improved shortly before he retired. The running of the school under the original deed was with the Haberdashers and a local group of Visitors, six clergymen and four laymen. There was always friction, with the Haberdashers controlling the endowment and the Visitors suspicious that it was not all being spent on the School. From his first day Collins landed in the middle of disputes between the Governors and the town now formed into a Town Committee. By 1872 a new "scheme" had been devised but its implementation was delayed by the Haberdashers until 1879. Under this the free element for eighty scholars of the original foundation disappeared to be replaced by fees of £1 per term in the Newport area and £2.50 otherwise; masters were allowed to keep boarders in approved houses thus supplementing their earnings; Greek became an optional extra at £1 per term and there were examinations for admission.

No one was happy, the new governing body falling out with the Haberdashers; Collins fuming because Greek declined as a subject and was, he alleged, the reason for the decline in numbers; the town was unhappy about the loss of free places and the lack of provision for girls.

More useful would have been a new building on a new site. Section 30 and 34 of the new scheme provided for this and a girls school, combined if necessary, but despite many public meetings in the 1880's and 90's they were never implemented. Sir Thomas Boughey of Aqualate Hall offered a free site up the Wellington Road but became fed up and withdrew it.

In any case there was little capital to build a new school as the agricultural depression reduced income to £800 pa and fewer parents could afford education. So Collins continued to find himself without playing fields, with three classes in one room, no space for science and insanitary conditions for boarders.

Eventually in 1901 alterations were sanctioned to the original building, including a dividing partition in the *"Big School"*, laboratories, a heating system, rear garden and dining accommodation. The next year, 1902, saw the Education Act that was to revolutionise secondary education under new Local Education Authorities such as Shropshire County Council. Both were too late for Tom Collins or perhaps a reason that he should go?

The crucial point was after thirty years in office there were only 55 boys in the school in 1904 well below the original *"free eighty"*. If the Grammar School was to be used as the basis for the great leap forward in secondary education then new men were needed as well as new ideas and investment, otherwise the new Authority would start afresh as they did in Newport with the Girls High School, and in other Shropshire market towns such as Wellington.

His achievement was to impose on an ancient foundation and a small market town the educational principles that had revived the major Public Schools in Victorian England, an achievement based on his own powerful personality. Of course nostalgia clouds the perception but he does come through on his own. A good teacher though perhaps not a great scholar. He had the aura of a good sportsman that enhanced his reputation and eased discipline. Within the code he set education became healthier, there was pleasure and optimism and achievement not just amongst the high flyers but with those who went on to become farmers and businessmen and community leaders.

Some years earlier he had read a paper at a conference of Head Masters in which he opposed corporal punishment. The cane, he said, should never be used. It encouraged lying and cheating, far better was fairness and justice based on honour and forgiveness. At his last

Speech day, graced by Lady Boughey, at her request, he recalled that he had no discipline that meant a boy did not smile or went to school as if to a funeral. *"I never ask a boy to do anything but he willingly does it"*. In 1904 at a dinner in the Royal Victoria Hotel, the Old Boys and staff presented him with an Address, a silver cup and a cheque for £90 and he reiterated his belief in honesty and truth, love and participation in sport and the abhorrence of corporal punishment.

> *"I hope when I die the words "Newport School" may be found written on my heart".*

He was made a member of the Haberdashers Company.

Numerous Old Boys recalled *"Tom"* in later years; how he would dismiss a class in a rage and refuse to teach them; how he would extemporise in Latin to fill gaps in the timetable; how everyone knew when a half-day holiday was due since it always coincided with a sporting excursion with the Rector, the Rev. Ward Travers Burges. How he would take a roll call in the Hall before Sports Day when each boy would have to name the events in which he wished to compete and his colours. How he would deal leniently with juniors with a growl of *"You young rascal!"* said with a long, lingering "a". How he would swing out of his house, gown billowing, carrying under his arm his own textbook "Gradations", Latin pieces for translation into English! In those days the 1st Class was the Sixth Form; the 6th class was the lowest.

> *"During my four years at the school, I can only remember three or four boys who were caned. This made it an event of outstanding importance. Venial offences counted but little with "Tom". But what of duplicity, deceit and dishonesty? He loathed them. Then the Sword of Damocles descended upon the unhappy culprit with dire vengeance, in the shape of a stout cane wielded by a powerful and stalwart arm".*

> Dr J.R.Pooler. 1930. Novaportan.

One of his most famous pupils was Charles Silvester Horne, the first nonconformist Member of Parliament. In his biography W.B. Selbie quotes the following description of Collins by Leonard Horne:

> *"In those days the Headmaster of the Grammar School was Tom Collins whose manly character, energy and good nature exerted a very strong and healthy influence. He fostered games which, however, never assumed the importance attached to them in boarding schools; and he saw that a good all-round education was given, though his own chief interest was in teaching Latin and Greek. An exception must be made of science of which the boys learnt little at that time".*

In return Collins obtained financial security, £315 pa by 1903, which gave him a gentleman's existence and status which he might have lacked in a larger community. However, at retirement the funds of Adams Grammar School was so low that he did not receive a pension.

After his retirement numbers rose quickly, 110 in 1906 to 170 by September 1908.

Having secured the headmastership Tom Collins duly married Emily Mary (Minnie) Elkington at Edgbaston Parish Church on 11 April 1871. Elkington was an important name in the Birmingham electro-plating industry and in the medical profession a branch of which was already settled in Newport at this time.

> *"....nothing could have been happier than my married life for five years. No man ever had a sweeter partner of his joys and sorrows. Alas! My happiness soon came to an end, for in giving birth to a third child she was suddenly taken from me, leaving me with a daughter and a son."*

His daughter was Ethel Mary Collins who in 1900 married the engineer son of Edward Hodges the Newport solicitor. Like her father she was robust, high spirited with a strong sense of humour and friendliness which made her home a centre of social activity. She died in 1936 aged 63. His son T. B. Collins pre-deceased him, aged 54, in 1927. He was educated at the Grammar School. A Careswell Scholar he obtained a mathematics degree at Christ Church, Oxford and taught at Woodford and Cranleigh. Neither had children.

In September 1879 Collins married the daughter of Doctor Henry Groves, Cookstown, County Tyrone, Ireland. He went fishing for many years in the summer holidays to Donegal just to the north of Tyrone, and in Lough Erne. The 1881 census names her as Lola aged 22, which means she was barely twenty when they married and he was thirty-eight. In May 1885 she is secretary to the Church Restoration Bazaar, and in June 1888 presented the prizes at Speech Day. She is in the 1891 census, *"Lola Melsina, wife, 31,"* but is never mentioned again certainly not in his autobiography. Newport folklore has it that Collins found her with another Master and turned her out.

Lady Cavagnari, the sister of the second Mrs Collins, by a strange coincidence, died in 1934, the same year as Tom Collins. She had married Sir Louis Cavagnari the son of a General of Napoleon Bonaparte. He was murdered in Afghanistan in 1879, an event which led to the second Afghan War.

Collins was a keen outdoor sportsman, particularly shooting and fishing and probably shot and caught more fowl and fish than anyone in the County. He certainly had the leisure with long holidays and half days. It was not just the sport but the social side that attracted him. There was Sir Thomas Boughey on the Aqualate Estate; gentlemen farmers; the sporting Rector but also Charles Oakley, who was a bank tender on the canal, a well-known character who became a firm friend of Tom Collins and went on many of his sporting expeditions. As we have seen he travelled to Norway and Ireland also to Scotland and the Orkney Isles. He fished and shot all over Shropshire, Suffolk, Dorset and Warwick and probably elsewhere. There were pigeons, partridge, grouse, hare and rabbits. There were different kinds of guns, accidents with guns, shooting round dogs over dogs, different types of dogs, barbed wire, drag-nets, gin traps, poachers, *"a dishonest but exhilarating way of making a living"*, tenant farmers, catapults and vermin – foxes, stoats weasels, rooks and even cats. He knew what to fish, where to fish, the pike, perch and trout; the vitality of the carp the use of the wasp grub and how to obtain it. The latter involved cyanide of potassium in water poured down the wasps nest. Apparently the wasps turned over on their backs and expired!

> *"For many years I have had a very good rough shooting of about 1,000 acres close to Newport. I kept no keeper had the ground well bushed, and trusted to the tenants who farmed the land to look after the game for me, and not in vain did I trust them. In one year I killed 426 partridges, 90 pheasants – all wild birds – 40 hares, and about 70 rabbits, besides several duck, snipe and various".*

Collins and his friends pursued their sport at leisure and in comfort accompanied by man-servants and sometimes a housemaid and a cook. Sir Thomas Boughey's shoots were managed to perfection:

> *"A cart drawn by a donkey – he had a first-rate one –*
> *or pony accompanies the party to carry the hares and*
> *ammunition; when the game is put out at lunch-time,*
> *it is all covered with a light gauze to keep off the flies,*
> *and then what a lunch! – not in a marquee erected for*
> *the occasion, but under the lee-side of some neighbouring*
> *hedge. No champagne or sparkling wine (than which I*
> *think there is no greater mistake at a shooting lunch),*
> *but the best of beer or whisky and soda, with a glass*
> *of brown sherry to finish up with, and then just one good*
> *cigar before we again pursue the little brown birds."*

Servants were essential for getting over barbed wire, the curse of the shooting man.

> *"....so at last I procured a piece of leather about a yard*
> *square which my man carried, and as occasion*
> *required placed upon the top."*

As with cricket he deplores change, the simple days of one man and his dog with the old muzzle-loader, shot-flask and powder-horn now replaced with elaborate social rituals which few landowners at a time of severe agricultural depression (1903) could afford. Even the Newport Coursing Meeting held at Aqualate, had been ruined by *"riff-raff"* and bookmakers. It does not seem to have prevented him enjoying himself.

On his retirement Tom Collins had determined to return to Birmingham, his Club and fishing. He was persuaded to stay and lived at Musgrove House, opposite the Grammar School gates until his death. He had already been involved in public affairs since as headmaster he had automatically been vice-chairman of the Marsh Trust. This Trust set up originally in 1764 when the marsh was enclosed had been reformed in 1854 to administer the land and use the profits for the benefit of the town. By the time he retired Collins had been a Trustee for thirty years and though the Trust had done many good things, such as building Granville Avenue, demolishing old property, erecting public conveniences, paving the streets and putting in sewers, its functions had been overtaken by the Urban District Council set up in 1894. In fact at one of the last meetings of the Marsh Trust in January 1926 he opposed the building of public toilets. His former pupil C.W. Smallman described him as the *"Forces of reaction"* :

> *"They all knew their friend Mr Collins. He could not hear*
> *and should not make statements which were not true to facts".*

He campaigned for the abolition of the Trust and its absorption into the District Council. This did not prevent him getting very irate with the UDC and disapproving of the conduct of certain councillors. Writing in 1928 in support he said:

> *"I am sick to death of the thwarting interference of the*
> *Charity Commissioners, I have come to the conclusion*
> *that I must support the resolution of the Council on*
> *being the most beneficial to the town".*

By Act of Parliament 1930 the Trust was abolished and decided to *"fade away"* so there were no photographs, dinners or speeches.

In 1916 he resigned as Chairman of the Gas Company. The works had been built on Marsh Trust land in Avenue Road in 1835 and when the lease was up the Marsh Trust and the Company transferred the business to the Urban District who ran it until nationalisation in 1948. Writing to the "Advertiser" in December 1922 Collins opposed the laying of gas to the new council housing at Vauxhall Crescent. He thought they should stick to oil-lighting as gas was dangerous and expensive, his own gas bill was £30pa. Strange reasoning from the ex-Chairman of the Gas Works! He was a founder member of the Literary Institute, a Freemason and Land Tax and Income Tax Commissioner for fifty years. He was a Director of the Market Company and also a Justice of the Peace but by 1921 seldom sat, because of increasing deafness.

In 1904 he was asked to stand for election to the Newport Urban District Council and agreed on being assured he had the support of the working man. He also determined to canvass the electors on the principle if you want a person's vote you ought to pay him the compliment of asking him for it. He therefore canvassed the whole town issuing handbills and polling cards and using vehicles to bring in voters and held a public meeting in the Town Hall. Numerous ladies recorded their votes. Not surprisingly he topped the poll by 119 votes. He did the same in the 1907 election. In 1904 he was immediately proposed as Chairman of the Council but missed out because two of his supporters, Smallman and Brittain, missed the meeting by getting into the wrong train from Ludlow races! When it came to street lighting Collins opposed the use of oil even though he was the Chairman of the Gas Company. No declaration of interest? He supported the *"working mans right"* to street hydrants even though this was detrimental to improved sanitation. In fact he opposed the new sewerage scheme because of the burden on the rates (a 1d rate brought in £48.) and the damage to the High Street. He certainly had romantic notions of the needs of the working man a concept he never defined. In April 1910 he stood down. Popular in the town maybe but not in the Council. He vented his famous sarcasm on his colleagues:

> *"These Urban Councils of small towns are not, I think, famous for their wisdom and sagacity, and certainly the proceedings of the Newport Council have not been characterised by the prudence one would have expected from so eminent a body."*

Despite his eminence he was never elected Chairman of Council or committees and was it pique that coloured his view that:

> *"In small towns, from my experience, people of position stand aloof from the management of the affairs of the town in which they live. They either don't care about giving up the time such management requires, or they consider it derogatory to their position to meddle in such matters. The result is that Urban Councils in small places are generally made up of tradesmen, who, considering the interests of their trade as the summum bonum, do not exhibit that independence of character that you might expect from people in their position."*

In the 1910 General Election with all the controversy over the Lloyd George budget and the threat to create hundreds of Peers to overcome the opposition of the House of Lords, Collins supported the Conservative and Tariff Reform. Unfortunately the meeting ended abruptly when Collins was accused of telling a lie. In February 1912 he chaired a meeting of the Womens Suffrage movement addressed by Miss Elkin of Girton College. His attitude was that lady ratepayers should have the vote – they had in fact had the vote for years on local matters – but not wives as this would cause domestic friction.

By 1924 he was very deaf with poor sight and refusing public invitations. In March 1925 a servant girl was charged with stealing £5 from his wallet. At the court Collins made an impassioned plea for mercy so much so, that at the close *"subdued applause could be heard in the Court"*. This touch of histrionics familiar throughout his life led him to be compared to Sir Edward Marshall Hall, for eloquence. *"It was a wonderful appeal by an old gentleman like Mr Collins who was practically blind and deaf"*. The girl was bound over for twelve months. He was now contributing to debate by letters to the "Advertiser" as in November 1930 when he supported the building of the Cottage Hospital but pointed out its main fault in that the very poor would not be admissible because they could not pay. He likened it to a Nursing Home rather than a general hospital. In this he was correct and echoed the belief of the majority of the town.

On 16 October 1931 at the age of 91 he wrote regarding the financial crisis and the proposed National Government:

A Call to Newport.

> *As one of the oldest inhabitants of Newport, who for more than sixty years has taken the deepest interest in the welfare and prosperity of the town, I hope I may be allowed, without being thought presumptuous, to write a few lines on the coming election, especially as owing to the disabilities of old age, I am unable to record my vote, or take any active part in it.*
> *The previous social government, by recklessly promoting the dole (very proper no doubt within certain limits), and many other unpolitic measures, were guilty of wilful and wanton extravagance, and brought this country to the very verge of financial ruin. The present National Government has done its best to remedy this dreadful state of things. By increased taxation and other drastic procedures they have hit most of us very hard. But it was absolutely necessary, therefore we must grin and bear it as best we can and hope and pray for better times to come.*
> *I do most earnestly beg and exhort the electors of Newport, almost with my dying breath, before recording their votes to consider carefully what they are doing. If the National Government is still kept in office, things will undoubtedly Improve. Tariff Reform will be introduced, and this will be an enormous factor in improving the trade and industries of the country. If by their votes they let the Socialists again take the reins of office, then all I can say is "God help us". The country will be ruined, and what was once the envy of all nations will become the jeer and laughing stock of the world instead.*
>
> *Tom Collins.*

This brought a reply in December 1930 from *"Localist"* which recalled the political days of Stanley Leighton and Kenyon Slaney when canvassers were lassoed and there were scuffles up country lanes:

> *"Mr Collins remembers Newport in the spacious days, when the little town had its own "smoking chimneys" and heard the swirl of the big saws and the hum of the foundry fans – not great things but they were the main note and rhythm of days of contentment."*

Collins was still in good health though his sight and hearing were failing. Nevertheless he had an excellent memory and mental functions playing bridge and translating nursery rhymes into Latin.

Tom Collins died at Musgrove House, High Street, Newport on 16 March 1934 aged 93. He had resided with his sister Miss Collins aged 92, while two other sisters, widows, were over 80. Miss Francis Collins, who had come to look after her brother nearly forty years earlier, died at Chetwynd Aston in December 1939. Her two sisters were then 94 and 91.

In an appreciation the "Advertiser" wrote he was: *"thoroughly human, warm hearted, decidedly passionate, but ever just."* He had forgiven those who owned up while his sarcasm towards any mean, ungentlemanly action, could cut like a knife. He was a person of deep religious feeling, which dominated his life. Straight and upright he was every inch a man and a gentleman. W.S. Brookes the Headmaster of what was now Adams Grammar School, wrote of his advanced age which had bowed his splendid frame. He had a flashing spirit, gaiety, and gave an uncompromising challenge to public wrongs and injustices. He had a wide experience of humanity; he was *"a wonderful teacher, in that vast school of humanity."* The Archdeacon of Gibralter, the Ven. Lonsdale Ragg, a pupil fifty years before, described TC as a *" generous and understanding optimist."*

In July 1936 a memorial ceremony was held at Adams Grammar School. The memorial was a handsome, carved, oak lectern and bible, carved by Gertrude Hermes the sculptor and engraved, *"In memoriam, Tom Collins M.A., Headmaster 1871-1903."* It was unveiled by Dr Josiah Oldfield and presented by the "Old Boys". In his eulogy the Doctor described "Old Tom" as a great man, not because he was a great scholar but because he had the power and capacity to make great men. He encouraged the best that was in them; he was not a great classical scholar but he taught the love of Greek; not a great cricketer, he liked to put his great shoulder into the blow; not a scientific cricketer but he induced others to become players. He was religious but one of his mannerisms was to say his prayers into his top hat as he came into church, a practice he knew amused people; he said his prayers as if he was the equal of God.

"He was so conscious that everything he did was the best".

His gown would swing over his shoulder as though he was a great victor of the past; it was not arrogance, just that he was a fine fellow. His greatness lay in the development of character; *"I hate a bully, I hate a cheat, I hate a sneak, I hate a liar."*

*"In memory of a great master, who taught courage
and purity, I unveil this memorial."*

Tom Collins, a teacher of Christian principles, discipline, friendship and honour. A confident, optimistic product of the Victorian Age when it was possible to believe that such qualities would ultimately prevail.

A final story which always made Tom Collins chuckle was an account in The Newport Advertiser of his part in a cricket match where it was reported *"In the first innings he made one run, in the second, he was not so successful"*

NOTES.

Eleven.   Tom Collins.

1. Collins, Tom, *School and Sport,* London, (1905)
2. Taylor, David and Ruth*, Mr Adams` Free Grammar School,* Phillimore, (2002)
3. Selbie, W.B.*, The Life of Charles Silvester Horne,* London, (1920), p. 3ff.
4. Mate, C.H., *Shropshire, Historical,* (1906).
5. Meredith, J.R*., Adams Grammar School 1656-1956,* Newport, (1956)
6. Miles, Malcolm, *Tom Collins – A Confident And Optimistic Product Of The Victorian Age,* Shropshire Magazine, August, 1984.
7. Miles, Malcolm*, Newport Literary and Social Institute,* Shropshire Magazine, October 1983.
8. Miles, Malcolm, *Tom Collins the Purge,* NMDA, 16. March, 1984.

NMDA., has extensive cover from 1871 of TC`s many activities and interests, including the Grammar School, cricket, Urban District Council, Marsh Trust, Gas Company, Literary Institute et al.

Tom Collins and Bridge.

Tom Collins was very fond of bridge and this poem must have been written shortly after 1926 when he was 85 and his sight and hearing were failing. The Rector was the Rev. William Manning Salt. Lady Shand was Lady Isabel Eleanor Louisa Shand wife of Sir Charles Shand, a County Court Judge, who lived at Banshee House, then Banshee Lodge, and who died on 6 April 1942 in Bath when the hotel where she was staying received a direct hit in a bombing raid. Mr "Shuker" was John William McLellan Shuker headmaster of Adams Grammar School 1903-1926. His "fair daughter" was Ethel Mildred Hodges 1871-1936 a prominent social figure in Newport. Mrs Brooks was the wife of Walter Samuel Brooks headmaster of Adams Grammar School 1926-1946.

The Rector comes first he is cautious and sure
His looks tell you nothing, he`s always demure
When he holds some good cards, he quite often says "no",
And then bides his time to drop down on his foe,
They go down 300 a nice little start
For the Rector, who chuckles deep down in his heart,
His victims with sorrow and chagrin declare,
That in future of parsons, they`ll always beware.

Next comes a fair widow, ycleped Lady Shand
She is always most ready at bridge for a hand,
Her play is quite good, her declares are all right,
She would like to be playing from morning till night.
Her kindness is matchless as well as her looks,
We read of such women sometimes in our books,
But in actual life they`re exceedingly rare,
For the kindest of women are not always fair.

Mr Shuker has left us, his loss we deplore,
And we grieve that he`ll come to our meetings no more,
Very clear and long-headed he played a good game,
And was always most welcome whenever he came,
At Falmouth I hear he plays bridge now and then,
With smart Cornish women and smart Cornish men,
Though they think they can easily vanquish my friend,
They`re certain to lose and shell out in the end.

When its her turn to call, the Old Lady says "no",
Nine times out of ten she will always say so,
But once in ten times she will make a declare
And then her opponents had better beware,
For as sure as the night follows close on the day
At the end of the rubber they`ll both have to pay.

Mr Jackson is next - a cashier at the bank,
Among the best players entitled to rank,
Keen as mustard, he guesses his foes are in trouble,
And then smiling calmly he gives them a double,
I am told that at tennis, he is as keen as can be,
Though wounded in battle, he has a stiff knee.

Next comes my fair daughter, first-rate at the game,
Because of her great size called "Tiny" by name,
At bridge, she is cunning and up to all dodges,
Though her pet name is "Tiny" her real name is Hodges.,
Auction bridge is her pastime, her only delight,
She has afternoon parties and others at night,
If she fails to get four, then not play she would rather,
Play a dummy and rook of his pence her poor father.

Herbert Jones is the next who appears on the scene,
It`s only of late to our parties he`s been,
A tyro at first he experience gains,
And will be first rate for he always takes pains,
If the devils is said to assist the beginner,
He ought to do well and come out a good winner.

Mrs Brooks seldom comes for as Headmaster`s wife,
To her husbands success, she devotes all her life,
Hence his boarders are all, you can well understand,
With care for and treated with no niggard hand,
She plays very well and I wish she`d play more,
The reason she does not I`ve noted before.

Then Emmeline comes in a motor from Eaton,
She plays very well and is not easily beaten,
She oft times comes here and oft brings me a cake,
No fuller in London, its equal can make,
If fortune does favour the brave with good luck,
She ought to do well for she has plenty of pluck.

Last of all comes Tom Collins, the damndest old fool,
At bridge who was ever once head of the school,
When the rubber seems over, in spades he goes four,
When he ought to say nothing and pass and no more,
When doubled his partner turns faint in his chair,
And rushes to open the window for air
TC smiling grimly says "Perhaps I`m a Lubber",
But at least for the present I have saved you the rubber!

The Novaportan

TOM COLLINS.

"If a man love the labour apart from any question of success or fame the gods have called him." In these words of Stevenson we may envisage the genius of the scholastic life of "Old Tom." It is difficult within the bounds set by our national reserve adequately to picture for those who knew him slightly, or not at all, the reverence and abiding affection inspired by their old Head in those who knew him in his prime. Justice, humour, humanity friendliness, were the distinguishing characteristics of his rule. Coming to Newport after a regime of harshness and rigidity which had only succeeded in defeating its own object – orderliness and discipline – his yoke was easy and his burden light, yet his success was immediate, order was established and discipline maintained. Boys obeyed yet hardly realised that they were obeying. He had his own burdens to bear, in school and out, yet few of us ever saw signs of stress or storm, and none of us suffered from it unfairly. He was always "just" even though occasionally he had to be a "beast." But if those occasions were rare they were all the more impressive and memorable. Cheating, lying and other forms of unfairness became the only capital crimes, to be punished with the utmost rigour. In the days of his predecessor canings were of no account, the ordinary occurrences of normal school life; in the days of "Tom" they became "events," carried out before the whole school, ever to be remembered by every boy in it and a lasting disgrace to the delinquent, though hardly more cutting than the lash of his scorn of the deceit which called for the punishment. But these were rare indeed – in five years the writer witnessed three only. Generally speaking, his sense of humour dominated everything, even his punishments, which were sometimes Gilbertian in the way they were made to fit the crime. Who of the older generation has not seen that gnawing of the moustache and twinkle of the eye that presaged the inevitable chuckle at some more or less audacious remark from some boy or other? There was an unwritten law that boys in the top class must not fight. On one occasion a first class boy going into the playground found a boy, addicted to bullying, annoying a very young and timid new boy. Told by the senior to stop it, the bully squared up and offered to fight. Observing the unwritten code, but by no means averse to a scrap, the senior got hold of the bully and rushed him face first into the thorn hedge round the Head`s garden. The whole episode had been witnessed by Old Tom from the garden. In his stentorian voice he ordered both boys to appear before him in the library. The senior duly presented himself and was received as follows: - "You are in the first class and have been fighting." "No, Sir," was the answer, "only wrestling." "Oh," said the Head gnawing his moustache, "where did you learn wrestling – Cumberland?" "No, Sir," replied the boy. "Be off with you," said Old Tom. But for months after that boy was "Bruiser" to the Head, out of school hours. The bully did not get off so lightly. After a few amused enquiries as to the state of his face, he was penalised a half-holiday for damaging the Head`s garden fence.

In those early days "Tom" played football, but it was plainly "pour encourager les autres," for he had not the slightest idea of football science or even of the rules. He had only one rule:- follow the ball wherever it goes. But his cricket was a different proposition altogether. A Cambridge Blue, he was an inspiration and a tower of strength to the eleven, for, at that time, masters played in school matches. And at practice he was virtually the cricket coach. The annual fixture with the town club was the match of the season, and, with the aid of "Tom," was always a very near thing. The Old Boys` match was another great occasion; for it was an all-day match and a first-class luncheon was provided by the Head for both teams and many friends. Perhaps it was on these and similar occasions that his Old Boys learned to know and appreciate their old Chief as they had never done before. With such active and personal interest it was inevitable that the standard of athletics was high for a comparatively small school. In the short period (five years) that the writer was at the School there were two future Welsh International footballers, two future County cricketers, and an amateur high-jump champion – all contemporaries. Nor was the other side of school life less memorable. One boy secured the first place in all England in the Cambridge Senior Local, and, in the same period there were boys at the School who subsequently became respectively – a Bishop, a Principal of a Theological College, the Keeper of Cairo Archaeological Museum, a world-renowned Pulpit Orator, and others distinguished in the medical profession and civil service. Such records are eloquent of the inspiration and wisdom which characterised the guidance of this comparatively small number of boys – round about 120, if I remember rightly, at this period. But to produce distinguished Old Boys was not Tom`s real ambition; his objective was always the useful and upright citizen, in whatever walk of life he might be chosen. That he achieved success hundreds of living witnesses can testify. "Himself a man he made men."

Probably few of us realised during our schooldays our great privilege. Only in after-life did many of us get to know him best. Then, when he had thrown off the semblance of authority and we had, perhaps, arrived at a wider knowledge of affairs, we learned to know him, not as the Headmaster, not as the disciplinarian, but as the intensely-human and life-long friend. One personal reminiscence I would like to relate, because I think it demonstrates this as no mere statement of the fact can do. At the end of my school career I ranked as third boy in the school. Unquestionably inferior to the leading pair in most subjects, I sat for the usual midsummer examination; reasonably safe for a good place, but with no hope or even thought of anything better. Now, I was in the cricket and football elevens, and my two superior colleagues never played atall. After the examination the Old Boys` Match came along, and, entering the luncheon tent, I came across the Head. After the usual amused greeting, he said; "Who do you think has won the English Prize?" I said "I don't know, Sir." "Why you, you rascal," was the reply, "and I am glad of it." That was an illumination. Old Tom had been interested – he was glad I had won something. A trivial incident, perhaps soon forgotten by him, but a life-long memory for me, perhaps the first real revelation of what his boys were to him, and what he was to them. This was merely my own personal experience; many others must be able to recount similar incidents. Small wonder that our late Head has had the abiding place in our hearts which to him was a joy and consolation during the afflictions during his declining years. Just before his death I wrote to him congratulating him on yet another birthday. As many of you know, at that time he was only able to dictate his letters. His reply concluded as follows:_ "Yours very truly, Tom Collins, otherwise "Old Tom," and very proud of the name."

His work was done in a small and comparatively unknown school and his fame was never widespread, but in all essential he was one of the "elect", a Great Headmaster. Truly, "apart from any success or fame, he loved the labour. The gods have called him."

H.W.Pooler. M.B

12. SARAH JANE MILLS AND MEREVALE.

Market towns were favourite places for private schools. They abound in literature and Newport had many such schools for girls and boys in the 19th Century. They drew children of all ages, locally, and depending on reputation, from a much wider area. It was suggested in 1888 that Newport was a centre for so many schools because it was a healthy locality, pleasantly situated and had a good railway. They might have added also that there was a plentiful supply of large town houses at modest rents to suit the pockets of the spinster ladies, widows and poorer clergy who seemed to make up most of the proprietors. There cannot be many large houses in Newport that have not at some time been home for some form of educational establishment.

Of course many believed the education of girls was not necessary and what was provided was often limited, as Mrs Gaskell describes in *"Cranford"*, really the small country town of Knutsford in Cheshire. The mistress of the Ladies` seminary, to which all the tradespeople in Cranford sent their daughters, saw a solid education as *"fancy work and the use of globes"*. The skills of the ladies of Cranford consisted of making decorative spills or candle lighters, delicately wrought garters and cards on which sewing-silk was wound in a mystical manner. These were the only arts required. By the time of Merevale, Miss Buss and Miss Beale had changed attitudes but it had taken a century.

To put Merevale into perspective it is interesting to look at what existed for girls in Newport from around 1800. In 1797 Jane and Elizabeth Bennett had a Ladies School at Weston House in the High Street. [ex Masons Butchers]. Between 1869 and 1882 Elizabeth and Jane Collier, two spinster sisters formerly of Penkridge, also had a school there. In 1871 there were twenty girls down to 7 in 1881. Miss E Justice had a Ladies Seminary in the High Street from 1828 to 1836. Miss Egington and Miss Whitfield, and later the Misses Harding, had a Ladies Boarding School at nearby Meretown, in Staffordshire. There were others, Ellen and Francis Weaver at the Old Hall, Mary Anne Pritchard at Chetwynd End, Elizabeth Keeling at Mount Pleasant, Mrs and Miss Mary Anne Stevens, Ladies Seminary, St Marys Street 1828-1844. Frances Atkinson and Caroline Cooke both in their 40`s had a boarding school near Gower House [Henshalls Insurance] in 1849 and from 1855 to 1860, when they gave up the lease, they were at Stanmore House, 93 High Street, opposite the church. Miss Helen Bradbury also moved about town with her school being at Chetwynd End in 1840, Aston Terrace in Station Road in 1849, Prospect House on the corner of Wellington Road in 1861 and at Beech Grove, behind the Grammar School when she sold up in 1884. In 1861 she had three pupils one of whom was her niece Agnes.

In the 1870`s and 80`s Miss Elizabeth Siderfin had a young ladies school next to Roddam House. In 1888 the Misses A.E. and B.A. Thompson set up a boarding and day school at Berkely Villa, Aston Terrace. Their father, a prominent local businessman, had died shortly before. Next door at The Laurels Mrs Milner in 1893 received a *"limited number of pupils"*, with the violin taught by Senor Mancini and pupils prepared for local examinations. In 1901 Mrs Smith had a school for young ladies with a preparatory class for boys at Gower House. She called it *"Newport High School for Girls"*. In January 1906 a *"High School for Girls and School of Music"* was opened at Ivydene in Lower Bar by Mrs Maddox formerly Miss Frood of Merevale. This was an offshoot of the boys` school at Rosement. The Maddox`s left in 1910.

The most important girls school preceding Merevale was probably that of Mrs Jane Sillitoe between 1857 and 1874. This was at Beaumaris House now senior boarding accommodation for the Grammar School. She kept a substantial teaching and domestic staff and had 18/19 pupils from as far away as London and Australia. The building became the Rectory in 1874 and Mrs Sillitoe moved her school across the road retaining the name "Beaumaris House".

Few of these schools, whether for boys or girls, had any permanency, perhaps many reflected not a vocation, but a need for a certain social class to find an income and status without the indignity of it being labelled work. None outlasted their proprietors and they were always bedevilled by financial crisis.

Merevale emerged out of several Ladies establishments. On the 22 November 1884 Mrs Winter advertised that she was leaving Park House (now Masons Place) where, with her daughters, she had had a school for many years, for more commodious premises, and that after Christmas her school would be carried on at Merevale House, Chetwynd End. Chetwynd End was not then part of Newport and Merevale was hidden behind a cluster of smaller properties overlooking the Strine, the canal and the countryside stretching into Staffordshire. Since the beginning of the century Merevale and its neighbour, Castle House, had been connected with the Cobb family who between the houses and the canal bridge had a timber and builders yard. Their most notable work is the Town Hall or Corn Exchange in the main High Street. They took their work home and throughout the grounds are individually carved stones, an archway supported by two pillars from the seventeenth century Butter Market which they demolished in 1860, and enough material to construct a castellated terrace which gives Castle House its name. The medieval High Street climbed from here to the church an ideal setting for a genteel school.

> *"Merevale House, Chetwynd End*
> *Newport Salop.*
> *Mrs Winter*
> *Who is leaving Park House for more commodious*
> *Premises respectfully announces that her school for*
> *Young ladies, will after the Christmas vacation, be*
> *Carried on at Merevale House, where she will have*
> *Vacancies for a few more pupils."*
>
> Newport Advertiser 22 November 1884.

Kelly`s 1891 Directory of Shropshire lists under Chetwynd End *"Winter Sarah (Mrs), young ladies` boarding school."*

> *"High Class School for Girls, Merevale House, Newport, Salop.*
> *Conducted by Mrs and Miss Winter*
> *Resident English and Foreign Governesses, Pupils*
> *prepared for Cambridge Local, College of Preceptors*
> *and other examinations*
> *Thorough Education and Home care*
> *Masters attend for organ, Violin, Painting and drawing,*
> *singing, Mathematics, dancing and Calisthenics.*
> *Ladies wishing to receive lessons in any of the above*
> *subjects may apply to Mrs Winter.*
> *Next Term January 20th."*
>
> Newport Advertiser 2.1.1892.

By 1893 the school had been taken over by Mrs and the Misses Maunde

> *"Merevale, High Class School for Girls; Mrs and the Misses Maunde;*
> *Cambridge Local, College of Preceptors and other examinations.*
> *Miss Maunde gives private lessons in French and German. Miss*
> *Crystal Maunde in music, violin and piano. Governess pupil*
> *required, small premiums,*
>
> Newport Advertiser 1895.

In January 1895 Crystal Maunde married Surgeon Captain Duggan of Edinburgh, an army surgeon. Mrs Maunde died at Merevale aged 62 on 28 February 1898. In September Mrs Mills purchased the school her husband being music master. At this time Mrs Mills had a small school at East Retford in Nottinghamshire. One view is that after the death of Mrs Maunde, Mrs Mills was approached by the parents to take over the school. She already had several little boarders at Retford, some orphans and agreed to do so, on condition she could bring them with her. Her eldest daughter Mabel, `Mabs`, was born at Retford in 1889. Her other daughter Josephine or `Joie`was born at Newport in 1900. By September 1898 Mrs Mills had purchased and was the principal of Merevale College. Her husband, Mark Mills, became music master at Merevale and also organist and choirmaster at Church Aston Church. He was a founder member of Newport Bowling Club

There were 28 girls on the roll rising to 62 by the Autumn Term of 1901 both day and boarding. In 1899 the school had become a centre for the Oxford Local Examinations, had opened a Kindergarten from 4 to 8 years and was holding French conversation classes.

The 1901 Census shows Mark Mills aged 44 as professor of music, self-employed, and Sarah aged 45 with Mabel aged 12 and Josephena just 11 months a very late age to have a baby in those days. Annie Wass aged 24 the younger sister of Sarah was keeping house and there was a French governess. There were seventeen boarders including one boy, and three domestic servants. It proves her insistence on bringing boarders with her from Retford. One was Florence Wilson aged 17 but more interestingly were the Brown children, Lily (16), Gertie (14), Lizzie (13) and John (11). Their father John Thomas Brown, of farming stock, kept the Anchor Inn at East Retford, where in 1884 he married Anne, his deceased wife`s sister which was then illegal. Their mother Anne died in 1895 and their father the next year, 1896. The four children were orphaned but a trust had been set up and this was used to send them to the boarding school at East Retford run by Sarah and Mark Mills. In this situation Sarah Mills could not leave them. Mark Mills had actually witnessed the will of their father. The family still have the Common Prayer and Hymn Book given to young John Brown inscribed *"from his sincere friend Sarah Mills"*, 2 November 1902 and also the poetry book, a school prize, awarded to Gertie.

Mark and Sarah Mills

177

A more distinguished pupil was Ellen Mary Breese who lived with her grandparents at Avenue Road, Newport and attended Merevale for several years before proceeding to the Diocesan Teacher Training College at Derby. Ellen married Albert Enoch Powell at Newport Parish Church on 31 July 1909 and subsequently her son, John Enoch Powell, was christened there on 18 October 1912, Mrs Mills being his godmother and presenting him with a silver cross inscribed in Greek with her favourite text: "Stand therefore" (Eph. 6. 14.). While at Merevale Ellen taught herself Greek a language she passed on to her famous son Enoch Powell.

Mrs Mills was a vigorous, cultured, travelled woman of deep religious conviction. Behind her cultivated exterior lay a shrewd determination that enabled the school to survive until 1937. Her granddaughter recalls that while she may have been stubborn she often fell victim to any hard luck story from parents, and remembers the groans while balancing the books. Evidence suggests that Mrs Mills was quite able to resist parents and to tackle authority with skill and persistence. For example in June 1900 she won a law case against the Hayward family, prominent in business and Council, for fees, after their two girls had been withdrawn when Mrs Mills requested their hair to be held back. There were standards. The family continued to send their children there to the end.

She was a person of intense relationships so that differences could become bitter while friendships remained deep and lasting, endearing messages and photographs passing between her and pupils and former students. Her life was full of private kindnesses but above all she was a dedicated teacher.

In September 1904, because of the increased numbers, a new schoolroom was erected with a reception room, cloakroom and two classrooms. There was also a large room for painting. The old schoolroom was set aside for reading and for the transition room and the kindergarten. The classroom stood on the terrace, below which, were croquet and tennis courts and archery butts. Merevale was the home of Mrs Mills with the infants on the top floor; next door was Castle House with the boarders. The games field was across the main road down *'Green Lane'* which with its surrounding trees, large house and coach house, is still recognisable. As well as the Oxford Local, children were being entered for Trinity College of Music and Royal Drawing Society examinations.

The school took an active part in the social and religious life of the town with Speech Day, sports, drama and dance displays being popular and well attended events. It raised money for good causes the processional cross at St Nicolas Church being purchased by Mrs Mills and the girls.

Things became difficult after the 1902 Education Act (the "Balfour Act"). While unable to build a new school in the town under the Act, Shropshire County Council concentrated on bringing existing schools up to Board of Education standards. Mrs Mills had to spend £1,000 to satisfy County Council requirements. In 1908 the County was proposing a new secondary school for girls which would have undermined Merevale. In August of that year Mark Mills died at Llandudno aged 51 while on holiday. The shock was enormous and Mrs Mills was in a state of collapse for a year the burden of the school being shouldered by Mabs who was only 19. It is easy to see why, looking back, she described 1908 as the *"great cloud"*. The problem for the LEA was that only 30 to 40 of the girls at Merevale came from Newport, a good proportion being from Manchester and Liverpool. For Mrs Mills of course the profit lay in taking boarders.

An advertisement for December 1911 shows the school as a centre for the Oxford Local, Trinity College of Music and Royal Drawing Society examinations. There were *"moderate inclusive fees"*. It offered thorough tuition and home care in large houses, with extensive gymnasium, recreation grounds and a games field. A delightful photograph of July 1908 signed "Sally", that is Mrs Mills, and addressed to her sister Miss Wass in Leeds, shows the games field with the girls playing tennis and cricket. The grass is rather long, the skirts even longer, the bowling underarm, but the deportment is excellent! This was the month before her husband died.

The uneasy relationship between the County and the school continued into the Great War by which time Mrs Mills had been joined from a teaching appointment on Lake Como by her daughter Mabel, 'Mab' Mills, and had taken a partner, Miss Jessie McWean. In March 1917 there were 44 boarders. In 1919 a compromise was reached that satisfied neither side whereby the Salop Higher Education Committee took over Merevale College as a County High School for Girls with Miss McWean as headmistress and Mrs Mills as boarding mistress.

An item in the Newport Advertiser on Saturday 25 October 1919 reports that the "Committee" had interviewed candidates for the post of headmistress of the Merevale County School for Girls, Newport, and recommended that Miss J. McWean, B.A. (London), be appointed at a salary of £150 per annum with a capitation fee of £2 per annum, the minimum salary to be not less than £450 per annum, on the usual terms and conditions. It was further recommended that the Chairman of the Committee and Mr C.W. Smallman be authorised to act as governors and to sign cheques until a permanent governing body was appointed. The governing body was to consist of eleven persons.

So it became a public secondary school for girls under Shropshire LEA and the Board of Education. The curriculum included French, German, Latin, PE, Science, Cookery and

Needlework. Tuition fees, including school stationery, were £2.18.04 per term with reductions for two or more members of a family. There were fifty boarders. The colours and hat-bands of Merevale County School were red and white.

Free places were offered based on examinations and one of the first announced in November 1919 was M.E. Lewis from Newport Church of England School.

In January 1920 the County appointed governors to *"Merevale County School for Girls"*, and they extended and improved the kitchen for domestic science. They leased Castle House from Mrs Mills for five years at an annual rent of £50. There was also an agreement to purchase Merevale and the school furniture for £1,400. Mrs H.A.Cobb died at Atherstone in September 1918 and Mrs Mills wisely took up the option to buy both Merevale and Castle House, the latter for £650 in 1919 and Merevale in 1920 for £800. She had in a sense secured her withdrawal.

In July 1920 the County recommended that the nearby Rosemont School on the corner of Forton Road, with its large house and schoolroom, be leased for five years at £30 per annum with £350 to be spent on adaptations but, at the same time, they recommended the purchase of seven and a half acres of land in Wellington Road to build a new school, completion of purchase to be deferred for two years.

One pupil recalled how in 1920 the buildings were of wood and corrugated iron creating a terrible noise when it rained. The games field was across the main road down Green Lane with a pond in one corner that became a favourite haunt. PT was taken in a kind of shed in the grounds the sides being open which was not so good in windy and rainy weather. Miss McWean's office was wedged between the Hall and the Domestic Science room. The relationship between the two women was by now reflected in increased rivalry between the two groups of girls.

The school played netball against other, similar, schools such as Wellington High and took part in county tournaments. Plays and pageants were staged on the Merevale lawns, still a natural setting, one of the first being *"The Seasons"* starring Zellah Pitchford as *"Summer"*. Zellah was to re-create the school in the 1950's as Castle House.

The actual school was in Castle House, including a preparatory department for boys and girls under 10. Tuition came from Shropshire County Council. Mrs Mills retained the boarding side taking fees and some tuition fees for music, painting, dancing, shorthand and typing which were included in the boarding fee; she was entering boarders for examination under the title *"Merevale College"* while taking boarders for *"Merevale County School"* who received tuition from the Local Authority. In September 1920 it was being suggested that she should re-open her Ladies School and in October 1921 came the following notice:

> *"Mrs Mills wishes to announce that having purchased Chetwynd Bank Newport (formerly in the occupation of Dr Evans and adjoining Merevale) she hopes to re-open Merevale College as a Private Boarding and Day School in January next and will be pleased to send Prospectus as soon as possible to friends in the neighbourhood on application...".*

Newport Advertiser 8 September 1921

She had hoped to work as a housemistress but the number of boarders fell to 20 and she could not even meet expenses. Failing to get agreement with the County Council she reluctantly started up her school again in January 1922 at Bank House in front of Merevale, now a nursing home, and was accepted as an examination centre.

Those at the school at that time can remember the tension between Mrs Mills and Miss McWean manifested in boarders not being allowed to speak to day-girls. Relations with the County Council were bitter. The joint scheme had not worked. There were physical and financial problems but the greatest was the difference of outlook and attitude of the two women. Mrs Mills was in *"no mans land"* a phrase all too familiar to that generation.

The County Council lease on Merevale ended in July 1924 and from 1 August the County rented temporary premises at the Congregational or British schoolroom and used the disused Primitive Methodist chapel opposite as a gym until the new High School was completed on the Wellington Road. Fortunately they were able to use the playing fields on the new site during this period. The preparatory department was in Miss McWeans house in Wellington Road. Doris Beynon was the entire 6th Form.

In August 1924 the demountable buildings at Merevale, which belonged to the County Council, were sold, one housing an assembly room, kitchen, cloakroom and pantry; another four classrooms with radiators; also sold was a four-bayed galvanised gymnasium 60' by 24'. Mrs Mills received £77.10.00 for dilapidation to Castle House. The County Council pursued her over drainage and pollution at Castle House but she defied them, the local County Councillor expressing himself surprised that it was allowed to be used as a school at all. Mrs Mills he said was *"a very clever lady. She had been able to defy the Board of Education and the County Council for 5 years"*. Nevertheless by 1929 the school had expanded to 40 boarders.

Meanwhile the new Girls High School opened in September 1925 at a cost of £12,793 supporters of Mrs Mills describing the buildings as *"palatial"*, a *"white elephant"*, a burden on the rates and expensive in fees and books and uniform. Merevale was good enough, they said, to take girls from Scotland and Paris. These remarks made at the official opening of the High School were considered in bad taste. It is difficult now to understand the opposition but there was considerable disapproval of the High School amongst townspeople partly out of respect for Mrs Mills and the sense she was being betrayed, also because of cost, but also because facilities at the new school were limited, the preparatory department continued to be housed at the British School along with the domestic science classes from the C of E school and it was not until 1935 that A level subjects were available, particularly science, while numbers did not reach the 100 until 1931. Mrs Mills had 67 at that time and it was not a burden on the rates.

Miss McWean was Headmistress with ten staff and 88 pupils. Most of the Newport girls went with Miss McWean. Fees were £10 pa.

Staff at Merevale 1922.

Miss McWean second from left.

At Speech Day in June 1927 Mrs Mills recalled the origins of the school. She talked of the *"sudden upheaval"* of coming to Newport in 1898. There was she said, nothing elaborate at Merevale; drill rooms were simply fitted, with a stage for plays; there was no fitted laboratory but the room contained all the basic apparatus needed for botany and elementary science; there were tennis courts and an excellent playing field for hockey and cricket. Examinations included Trinity College of Music, Royal Drawing Society and Pitmans Shorthand. There was a PE Mistress and a mistress of Lower School.

Merevale continued as the home of Mrs Mills and the kindergarten boarders. Meals were cooked there and wheeled over to the dining room. Castle House had the junior boarders upstairs. The gym was on the terrace. The main focus of the school was now Bank House with the kindergarten at the back and the junior and intermediate classrooms above. At the left front was the senior classroom with the assembly and music room on the right and above dormitories for the senior girls. To the rear was a grassed quadrangle leading to a recreation room above the former stables. In 1930 there were 40 boarders and 8 staff and in 1932 67 children. Most were local, children of farmers, businessmen, clergy and doctors, now brought in by car or Dicky Beard's bus. Girls from say Eccleshall or Albrighton boarded weekly while examination candidates boarded no matter how "local". Boys remained until they were 8, girls until 16.

It was not a career school or a springboard for higher education, the emphasis being on domestic skills such as needlework. Girls had to provide one dozen handkerchiefs everything marked with the owners' name. They had to write home with letters being checked once a month for correctness. Fees were 17 guineas a term, or 16 if under twelve and £3.6s.8d [£3.40] a term for day pupils.

Staff lived in, sleeping with each dormitory. There was Miss Atkins who had one arm and acted as housekeeper and did the cooking and knitting; Miss Richards took music. Miss Hamm was there by 1928 and in 1934 became co-principal and partner, the property being vested in the new partnership. Miss Hamm developed TB and Mrs Mills, now 76 years old could not cope and numbers declined. It was hoped that Joie the younger daughter would return and continue the school but she had her own remarkable career teaching in Cairo, Jaffa and then Amman and turned down the offer.

In 1937 Mrs Mills, then 76 years old, retired and in September Castle House and Merevale were advertised for sale with vacant possession, Castle House being occupied by Captain Ernest Groom and in 1944 by Mr R G Carr ex-licensee of the Plume of Feathers. Merevale, became the home of Douglas Herbert Caird-Daley. In the war Bank House was leased to the Ministry of Works as the headquarters of the National Milk Testing Service. In 1962 it became the offices of Newport Urban District Council and then in 1974 a private nursing home. The outside structures, the dining hall and gymnasium were also sold.

Sarah Mills and "Dainty"

Mrs Mills and Miss Hamm retired to West Kirby, on the Wirral. Miss Hamm became a Church of England nun and Mrs Mills died at Moreton on the Wirral, on the 21 January 1942 aged 81. Her body was brought back to Newport Church where it rested before morning requiem celebration of Holy Mass. Sixteen choirboys sang at the afternoon service during which the processional cross she and the girls had given to St Nicolas` was paraded, draped in black. The cortege then moved to Church Aston for another service and burial near the door of Church Aston Church within earshot of the music played by her husband a third of a century before.

End of Merevale College

Mrs Mark Mills retires.

There is general regret in Newport and district at the decision of Mrs Mark Mills, the Principal, to close Merevale College, the educational institution in Chetwynd End which for many years has been a distinguished feature of the life of the town. The decision has been taken regretfully on account of advancing years.

It is some forty years since Mrs Mills, who in her early life was engaged in the teaching profession in London, came with her husband, the late Mr Mark Mills, from London, to take over an existing private girl`s school at Chetwynd End, and thus began her long association with the educational life of Newport. The school which she acquired proved to be anything but a flourishing concern, so, with the energy and enthusiasm which marked all her actions, she set about to remedy the existing state of affairs, and out of her efforts emerged Merevale College. From that time on continuously till the end of last summer term, except for an interval of five years when the Salop County Council leased the school buildings on the establishment of Newport High School for Girls after the War, Mrs Mills has been in supreme control. Even during the five year interval she acted as housemistress and had care of the boarders attending the new school.

The Merevale tradition.

Under Mrs Mill`'s wise direction, the College achieved an enviable position among educational institutions in the district, and drew pupils form both sides of the Shropshire-Staffordshire border. The standard of efficiency developed with the years and many notable successes both on the academic and commercial side. The principal lavished infinite care on the girls and small boys who were placed in her charge, and it may be regarded as an indication of her pride in the warm feelings of affection which her younger proteges accorded her, that, on relinquishing the active management of the school, she preferred to close it down completely rather than dispose of it as a going concern to someone not nurtured in the Merevale tradition.

A staunch, yet broadminded churchwoman, Mrs Mills has always strongly supported Newport Parish Church, but she has lost no opportunity of co-operating most cordially with the Free Churches of the town in any good work. A notable instance of this is the fact that it has been her invariable practice for years past to lend the beautiful College ground to the Newport Methodist Circuit for the annual fete. The scholars and staff, too, have organised many successful efforts in aid of Foreign Missions. Newport people will join with the many hundreds of girls who have come under her kindly and beneficent influence, in wishing Mrs Mills a long and happy retirement.

Newport and Market Drayton Advertiser 17 September 1937.

Death of Mrs Mark Mills

Former Principal of Merevale College.

Her many former pupils and friends in the Newport district will learn with regret of the death of Mrs Sara Jane Mills, formerly proprietress and principal of Merevale College, Chetwynd End, Newport, which occurred at Moreton, Wirral, Cheshire on Wednesday night at the age of 81. She had been in failing health for some time, having undergone a serious operation some time ago.

Mrs Mills whose maiden name was Wall [sic Wass], came to Newport in 1898 with her husband the late Mr Mark Mills on purchasing from Miss Maunde Merevale College, a private school for girls, originally founded at Park House by Mrs Winter. She continued to conduct the school very successfully for many years, her husband, who was also organist and choirmaster at Church Aston Parish Church, assisting her as music master until his sudden death while on holiday at Barmouth {?} in 1908. During the Great War the Salop County Council took over the school and its buildings from Mrs Mills and established there the Newport County Girl's High School under its first principal, Miss J McWean, Mrs Mills`s services being retained as house mistress and matron. A few years later, however, Mrs Mills, who still retained the ownership of the school buildings, decided to re-establish

Merevale College, and accordingly terminated the County Council`s tenancy, with the result that the High School was built in Wellington Road. She then again carried on her school till four years ago, when she retired and went to live at West Kirby, where she strongly supported the Church of St Andrew.

A lady of considerable culture, Mrs Mills had travelled widely, visiting amongst other countries, Germany, Egypt and Palestine, where her younger daughter was a missionary. An excellent headmistress, gifted with unbounded energy, she had the welfare of her pupils at heart, and took the keenest interest in them after leaving school. Of a deeply religious temperament, she was a devoted churchwoman, and strongly supported Newport Parish Church, where she and her boarders regularly worshipped. The handsome processional cross in the church was the gift of Mrs Mills and her Scholars, and is so inscribed. Through her influence, her school also warmly supported home and foreign missionary work. Of a most kindly disposition, she performed many private benefactions, and was greatly esteemed. She leaves two daughters, Mrs Horace Gibbs of Louth, Lincolnshire, and Miss Joy A Mills, a missionary with the Church Missionary Society, and several grandchildren.

The funeral will take place at the Parish Church on Monday at 2.30pm, and the interment will be at Church Aston Churchyard.

Newport and Market Drayton Advertiser 23 January 1942.

NOTES.

Twelve. Sarah Jane Mills and Merevale.

1. Miles, Malcolm, *The History of Castle House School,* (1994). This contains an earlier version of Mrs Mills and Merevale.
2. Miles, Malcolm, *The Stubborn Woman Who Battled For Merevale,* NMDA 3 August 1984.
3. NMDA, November 1884; June 1900; August 1908; September 1919; October 1921; June 1927; September 1937; obituary January 1942 et al.
4. Information on the Brown family is courtesy of Ruth Wright of Ontario, Canada.

13. THE SILVESTERS OF NEWPORT.

The best way to describe Dissenters, Independents or Congregationalists is to use the words of the biographer of Charles Silvester Horne, Newport's most famous nonconformist, who described him as an inspired radical and an incurable idealist, who spent his life in earnest service and devotion to great causes. Yet in no way was his outlook narrowed or his influence restricted in fact it gave him greater freedom and authority. This portrait is equally true of his predecessors the Silvesters and Hornes and the many good men and women who formed the "Independent" Church in Newport, Shropshire.

In 1800 Nonconformists still faced many restrictions on their civil and religious liberties; they were excluded from Universities (abolished 1871); they paid rates to the established church, (abolished 1868); they were refused burial in churchyards; they could not hold public office judicial, civil or corporate, (abolished 1866); they also fought the use of public money to subsidise Church of England schools despite the 1870 and 1902 Education Acts. In fact as late as February 1904, Nonconformists in Newport refused to pay the part of their rates going *"to the support of sectarian schools"* and were summoned before the magistrates where Sir T.F. Boughey refused them the right to speak in Court. Despite this by their example, through their church and their newspaper, the Dissenters became the conscience of their community.

In 1792 two brothers of the name of Silvester came out of Staffordshire to the country town of Newport in Shropshire. One was Moses Silvester of the bank now known as Lloyds, the other Henry Price Silvester founder of the business now known as the Newport Advertiser. Why did they come? Well on 3 December 1793 Moses married Elizabeth Brown of Newport, a good enough reason; perhaps it was a business opportunity; maybe it was because they were dissenters, Congregationalists, facing violence in urban areas and leaving Wolverhampton for the relative peace of a country town.

Moses Mitchell Silvester a Congregational Dissenter came from Wolverhampton in 1792 as a clerk to what became the Shropshire Banking Company. He also seems to have been a corn merchant, a cider and porter merchant and a carrier three times a week to Stone. The business of the bank was transacted in the lower part of the yard before entering the garden and finding no Independent Church in the town he began a small congregation and Sunday School in a large room over the bank offices behind his home. In 1765 a Mr Jones gave to a Captain Scott, a long serving soldier who founded many churches after leaving the army and before his death in 1807, land between the bank and the Grammar School on which he built a chapel. Moses found the building was still there being used as a day school and obtained the consent of the Captain to re-open it as a chapel. Some time later he purchased it. The success of the chapel did not meet with the approval of the headmaster of the Grammar School, the Rev. Joseph Scott (1773-1818), who annoyed at its proximity to his school and his pupils, offered to take it down and rebuild it at his own expense in another part of the neighbourhood. It was rebuilt in Beaumaris Lane in 1803 on land at the bottom of the "Bear Meadow" to the rear of the former Bear Inn that by then was the house of the lawyer Thomas Morris and is now Beaumaris House. This was a one-storied brick building capable of holding 50-60 people and approached down Salters Lane or through the garden of the bank there being no New Street. It was converted into two cottages only recently demolished.

When numbers increased he instigated the building of the Congregational Church in Wellington Road, now Trinity Church, though he died before it was opened in 1832, at which time he was manager of the bankers "Hordern Sons and Company" in the High Street. His son William was also a corn merchant and succeeded his father as manager at the bank, then the "Shropshire Banking Company", until at least 1861, and, with his two sisters, continued active in the Congregational Church and Sunday School.

> *"Thus, Mr Silvester, who revived this little cause,*
> *resembled Moses, who having led the Children of Israel*
> *to the borders of the promised land was gathered to his*
> *fathers, ere they entered it..."*

Short History of the Congregational Church, 1907.

Henry Price Silvester was established as a printer and bookseller in Newport by 1795. He was 22. Soon he was married with five children three of whom died young, and even though they were dissenters, were buried in the aisle of Newport Church. Two boys survived, Henry, born 1803, and Charles, born October 1809 and a sister, Harriet Amelia, born in 1815. In 1814-15 Henry Price Silvester was a member of the Newport Patrol set up to guard the streets at night during the Napoleonic Wars. He was also a subscriber to the coffee room and the oyster club at the Red Lion.

> *"..... bookseller, printer, stationer, binder and commissioner*
> *for taking special bail, and manufacturer of the composition*
> *roller for inking metal types. High Street."*

1822 Directory.

The business was at 23 High Street with the printing works up the yard at the side, still visible from the tennis courts. In 1961 it was transferred to Bellmans Yard and later the printing and newspaper split, the latter going to St Mary's Street.

By 1828 he had the additional roles of post-master and vendor of patent medicines, in 1829 he was *"druggist and tea dealer and perfumier"*, and by 1835 he was the actuary of the Savings Bank next door.

> *"Mr. H.P. Silvester, Post-Master, High Street. A horse post*
> *leaves every morning at half-past three, and meets the*
> *London and Holyhead Mails at Shiffnal, and returns every*
> *morning at four. A horse post is dispatched at six o`clock in*
> *the morning, to meet the Manchester mail at the Spread*
> *Eagles".*

The Salop Directory 1828.

Dissenters may have faced religious discrimination but they were trusted with money. By 1840 with increasing illness Henry and Charles came into the business with their father retired and listed as "Gentry". He died aged 78 in April 1851. Though not as prominent as his brother in the church he is listed as one of the members who remodelled the church in 1839 when faced with declining numbers.

Henry Silvester	65	Postmaster
Anne Silvester	65	
Henry Silvester	35	Printer
Charles Silvester	30	Printer
2 apprentices		1 female servant

1841 Census.

One of the apprentices was Alfred Zeigler aged 15; was he related to the artist Henry Bryan Zeigler who painted a picture of Newport High Street in 1840, a picture strangely still in the possession of the Hall/Silvester family?

The youngest son Charles after leaving the Grammar School worked in his father's office in the bookbinding department and subsequently took positions in Bristol and London to obtain experience. Henry, the quiet one, stayed at home and Charles had to return home on his father's illness. He gave up the Post Office and often refused other business if it meant working on Sundays. In 1842 they were booksellers, stationers, printers and music and musical instrument sellers as well as commissioners for bail and vendors of patent medicines. They expanded into account books and other specialist printing.

But dramatic changes were on the way in technology and politics. There were various taxes on newspapers through the politicians' fear of the masses. Stamp Duty imposed on newspapers at a 1d a sheet in 1712, had increased to 4d a copy in 1815 in the troubled times of the Napoleonic Wars and was not finally abolished until 1855 just as Charles Silvester was enlarging the business. Newspapers had to carry stamps this allowed them to be taken free through the post. In reality it was a tax and no advantage except to London papers like *The Times*. Though there were provincial weeklies, dailies were too expensive and did not survive long. Abolishing the Stamp Duty destroyed the monopoly of *The Times* and made newspapers cheaper for a vaster audience. Almost overnight papers went down from 5d to 4d and very soon to 1d. This was part of the Victorian movement to Free Trade. It was also because the 1850's were prosperous and the prospect of revolution and disorder diminished. There were other taxes, on advertising, removed in 1853, and duties on the printing paper which lasted until 1861.

There were technical changes, the telegraph, the cable and Reuters meant provincial newspapers could get the news as quickly as London. By the 1850's there were rotary printing presses, printing on both sides on continuous rolls of cheap, wood pulp paper. The age of the local newspaper had arrived. The *"Newport Advertiser"* was born.

The first edition was a modest affair on 1 December 1854, the *"Newport Advertiser and Monthly Record"*, partly printed in London, illustrated and published once a month. On the 18 August 1855 it was enlarged and made a weekly and further enlarged six months later. The paper received immediate support not only in the Newport district but around Market Drayton and as it became known its circulation increased. By now it was the *Newport Advertiser and North Shropshire Herald* price 1d published on a Saturday morning. In 1858 its circulation was 1,700, in 1861, 2,400 and by 1863 it was claimed to be 3,000 weekly.

> *"A first–class family paper, with an ordinary weekly issue of upwards of 2,400 copies, circulates among the Clergy, gentry and commonality of Shropshire, Staffordshire and Cheshire. While it declines attaching itself to any party, it discusses, in its leading articles, all the political and social questions of the day in a calm and dispassionate spirit, it devotes a portion of its columns monthly to an impartial review of new publications, literary and musical, and publishes a resume of the latest news, with the state of the markets. The advertisements on its columns are brought before the eyes of numerous and select circle of readers, and for the general body of Metropolitan and local advertisers it is the best agent in the district."*
>
> July 1862.

The great leap forward was too much for Henry Silvester who retired at the age of 51 when the newspaper was introduced. He went to live at Millington a quiet hamlet near Knutsford. Never very strong he outlived all his family, dying in August 1887 aged 84. He was the gentlest of all gentle souls and unfitted to grapple with the work and difficulties of life never mind business. A careful and excellent printer the pace and upset caused by the introduction of the newspaper and the constant exposure of the publisher to the dangers of libel meant he could not adapt to the change. He gladly retired. He was buried next to his brother in Newport cemetery.

Being what he was Charles Silvester never professed to write for the paper and being a minority group always excluded anything and everything of an offensive or contentious nature. There were lots of advertisements and notices and regurgitated national and international news and though there were some voluntary contributions there was at first little "local" or literary. There was an element of chapel news and teetotal and missionary items.

Until the paper became established it was excluded from public bodies so a large source of copy was denied them. A few years later the reporter was one of the few attending such meetings:

> *"Vestry Meeting: The consequence on Thursday was that*
> *instead of an animated meeting like those of former years*
> *there was great difficulty in raising a meeting atall and the*
> *business of the Parish had to be transacted by a ratepayer,*
> *the rate collector and the Reporter. The various*
> *propositions were " carried unanimously".*

Newport Advertiser 9 March 1872.

The *"Reporter"* in this instance and throughout the 60`s and 70`s, albeit part-time, was John Norris who was in fact the Newport postmaster. One of the best known men in town he was conscientious in local affairs and his involvement and knowledge made him an ideal correspondent and some of his reports are classics.

Whoever wrote the leaders, on big issues the paper became very influential. Between 1856-59 its coverage of the clearing of the cattle markets from the streets and the creation of a Market Company with an indoor and outdoor market and community facilities was eloquent and decisive:

> *"The spirit of improvement is hovering over our town,*
> *seeking a convenient spot where she may alight, and where*
> *she might exert her utilitarian influence for the well-being*
> *of the community:- shall we scare her from the*
> *neighbourhood by our want of harmony, or shall we*
> *endeavour, in a spirit of unity and brotherhood, to*
> *facilitate the introduction of those valuable results that*
> *will undoubtedly spring from her labours".*

Editorial, Newport Advertiser, 7 February 1857.

The paper published letters from all points of view, reported detailed arguments from every meeting, displayed public notices, gave lists of subscribers and printed the Act of Parliament. It appealed for harmony and unity of action for the mutual benefit of all. It is hard to find before or since such an impartial and balanced presentation of an issue. It could only have been done by the Silvesters.

Charles Silvester	Head. Unmarried	51
Anne Simpson	Niece	23
Mary Podmore	Niece	22
Francis Horne	Scholar. Visitor	15
1 female servant		

1861 Census.

Charles continued to improve the business, installing new printing machinery that could produce new lines such as ledgers and cash books and in the same year, 1862, stocking a wide range of accessories like albums, stereoscopic slides, inkstands, souvenirs and wedding and birthday presents, aimed at the readership of his new paper.

The Silvester family was expanding through church connections. Harriet Amelia Silvester (1815-77) married Leonard Simpson of Toxteth, a Liverpool docks official at Birkenhead. Their daughter, Anne, acted as housekeeper to Charles and married in 1882 the Rev. Joshua Sidebottom a Congregationalist Minister who was pastor in Newport and ran a small school in Avenue Road. Her sister Harriet Simpson, another niece of Charles Silvester, married Charles Horne also a Congregationalist Minister.

Leonard Simpson, the father of Mrs Horne, illustrates how members of an apparently closed and restricted religious sect, were remarkably worldly people. A poor boy, he worked himself up to be Superintendent of the Government Tobacco Warehouses in Liverpool, the largest in the world. His beliefs and character underpinned the responsibilities of the post and he even gave up smoking to avoid any suggestion of abusing his position. An extrovert who had a gift of humour and exaggeration that illuminated his Sunday School teaching he also had a great curiosity fitting an age of scientific and technological progress. His working life began by being rowed to work across the Mersey, encompassed the opening of the first railway and the death of Mr Huskisson as the first railway victim, the steamship replacing sail, and the consequential development of Liverpool as a huge transatlantic city. He had all the attributes of his fellow Liverpudlian, Mr Gladstone, without his stuffiness. He died aged 83 in 1896.

The need for more reliable help became pressing and on 1 March 1866 Charles Silvester and Charles Horne went into partnership in the printing and publishing business in Newport, Horne giving up the Ministry. In 1869 Charles Silvester retired and Horne went into partnership with Samuel Bennion a man running a similar business in Market Drayton. In September 1869 six of Charles' employees presented him with a gold pencil case and the accompanying letter on silk, printed in black and white, is in the newspaper's archives:

> *".... as a slight expression of the goodwill and esteem entertained by us toward you, and also as a recognition of the desire you have always evinced, during the time we have been in your employ to promote our best interests and social welfare."*

The signatories were James Bennett, Henry Lunn who had his own family orchestra and founded his own printing business, George Cartwright, Francis Evans, Edward Bradbury and William Stanton.

> *"Mr Silvester, in replying, said his duties as actuary of the savings bank rendered his retirement necessary, and he rejoiced to think that he had procured such a man as Mr Bennion, of Market Drayton, as his successor."*

On 29 May 1878 Charles Silvester died *"a man of fine presence and saintly character."* The Church history records that with Mr Mark Thompson he had gone to London to the May Meetings of the Congregational Union, was taken ill there, and died suddenly. Another version was that through friendship he came to edit the paper while Charles Horne was away, caught a chill on the train and died. He had been a church deacon for thirteen years, secretary and treasurer of the Day and Sunday Schools and of the British and Foreign Bible Society. He was also the actuary of the Savings Bank, which became The Trustee Savings Bank (TSB).

> *"Silvester and Horne's, general printing, stationery and binding establishment. Hand and posting bills, catalogues, circular letters and notes, cards, pamphlets, club articles and every other description of printing, executed with neatness, accuracy and despatch.*
>
> *Machine printers, publishers, book-sellers, stationers, binders, account-book manufacturers, etc, Advertiser office, Newport.*
>
> *Ledgers, journals, cash and day books, etc, made to any pattern in Russia, Vellum, Calf etc with all the latest improvements and of the best materials and workmanship.*
>
> *Bibles, church services and prayer-books; companions to the altar etc in the most novel style of binding. Machine ruling to any pattern, carefully and neatly executed".*

Newport Advertiser 13 June 1868.

On the 22 October 1901 a tablet to the memory of Charles Silvester was unveiled in the Congregational Church by his niece Mrs Sidebottom who had been practically a daughter for 28 years:

> *"In loving memory of Charles Silvester, a generous supporter of this church from the time of its erection and a devoted Deacon and leader of the choir for many years. Born 1809. Died 1878. The memory of the just is blessed. This tablet was placed here by his niece Anne Sidebottom."*

An editorial in the "*Advertiser*" written by Charles Horne, described him as:

> *"A man of strong character. His resolute will was strengthened by fixed principles and deep convictions, and his sense of duty was so irresistible that he would have been ready to sacrifice anything to it. He was eminently a religious devout man of the Puritan type....Throughout life his punctuality, order and perfect correctness were remarkable".*

From now on advertisements would read *"Horne and Bennion, Newport, est. 1785"* while in Market Drayton it would be *"Bennion and Horne, est 1800"*, a tactful compromise.

The Silvester Monument in Newport Cemetery

In July 1867 the paper added *"and Market Drayton Chronicle"*. In October 1869 the Newport and Market Drayton papers merged as the *"Newport and Market Drayton Advertiser"* under the partnership of Charles Horne and Samuel Bennion. It was a practical and sensible merger of similar interests that encompassed retail bookselling and stationery, manufacturing stationery, wholesale provision, bookbinding, printing and a range of newspapers covering a large part of Shropshire and Staffordshire. The printing was concentrated at Newport.

Thomas Platt Bennion was a bookseller in Drayton in 1851 though the business claimed to have been established in 1800. It was he who started the Market Drayton paper in 1855 a year after Newport. There was also a Samuel Silvester bookseller, printer and stationer in Drayton at that time. Thomas Bennion was succeeded by Samuel, then Archie Bennion and Edgar Bennion, who lived in Newport.

In 1879 the Advertiser had a circulation of 6,000 and was published on a Saturday morning at a cost of 1d. Ten years later they had added the "*Stone and Eccleshall Advertiser,*" published on a Friday afternoon for Saturday. Both were printed in Newport.

> *"These papers have an extensive circulation throughout Shropshire, Staffordshire, and Cheshire, comprising a rich and prosperous district – Agriculture, Mining, and Commercial in its character".*

Advertisement, "History of Tong" 1894.

In 1895 with no one from the family to succeed and the original religious impulse gone the basis of the business was broadened by the formation of Bennion, Horne, Smallman and Co. of Newport, Market Drayton, Shifnal and Stone but based in Newport. Publications now comprised the *"Newport and Market Drayton Advertiser"* (and Shropshire, Staffordshire and Cheshire Chronicle), *"The Stone, Longton, Fenton and Eccleshall Advertiser"* (and Uttoxeter, Cheadle and Stafford Gazette) and also the *"Shifnal, Oakengates, Ironbridge and Madeley Advertiser"* (and Dawley, Much Wenlock, Coalport, Coalbrookdale, Broseley, Albrighton and St Georges Gazette). 64 columns for 1d.

> *"In addition to being the recognised organs of local towns, these papers have an extensive circulation generally throughout Shropshire, Staffordshire and Cheshire, comprising a rich and prosperous district – Agricultural, manufacturing, Brewery, Mining and Commercial in character. Being independent in politics and religion, they are taken by all parties; and, as well-established local papers, they are seen by all classes. They are excellent mediums for Advertisers, by whom they are well supported."*

Charles Horne.

Charles Horne was born in Moreton in the Marsh on 1 May 1829 and educated at Springhill College, Birmingham that produced several eminent nonconformist scholars. He graduated MA London. He was ordained as a Congregational Minister and his first church was at Odiham, Hants and later Cuckfield Congregational Church, Sussex. His career change came when nervous strain obliged him to give up the ministry and through his wife he joined the Newport newspaper. The paper had then been in existence 12 years. His partnership with Samuel Bennion of Market Drayton not only widened the business but allowed Charles Horne to concentrate on editorial and journalistic duties not easy as a liberal and nonconformist in a conservative town dominated by cliques.

> *".... nonconformity was a very unfashionable thing in Newport, and the church could only afford a small stipend...so Ministers came and went without leaving any very permanent mark."*

"Life of Charles Silvester Horne." p 5.

A strict puritan, a strong character, literate, intellectual and modest and very nervous in public, he forced himself to take a role in public life and fought many campaigns against privilege and prejudice. An ardent politician, intensely patriotic and devoted to the cause of progress people relied on him in public and private matters yet he was a man of few words, modest and retiring, content to be felt rather than seen or heard. His circle was limited to the chapel. He was essentially a scholar and a gentleman and this is evident to anyone who reads the paper during his thirty-seven years of editorship.

The biography of Charles Silvester Horne, the son of Charles, described life at home with his father and the newspaper:

> *"During his boyhood the home life was very much under the domination of the newspaper which his father edited. The whole family was sometimes involved in proof-reading – an excellent training in accuracy and correct expression – and at a very early age Horne became familiar with the processes of printing, and used to set up in type his own compositions, both in prose and verse. But the paper also led naturally to politics, and under his father's wise guidance the boy began to acquire the taste and enthusiasm for politics which remained with him throughout his life. Though known as an ardent Liberal and Nonconformist, the elder Horne was accustomed to write with a sobriety and fairmindedness which, except, perhaps at election times, commended his paper to many whose politics were of a different complexion from his own. He always recognised that there are two sides to most questions, and tried to understand opinions which he could not share. His weekly "leaders" won him very considerable influence in the locality, and men looked to see what he had to say on matters both of local and national interest. In those days politics were very lively. Newport was a stronghold of Conservatism, though it contained a good many Radicals who found their inspiration in the Birmingham of Dale, Chamberlain and Bright."*

"Life of Charles Silvester Horne" p 4-6.

It was said at election times that the wise nonconformist closed his curtains!

He was a Poor Law Guardian; founder of the annual treat for the poor; he was on the School Attendance Committee and a manager of the Grammar School. In August 1896, in a bye-election caused by the removal of Dr C.E. Baddeley for non-attendance, he was elected as an Urban District Councillor and was Vice-chairman at his death. He was the actuary of the Savings Bank and created the Penny Bank.

One of Charles' main interests was education not surprising given the long conflict between the nonconformist *"British"* schools and the Church of England *"National Schools"*. Like the Quakers, the nonconformists had long been excluded by law and religious doctrine from main stream education such as universities and public schools and, like the Quakers, from many other areas of public life so that education was one means of advancement. Freedom of entry therefore to an endowed school like Newport Grammar was essential and Charles Horne was in the middle of disputes between "Town" and "School" over reform of the school in the 1880's. In fact much of our knowledge of the disputes comes from his meticulous reports of the debates in the *"Advertiser"*. All his sons went through the school and he himself became a manager.

The Congregationalists had formed their own "Infants" school, though it took older pupils, in Wellington Road in 1847. They tried manfully to maintain a mixed school in the 1870's and the plaque over the door still proclaims "British School", but it failed through lack of subscriptions and became the infants outpost of Newport Junior School. As the Junior School then took children of all denominations he was anxious to keep an eye on its teaching particularly as all nonconformist and Liberal adherents in the country were up in arms over the 1902 Education Act. In 1900 he paid a visit to the Newport National School:

> *"Feb 20. Visit from Mr Horne this afternoon. He is the editor and publisher of the Newport and Market Drayton Advertiser Newspaper, and other publications. He takes a great interest in the education given and the welfare generally of elementary schools. He came to look round while object lessons were on and elementary science was being taught. He seemed very pleased with his visit. He was pleased at the practical nature of the instruction. No doubt it will help him to rebut the idea that the present education we are giving in our school is too bookish and unfitting for their future station in life as argued by some."*

School Log Book, 20 February, 1900.

Charles Horne later became involved with the affairs of the headmaster, Mr Carr, who was in dispute with the Attendance Committee over leaving ages and later was dismissed for hitting a child. To the *"Advertiser"* Mr Carr became something of a martyr and was described as being:

> *"A marked man, and for his liberalism had to leave the school."*

As a Councillor, Horne campaigned for the merger of the Marsh Trust with the Urban District Council. The Trust had been set up in 1764 to administer the Marsh Estate on Audley Avenue and to use the income for the improvement of the town. With the advent of local government in 1875 and in 1894 its duties were overlapping and irrelevant. Charles Horne used an advertisement in his newspaper to push his candidature and policies, reinforced at a public meeting in December 1901 by a long, witty, speech. However the merger did not happen until 1930.

He fought hard, with the local doctors, for improved water and sewage, and when in 1896 the town had been surveyed, the engineer appointed, and the money borrowed, the *Advertiser* trumpeted the improved sanitation, not only in Newport, but also Stafford, Stone and Uttoxeter, as *"the approaching triumph"*.

Charles died 25 March 1903. His son Charles Silvester Horne wrote:

> *"We have been much comforted by the wonderful demonstrations of love and honour in which he was held everywhere.....He was so gentle and shy and retiring, and yet so able and strong and true. He had known religious doubt and mastered it."*

"Life of Charles Silvester Horne" p 186.

> *"Mr Charles Horne, for many years a respected member, Deacon and officebearer of the Church, died March, 1903, and his loss has been severely felt by all who knew him."*

"Short History of the Congregational Church."

Charles Horne	Mar	41	Printer, bookseller, employing 2ass, 4 men, 7 boys	Moreton in the Marsh, Gloucester
Harriet S	Wife	32		Liverpool
Leonard	Son	10	Scholar	Hants
Mary	Dau	8	Scholar	Westbury on Sea.
Frederick	Son	7	Scholar	Cuckfield, Sussex
Charles Silvester	Son	5	Scholar	Cuckfield
1 Ass. 1 F. Serv.				

1871 census. Living next to Adams House, High Street, Newport.

The Horne Family
Top left: Charles Horne, Harriet (Wife, with Margery Hall on Grandmother's knee),
Mary Elizabeth Hall (Daughter, with Thekla Hall on knee), Mr. Simpson (Father of Harriet).
Front: Frank Hall, Winifred Hall, Joyce Hall, Nora Hall.
Photograph courtesy of Ann Warner-Casson.

The Horne family.

Harriet Horne, wife of Charles Horne and grand-daughter of Henry Price Silvester, died 29 November 1914, after an *"unostentatious life"*, at the Gables, Granville Road, Newport, the home of her daughter, Mrs Hall. The daughter of Leonard Simpson of Birkenhead and a Silvester on her mother's side, she was a woman of strong character, keen and enthusiastic, with a Puritan strictness and self-repression, who provided a home of high ideals and devotion, where religion and education were of supreme importance, and money, if there was any, was a means to an end.

Leonard Horne, MA, CBE went to the Grammar School where he passed first in all England in the Cambridge Senior Local Examination; he entered the British Postal Service. He died aged 73 at Muswell Hill, London, on 2 June 1934.

Fred Horne. He attended the Grammar School, studied farming, then, through ill health, farmed in Central Queensland, Australia between 1881-8. He farmed Honnington, Shifnal as a tenant of Kenyon-Slaney for 15 years though it did not stop him contesting Ludlow in 1903 and 1906, and Barkston Ash in Yorkshire twice, as a Liberal.

"We had a very big meeting at Craven Arms last night. There was some disturbance at first, and the police turned two or three drunken men out. After that it was absolutely unanimous and most enthusiastic."

December 14, 1903.

He was an authority on agricultural legislation and advocated security of tenure, compensation for disturbance and changes in land law. He promoted Shifnal Agricultural Improvement Society and was a member of Shropshire Chamber of Agriculture. He entered government service as a Smallholder Commissioner until 1924 at £800pa. He was awarded the OBE in 1918 and died aged 63 in February 1927 at Maidstone. He married Jean Picken Thomson, The Manor, Shifnal who died aged 87 in February 1954 and had a son Ralph and a daughter Mary Silvester Horne.

Mary Horne was the only daughter of Charles Horne and married Richard Nicklin Hall a solicitor from Dudley in October 1883. Because of ill health he became an archaeologist in Rhodesia (Zimbabwe) and the curator of the ancient ruins there. He died on 18 November 1914 at Bulawayo aged 61. Mrs Hall took her five daughters (Winifred, Norah, Margery, Thekla and Joyce) back to Newport to look after her ageing parents at first over the newspaper offices in the High Street then at The Gables, Granville Avenue. She died 12 April 1922. At her death her daughters went to live at 58 High Street, Newport, over Brittains' shop.

Of her children Margaret Silvester (Margery) Hall died aged 93 in 1986. Having trained at Queen Charlotte's Hospital and become a highly qualified maternity nurse, she was one of the first nurses to be employed at Annabelle Lady Boughey Cottage Hospital and was later matron at the Roddam Nursing Home retiring when it closed with the foundation of the National Health Service in 1948.

"Miss Margaret S.Hall, SCM MTO. Maternity nurse, 58 High Street, Newport. Tel:115".

Newport Advertiser 2 July 1937.

Winifred Hall had a kindergarten and preparatory school above Brittains' shop at 58 High Street with about 16 pupils in 1931. She had a similar school for two years in Wolverhampton in 1934 but returned to Newport and re-opened her school but retired through ill health and died in December 1937. Miss Pitchford, who founded Castle House School, worked under her and took over the school.

"Kindergarten and Nursery Class. Will be started in September, (Date later). For particulars apply Miss Winifred Hall, 58, High Street, Newport, Salop".

Newport Advertiser, 23 July 1937.

"Kindergarten and Nursery Class for boys and girls. Mornings only. Private lessons by arrangement. Miss W.Hall, 58 High Street, Newport."

Newport Advertiser, 1 October 1937

Winifred died New Years Eve 1937 aged 50 at 58 High Street. Her obituary records a *"sterling public career"*, devoted to the poor. Educated at Merevale College she was a strong Congregationalist and a Newport and Wellington Guardian.

Thekla Hall who died aged 101 in February 1996 was educated at Merevale College and Hiatts College, Wellington, until 1911 when she left to train in secretarial work in London then in social work at Birmingham University. During the 1914-18 War she was a WAAC and served with the British Expeditionary Force in France and was later seconded to the American Expeditionary Force. For six years she was private secretary to the British Consul in Sao Paulo, Brazil, then did social work in Canada and for 25 years in South Africa.

> *"Before the 1ˢᵗ war hardly any one in Newport dare be a Liberal – outwardly. This, because the Sutherlands had a finger in most business interests. My family were Liberal."*

The married sister, Joyce Hall (Evans), left home at 16 in 1906 to work as a governess in private families in France, Russia and Belgium and then as a missionary in Madagascar for many years. She appeared in the Guinness Book of Records as the *"Longest Diary-writer in the world."*. She had twin sons, David and Frank, and a daughter Olwyn.

Charles Silvester Horne.

Charles Silvester Horne was the youngest son of Charles Horne and the most famous. He was born in Cuckfield in 1865 and came to Newport when only six weeks old when his father took over the *Advertiser*. He proceeded easily through the Grammar School and at sixteen was top of the school and preaching his first sermon at the "Outwoods" mission in the village of Moreton, Staffordshire.

> *"It was at Newport that Silvester Horne was educated and spent the whole of his boyhood. Though just on the border of Staffordshire, and within easy reach of a busy industrial district, Newport itself is a purely agricultural market town of some 3,000 inhabitants. Its chief distinction is an old endowed grammar school, where an excellent education is provided at a moderate cost. At this school the Horne boys were brought up, and the eldest brother Leonard writes of it as follows: "Charlie passed through the school, rising from class to class with too little exertion, his quick intelligence and retentive memory making everything easy to him. He did not distinguish himself, however, except in English, where he showed real power of expression and the faculty of committing to memory long poems and speeches in the plays of Shakespeare. He played cricket and football with zest and success. The boys who attended the school were largely sons of farmers of the neighbourhood and of the professional men and tradesmen of the town. But there was also a large contingent of the sons of labourers and artizans who entered with scholarships from the elementary schools, and this fusion of classes was probably one of the influences which helped to make Charlie so much at home with all sorts and conditions of men, and especially with the congregations of little village chapels up and down the country"."*
>
> "The Life of Charles Silvester Horne" W.B.Selbie.

He was immersed in the nonconformity and liberalism of his father and chapel, and being too young for an English university went to Glasgow and then in 1886 to Mansfield College, Oxford, then in its first year. In 1888 at the age of 23 he was at Allen Street Church, Kensington where in 1892 he married Katherine Cozens-Hardy the sister of an Oxford friend and daughter of a supporter of Kensington Chapel.

"Quite a furore has recently been created in Congregational circles by the preaching of the Rev.C.S. Horne. Mr. Horne who comes from Gloucestershire is only 23 years of age. He has a pale boyish face, and deep-set, pensive, sepulchral-looking eyes. He is a graduate of Glasgow University and has not yet finished his theological training under Dr Fairbairn at Mansfield College."

Quotes: *"his simple, but polished utterance".*

Newport Advertiser, 20 October 1888, quoting a London newspaper.

They had three sons and four daughters, one son being Kenneth Horne the broadcaster. By 1903 he was at the prestigious Whitefield Chapel in the Tottenham Court Road a city centre mission. In 1909 he was the chairman of the Congregational Union of England and Scotland and in January 1910 was elected member for Ipswich the first Minister of religion to be elected since the time of Oliver Cromwell. He had previously contested a London County Council seat and helped his brother in elections in 1903 and campaigned vigorously in the 1906 Liberal landslide.

Sir D.F. Goddard (L) 6,120. Majority 262.
Rev. C. Silvester Horne (L) 5,958.
A. Churchman (U) 5,690.
B.H. Burton (U) 5,645. First two elected. No change.

Though there were political factors that took him into Parliament, such as the opposition to the 1902 Education Act, the need for religious equality and the dislike of the privileges of the House of Lords where no dissenters sat, his main motivation was public service and the need for social reform:

"Silvester Horne himself was so convinced of the need for the Church's witness on public questions that he went into Parliament, and probably shortened his life thereby."

"A Popular History of the Free Churches" p 443.

Horne was often criticised for the political complexion of his religious meetings and preaching but was unrepentant about the necessity of bringing religion into politics. Perhaps this was to be expected given the social conditions around the Tottenham Court Road Mission and his immersion in the writing of Charles Booth and the work of William Booth and the Salvation Army.

He found time to write a novel *"A Modern Heretic"* in 1894, poetry, hymns and his collected sermons. He also wrote *"The Story of the London Missionary Society"*, *"The Popular History of the Free Churches"*, 1903, and *"The Life of David Livingstone"*.

He was a great walker, golfer and cyclist, going on cycling tours even for his honeymoon! In 1911 he visited the USA but he was already ill given the massive programme of legislation through Parliament and the Marconi share scandal, and in January 1914 he retired from

Whitefields and went on another trip to the USA. He gave a series of lectures at Yale University and then went from Boston to Niagara and then by boat to Ontario. He died on board in view of Toronto on 2 May 1914 aged 49. His body was brought back by his wife for burial in Church Stretton where for the last few years they had lived in the "White House".

In September 1918 the Silvester Horne Institute was opened in Church Stretton at a cost of £2,600 as a national memorial. It is odd that the one memorial to the family should be in Church Stretton not Newport.

"Mr Charles Silvester Horne was the third and youngest son of the late Mr Charles Horne M.A. for many years editor and one of the proprietors of the "Newport and Market Drayton Advertiser". When he was an infant only six weeks old his mother brought him to Newport, where the years of his childhood, boyhood and early youth were spent. At an early age he was sent to Newport Grammar School, of which Mr Tom Collins M.A. was the popular Headmaster.....He lived up to the honoured traditions of the school, was diligent in study and keen in sport. He never lost his love of his alma mater; time seemed to enlarge rather than to diminish his affection for his old school; and whenever he came down from the university for his summer vacation, he always played in the annual cricket match:- "Past v Present". He encouraged the boys to love their games and never failed to give a valuable prize at the annual athletic sports. He also presented the handsome Challenge Shield, now competed for by the "Houses". When the old Novaportian Club was initiated he assisted in its foundation, attended its annual meetings in Newport and London, unless unavoidably prevented and was President in 1913, but was unable to attend the Newport dinner on account of indisposition".

"The flag was hoisted at half mast on the Parish Church Tower. The Grammar School flag was also run up at half mast and a similar sign of mourning was displayed at the School Cricket ground in Audley Avenue."

Newport Advertiser 9 May 1914.

A plaque was erected to his memory in Big School.

Charles Kenneth Horne. 1907-69.

The son of the Rev. Charles Silvester Horne he married quietly in September 1930 Lady Pelham-Clinton-Hope younger daughter of the Duke of Newcastle. He had been a graduate at Cambridge with the bride's brother. They went to live in a suburb of Birmingham where he was employed by Triplex Glass later becoming Chairman of Triplex and Chad Valley Toys, Wellington. He gave up business after a stroke to concentrate on comedy.

He appeared in "Much Binding in the Marsh", with Richard Murdoch and Sam Costa, "Beyond our Ken", "Round the Horne", with Kenneth Williams, and "Horne A`plenty". He died while making a speech just after completing the last series of "Round the Horne".

The Newport Advertiser 1854-2004

After the death of Charles Horne the Advertiser continued under Charles Smallman and was rationalised into one edition enlarged in 1909 to twelve pages and in 1912 had photographs from its sister paper the Shrewsbury Chronicle. There was a major change in philosophy for

Smallman was a staunch Conservative and was supported by the money of Sir Beville Stanier a local landowner and Conservative MP for North Shropshire who in 1908 purchased the Shrewsbury Chronicle as well as the Advertiser to boost his political ambitions. By 1909 Smallman was manager and editor and in 1913 purchased the paper and the printing works under the title "C.W. Smallman". In 1916 the stationery and bookselling business was sold and Smallman edited the paper from next door at 21 High Street. New electrical equipment went into the printing plant that was handling the Shrewsbury Chronicle as well. In 1919 Smallman absorbed the printing business of A.S. Hall, 75 High Street. That same year the veteran reporter, T.P. Marshall died and his son Robert came as editor. In 1920/21 Smallman retired and sold the business to David Rowlands of Welshpool who continued to publish from 21 High Street under the banner of the Shrewsbury Chronicle Ltd, Smallman staying on as a director.

Charles William Smallman was a Newport boy whose family is still in town. He was the eldest son of Charles Smallman a market gardener in Upper Bar, Newport, and served his apprenticeship as a printer with Horne and Bennion. He became a printer and bookseller in The Square, Shifnal and acted as a reporter for the Advertiser. He held many public offices being a County Councillor, where he chaired the Education Committee, Chairman of the Urban District Council, a Marsh Trustee and Guardian, director of the Market Company, a freemason and churchwarden and one of the first to have a car in Newport. He died 25 March 1939 while living with his daughter in Manchester.

C.W. Smallman M.J.I.

In June 1920 David Rowlands proprietor of the Montgomery County Times purchased the business of C.W. Smallman including the Shrewsbury Chronicle, the Advertiser and the extensive jobbing printing business at Newport. By 1927 the printing of the papers was done in Shrewsbury involving the editor in weekly trips to supervise the final details. John and Llewellyn Rowlands assisted their father.

In 1926 the paper began a football competition with a £2 prize for forecasting eight results on games such as Rhyl v Oswestry, Oakengates v St Georges or Burton Town v Shrewsbury. In 1928 the paper started to appear on Fridays. In May 1937 the paper organised a "Coronation Excursion" to London and in 1938 advertised a summer trip to Devon at £1.30 including a steamer trip, a far cry from the sobriety of Charles Horne.

David Rowlands died aged 74 in December 1939 and was succeeded by his son John who was killed on active service in 1944. In 1945 the business was sold to Morley Tonkin under the title "Powysland Newspapers" many local papers being absorbed such as the *"Bridgnorth Journal"* and the *"Staffordshire Advertiser"*. Advertising disappeared from the front and in 1981 the paper became tabloid. In 1960 the printing works and the editorial moved from the original site in the High Street to Bellmans Yard though the paper was now printed in Welshpool. On the death of Morley Tonkin in 1979 the two elements of the business came apart, the printing works were sold and the newspaper went to the Midland News Association who had founded a new evening paper, the *"Shropshire Star"*, at a modern works in Ketley in the new town of Telford. The editorial moved to St Marys Street where in 2004 it celebrated its 150 years in journalism.

For nearly one hundred years the Advertiser was served in turn by two reporters whose characters and characteristics became embedded in local mythology and indistinguishable from the medium they loved. Both had deep roots in the community, profound local knowledge, literary pretensions and impeccable news standards. Thomas Paine Marshall, at the Advertiser from 1874 to 1919, was named after the radical writer of the French Revolution and had a dry northern wit and a sharp eye for a story. He was a great raconteur and a teller of dialect tales. Frank Lawton, 1920-1968, was a much gentler person but with a keen sense of humour and a passion for the community he reflected. His catchphrases became legendary particularly his custom of reporting every death as having "cast a gloom" over the neighbourhood. Hence his title "Cast a gloom". Yet TP thought nothing of walking to Market Drayton and back to deliver "copy" while Frank cycled everywhere or, allegedly, if in a hurry, ran at the side of his cycle, to cover a story.

Local newspapers could be satirised and P.G.Wodehouse did this as the *"Bridgnorth, Shifnal and Albrighton Argus"* incorporating the *"Wheat Growers` Intelligencer and Stock Breeders` Gazette"* and there is an element of truth there, but the *"Newport Advertiser"* is invaluable for the length and depth of its reporting and its range of subjects whether it is describing the clearing of the cattle from the medieval streets in 1858, the dramatic fire at Aqualate Hall in 1910, Pat Collin`s street fair in 1895, or the arrival of the evacuees in 1939. The accounts are so precise and evocative as to make them historic documents of the highest order. Matches and dispatches, dances and dinners are minutely recorded to the merest *"Hear,Hear"* and *"Applause",* so as to make visits to the archives unnecessary. In the pages of the newspaper through men like Charles Silvester and Charles Horne, Tom Marshall and Frankie Lawton, you can share and participate in the past with complete confidence.

The Advertiser Office
23 High Street, Newport

Thomas Paine Marshall

On the 6 July 1919 at the age of 69 a remarkable man with a remarkable name died in Avenue Road South, Newport, Shropshire, in a small unimposing terraced house. He was Thomas Paine Marshall an intrepid reporter, writer, commentator and wit, who had joined the Newport and Market Drayton Advertiser forty-five years earlier in 1874. He was named after his great, great uncle, Thomas Paine author of the "Rights of Man".

Tom Paine was born in Thetford, Norfolk, the son of a Quaker corset maker. He pursued many careers, corset maker, teacher and excise officer. He moved to Lewes where he became involved in politics and was dismissed from the Excise Service for requesting more pay. He published a pamphlet supporting his case. He met Benjamin Franklin who encouraged him to go to America.

Paine settled in Pennsylvania as a journalist. In 1776 he published a pamphlet *"Common Sense."* attacking the British Monarchy and supporting American independence. He served with George Washington's armies and travelled to France to raise money for the American cause.

He played no further part in American politics but returned to England where he wrote *"Rights of Man"* which attacked hereditary government, suggested all men over twenty-one should get the vote and recommended things like family allowances, pensions and the abolition of the House of Lords. With the French Revolution across the Channel this did not go down well with the Government and Paine was forced to escape to France before he could be arrested. In 1792 he became a French citizen and was elected to the revolutionary National Convention though surprisingly, given what he had written, he opposed the execution of Louis XV1, was arrested and only escaped the guillotine through the intervention of the American Minister. While in prison Tom Paine wrote the *"Age of Reason"* questioning the truth of Christianity. This lost him a lot of support in America where he had returned to live in 1802. He died in New York on the 8 June 1809.

Thomas Paine Marshall was born in Maryport, then Cumberland, on the 18 May 1850. He joined the Advertiser at Market Drayton working there for about twenty years before moving to Stone, then to Shifnal and then Newport. This illustrates the extensive coverage and success of the weekly and its influence over a wide area. He had been on the staff of the Barrow in Furness Times and before then was in the office of Oliver and Boyd in Edinburgh. Country reporting was a laborious task involving long journeys on foot through stormy nights and seeking the public interest was often unpleasant work. He brought with him the north country integrity and capacity for hard work and its gritty humour. He was an excellent writer no ordinary hack. His knowledge was extensive and his views were eloquent and forceful. He was a Shakespearean critic and wrote a series of books for schools and examination use. His historical knowledge was great and he wrote on philology, place names, and local history for local and leading magazines. His historical books included the "History of Tong and Boscobel" and the "History of Market Drayton Church". He wrote school texts on Kings and Queens and poetry as well as being a poet himself.

He was preaching amongst the sailors and colliers of Cumberland when he was seventeen. He was a strong temperance advocate and a churchman of broad views and lectured on many subjects to large classes.

His radical and republican name and his interest in his lineage and his passion for tracing his aristocratic past sit uncomfortably together. He was the son of John Robson Marshall and Margaret. His mother claimed to be the daughter and eventual heiress of the last of the *junior* branch of the ancient Lord Audley of Healey Castle and in direct male descent of James, Lord Audley who was killed in the battle of Blore Heath in 1459. The Yorkist leader at that battle, the Earl of Salisbury, was also a direct ancestor of TP. Another interesting claim was that his paternal grandmother gave him direct descent from Hotspur, Earl of Northumberland who was killed at the battle of Shrewsbury in 1503 and was immortalised by Shakespeare. Moreover TP could trace his descent right back to the Norman Conquest and through the female succession to James 1V of Scotland and Henry V11 of England. A heavy pedigree for a descendant of Tom Paine to bear.

His descriptive and humorous writing was of a quality that was seldom found in the provincial press then and now. He describes a visit to Newport in the hot summer of 1900 in perhaps flowery language, full of biblical and classical allusions:

> *"There was no bustle neither was there inanition and though there was here and there a section of the main street where a sheep might have been turned to graze among the "petrified kidneys" [granite setts] the women filling their pails with water at the hydrant stands, redeemed the thoroughfare from any suggestion of the ultima thule or rus in urbe".*

A country town with cartloads of coal; the bakers van *"with its sober body and its gaudy lettering"*; *"the grand old lime trees on the causeway which are to Newport what her hair is to a woman"*; you could smell the scent of the new-mown hay: *"We do not acknowledge that Newport has the country in the town; but she can hear the voices of the country"*. The shopkeepers have sun-blinds, the gnats are vicious; flies and wasps converge on the shop goods; there is an organ playing, with two monkeys: *"all terribly prosaic"*, *"a strange drowsiness steals over you"*. The deceptive lethargy of Edwardian England.

He wrote humorous articles week after week under the pseudonym of "George Aspin". Dialect tales of events in Newport, Hinstock and Gnosall and other villages. These involved "Uncle Joe" and cousin "Pheeby" on visits, one in 1911 to Newport May Fair. There are descriptions of fairground rides now hard to imagine; sarcastic comments on the state of the High Street, and the philosophising of the idlers on the Town Hall corner; allusions to well known characters that have long since ceased to be "characters". Humour, that was immediate and understood; rich, sharp and playful.

His articles on the history of the town, the Guildhall and the Butter Cross are generally acceptable and if he reaches conclusions that are now to be questioned it could be that he had sources now denied us. He argues the origin of "New Port". Port could mean a "gate" and gate in Old English was a way or a street thus "Oakengates" and "Cross gates". Newport in this sense is "new road". TP suggests another derivation as in "port" meaning market privileges. So a "portman" was a burgess and "portreeve" in some towns means a "Mayor". So Newport means "new market".

A great raconteur TP had his own favourite stories. One was about the burial of a member of the Clive family at Moreton Say when the Clive vault was opened. He saw the coffins surrounding the interior and the name plate of one becoming detached he discovered it was of Robert Clive thus proving that Robert Clive was buried there. As Clive had committed suicide his burial place had long been disputed. On another occasion while walking from Newport to Market Drayton he was asked, while passing Hinstock Rectory, by the Reverend John Ellerton, to take a manuscript to Bennions at Market Drayton to be printed; it was the hymn "The day thou gavest Lord is ended".

There are several descriptions of Tom Marshall including one in the Advertiser in March 1944:

> *"No TP emerged from the "Advertiser" office ready to buttonhole the first person he met and in that Cumbrian brogue of his air his views on "shoes and ships and sealing wax, or cabbages and kings"."*

W. Leese writing in the "Shropshire Magazine" March 1951 remembers:

> *"About noon, when business was at its height and the hubbub and noise of buying and selling loudest, T.P. Marshall,*

> *would stroll leisurely through the crowd in quest of the day's quotations.*
>
> *His humorous articles in dialect on Hinstock Flower Show, Gnosall Wakes or other events in surrounding villages were signed in the "Advertiser" "George Aspin" and country readers especially were tickled with amusement by TP's wit."*

Tom Marshall died on the Sunday morning of Peace Thanksgiving Day and had in fact been preparing to cover the Thanksgiving Service. His death was a great shock to the newspaper and journalism in general and is reflected in his obituary. His prodigious output had made him known and popular over a wide area of East Shropshire and Staffordshire which the Newport weekly covered in those late Victorian years. To quote the familiar phrase of another well-known journalist, Frank Lawton, who succeeded him, his death "cast a gloom" throughout the border.

His death is even found in the Log-book of Newport Junior School 8 July 1919:

> *"Owing to the sudden death of Mr T.P.Marshall, Miss Rabone was absent for two days yesterday and Friday".*

Miss Rabone who had taught at the school since 1906, became Mrs Robert Marshall two months later, in September 1919. Robert Marshall, son of TP joined the Advertiser in 1919 from the Wellington Journal on the death of his father and became editor in 1920. He collapsed and died in October 1934 aged 55 while on a walk to Church Aston. Mrs Marshall was headmistress at Sambrook school. They had one son Tom Audley Hilton Marshall who in 1946 was a Captain on the staff of the Military College of Science and later Chief Engineer and technical controller of Anglia TV. He was an Old Boy of Adams Grammar School and returned in April 1965 as the guest speaker at the Speech Day.

T.P. Marshall had one daughter, Miss Sarah Edith Marshall, who went to Merevale College and Whitelands Training College. She became Head of Newport Infants School on 4 November 1919 an eventful year for the family. She found the school run down and often staff-less through war, illness and neglect. The Inspector reported that the school was *"practically inefficient"*, the children *"imperfectly prepared"* and the original nineteenth century gallery, or tiered seats, still in place. She replaced this with a happy, enthusiastic school. She retired on 9 April 1952, after 32 years, when the infants department was transferred to a new school in Granville Avenue. Miss Marshall resided for years at "Coniston" in Granville Avenue with her teaching colleague, Miss Rich.

Like her father she claimed descent from nobility, the Earl Marshall of England, and from royalty, William the Conqueror and James 1V of Scotland, as well as Rob Roy.

All this is a far cry from the revolutionary republican, Tom Paine.

Newport and Market Drayton Advertiser

22 June 1912.

Haymaking at Newport.

T.P.Marshall.

"I know I've got it" he doubled himself up and sneezed. He was one of two men who were lounging on a seat in Audley Avenue where the wind was making rustle music in the leafy limes. The tall man, with a nose and a black moustache, and eyes as round and as staring as an owls. His friend was a little fellow with pink cheeks, thin lips and a straw hat. He was a bundle of nerves, he fidgeted with a Kodak and his finger was itching to take a snap. The subject was there across the road "Landscape and Life". To the left the red-bricked façade of the Workhouse Infirmary, and beyond it the choir of green linnets their song a cascade of liquid notes. To the right, shut off by a wall of tremulous green "Gods Acre", its white memorial stones the ghosts of the buried dust of fifty years. The foreground a long, level meadow where the grass which had been nourished by the rain and ripened by the sun, was either waiting for the scythe or had already been cut.

The background an upland. Beyond the line of the horizon, Staffordshire. In the middle distance a white-sleeved man was wielding a scythe. A swathe of grass followed the flash of its long, keen blade. Between him and the hurdle fence against the Avenue three sturdy men were tossing the grass he had already mown. Old Sam came along the road for his accustomed walk. He halted, leaned forward on his stick, looked at the haymakers and said "They wunna get it in". "I`ve got it" snapped the man with the nose and he mopped his brow with his pocket handkerchief. Sammy turned and looked at him, shook his wise old head and tottered away muttering as he went "The blue Beelzebub, poor chap".

The air was thick with birds where the men were plying their forks. An animated picture of feathered life foraging for food. Now in a circle high overhead anon darting down to dash through the shower of grass as it fell from the shaking forks. Everywhere swarms of insects winged and wingless the denizens of the silent city of the meadowland. A starling screeched from the leafy shelter of the pollard lime in Nearful field. A rook crossed the line of vision like an imp of darkness carrying in its beak a morsel from the Workhouse piggery. The haymakers paused to wipe the perspiration from their foreheads and to rest on their forks. The little man with the pink cheeks got his camera into position. He had found the opportunity for a good snap, but he was foiled for his companion gave a mighty sneeze which shook the seat beneath them, when he cried "O dear I've got it". The pink cheeked man frowned and said something which is never printed in a dictionary. But the world went on all the same.

The mower who had paused to use his whetstone was again swinging round the blade in the track of which the long grass fell. The men with the forks *were again submitting the crop to the alchemy of the sun and the dashing birds were ceaseless in their murderous task in the meadowland won by the rude forefathers of the hamlet from the primeval marsh. The soil, which had fed the grass, had been nurtured by the life sweat of the men who made the way for Newport on that away back landscape of time on which we see men as trees walking on the edge of the Avenue, cut through the heart of the land reclaimed from the bogland before the coming of Neolithic man.*

The Avenue with its long drawn lines of lindens just now leafier than they had ever been within the memory of living man. The Avenue, Newport's pleasure ground where the youth and the lusty manhood of the town resort for recreation and for sport, along the sheltered paths of which both young and old are fond of sauntering in the sunshine of the afternoon and in the mellow glow of the eventide. The Avenue, Newport's "Via de la Rosa" the white stones shut in by the wall of green tell us why.

Old Sammy came down the road again, thoughtfully and slow. The wind was still blowing but the spells of sunshine were fewer and longer between. The veteran paused once more to look at the haymakers and as he was doing so one of them put out his hand and looked at it. "Didna I tellya" cried the old man "You wunna get it in!". "I've got it" groaned the man with the nose and he pulled a face like a fiend. Sammy looked at him and stumped off saying "Poor chap, poor chap, and so nigh the Wukhus". The man with the Kodak turned to his friend and demanded "What's up with you?". "Confound you what is it that you have got?". "The hayfever" moaned the man with the nose. Then the rain came down in a torrent.

NOTES.

Thirteen – The Silvesters of Newport

1. Selbie, W.B. *The Life of Charles Silvester Horne*. Hodder and Stoughton. 1920.
2. Horne, Charles Silvester, *A Popular History of the Free Churches*. 1903.
3. Malthouse, G.T. *Short History of the Congregational Church in Newport*, Shropshire. 1907.
4. James, Tom. *Hot Metal to Mac*. 1998.
5. Mate, C.H. *Shropshire Part 11. Biographical*. 1906.
6. *Newport and Market Drayton Advertiser*, archives from 1854
7. P.G. Wodehouse. *Pigs Have Wings*. Penguin Books. 1957. P144.
8. T.P. Marshall - NMDA. Most of the information comes from articles, reports and stories written by TP or under the pen name of "George Aspin".

14. The Underhills.

The Underhills were members of that 19th Century breed of practical, inventive mechanics and engineers beloved of Samuel Smiles, who beavered away in small workshops to the admiration and bewilderment of the locals and sometimes to the wonder of the world. The Underhills did not produce the sun and planet or the separate condenser of James Watt, or the locomotives of George Stephenson, but every market town appeared to have such a family and their influence persisted well into the 20th Century.

Thomas Underhill of Albrighton married Anne a daughter of John Baddeley of the prolific Baddeley family of Tong. George Baddeley was a blacksmith and his son John a clock and watchmaker. Another sister, Martha Baddeley, married Robert Webster of Shrewsbury, a clockmaker but also an ironmonger, brush manufacturer and, in 1792, inventor of washing machines. There grew up a network of families skilled in metal, practical, adaptive and inventive. They moved west into the market towns of Shropshire and east into Wolverhampton. In 1862 H and J. E. Underhill were solicitors in Wolverhampton and in the 1870's were Clerks to Wolverhampton Town Council. G and W Underhill were also iron merchants in the town. There were also links with South Wales, while one member of the family is reputed to have worked with James Brindley on the Bridgewater Canal. The family names persisted as christian names such as John Baddeley Webster and George Baddeley Underhill.

The Newport Underhills followed both the legal and engineering traditions.

George Baddeley (1730-85) a son of George the blacksmith was a clock maker in Newport and in 1771 bought property on the site of the *Fox and Grapes*, now the Market Hall, for £270. The premises had formerly been occupied by Thomas Webster a hatter who was related to George's first wife Mary Webster. George died in 1785 and left property in Newport, Smethwick and Harborne to his sons George and John and his daughter Anne Scott.

Meanwhile in 1782 Anne and Thomas Underhill had a son William who on 18 April 1814 married Elizabeth Scott witnessed by Robert and Susan Scott. Joseph Scott, the son of Robert Scott of Newport, Gent., was Headmaster of the Grammar School between 1773 and 1818 and formerly curate at Forton. He had a brother Samuel who was a grocer and also Master of the Royal Free English School in 1771. Robert Scott was a grocer while his sister Susan married a Northwood, another family of watchmakers. William and Elizabeth had a son William Scott Underhill [WSU] named after his uncles.

Between 1822 and 1841 William is listed under many trades; watch, clockmaker and jeweller; brazier, tinplate worker and nailmaker; tallow chandler, tea dealer, hop dealer and oilman; ironmonger and grocer. In 1841 he is at 71 High Street aged 55 with his wife, son William Scott Underhill (23), Martha (10) and Elizabeth (20). On 28 September that year Mary Elizabeth Underhill married John Joseph Dean of St Clement Danes, London with William Scott Underhill, Elizabeth Dean and Robert Scott as witnesses. This was to be important later.

In 1844 the business is listed as William Underhill and Son, ironmongers, iron merchants, wrought iron gate and hurdle manufacturers, nailers and grocers. At this time William had taken over the grocery business of Robert Scott but in 1854 when William was retired, WSU transferred it to William Henry Foxall who had served his apprenticeship with Robert Scott and who traded as Foxall and Williams at 73 High Street until the end of the century. The Underhills, father and son, were in a group of private shareholders who under The Watching and Lighting Act of 1833-4 in 1835 constructed the gas works in what is now Avenue Road to provide street lighting. In 1849-50 WSU was the manager of the works.

In 1849 William Underhill is listed as retired and living in Church Aston. Bagshaw in 1851 quotes *"Mr Underhill has recently built a neat villa residence on elevated ground a short distance from the village, which commands a pleasing view of the country."* This was *"Highfields"* now a housing estate and for many years the home of the Liddle family. His will of 1851 proved at Lichfield in October 1855 left all his property to WSU subject to a legacy of £3,000 to his daughter Martha Susan Underhill and £1,000 to his grandson John William Dean. These simple conditions led to repercussions fifty years later illustrating the problems of financing enterprises before a strong banking system. For £2,000 of the legacy was left in the business with income going to Martha and her husband, after 1855, Charles Baddeley. Martha died the next year and there were no children and the remainder of the legacy was never repaid.

William Scott Underhill was born in 1817 and attended the Grammar School from which he was removed by his father at the age of twelve for a more practical education at the English School. The vast majority of boys at that time left the School about that age for the same reason so that the Upper School had only three pupils. In 1849 the business with its varied strands is his and in 1851 he is in the family home, above the shop, in the High Street, aged 34, unmarried, with three assistants, one apprentice and two female servants. Independent from his father he began to make changes the first being to find a wife. When they married on 3 February 1853, he was 36 and Martha Holland 21 but she was the daughter of John Holland a prosperous, self-made auctioneer and public figure who was involved in various legal settlements with WSU. He transferred the grocery business and began to concentrate on manufacturing on a site owned by his father behind 24 St Mary's Street. [Sketchleys 2004]. There was already a blacksmiths shop there. He took on public duties becoming in 1854 a Marsh Trustee under the new Act of Parliament of that year and in 1858 a Director of the new Market Company, again set up by private Act of Parliament, where he had a substantial holding of £200 shares.

It was a good time to enter the agricultural machinery business. Farming was beginning a golden age. Improvement and progress were in the air. In September 1853 he took a large advertisement for cast-iron land rollers, balance lever horse rakes, wrought-iron cultivators, ridge or moulding ploughs and turnip seed drills. He used the new local newspaper as soon as it began publication:

> *"High Street Newport Salop. W S Underhill begs to inform the inhabitants of the town and surrounding neighbourhood that he has enlarged his ironmongery establishment and begs to assure them that all orders committed to his care shall meet with prompt attention. His stock consists of Bright and*

> *Blank registers; stoves, Yorkshire and other grates, kitchen*
> *Ranges, fire irons, fenders and electro plated goods;*
> *Moderator and other lamps, japanned ware, cutlery etc etc.*
> *Iron bedsteads, cots, mattresses etc. Established 1795."*

In August 1856 he advertised his *"St Mary St Iron Foundry and Implement Works"* where may be had castings and forgings of every description and St Mary's Ironworks it remained even when he moved site. A year later he was seeking a man to take charge of a portable steam threshing machine – *"portable steam engines with combined threshing machinery can be seen daily at work."* By 1861 he described himself as ironmonger and brass foundry owner; he had four sons living, with one son, Henry George, having died aged two in 1858. In April 1862 at the International Exhibition he showed an oil cake mill, ridge plough, a general purpose plough, a threshing machine with corn elevator, patent wire fencing, horse rakes, cow cribs and cattle troughs. In 1862 he went into partnership with Bruckshawe of Market Drayton. In 1867 at Lichfield Trials and the Paris Exhibition he demonstrated the *"Zig Zag Wheel Traction Engine."* In 1937 John Scott Underhill recalled his father exhibiting a steam traction engine at the Paris Exhibition of 1867. It paraded the town and afterwards was used in the fields in Station Road.

There were signs that the St Mary's Street site was becoming restrictive when in August 1865 the 70 foot foundry chimney collapsed across Briarwood's at 28 and Brooke's at 26 St Mary's Street. Trade was also beginning to fall causing an excursion into the new fad of velocipedes.

> *"A few weeks back some amusement was caused by the*
> *passage of a velocipede through the town on a Saturday*
> *afternoon, at the time of the Market gathering. It was*
> *made at St Mary's Works at this town and others have been*
> *turned out since. They seem likely to become numerous*
> *and several young men and lads are getting good*
> *command of them and can travel fast."*
>
> Newport Advertiser. 13 March 1869.

> *"2, two wheeled velocipedes arrive at 1pm having set*
> *out from Chester at 7am i.e. 10 mph – went on to*
> *Wolverhampton after meal at "the Vic" – accompanied*
> *to Pave Lane by Mr James (Foreman of St Mary's Works)*
> *on a 3 wheeled velocipede – next day he rode to Shrewsbury."*
>
> Newport Advertiser. 27 March 1869.

> *"Great Exhibition of Velocipedes, Agricultural Hall, London.*
> *Silver medal for Velocipedes was awarded to Mr Underhill*
> *of this town. We believe the competition was very severe,*
> *including representatives not only of this Country but also*
> *from France and America."*
>
> Newport Advertiser. 19 June 1869.

In January 1936 Moses Taylor then aged 83 remembered buying a bicycle from William Underhill to ride to work as a bricklayer. It was wholly constructed of iron with solid tyres but though it was primitive, he said it made a vast saving in time and energy.

WSU was also on the move:

> *"New Foundry. Our townsman, Mr Underhill is erecting fresh workshops in a field near the Gas Works. The first portion completed was the foundry, which was greatly wanted for the manufacture of Velocipedes which are being sent in great numbers from St Mary's Works throughout the United Kingdom and even to the continent. On Thursday evening Mr and Mrs Underhill and a few friends and the workmen, met to give the foundry a formal opening. This was done by casting the centre of some velocipede wheels. The Company then drank the health of the proprietor and prosperity to his enterprise, the men cheering the toast lustily. The foundry is a roomy brick building 46.5 feet by 33.5 feet; it is roofed with galvanised iron, supported by iron girders. Those who have worked in the confined space in St Mary's Street will feel the advantage; and when the adjoining workshops are finished the establishment will be very complete and convenient."*

Newport Advertiser. 27 March 1869.

It appears that he gave up making cycles when the new factory was opened. Meanwhile he was still exhibiting, a report of July 1870 describing how in the last few days he had sent to Oxford a large quantity of machinery for exhibition at the Royal Agricultural Show. It comprised fixed and stationery steam engines, threshing machines, reapers, drills, ploughs, hoes, grubbers, "etc"; there were also carts, velocipedes and bicycles. The whole filled eight railway trucks, weighed twenty tons and was valued at £1,000.

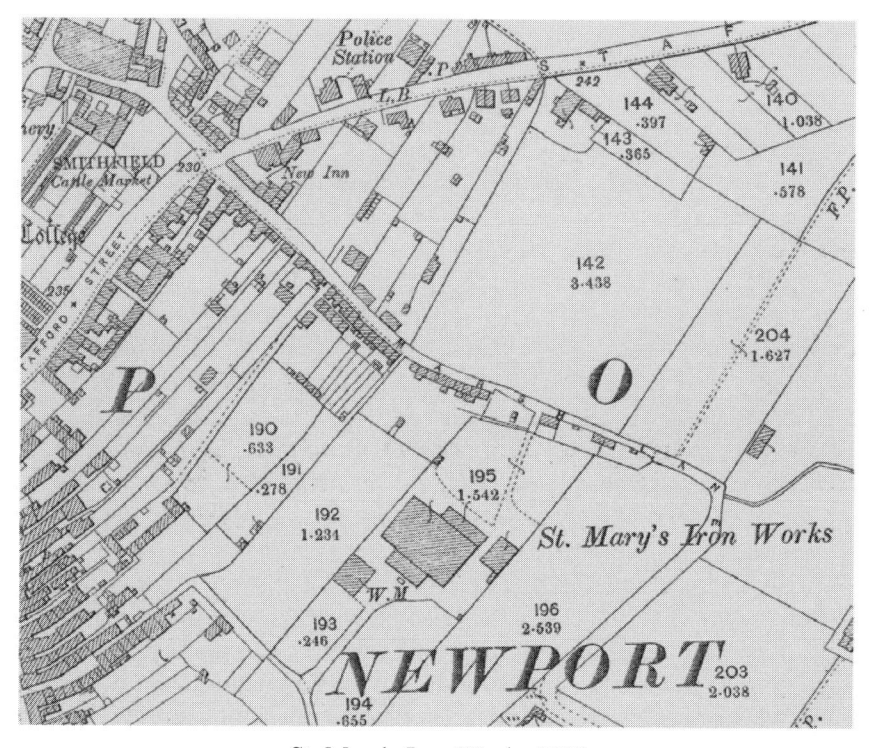

St. Mary's Iron Works 1902

William Scott Underhill finally removed to his new works on 3 December 1870 letting the St Mary's Street site to *"St Mary's Wholesale Ham and Bacon Factory"* proprietor Thomas Fieldhouse who had a pork shop next door.

"W S Underhill, respectfully gives notice of the removal to his new works, Upper Bar, from this date. He also takes the present opportunity of thanking his numerous friends and customers for past favours and informing them that his new and extensive premises will enable him to execute all orders with promptitude and despatch.

December 3rd 1870
St Mary's Works
Upper Bar
Newport Salop.

PS. Orders may be left as usual at the shop in High Street.

WSU now advertised extensively as a *wholesale ironmonger* as well as an ironfounder and agricultural engineer and the prosperous home market and the double-tracked London North Western Railway which reached Newport in 1849, allowed him to export. In 1879 he was making steam engines and boilers and in 1880 advertised vertical engines and boilers and two 14hp steam engines.

In the 1881 census he is still living over the shop at [71] High Street with Martha, John Scott, aged 29, solicitor, William, 25, ironfounders assistant, Robert Scott, 22, ironmongers assistant, George Baddeley, 20, articled clerk and Elizabeth, 19 and Martha, 16. Living in were a shop assistant, a cook aged 17 and a female domestic aged 17. This was a large house with workshops and cottages down the long burgage plot to Beaumaris Road. He is described as an ironfounder master employing 40 men and boys. This is a large concern by any standards and explains the influence and respect he had and why he always topped the popular vote.

In public life he was a shareholder in the Gas Company, a director and shareholder in the Market Company, a Marsh Trustee with its large land holding and income, a Burgess and when local government was reformed he was immediately elected to the Local Board. His skill and knowledge were indispensable in local affairs but there was often conflict between his public and private interests which would make him fractious and irritable leading to feuds and litigation. This was certainly true after 1870 when his new works led to arguments over the widening of Marsh Road [Audley Road] which would have been to his advantage and to pollution in the Marsh Brook which ran below his factory. In 1880 he wanted a tramway over Marsh Trust land from the railway to his factory while the Trust was proposing to run the sewage and drainage of their new road, Granville Avenue, into the Marsh Brook through his property. Both sides were suffering from the agricultural depression and WSU was ill. The Trust suffering from declining agricultural rents was trying to open up the estate to building development while WSU was facing declining orders from farmers. In April 1882 he walked out of a meeting of the District Board in a dispute over the number of newly elected members on committees. He wanted more "new blood."

In 1882 he also resigned from the Church Restoration Committee. A former church-warden and one of the oldest and most regular attendants at the church he had long been a *"free seater"*, that is he opposed the allocation of pews to owners of property. In 1837 the church had been re-pewed and galleries inserted allowing accommodation for 1,500 of which 600 were free. Over the years these had been reduced and when in 1882 it was proposed to remove the galleries Underhill was outraged and wrote to the Bishop outside of the committee. When this action was questioned he retired blaming the person he thought responsible for also having him pushed off the committee set up to construct the new Granville Avenue:

> *"Had that scheme been carried out in a way I wished, the road would not have been in the mess it is – it would today have been an accomplished fact, and many houses would have been built."*

His most notable dispute was with the Newport Schools Committee. The Committee was raising money to build a new National School in Newport and in 1869 organised a fete in Chetwynd Park at which Blondin was to do his famous tightrope walk. They borrowed scaffolding from WSU. Unfortunately the bad weather that prevented Blondin's walk also blew down the wall at the new factory WSU was erecting, a wall that should have been supported by the scaffolding. He refused to pay his ticket money and his donation. He lost the case but was only ordered to pay back the ticket money.

William Scott Underhill born 24 February 1817 died on the 14 December 1884. The brass lectern in Newport Church is to his memory. His executor was Martha Underhill and his estate was valued at £10,654. He was buried in the family vault in the churchyard even though it had been closed for burials. The funeral was preceded by the Head Borough (W Harris) in his regalia, WSU having been the last High Constable of the town. His coffin was carried by six workers who had over 25 years service each.

His sons were all notable sportsmen. In 1879 John Scott, Robert Scott and George all played for the Newport Football Club which after four matches defeated the Engineers FC (Shrewsbury) to win the Shropshire Challenge Cup. Over 1,000 watched the game. The engineers were a rather "rough" working class side while Newport consisted mainly of middle-class ex-Grammar School pupils. In 1880 they entered the English Cup and after winning two games were drawn against Aston Villa and knocked out.

Now it was time for the boys to stop playing, leave home, get married and run their own affairs. An agreement was signed by all parties and a partnership entered into whereby William would run the ironmongery side, Robert Scott the foundry and John Scott would handle legal matters. Mother stayed on at the shop. In August 1888 they had Stand 6 at the Agricultural show at Victoria Park with 89 different exhibits such as steam engines, agricultural machinery, iron fencing, wrought and cast-iron work, dairy utensils and other ironmongery. They also had a telephone. In March 1895 they had a telephone line via Brittain's candle factory chimney between the High Street shop and St Mary's Works.

At the Agricultural Show in 1895:

> *"Messrs W and R S Underhill Newport and Eccleshall had*
> *a distinctly good and varied display of agricultural*
> *implements and machinery, and exhibited a number of medals*
> *won by the enterprise of the Firm. They had on view a*
> *drawing room, handsomely equipped. Their agricultural*
> *implements included a four horse-power engine and boiler (£85)."*

> Newport Advertiser. 3 August 1895.

They had opened a depot at Eccleshall in February 1886. In 1896 they went back into the cycle business leaving the Avenue Road factory and returning to St Mary's Street:

> *"St Mary's Street Engineering Works, Cycle Department.*
> *Stand No 1 Newport Agricultural Show. Messrs W and*
> *R S Underhill beg to announce that having engaged a staff*
> *of skilled artisans for the especial manufacture of high*
> *class cycles they are now prepared to receive orders for*
> *the following for delivery on or after Saturday August 2nd:-*

The "Lady Newport", an ideal ladies cycle fitted with all the latest improvements.
The "Dorothy" a juvenile safety. A little gem lightly built and easy running.
The "Baronet" a perfect light roadster fitted with all the latest improvements.
The "Audley" a special high class roadster highly adapted for touring.
The "Artisan" a strong built popular cycle much recommended for country roads.
All cycles are made of the very best materials and workmanship throughout and are thoroughly up-to-date in every respect, and each cycle is guaranteed against imperfect workmanship and defective materials for 12 months.
Cycles for hire!! Cycling taught (if preferred) in a spacious room 50 feet by 30 feet by an experienced rider. Gratuitous lessons until perfect given to intending purchasers. W and R S Underhill having a large assorted stock of cycle fittings and accessories can effect repairs at short notice. NB Cycles may be bought upon the deferred system of payment to suit the convenience of purchaser. Prices and terms upon application."

In June 1898 the partnership between the brothers was dissolved, William taking the engineering and cycle business and Robert Scott the ironmongery. In 1899 it is William advertising cycles and engineering equipment from St Mary`s Works behind Burleigh House

"St Mary`s Street Ironworks, Newport, Salop. W and R S Underhill, agricultural engineers, ironfounders, implement agents, fence makers etc, beg to advise their numerous patrons and friends of their removal to the above central and convenient premises."

Newport Advertiser 4 April 1896

In October 1899 William died aged 44. He was the second son of WSU. In 1882 he had married the eldest daughter of W. E. Addis of Forton. They lived next to the Elkingtons and Baddeleys in the High Street with, in 1881, five daughters between 10 weeks and 7 years and two servants. At his death they were living at Burleigh House in St Mary`s Street. Like his father he had been a churchwarden and Marsh Trustee. In 1900 his business had been amalgamated with the Shropshire Engineering Works of William Waterhouse and that of A and W. J. Massey in the Lower Bar Foundry in Salters Lane.

Robert Scott Underhill was unmarried and living with his mother at the ironmongers shop in

1891. Soon after he married Catherine Hall a farmers daughter from Forton but who had actually been born in America, and his mother moved back to 38 St Mary`s Street the Holland family home. RS died aged 48 in September 1906 leaving his wife Catherine with two young children. Robert was the third son, a county footballer and inventor with patents for disinfecting flushing tanks and for platform trucks locking system. The shop was taken over by W. F. Holloway an agricultural engineer from Lower Bar.

John Scott Underhill the eldest son died on 18 May 1942 aged 88 at Dog Bank, Church Aston. He was one of the most familiar, conspicuous and picturesque figures in Newport. In dress he was a real Beau Brummel, spruce and elegant sporting a fawn bowler and white cravat long out of date. *"Johnny Underhill the solicitor, used to exercise as he walked down the road and always wore spats."* He entered the Grammar School aged 7 and could recall the school being lit by gas in 1864. He lived long enough to see electricity come to Newport in September 1931. In 1871 he is living with his grandmother Catherine Holland. That year he obtained a Careswell Scholarship and went off to Christ Church College, Oxford where he graduated M.A. He was articled to his uncle in Wolverhampton and set up in Newport in 1879. He was 25. He picked up a string of public offices, Clerk to the Local Board, the Highways Board, and the Marsh Trustees, the Burial Board and Pensions Committee. In 1895 he became Clerk to the newly created Urban District Council and held office until 1936. He was working to the end. He was buried at Church Aston with a traditional funeral that only men attended

Like his brothers, he was a keen sportsman particularly cricket and football and though sparsely built he had a strong physique. He had an old-fashioned geniality and courtesy. He married twice and was survived by his wife and one son and daughter, his second son Gerald had died in London in 1914 where he worked in a drapery business, while Cyril Scott Underhill, the youngest, died of wounds in France in 1916. "Sunny little Cyril" sportsman and cricketer had trained as a teacher.

The fourth son of WSU was George Baddeley Underhill who died in January 1931 in Edgbaston, Birmingham after being knocked down by a car. He had taken articles in Stafford where he practised before going to Birmingham. It is this brother who reveals another side to a prosperous, respected, middle-class, professional Victorian family.

We have some early indications. We know that at his death in 1884 William Scott Underhill was heavily indebted to Lloyds Bank; we know in 1898 and 1905 actions had been taken in Chancery over the conditions of the will of William Underhill; we have a hint about John Scott Underhill's approach to money when he is replaced as Clerk to the Marsh Trustees in 1898 because accounts had not been audited, ledgers not made up and there were deficits. Underhill refused to give up documents. The legacies left in the business had not been repaid after the death of WSU in 1884 and by 1899 had become consolidated in one sum of £6,160. In 1905 property that had been used as security was sold and the money used as a substitute security for the debt. In1909 George Underhill came to realise the financial tangle created by his elder brother both in his own business and that of the family. The family property was extensive with the engineering works, land and houses; a residence, land and several cottages in Church Aston, other houses in Newport and the stock and plant at the works and the ironmongery. But there were heavy trade liabilities and the bank had a floating charge by way of a second mortgage over the entirety of the property. JSU handling the estate sold shares ostensibly to relieve the bank but no accounts were ever rendered. He was also raising money by using deeds of the estate as security.

Nominally the executrix Martha Underhill, widow of WSU, was the owner of the business but in reality the two brothers William and Robert Scott were running things, drawing what they required usually in cash. Three homes and families were living off the estate with little accountability. In 1893 Mrs Underhill faced bankruptcy. To overcome this and make the brothers more liable and responsible they formed a partnership each to run their side of the business. In this way creditors were mollified and eventually paid off. The bank was still indulgent and allowing overdrafts on the Church Aston house which was still being used a security for other loans. It was this property also that was charged by the will of WSU to repay the legacy to his sister hence the actions in Chancery. William and Robert professed little knowledge of these financial affairs while mother said *"she left everything to Jack."*

John Scott Underhill was using the family property and clients' money to speculate in businesses varying from guns, coal mines and building firms in Shrewsbury and Liverpool. No coal was found and the shaft flooded while the gun Company went into liquidation. He had day to day business debts that were patched up by the family and the bank anxious to keep him going for the sake of the whole family estate and because of his high public profile and public offices. For JSU to be caught using clients funds would have been disaster.

By 1900, within three generations, the energy, initiative and achievements of William Scott Underhill had been dissipated. Martha his wife died in 1928 aged 93. John Scott died in 1942 aged 88 a character and an institution. There are now no Underhills in town yet William Scott Underhill did survive in a way that brought the world to Newport for nearly one hundred years.

NOTES.

Fourteen. The Underhills.

1. Document: Abstract of the title of C.C.Barrow to property at 24 St Mary's Street, Newport. M.F.Miles. This indicates the legal and financial problems of the business.
2. Elliott, D.J., *Shropshire Clock and Watchmakers*, p. 125.
3. Griffiths, *Guide to the Iron Trade of Great Britain 1873,* David and Charles, (1967)
4. Biographical information courtesy of Mr Godfrey Marks, Bradford upon Avon, Wiltshire
5. NMDA. From 1855: advertisements, public notices, business reports, obituaries particularly of WSU and JSU.

William Scott Underhill. Obituary.

Mr Underhill was a native of the town, and his active connection with its affairs extended to the long period of half-a-century. And this half century here as elsewhere, has been one of remarkable progress in many ways, and in most of them Mr Underhill was not merely an interested spectator but an active promoter. We are not sure of the order of these accomplishments, but we may name such enterprises as the introduction of gas; the substantial paving of our broad streets; the erection of the noble Market House with its adjacent Smithfield, in their central position; the great expansion of the means of education, including the revival of the Grammar Schools prosperity; the restoration of the Parish Church on two occasions, the last being now in progress; and the making of the railway, which connects us with the outer world. Newport in old days had more than one benefactor whose liberality far surpasses any more recent benefits; but it seems safe to say that in all the centuries since the conquest, nobody of its citizens has ever by united efforts accomplished so much for its advancement as the able and enterprising men with whom Mr Underhill was associated in the first thirty years, especially of his business life, in the town.

It was as far back as 1835 that Mr Underhill joined his father, the late Mr William Underhill of Highfield, in business as ironmonger and grocer. After some years he gave up the grocery, and turned his chief personal attention to a new branch of business then rising into importance. In 1850 he commenced business as an ironfounder and agricultural engineer. The few simple cumbrous inefficient tools of past ages no longer sufficed in any region of production. The extension of steam and the invention of machinery had given a miraculous impetus to manufacturers. Clever men everywhere began to ask if agriculture might not be similarly aided, and the age of machinery set in. It was under these circumstances that our townsman opened his works in St Mary`s Street which were then superseded in 1870 by the large commodious works which flank the Avenue Road. Mr Underhill came of a family several members of which had displayed much inventive and mechanical ingenuity. Of this the family, we understand have some interesting memorials. One of them was the intimate associate and fellow worker, with the great engineer of the Bridgewater Canal; and helped him in preparing the levels and the construction of the works. Probably it was possession of the same faculty, which led Mr Underhill in this direction. Certain it is that he achieved considerable success in his new line of business. Thus his exhibits won a gold medal at Lille (France) in 1862, an honourable mention at the Paris Exhibition, and the highest distinction awarded at our own Universal Exhibition in 1862. He acquired a name for cultivators and iron fencing; but his greatest achievement was made (in conjunction with Mr Bruckshaw) when they produced and patented the Corn Elevator, which is now such an indispensable adjunct of the threshing machine.

To those who knew the town atall, we need scarcely say that the deceased gentleman was public spirited, and took a leading part in the town affairs. He filled nearly all, or quite all the offices connected with the place. As far back as 1845, he was churchwarden and the clock in the tower is a lasting *reminder of his year of office. Before the organisation of the present police, Mr Underhill was High Constable for some years and was the last to hold the office. The introduction of gas was an important and spirited enterprise in its day and our late townsman took a very active part in the good work. Till his death he was a Director of the Company in his native town. (With Mr John Stokes he established gas works at Stone, Shifnal and Market Drayton). Mr Underhill had also a seat at the Board of another body which accomplished a great work for the town and the whole neighbourhood – we refer to the Markets Company. He was chosen one of its first Directors and retained his seat as long as he lived. It was the same with three public bodies, which have divided between them the management of the town. For nearly thirty years he had been one of the Burgesses, whose chief duty was the water supply and in 1882 he was made Water Bailiff. We related some time back how the control of the Town Estate passed out of the Burgesses` hands and with it the Marsh Trustees became what is now called the "local authority" of Newport, with extensive sanitary and other powers conferred by Special Act of Parliament. Mr Underhill took great interest in obtaining that Act, and under it he acted as a Trustee from 1847 till his death. He was most regular in his attendance's, scarcely ever missing a meeting and was often appealed to as to facts long ago accomplished. The last one of the most useful improvements Mr Underhill was engaged in was the widening of the Marsh Road. Most of our readers will remember how, almost single-handed, he struggled for this object and happily he lived to see it accomplished. Nothing that he did recommended him more than this, especially to the dwellers in that locality; and we have the impression that his advocacy of this matter had an important bearing on the gratifying result of his election to the local board last year. He had been a member of the Board from its origin in 1875. Up to last spring there was no contest. But on that occasion he was returned at the head of the poll. We must conclude with one other public service, which we have heard Mr Underhill refer to. Five and twenty years ago the Grammar School, to which we are so deeply indebted, had been somnolent. Our late townsman had there received part of his education, and he had boys of his own in the nursery, so that he was doubly interested in its efficiency. Such periodical examinations as are universal now were quite the exception there. But it struck him that these annual enquiries into efficiency were the kind of thing likely to rouse the school to fresh life. And by his endeavours a deputation waited on the Governors, who consented to make the experiment, and having made it were so satisfied of its usefulness that it continues to this day.*

Newport Advertiser. 20 December 1884.

15. Audco and jobs.

In March 1996 the local newspaper reported that the future looked bright for Serck Audco Valves after a record-breaking year for the Newport based company. The firm was entering 1996 with a healthy order book and an expected turnover of more than £18 million and the signs were that this success would continue. Managing Director Keith Hollingworth said the reason for the company's on-going growth and success was its major investment programme, over £1 million a year had been re-invested for the last six years. *"The company is profitable and is poised for further growth, new products and increased market penetration world wide."* Such investment, he said, was vital if Serck Audco was to retain its place as a key player in the world market. His philosophy on why the firm was so successful was simple; *"We have experience of making valves of nearly 100 years."* The company was now concentrated on one site the original Underhill foundry in the Avenue Road having become Safeway's [Waitrose 2004] Supermarket. This had allowed the installation of a hi-tech system giving a planned factory-wide integrated computer network spanning every aspect of the customer's order from estimate and design through to manufacture and shipment. Over the previous three years there had been major investment in plant and machinery on site with computerised machines fed by computerised design engineering which allowed designs to be tested and modified to give precision engineered products.

The company employed 210 people most of them local with more than twenty years service. It gave, said Personnel Manager Vicky Langford, a *"family business feel"* to the company. There was a strong commitment to local schools and colleges, to universities, as well as on-site training centre. An *"electronic catalogue"* was coming on-line to enable customers to see how the valves were produced and how they worked. This was in addition to displays at exhibitions all over the world including China, Russia and France. This huge investment on state of the art technology was to ensure the firm's place as market leader. *"It doesn't matter where you go in the world, the word Audco is known. Wherever they are producing oil or piping gas you'll find Serck Audco valves."*

William Underhill would have been pleased because exactly one hundred years earlier, in 1896, the foundry he had opened with such optimism had closed and his family had vacated the site. He would have been pleased that from the ashes such a modern enterprise had emerged and brought jobs and prosperity to his beloved town.

Yet wait, three years later in April 1999 the same newspaper had shock horror headlines such as *"Audco closure stuns Newport"*; *"MP pledges help for Audco workers."* It looked as if history was about to repeat itself but this time, as had happened in 1906, there did not seem to be anyone willing to ride to the rescue.

In April 1896 the Newport and Market Drayton Advertiser was excitedly reporting the news that the large and commodious buildings containing St Mary's Engineering Works erected by the late W. S. Underhill which stood on nearly a quarter of an acre of land, had been acquired by Mr Samuel Robinson late of Fulham, London. Mr Robinson it seemed had entered into residence at Hugon Villa, Newport. It was believed that he intended to develop the manufacture of a new principle of steam engines, upon which he had been experimenting for many years with a view to economising on the use of fuel. This invention which would revolutionise the existing type of engine was on its way through the patent office. It was hoped that this would bring employment and would be entirely due to the efforts of Mr George Underhill who had persuaded Mr Robinson to locate himself in Newport. George was the solicitor brother who had been landed with the task of sorting out the financial problems of the Underhill family.

> *"St Mary`s Engineering works and ironfoundry, (late Mr Underhills). Messrs Robinson and Molyneux beg to notify to the public that they have purchased from the representatives of the late William Scott Underhill, the above engineering works and foundry and the good will of the business, for so many years carried on by him and his representatives. Messrs Robinson and Molyneux trust that by strict attention to business, efficient workmanship and promptitude in the execution of all orders entrusted to them to merit a continuance of the favours so long shown to Mr Underhill. It is Messrs Robinson and Molyneux`s intention to enlarge the works so as to undertake every kind of engineering and foundry work. Special attention will be given to repairs to agricultural machinery of every description. 2nd April 1896."*

Newport Advertiser. 4 April 1896.

In June 1896 Mr E.R. Molyneux celebrated his marriage with a dinner at the works. Here Mr Robinson was referred to as a native of South Staffordshire and his invention was described as a valve to prevent the loss of steam in locomotives and other engines. The valve, he said, was very useful but not a shadow of what was going to be displayed in the works. He would convince the world that James Watt had made a mistake in his condenser which had cost the Country millions of pounds.

The first casting of the *"Quadruple Steam Cylinder"* which Robinson forecast would dispense with condensers and save 60% of fuel was unfortunately delayed for nine months by the lack of a competent moulder. Mr Robinson was in trouble for in February 1898 Ernest Morton Molyneux now living at Chetwynd Knoll a large house of the Burton Boroughs, issued a disclaimer saying he was not responsible for any debts or goods ordered by Robinson and in April Robinson admitted a claim for £14.50 wages due to William Cattell and was given two months to pay. Robinson had lost his house under a distress warrant and was now locked out of the works. At his bankruptcy application a receiving order was made and his patent was said to be worth £25,000. At a meeting of creditors at Stafford in January 1899 Robinson was said to owe £20,000. His examination showed that he began engineering in West Bromwich in 1872 moved to London in 1884 to work on his invention, purchased St Mary`s works in 1896 and in April 1897 was sold up by G.B. Underhill, solicitor, the man who brought him to Newport! His patents were sold in September 1899.

In February 1899, on the orders of Molyneux, there was a sale of machinery and second-hand implements at St Mary`s Works, but by June he was trading again as Molyneux and Haigh making all kinds of engines, forgings and castings, fencing and gates, then Haigh and Molyneux until the partnership was dissolved in October 1899. Haigh tried to continue on his own as *"Newport Salop Engineering Company"* but in October 1901 it was all put up for sale at the Grand Hotel Birmingham and withdrawn at £3,100. Haigh, from Liverpool, was only 26 years old. In February 1902 Haigh was sentenced to twenty one days at The County Court and also sued by R. S. Underhill for non-payment of goods and later for non-payment of rates. In April/May Newport Engineering Company was put up for sale and bought by Wheatcroft and Co., engineers and iron founders making machines for tubes.

> *"St Mary`s Works which used to be such a busy hive of industry ..has been sold to a new firm styled Wheatcroft Ltd and work has been commenced… by the new firm..in a promising manner."*

Lunn`s Indicator for 1902.

In November 1904 Wheatcroft formed a syndicate with H.A. Saunders, G.I. Muirhead, a local builder, and H.G.U. Elliott, a local solicitor. Saunders put up £1,500 and bought up the debts of the previous company but they were always short of capital and figures showed a heavy loss even though there were orders with the South Australian Government for the supply of drawings and plant for casting socket pipes. Saunders and Wheatcroft, who acted as works manager, disagreed, and Wheatcroft resigned. The syndicate was dissolved due to the financial position and lack of capital and the business and assets were transferred in November 1906 to a new company *"The Audley Engineering Company Ltd."* The future had begun and the words valves and plugcocks had become associated with the business. Their advertisement read; *"support local trade, save railway charges and delays in transit."*

The first meeting of the directors of the Audley Engineering Company Ltd was held at the offices of Messrs Carrane and Elliot in Newport. The object of the company at that time was the making of machinery for the manufacture of tubes, cock making, being a sideline to fill in with the other product. Henry Arthur Saunders of Aston Grove, Newport was the main shareholder having bought the majority holding in the previous company. There was no public issue of shares and shareholders were limited to fifty, these included George Ingram Muirhead, the builder, H.G.U. Elliott, solicitor, Sarah Elisabeth Plant, widow, of Netherton, Worcester and later Walter Wheat a coal merchant in Newport, E.F. Bennion stationer and newspaper proprietor, Samuel Smith ironmonger and other smaller investors. Saunders was managing director and Elliott secretary though for economy these two offices were later amalgamated. The works were leased from Mrs Jane Molyneux at £85 per quarter. Muirhead soon went bankrupt and sold his shares to Bennion. In July 1909 an agreement was made with Mr R.W. Leach to establish at the works the steam pipe trade and to give the company the benefit of his special knowledge for one fully paid up share (£1) for each £10 of trade done in the first year and each successive years. He was also given 5% on orders the agreement for ten years. Mr Leach therefore had no part in its early beginnings and only became interested when it became a limited liability company in 1906. Mr Leach was manager of the Langloan Works of Messrs James Allen and Sons, near Coatbridge, Glasgow. His business was making tubes while Mr Saunders business was tube machinery. By way of business they came to hear of each other but there appeared to be no particular business significance but as they came to know each other Mr Leach joined in a consultative capacity carrying on his business commitments in Wolverhampton at the same time.

Henry Arthur Saunders died in October 1909 aged 53; he came from Pontypool to Audley Engineering and his efforts pulled the firm through from a very poor start. He was buried at Church Aston.

RWL was asked on what terms he would come to reside in Newport and superintend the company while keeping on his own interests. On 1 November 1909 he became director and managing director at a salary of £156 pa, £50 expenses for the Wolverhampton office, which became the company office, and £10 per cent on net profits for ten years. *"The genius who has made it the thriving concern it is today." (1938)* had arrived. He did not relinquish his other businesses and he continued to devote half of his day to each; he was helped by Mr N.B.Saunders son of HA, becoming secretary at £20 pa and clerk at £1 per week. By 1910 the debit had been reduced to £730 but more important new equipment was being brought in, a machine for automatically tapping and boring small cocks, for £200; three new lathes at £120 each; schemes for new foundry plant at £400, new gas plant for £900 and in 1914 plugging lathe, tool room lathe, disc grinding machine and fencing for the tool room. More important RWL worked out the financing even offering to provide the money himself. New machines reduced costs.

In March 1912 it was reported that the 60 employees were still out of work owing to the lack of coal through the miners strike. 1912 was a year of tremendous industrial unrest. In 1914 during a court case with the Urban District Council John and Joseph Pennington were quoted as owners of the property with Audley Engineering as occupiers.

In August 1914 N.B. Saunders, now a director immediately joined up; his job was kept open and two thirds of his salary paid. It was *"put on record their appreciation of the manly spirit exhibited....wished him god speed."* 26 staff out of 50 had volunteered and the management agreed to pay 5/- to 10/- per week towards a relief fund raised in the works in aid of the families of employees serving their country.

To a lack of dividends and loss on accounts was added the wartime disorganisation of labour and shortage of manpower. The company had about 80 on the payroll including a number of girls who were employed in the machine shop. In October 1915 the Company was advertising for women workers. Women also came in at the top, Mrs Kate Saunders being elected a director and chairing the meetings. This she did until 1921 when she went to South Africa.

War concentrates the mind. From making cast iron cocks and valves the works were given over almost entirely to one product, anchor plummets for mine sinkers. Mr Leach realised that specialisation was the name of the game. Also needed were better finance, modern plant and his full time attention. In December 1917 with no dividend in view, with heavy depreciation and increases in taxation there was a need for efficiency, reorganisation and capital. RWL put his salary due as a director since the death of Saunders into the purchase of ordinary shares. Shares were reorganised with an issue of new Preference shares. New directors came in such as A.E. Whittingham from the Newport family of builders with a holding of £1,000. More importantly Mr Leach severed part of his other business connections and decided to devote most of his time to the Audley Company. This was no inconsiderable sacrifice for it involved the surrender of four lucrative agencies as well as other business interests. Thinking of specialisation in 1917 he began experimenting with lubrication cocks for compressed air but these were put aside till the end of the war.

One strange purchase in May 1918 was a steam laundry in Wellington for £2,110. It was thought to be a good investment and an outlet for the sale of small cocks to the laundry industry. It was sold in 1920 for £1,750. Still hanging over the new company were the remnants of the old. Part of the former business had been at the Lower Bar Foundry in Salters Lane which historically had made hydraulic ram pumps still to be found in the surrounding countryside. In 1921 the assets were sold and the works let for £75 pa to a new company *"Foundry Equipment and Pattern Company"* making wooden and metal patterns. Leach and Saunders had shares in this which they held in trust for Audley Engineering. In 1922 this was liquidated a clearing up operation as defined in a resolution of January 1922:

> *"Resolved that the policy of the company should be to broaden
> company's connection by selling specialised and patented
> article allied to the company's usual manufactures and now
> being put on the market by the company to all large customers
> direct and that in such case the goods supplied should be marked
> "Audley" to advertise the company's name."*

This policy arose out of negotiations which began in 1920 when RWL received an enquiry from America asking him to quote for a number of cocks to their drawings of models. He realised that the American firm was thinking along the same lines as he was and he set out to make terms with them not only for the license to make but also to sell. In July 1922 came an agreement for licence to manufacture Merco Nordstrom lubricated plug valves together with the use of the patent right. There was also a licence to manufacture cocks with the Thos Eatons patent. In 1923 he retained the sales of the Merco valves on commission.

The boom and high prices that followed the 1914-18 war gave way to a slump of the twenties and then the world depression of the thirties. The response by RWL was a world wide sales campaign while at home he modernised the plant whenever he could. Agents were appointed throughout the country and in Holland, Denmark, South America, Newfoundland and Canada. Most of these places were visited during the inter-war years. In 1923 he was in South Africa then followed trips to California where he obtained rights for that part of the British Empire outside the American continent, followed in 1926 by a visit to San Francisco for a long term contract that secured the European rights. In 1923 also was an agreement with the Oil Well Engineering Company for increasing the sale of the company's products to the oil industry and with the Scottish Tube Co Ltd for sales to South Africa and New Zealand. In 1926 the company exhibited at the British Industries Fair with encouraging results. H.B. Leach, brother of RWL, became a director and London agent with a London office.

At home the company continued to invest in equipment and plant, a foundry cupola, boring and turning mill, and a gas engine. In 1928 £1,893 was spent on a Holt radial drilling machine, a Borroughs calculating machine, a 9HP Standard motor car (£195.3.9) and a 110 HP National Gas engine. They also bought the works and began to plan a new access which up to then had been by a lane through the Gas Works. They eventually purchased Hen Meadow in 1928 from the Marsh Trustees, a strip of land which allowed access on to Audley Road gave more space and an impressive entrance to the works. RWL constantly improved the product, in 1925 introducing a new and novel type of parallel plug and in 1926 still registering patents for valves including improvements to lubricated plug valves not only in this country but in South Africa and Australia.

The report to the Twentieth Annual meeting in March 1928 was quite cheerful:

> *"The baby we started with in 1906 was not very robust, but with
> the passing of the years it has gradually gained strength in
> spite of setbacks, until we can now congratulate ourselves
> that it is a sturdy young man with the years before it."*

Though like everyone else they had suffered from the coal strike and general strike of 1926 the company was in a *"sound financial position"* with a total capital invested of £9,465, fixed assets of £9,000 and a credit balance of £7,597. Dividends, held back for many years, were recommended at 6% Preference shares and 10% ordinary.

> *"On our 21st birthday we can look forward to a bright and
> prosperous future."*

For the August holidays employees were given a bonus of half a weeks pay. The salary of RWL was increased to £1,500 and that of N.B. Saunders to £750.

The next two years were ones of optimism and expansion. There were now sales agencies in Norway, Sweden, Finland, Austria, Hungary, Czechoslovakia, Canada, South Africa and Australia. Through M. Jules Pinchaud a subsidiary company was being formed in France the, *"Societe Francaize du Robinets` Audley"* with a capital of £750. In 1929 £31,885 was spent on new machinery and £1,649 on materials for new stores. Later in the year another £2,634 was spent on machinery. In May 1930 the company was installing buildings and plant for the manufacture of "Audco" lubricants and appointing a chemist at £500 pa. Extensive work on the pattern shop included £378 for the foundations, £511 for the steelwork, £368 for the pattern stores, £347 for pattern machinery and £137 for electrics. At the same time an office was built for a planning department at £167, the new roadway to Audley Avenue was put in at a cost of £149 while sidewalks and an entrance gate cost £25. Four Ford cars were bought, part exchange, for £284 and a Staff group pension plan was inaugurated for all employees.

All directors were active members of staff. Sales visits were numerous; to Roumania cost £156; two directors to Germany, £49.18.00.

In October 1929 came the Wall Street crash in the United States and over the next few months the repercussions were felt in Europe as trade diminished and the USA called in debts. The Directors report of 1930 reflected this. There had been a slight increase in profit but increased capital expenditure was bringing less profit increment and increased spending on sales in new territories was bringing diminishing returns as trade collapsed. There was no point in increasing output. There had been a drop of £20,000 in orders from the chemical industry and though this had been partly offset by new customers, orders in the last three months had been 40% down. There was little optimism going into 1931 and a need to cut out deadwood which it was stated coldly, was what *"depressions are for."* In December 1931 there was a reduction in salaries of all directors and staff earning over £3 a week. R.W.Leach was reduced to £1.303, N.B. Saunders to £675, W.H. Bateman to £675 and F.Bird to £405.

The Report for 1931 showed the effect of the slump. Orders were declining in the face of establishment expenses which had been built up for expansion. The cost of increased sales activity was out of proportion to the results. The cost of installing the lubricant plant had been offset by not having to purchase expensive imports from the USA. There had been a profit of £3,385 but after tax this was a loss of £159. Two debenture holders were calling in their money, staff pay had been reduced, no dividends had been declared, but sensibly, new equipment continued to be bought £400 being spent on new machines in 1933.

There were several consequences of the depression in Europe which hit the "Audley". One was the decline in orders and linked to this, the rise of dictatorships and the move to protectionism, that is the banning of foreign imports. In 1932 the German agents simply defaulted with a loss of £610. August of that year was the lowest for sales in eight years. Certain markets were simply closed though the company kept the sales organisations going in the hope that new designs of valves would increase sales without having to rely on an improvement in world trade. There were in fact 2,800 more customers but lower turnover and losses.

One of the unsuspected difficulties was protectionism with several of the countries passing legislation forbidding sales. In Germany the difficulty was brought about by the currency restrictions following the rise of Hitler and National Socialism; in Italy it was the reaction to sanctions imposed by the Italian invasion of Abyssinia as well as currency restrictions; in France it was the Government's determination that all the equipment for the very big oil refineries should be manufactured in that country.

Arrangements had to be made to get round these trade barriers by setting up in the countries concerned. Valves would have to be made in France, Germany and Italy. In May 1933 an agreement was reached with the French Company through M. Pinchaud for the exclusive right to manufacture only in France and to export valves only as part of complete units. The French were to pay royalties to Merck and Audley and also for technical services. In January 1934 a subsidiary company was set up in Belgium *Society Belge des Robins Audley,* with Audley Engineering having 77 of the 100, 500 francs shares. The company took over all the assets belonging to Audley but all goods had to be purchased from Audley Engineering at wholesale prices. M. Bureaux was to manage and be allowed to run his own merchants business. It made a profit of 15,000 francs in the first four months. Negotiations were also going on in Germany to manufacture and sell on licence as the German Government was forbidding the export of their currency to pay royalties. Operations were being considered in Italy and Spain.

The Avenue Road site was becoming too small particularly with the erection of a new foundry and centralised stores. Various neighbouring cottages were bought up in the old Marsh Road [Audley Road]. This gave 7.5 acres for development and to cope with what was described as the Company's *"middle-aged spread"*. The new foundry began operation in June 1934 and cost £7,000. The foundry was opened by J.S. Underhill who had opened his fathers' foundry on the site in 1869. It produced 1.5 tons and was operated by electricity. The foundry was built and designed by the Company.

In July 1936 the Company purchased Pen-y-Bryn a large house with five acres of land in Station Road, for offices at a cost of £1,700. Originally known as Chetwynd Aston Villa the name was changed after 1894 when Chetwynd Aston was absorbed in Newport. It was estimated that the cost of running Pen-y-Bryn was £700 more than having offices on site so the property was sold and an office block built at the factory. In May 1952 the company applied to the Urban District Council to build eleven detached houses at the rear of Pen-y-Bryn mainly for staff. The house was occupied by employees until 1956 when Queens Drive was built. In 1963 the house was demolished and Princess Gardens was developed.

1934 was stated as being the most successful in the Company's history with profits after tax of £50,503 and assets of £68,192:

> *"....the financial strength of the Company from this brief review will rank amongst a privileged few, and it should be the ambition of all of us to keep in this happy position."*

This happy state was reflected in an interim dividend of 30% on ordinary shares free of tax, an investment of £2,500 in Gilt Edged Securities and increased bonuses and salaries to staff.

> *"If one calls to mind the position of 10 year's ago, when we were barely making ends meet and the sums which have been paid out in the years between, I think that we can at least claim this has become a successful company. We have passed through one of the greatest depressions since what is known as the industrial age began which would have been difficult but for the nature of the product we specialise in.*
> *In the last two years ordinary shareholders will have received more than the equivalent of forty years interest at 5%.*
> *As to whether the trend is healthy or not depends upon the foreign political situation. In my opinion trade will be active either way but the continuance of prosperity is a factor of the spiritual outlook of the nations of the world."*

Directors report 1935.

Sales were £87,933, assets £89,115 and undivided profits £58,241. A £5 subscription was sent to the Conservative Party.

In 1936 a new Company was formed, *"Audley Engineering Co Ltd"* with a pro rata distribution of shares to existing holders plus £2,800 in cash. R.W. Leach and his family held over 42,000 preference shares out of 60,000 and a similar amount of ordinary shares. Kenneth Leach son of RWL was now a director and visited the USA overspending on expenses of which £75 was by Mrs Leach but this was approved *"on account of the value of social contacts on a visit like this."*

In 1938 the firm employed 250 manual workers and 70 clerical and administrative staff with a wage and salary bill just short of £1,000 per week. Workers had their fun; in July 1926 a cricket match was played on "The Oval" at the rear of the works between the "Truckers" made up of Bunny Bolton, Jock Towns, Boko Atwoods, "The Master" Jones and Bow-wink Harvey, and the Fitters, consisting of Toby Jones, Teacan Cummings, Dab Breeze, Nagger Jones and Chequers Simmell; the result was Fitters - 74, Truckers - still batting - 68 - Bunny Bolton 52 not out. They entered factory floats in the carnival and other celebrations. Joe Barnett reminiscing in 1987 recalled how in 1929 he travelled by motor cycle from Wolverhampton parking his bike by the Gas works. A field and a dirt track separated the works from Audley Avenue. The Thirties slump meant that workers often worked two or three days in the factory and the rest of the time in the offices.

On 18 February 1938 The Newport and Market Drayton Advertiser wrote a *"Special"* on the *"Romantic rise to Eminence"* of Audley Engineering Company and its part in the national defence programme.

War was recognised as a possibility:

> *"The Secretary was instructed to send a letter to the Secretary's of the Admiralty, War Office and Royal Air Force offering their services in connection with the development of the Government's Defence programme."*

25 May 1936.

In April 1939 the Company allocated £350 for an air raid shelter and by October, after war had been declared, they were already making losses due to the uncertainty of exports and having to pay large premiums (£412 rising to £525) for Compulsory War Risks Insurance. The first weeks were uncertain before it was clarified what could be or could not be exported. Valves and Cocks had no restriction while export of lubricants was prohibited. Prices were rising to cover war risks and ARP arrangements while money was put into War Loans. Strangely in May 1940 the Company received royalties from Italy and France while other foreign debts were being written off.

The Company kept separate accounts for ARP expenses:

1940.	ARP shelter	£179.06.01
	ARP equipment	£303.15.03
	Blankets	£311.04.02
	Sundry expenses	£1,447.17.00
1941.	ARP expenses incl. ARP "wages"	£1,951.03.08
1942.	ARP expenses	£536.08.10
1943.	ARP expenses	£1,999.15.04
1944.	"	£1,183.10.04

Against this was set a government grant towards the air raid shelter of £383.

When war came the Company was not faced with a great upheaval it simply moved its valve production up a gear to cater for war needs. It was this smooth transition and the secrecy of the work that made many believe that the firm was never engaged in *"war work"*. Nothing was further from the truth.

In the early stages of the war vast quantities of valves were needed for extensions in the explosives industry such as toluol production. At one period in 1942 the Company was asked to produce a large number of special valves for making "block-buster" explosives, a task completed in record time. Another big demand came from the building of new aerodromes, many in the Newport area, each of which required quantities of valves for the distribution of petrol. There was a large demand for valves for main line distribution of petroleum products, for production and refining. Thousands of valves were supplied for installation in British tanks. Valves were also required for poison gas factories.

There were more humanitarian uses of valves, for the production of penicillin, mepacrine (the substitute for quinine), and DDT, which was widely used to prevent epidemics such as typhoid. Valves were also used for the production of blood plasma and in the making of rayon and nylon for parachutes.

The more spectacular products were valves for PLUTO and FIDO installations. Pipe Line Under The Ocean was the cross-Channel installation for moving fuel to the beaches of Normandy during Operation Overlord. FIDO was the acronym for the apparatus to disperse fog at aerodromes. Another valve was used in voice pipe controls in submarines.

In December 1940 K.M. Leach reported negotiations with Lilleshall Estates Ltd (Mr H Ford) to transfer the production of 25-pounder gun trails from their bombed-out West Bromwich factory to a new building next to the tool room at Audley. In return K.M. Leach would manage the plant and the Company would be allowed to purchase the building at 50% cost at the end of the war, this they did in May 1946 for £959, converting it to a new packing and despatch department

In 1943, when the Russians began to advance, transportable power stations were required and thousands of stoker links for these were supplied from Newport. Special tools were made for the production of Rolls Royce and Merlin aero-engines as well as castings for machine tools for tanks and motor-vehicles.

Without the specialised products of Audco no petroleum, explosive or chemical plant would have operated or the vast amounts of dehydrated foods- powdered egg and milk – been made.

Directors assumed other roles in the war, K.M. Leach as a Home Guard Commander, N.B. Saunders as evacuation officer as well as Chairman of the hospital and Councillor; F. Bird was the Head Fire Guard. Employees were active in the Home Guard, Fire-watching and Civil Defence squads.

In December 1945 the Comforts Fund was wound up. During the war collections had been made in the works, and doubled by the management, to provide gifts for workers in the forces. It had a surplus of £28 that the management doubled and gave it to Mr Talbot an employee who had been disabled.

Personnel changed during the war. In 1939 N.B. Saunders left having purchased a business in the south of England. He retained his directorship and was replaced as Secretary by F. Bird. In March 1941 R.W. Leach resigned as Managing Director to be replaced by his son Kenneth. His brother H.B. Leach died that year. Robert William Leach died at Brookfield, Chetwynd End, Newport on 29 April 1944 aged 66. Born at West Bromwich he came to be not only managing director of Audley Engineering but its presiding genius. Deafness prevented a more public life and he was happy with gardening, water colours and angling. He had constant ill health and his trips abroad were often for convalescence as much as business. His son Kenneth now became Chairman. His younger son Robert Murray Leach also suffered from ill health causing him to retire from industry and to return to Newport and set up Chetwynd End Nurseries. He died aged 30 in 1948. Four of the seven directors were engaged in the business, Mr K.M. Leach, E.B. Leach (Technical Director and second son), P.Meredith (Sales Director) and J.W. Taylor (Work Director).

Kenneth Leach was planning his post war export strategy in November 1944, like his father before him he had in mind the possibility of working in conjunction with other manufacturers whose products were complementary to the Company`s, this would mean overseas markets would be more actively and economically worked as well as giving better sales service to customers. Negotiations were reopened with the USA and France and in June 1945 he reported on a visit to Paris where he discussed the condition of the French Company *"Societe Francaise des Robinets Audley"* with the new managing director Andre Collingnon. Considering the conditions of the war he found it in a satisfactory state. Andre Collingnon had joined the company in 1929 and succeeded M. Pinchaud in 1947. The French business went from strength to strength becoming Audco France SA in 1956 and then joining with Rockwell manufacturing of USA to become Audco Rockwell France SA in1960. Collingnon died in January 1961.

In March 1945 KML visited the USA and renewed the agreements with Merco Nordstrom Valve Co. The Annual report showed output down because of the shortage of labour and money being put into reserve for the anticipated post-war expansion. There was little hope of recovering pre-war foreign debts. The order book was full and little difficulty was envisaged in absorbing men and women on their return from the Forces.

In September/November 1946 Ted Leach went to the USA to study the manufacture, sales and developments of the Nordstrom Valve Division. He concluded that the *"Nordstrom organisation is not as far in advance of us as I had previously been led to believe."* The war had disrupted development and production and led to the rise of competition. As regards industrial relations the country was verging on a state of chaos with widespread strikes, disputes between unions and *"just plain racketeering."* But it would be wrong to underestimate the aggression and energy of the Americans in tackling problems, an outlook he thought the British could well adopt. Though the expenditure on their relationship with Nordstrom might at times be difficult to justify, he believed that the exchange of information and experience was essential and that it would cost far more in advertising expense to get only a portion of their publicity and standing in the industry.

> *"When once America becomes stabilised and production is again normal, we shall have to be ready for very serious competition in the World's markets."*

He appeared to get on well with the main executives W.F. Rockwell and W.F. Rockwell, Jnr:

> *"My conclusion is that the days of mistrust between ourselves and Nordstrom are past."*

Sven J. Nordstrom a pioneer of the lubricated valve with whom Audco had had a long relationship, died, aged 70, on the 11 December 1951. Mr Nordstrom, a Swede, went to the USA in 1901 and for ten years lived in Mexico. It was there he did his early work on lubricated valve development before returning to the USA.

In July 1947 they formed a new company in Belgium *"Societe Audco Belge"* discrepancies having being found in the original company. By the end of that year there were agencies in Sydney, Melbourne, Belgium, Finland, France, Gold Coast, India, New Zealand, Norway, South Africa, Spain, Sweden, Switzerland, and Trinidad and Tobago. In 1952 E.B. Leach visited the Middle East in connection with the large number of high pressure valves being installed in the new Iraq – Mediterranean oil pipeline.

The Chairman in October 1945 presented the directors with details of new plant he thought should be purchased as soon as possible in view of the heavy demands, particularly from the Oil Companies, mainly for steel valves. It was agreed to spend £20,000 including buying from the Ministry of Supply the machine tools and plant that had been on hire during the war. Extensions were made to the Machine Shop, the Core and Dressing Shop, Stores, Inspection and a new Foundry Washing Centre. A Gate Lodge was set up at the entrance to the works.

Light Drilling Section, Hurst Engineering Co.

To cope with demand in May 1946 the Company purchased 3,000 shares at £3.37 and took control of Hurst Engineering at Lilyhurst in Lilleshall. This was used for small valves allowing the main factory to concentrate on the larger sizes of up to two tons. In 1951 the whole of the assets were merged with Audley and Hurst ceased to exist. The Hurst Engineering Company had been formed in 1941 by a group of Birmingham business men for the manufacture of aircraft components required for the war effort, a secluded, ideal site, that had once been estate workshops for agricultural purposes. The war work had consisted of aeroplane propeller blades for Rotol Airscrews, but at the end of the war all contracts were cancelled and the company was left with nothing to do.

Core Shop 1951

The Audley Social Club was officially opened by Mr K. Leach on 15 December 1947 in a building at the corner of New Street and Beaumaris Road. Over the years playing fields were obtained and a pavilion built opposite the Avenue site mainly for football, tennis and cricket but also for minority sports like archery and judo. In October 1960 £4,300 was paid by the Company for St Mary`s Cottage, outbuildings and garden and land opposite from the estate of Tom Blakeman in Bellmans Yard. In 1962 a new social club was opened in Bellmans Yard and a modern version still exists [2004] even though the factory has closed. The Beaumaris building was demolished. The premises included a licensed bar, stage, and facilities for billiards, table tennis, and other indoor games. There was a bowling green adjacent to the Clubhouse. A photographic club and the Film Society also met there. The subscription was 3d per week deducted from wages.

Group Assurance and pension schemes, all subsidised by the firm, were open to employees. Many had returned after the war, to complete 20 and 25 years service by 1948, with two and sometimes three generations.

> *"At a ceremony in the works social club on Friday, seven employees of the Audley Engineering Company who have been with the firm thirty years or more, were presented with watches to commemorate their long service. The presentations were made by Mr Noel Saunders, a Director, who was supported by Mr Kenneth Leach managing director, and Mr E B Leach, a director. The recipients were: Mr George Cummings (31 years), Mr George Lewis (31), Mr Donald Breeze (30), Mr Stanley Hughes (31), Mr Edward Simpson (31), and Mr Thomas Ferriday (31). The arrangements were made by the secretary of the club, Mr H Haseley."*

Newport Advertiser. June 1951.

The company had a small fund to assist community projects within the town often called the "K.M. Leach Fund".

K.M. Leach in the Christmas 1952 edition of the works magazine "The Seal" wrote:

"We, at Newport, working in a modern factory set amidst the rural beauty of Shropshire, have every reason to be proud and thankful."

During 1955 production at Audley reached a peak and it became necessary to consider further expansion as the works site was almost completely developed. A new site at the top of Audley Avenue was purchased and a machine shop and auxiliary buildings were erected. Known as the Avenue Works it went into production on 20 August 1956. Until 1955 Audley was a private company with restricted shareholders who were connected with the management of the business. Taxation, death duties and growth made it necessary to change this status and the company amalgamated with Serck Radiators of Birmingham with whom they had been trading since at least 1939. Employing about 2,000, three times the size of Audco, Serck made heat exchangers, oil coolers and car radiators.

In 1961 the company changed its name to Audco Ltd and introduced the first of a new development in plug valves but in 1966 broke from tradition with a range of wafer type Butterfly valves known as the Slimseal range. This was followed in 1968/69 with new valves for the Chemical Industry known as Chemseal. Known by 1967 as Serck Audco, the company went on to merge with a sister company from Gloucester, Serck Jamesbury, in 1970, taking the name Serck Audco Valves. All ball valve production was transferred from Gloucester to Newport. With this merger the Leach family withdrew from management.

The Diamond Jubilee of Audco Ltd was held at the Royal Victoria Hotel, Newport in September 1966 when ninety guests from all over the world attended a celebration dinner.

"Export sales executives of Serck Audco Valves, Newport returned from Moscow at the end of a fourteen day international exhibition to report considerable interest in the range of valves the company has to offer. Of particular interest to Soviet engineers were the Chemseal butterfly valves – chemical industry valves launched only in July this year, and the JSL ball valves - now in production in Newport, following the merger

> *with Serck Jamesbury of Gloucester.*
> *It was the 1965 Chemical Exhibition in Moscow that started an intensive effort to break into the very difficult but valuable market and in the last eighteen months some good orders have already been received."*

Newport Advertiser. 6 October 1970

Things were not all smooth with a strike by maintenance men in March 1969 when negotiations for a pay rise broke down, leading to a lay off of 60 foundry workers and threatening 560 other employees. Nevertheless 1970 saw increased group sales of £25.7 million and profits of £1.8 million.

Serck Audco was one of four Shropshire firms to receive the Queen's Award for Industry in April 1970. This was the first time they had received such an award and it was made for technological innovation in group technology as introduced and practised by the company. This was a novel material and production control system using a Brisch numbering system for product rationalisation commonly called cell manufacture. It was introduced by the Works Manager Gordon Ranson and triggered off similar systems world-wide, not least in Japan.

The '70's were not easy for industry with strikes, three day weeks and roaring inflation. In May there was a 10% cut in the workforce, 120 employees were made redundant followed by another 40 in August. *"Sluggishness in the economy"* and lack of orders were to blame. A new foundry was erected much to the annoyance of Audley Road residents who thought the noise and vibrations should be removed to the Avenue works a mile away, but the same year, 1979, the company was asking for voluntary redundancy of about 40 people in the administrative and technical departments. It warned that if this was not agreed the reduction could be forced. The blame was put on increased operating costs but in August 1981 it was decreased orders that were said to be responsible for a four day week. Management too was unsettled with incompatible views and differences of philosophy within the holding groups Serck International and later BTR, leading to resignations. Newport often sat uneasily in an international production and marketing combine.

A Regional Study of Newport in 1971 by Leslie A Parker placed the Company in the context of its environment. The population of Newport was about 8,500 but expanding as new housing went up and moving towards becoming a dormitory, commuting town. Apart from Serck Audco Valves, industry in Newport provided no more than 250 jobs. There was conflict between those who wanted to retain the rural image of Newport and those who wanted to attract jobs. It was recognised that the importance of jobs and the capital investment made it impossible to move the site from the town centre for at that time Serck Audco employed 1,100 men and 240 women with men's wages at £20-33 for a 40 hour week, and the women's rate at £18. If you apply the multiplier of twelve, that is one income generates twelve more, the financial input to the locality by Serck Audco was enormous. 75% of workers were domiciled in Newport and given the lower shop and farm rates a pool of labour was always available. One spin off was that the bulk of the retained firemen in Newport came from the factory, they were near and always available; the company was co-operative since it was in their interest to have such a force available. For generations the fire siren on the factory was a familiar and comforting sound.

March 1985 found that it was still difficult for Serck Audco Valves to get a regular flow of orders from markets at home and abroad. While some notable successes had been achieved in Pakistan, Iran and Alaska there was fierce competition and it was a constant struggle to keep the factory fully operational throughout the year. The recession meant small orders were not being secured and day-to-day business was at a low level. Substantial orders often had a deadline which meant a lull in business afterwards, making smooth operation very difficult. Sales were a priority *"the life blood of the company"*, and the new managing director, Harry Wood, was a former Sales Director. Orders included one for the Alaskan oil field where deadlines were vital as transport could only get through four weeks in a year. There was regular business with butterfly and plug valves to the North Sea oilfields and a six figure order with Sui Gas in Pakistan.

The workforce had declined from 1,160 to 415 through investment in computerisation and streamlining of operations so that one machine, usually from Italy, now carried out nine operations on one component. Before nine loads would have been on separate machines. This had been achieved through a loyal and co-operative workforce.

Looking ahead meant a few months at a time:

> *"There is so much competition for orders. The opportunity to get quotations for business is only the first stage for then comes the real hard work to secure orders."*

Alan Cooney, Technical Sales Manager, 8 March 1985

Rationalisation continued. By 1992 the foundry was closed and castings were bought in. The Audley Road site of William Underhill was sold and the factory transferred to the Avenue works ironically opposite the cemetery. The old factory became a housing estate, at least it was called *"Underhill Close"*, and a Safeway supermarket. A commemorative plaque, and a lamp-post made from cast iron valves, was erected by the company and the Town Council, in a ceremony attended by the Chief Executive of BTR Valve group, Peter Talbot, who then controlled Serck Audco. Mr Talbot was a Newport boy a former apprentice at the works.

Twentysix jobs were cut in February 1998 and fifty in November.

Rationalisation was taking place at the top though the reasons were often not very transparent. By 1998 Invenseys were the parent company and the closure announcement followed a merger deal between BTR and the engineering giant Siebe. The closure statement read:

> *"With the resulting low demand for valves, the BTR Siebe Control Business, of which Serck Audco Valves is part, has had to undertake an in-depth review of its current operations and capacity.*
> *A proposal has been made to close the Newport factory, with the potential loss of 148 jobs, and consolidate the manufact--uring of Serck Audco products into other valve plants in Sussex and Texas."*

2. April 1999.

By the end of July redundancies were being made and the 142,850 sq. ft of factory were up for sale despite a short term order book of over £5 million and a wide range of large and loyal clients not to mention a highly skilled workforce and a modern computerised plant. As someone wrote - the workers at Serck deserved better. Yet in reality any protest was muted. The MP made the appropriate noises wrote the appropriate letters to the relevant executives, offered to lead any campaign but their were no votes in Audco, the Town Council did not even put the matter on their agenda. Perhaps it was true, as in 1938, that the affairs of Audco were a closed book to most Novaportans, in fact in 2000 most of the 10,000 population would not have known what a "Novaportan" was. Most were not living in Newport for its history or its jobs. As for the workers many were of an age to be content with a job well done, a career well spent and a package, including many Invensey shares, that would see them quite comfortably off. Today Invensey shares are worthless and it is difficult to be sympathetic.

The most inventive, productive and important period in the story of Newport People had been cynically destroyed.

Underhill Close

NOTES.

Fifteen. Audco and Jobs.
1. NMDA: information on the early years of Audley Engineering and its predecessors. article 18 February 1938; article 15 June 1945; supplement March 1985; reports on closure 1999.
2. *Where Novaportans Make Some Of The Worlds Finest Valves,* Shropshire Magazine, September 1951.
3. Serck Audco archives courtesy of Mrs. V. Langford. Minutes, conveyances, reports, extracts from the company magazine "The Seal".
4. Information from Mr.C.W.Perry, East Preston, West Sussex, May 1999.
5. Leslie. A. Parker, Regional study of Newport, Shropshire, unpublished, (1971).
6. Various: Serck Audco marketing and publicity material e.g. Audley Handbook 1957.

STORY OF THE
AUDLEY ENGINEERING COMPANY

*Newport's biggest
Industrial concern*

Romantic rise to eminence

*Its part in National Defence
Programme*

"Advertiser" Special

It is a curious characteristic of Novaportans that they take singularly little practical interest in affairs and institutions which concern them most deeply. This is a problem which members of public bodies cannot fail to recognise, and in no respect is it more patent than with regard to the Audley Engineering Company, which is, at one and the same time, the best known and least comprehended business concern in the locality. Here is a company which provides the means of livelihood for, at a low estimate, a thousand people in Newport and district, and which would be welcomed with open arms by communities ten times the size of Newport; yet to the average Novaportan of long residence the activities of the "Audley" are a closed book. It was with the idea of gleaning something of its past achievements and of its future aspirations that an "Advertiser" representative visited the Works on Monday and spent several interesting hours, moving from one department to another, threading a perilous way through intricate machinery which was working at full blast.

Importance to oil industry.

Speaking generally, one may assume that everyone knows that the Company produces valves. A valve, to the layman, is a tap for controlling the flow of liquids - usually water - in pipes, and that is a basis as good as any other from which to start. But if the pressure of all liquids was as easy to control as water there would be no need for the Audley Engineering Company. The household tap is probably the simplest form of valve - in purpose and in construction - made, and with that the Audley has nothing to do. Its concern is with taps which have to stand the pressure of all sorts of substances from crude oil to compressed air, often up to as much as three tons to the square inch. The oil wells of Rumania, Iran, Irak and Mexico, for instance, which between them provide the motive power for nearly the whole world on wheels, need valves which are capable of controlling the flow of oil gushing upwards at pressures of more than two thousand pounds to the square inch. It is literally true that the lives and fortunes of thousands may depend on the ability of a valve to withstand the terrific pressure to which it is exposed. The "gusher" at one American well got out of control ten years ago, and it has been burning continuously ever since.

Many firms, of course, here and abroad, are engaged in the manufacture of valves, but the eminence of the Audley product - known throughout the world as the "Audco" Valve - is based upon its novel construction and upon the fact that its working parts can be lubricated without taking the valve to pieces. Further, the particular lubricant used must have the property of resisting the action of petrol or other liquids which would wash away ordinary lubricants. In the evolution and production of valves possessing these unique features the Audley Company leads the way, and its goods carry the name of Newport (Salop) to every corner of the earth`s surface.

Where "Audco" valves go.

The market for "Audco" valves may be roughly divided into four industrial groups:- oil wells and refineries, the chemical industry, mining (gold and other minerals), and general industry. Oil concerns take valves of every conceivable size from little fellows with a few pounds pressure, the size of a Mills bomb, to great giants of valves which tax the strength of two men to lift. Yet all incorporate the same unique features, and are recognised as the "Rolls Royce" of their kind. The chemical industry, of course, makes peculiar demands upon valves, dealing as it does with all kinds of corrosive acids and gases. General industry provides a myriad of uses for valves, and "Audco" valves are to be found standing up to the strain involved in driving the "Queen Mary" from Southampton to New York in under four days as well as in such less spectacular jobs as ensuring the efficiency of central heating systems in the mammoth blocks of flats which are now springing up in all the chief cities of the world, and in the new Bank of England. Factories which manufacture soap, textiles, artificial silk and newsprint all look to "the Audley" to provide for their needs, and an interesting market is the gold-mining industry of South Africa, where valves are used for the powerful hydraulic drills with which the hard quartz is attacked. It will thus be seen that the market for the valves is almost illimitable and in every case it is an essential feature that they shall be flawless in construction and trouble-free in action. The Audley Company manufactures valves costing from as little as nine-pence to as much as £100 each

It is not without interest that the Audley Company is playing no inconsiderable part in Britain`s national defence programme by providing an essential part of the equipment for producing petrol.

Housewives to the rescue.

The principal basic material used is pig iron, with smaller quantities of bronze, brass, and stainless steel. The works has an enormous appetite for pig iron, amounting to more than 150 tons a month, most of it coming from the north and north-west coast and some from Essex. The shortage of iron due to the intensification of the defence programme was for a time felt acutely at the Audley and it was necessary - and in fact still is - to import a small proportion of supplies from Bengal, India. Until quite recently the metal was rationed to manufacturers, but that irksome proceeding is now fortunately unnecessary, due in no small measure to the successful harvesting of scrap from household and other hitherto unsuspected sources. Pig iron, it is interesting to note, costs roughly one penny per pound, while stainless steel, not noticeably different to the unpractised eye from pig iron in its rough *state, is purchased at two shillings per lb.*

The technical aspect of the manufacture of cocks and valves from the raw material to the finished article is a highly technical procedure and can find no place in the columns of a general newspaper. Suffice it to say that the gradual emergence of the valve from an ungainly block of pig iron is fascinating in the extreme. It calls for skill and ingenuity of a very high degree with machines that perform weird and wonderful evolutions. The component parts gradually take shape, and are tested for faults at every stage in their development, until at last the completed article, having passed through a dozen or more departments, is precipitated into the packing department ready for despatch. Careful packing is not the least important part of the process and our representative saw one consignment begin its long journey to Rangoon.

Chemical tests

Much of the work of manufacture is naturally of a more or less automatic nature, but there are some departments where it is of the utmost importance to assume nothing until test and re-test have proved to the hilt that such assumptions are justified. Many scientific and chemical means are employed in the laboratories to ensure that the ingredients in the alloy are in their right proportions, and that the lubricating materials comply with the proscribed formula. It should be realised that it is often necessary to conduct long and complicated chemical experiments to ascertain the correct lubricant for the particular liquid in connection with which the valve is to be used, and the Company now supplies twelve standard lubricants for different classes of work. There is nothing rule-of-thumb about this process, for even the apparatus to make the test has to be specially made. To every boy who has dabbled in "stinks" at school, the laboratories would be a virtual paradise, with this exception – that he would have to wait many days for the results. If it can be said there is romance in industry, this department is one of the most romantic imaginable.

Another department which is bound to excite the liveliest interest is that where skilled men are at work fashioning new and strange tools, designed to do strange jobs. The supreme virtue of men in this department is ingenuity, both in design and manufacture. They have nothing to do with the making of valves, and spend their lives transferring the blue-paper designs of draughtsmen into tools to perform a certain type of work.

Newport and Market Drayton Advertiser. 18 February 1938.

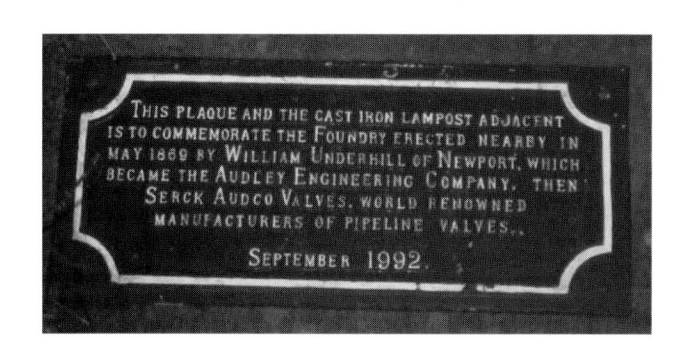

Malcolm Miles

Malcolm Miles is a professional historian born in Shropshire and has lived most of his life in Newport.

He has taught history at every level and was Head of History at the John Hunt School for 25 years.

His previous publications include Newport in Old Picture Postcards', History of Newport Market Company', History of Castle House School', Newport in World War II' and numerous articles and guides.

He is a popular lecturer on local history.

He has been involved in the public and social life of Newport, being an Urban District and Town Councillor for 33 years and also served as Mayor.

He is married to Sue Miles, equally well known, and has three children and three grandchildren.